GANGLAND:
THE EARLY YEARS

GANGLAND:
THE EARLY YEARS

James Morton

A *Time Warner* Book

First published in Great Britain in 2003
by Time Warner Books

A CIP catalogue record for this book
is available from the British Library.

ISBN 0 316 85936 2

Typeset by Palimpsest Book Production Limited,
Polmont, Stirlingshire

Printed and bound in Great Britain by
Mackays of Chatham Ltd, Chatham, Kent

Time Warner Books UK
Brettenham House
Lancaster Place
London WC2E 7EN

www.TimeWarnerBooks.co.uk

To Dock Bateson with love

Contents

Introduction

Between them they stole and they squandered millions. Not one seemed to think beyond his or her next magnum of champagne, next mistress, next lover, or the next coup. They revelled in the titles the newspapers gave them – the Napoleon of Crime, the Princess of Thieves, the Bravest of the Brave, the Plutocrat of Pickpockets and so on. With very few exceptions there were no thoughts of building an empire for their children or even setting themselves up for a comfortable old age. They were gamblers, whores and whoremongers. Most died broke, working for the Pinkerton Detective Agency as part-time informers, in prisons over America or Europe, or in the workhouse or its equivalent. They were career criminals pure and simple, but none were pure and very few were simple.

Take the Father of English Bank Thieves as an example. William Cauty, described as an elderly man of substantial appearance, and John Tyler, an old man also of respectable appearance but known as a returned convict, were charged with robbery of the London & Westminster Joint Stock Bank in St James's Square. Sergeant Whitcher, beloved by Dickens, saw them both on a park bench in the square on 31 May 1851. They went into the bank just before closing and were locked in with the other customers, giving them a chance to case the premises before being let out. They repeated the process for the first three weeks in June and then on 28 June walked out with the cash-box. Unfortunately the police had informed the bank staff and the box – which normally contained the bank's *ad hoc* reserves of between £20,000 and £30,000 – was empty. For good measure Cauty was also charged with stealing a box containing 40 sovereigns from Mary Allen, the landlady of the Grosvenor Arms in Lower Belgrave Place.

There was no such thing as prejudicial reporting in those days because before the trial *The Times* published a little eulogy of Cauty, describing him as:

> One of the most remarkable persons of his class and perhaps the only survivor of that peculiar and superior class of receivers and putters-up of bank and jewel robberies which flourished in the time of the old police but which is fast disappearing before the effects of the new police system.

He had been known to the police for about 40 years and was thought to have had £500,000 in jewellery and bank notes through his hands during the last 30 of them. In his early days he had been a croupier in gaming hells. Now he often travelled to America and the West Indies, paying for his passage by cheating at cards. He was believed to have had £50,000 from the bankers Rogers & Co. and £40,000 from the Custom House robbery. He was also suspected of being involved in the Andover Mail Robbery, that at the Bath Bank and one at Sir John Pinhorn's bank, as well as the South Western Gold Dust robbery. It was estimated that this man whose appearance as he approached 70 'is of a kind to disarm suspicion, being that of a country gentleman rather than an associate of thieves', had lived at a rate of £2,000 a year.[1]

On 13 July he and Tylor were each sentenced to transportation for 10 years – something which the Recorder accepted that, at their age, meant transportation for life. They had pleaded guilty to the bank robbery and Mary Allen's theft had not been proceeded with. Before he left the dock Cauty was allowed to make a statement and, as befitted status, did the decent thing and said that, 'none of the young men in the bank were any way concerned'.[2]

Nearly half a century later on 14 March 1900 William Pinkerton,

[1] *The Times*, 1, 5, 11, 14 July 1851. Arthur Griffiths, *Mysteries of Police and Crime.*
[2] *The Times*, 14 July 1851.

son of Allan, founder of the famous detective agency and then in charge of the Chicago office, dined with Eddie Guerin, the bank robber who would become one of the few men to escape from the French penal colony on Devil's Island and live to tell the tale. The reason he survived was, it would be said, because he had eaten his companions.

The next day Pinkerton wrote to his brother George in the New York office:

> Last night I met Eddie Guerin, bank sneak and all-round crook, at Chapin & Gore's restaurant, where he came looking for me. Guerin had just returned from Europe, he having been absent for 14 years. I found him but very little changed, excepting that he has grown broader and heavier than he was. He is a big, brawny, muscular looking fellow now, I should judge him about 37 years of age.

Guerin provided him with a round-up of just who was where and doing what in London. Details included the fact that Adam Worth, also known as Harry Raymond, was living in London and in better health because he had succeeded in stopping the haemorrhages in his head. Charley Allen had been released from prison and was still in England. John Curtin was in prison, and Guerin was sure Worth would kill him on his release on account of Curtin debauching Worth's wife while Worth was in jail in Belgium. Billy Burke was over there working with a man he thought was named Murtha. Dice Box McGuire, a Chicago pickpocket, had been in London for three or four years. Charlotte Dougherty, the wife of Horace 'Little Horace' Hovan, was there while he was serving his third sentence in France. Sophie Lyons, thief, con-woman, panel worker, in love with Burke, was also in London and she and Guerin had been to a dinner with Worth. She was not popular and Guerin said that there were a number of people in London who were ready to 'job' her.

John Carr, the bank burglar, had been released and was in England on ticket-of-leave. Carr was a 'big English pig', according to Guerin. He had hidden his money and could not get at it until his ticket-of-leave had expired, when he would be fairly well off.[3] Frank Dean, 'Dago Frank', was also in London but was a back number. He had to wait for Carr's ticket-of-leave to run out before he could get any money, thought to be around £1,000, which Carr had been hiding for him. Oscar Decker, one-time thief and forger, was in the East End, but old and not working. Frank Tarbox was in London, married to a woman with money, and Al Holman 'The Russian', 'Dutch' Alonzo and Billy Miller hoped to be out of prison in Holland in time for the World's Fair when great things were anticipated from them. 'Doc' Pat Sheedy was in Cairo but was expected in Paris any time. Guerin had brought a toy dynamo for Worth's children.

George Pinkerton had just learned of the whereabouts of some of the then cream of American career criminals. Adam Worth had stolen the Gainsborough portrait of the Duchess of Sutherland. Sophie Lyons, who would later marry the handsome Billy Burke, had escaped from prison in New York and was then cutting a swathe through London's demi-monde along with Guerin's one-time mistress, 'Chicago May' Sharpe, who would later have her former lover shot in Russell Square.

'Dutch' Alonzo was Dutch Alonzo Henne, who was regarded as having picked more pockets successfully than any other man in America and had been on Adam Worth's fateful Liège robbery.

Guerin had also told Pinkerton that he wanted a job on the race-tracks which the Pinkerton Agency policed, and that he intended to give up stealing. In Pinkerton's opinion:

> I will say to you I do not believe he will do this, he is a daring, desperate fellow and is always ready to take a chance to get money.

[3] In his autobiography *Crime*, Guerin refers admiringly to a Jack Carr as a receiver in Percy Street, off Tottenham Court Road. He regarded Carr, who had been in the trade for 40 years and who fenced some of the proceeds of the Lyons robbery, as being very fair. This cannot be the same man. Guerin was wrong about Decker; he and the receiver Carr were still working in September 1906. There had been a bank robbery in Liverpool and they were arrested in Sweden trying to dispose of the notes. They were both well over 70. Decker had been a long-time associate of Henry Wade Wilkes who unsportingly made a full confession of his activities as a counterfeiter while in custody in Italy in 1881.

Pinkerton suggested that he be given a cipher name, which was the way the agency worked. Old-time thieves were given jobs, but not wholly through altruism; they were the backbone of an invaluable informer system. Paid informants entered in the cipher book had names ending in Stone. Unpaid informants had names ending in Wood.[4]

What Guerin's information shows is the perhaps surprising mobility of the top-class criminals of the day – New York, Chicago, London, Egypt, France, Holland, Switzerland. Passports were not required and one of the better ways to avoid detection after a big job was to hop on a liner. The sea voyage also allowed the opportunity for a bit of card sharping, or deep-sea diving as it was known. The mug would be handled carefully and allowed to win until a final big money hand was played shortly before the liner docked. The crossing also provided the opportunity for jewel thefts. Nor was the traffic all one way. When James Lockett, the noted London safe-breaker and thief, pulled off a daring snatch in Birmingham in February 1905, the jewels were fenced in New York within the fortnight, almost before he was put on an identification parade and not picked out.

This then is an informal account of the developments in quality crime and the lives of quality career criminals, thieves, robbers, swindlers, forgers and murderers – some or all of those things – mainly British and American and French, from the end of the American Civil War in 1865 to the outbreak of the First World War in 1914. It also ends nicely with the year in which the fraudulent Joanna Southcott's box was due to be opened.

In 1792 Joanna Southcott, a farmer's 42-year-old daughter, proclaimed that she would be giving birth to the Second Messiah. The gestation, which would take ten years, generated an enormous following with supporters – or Southcottians as they liked to be known – totalling over 100,000. Later 19 October 1814 was announced as the date of birth and, amazingly, 17 out of 21 doctors who examined this 64-year-old woman announced that she was indeed pregnant. On the day of the proposed birth crowds massed

[4] For further details of the Pinkerton cipher system see Chapter 20, p. 303.

in Manchester Street, London, where she now lived. Three died during the vigil which produced no Saviour. Within ten weeks Joanna herself died of a brain disease. She did, however, leave a legacy of a box to be opened one hundred years after her death which, she said, would solve a great human crisis. Despite pleas from the dwindling band of supporters now known as the Panacea Society, the Archbishop of Canterbury refused to allow the box to be opened at the beginning of the First World War. When it was opened in 1927, in the presence of the Bishop of Grantham, it was found to contain a lady's nightcap, a pistol, a 1786 lottery ticket, a 1783 French calendar and, perhaps the most unusual item, a novel entitled *The Surprises of Love*. Her supporters maintained that the wrong box had been opened. However, the reality is that Ms Southcott was simply the spiritual grandmother of the many great swindlers, male and female, who will grace these pages.

Generally it was a gullible society as well. The showman William T. Barnum very successfully exploited Joice Heth. First, he announced that she was 161 years old and George Washington's nursemaid; then, when the public tired of this, he announced that she was in fact a robot. The trick was unmasked and a newspaper commented:

> [W]hat purports to be a remarkably old woman is simply a curiously constructed automat, made up of whalebones and numberless springs ingeniously put together and made to move at the slightest touch.

It was just one of many hoaxes.

The dates 1866 and 1914 seem to fit nicely, but they are not wholly arbitrary. During this time Britain, apart from the Boer War, enjoyed a long period of peace as did the remainder of Europe with the exception of the short-lived Franco-Prussian War of 1871. America had a small contretemps with Spain, but apart from that experienced rather over half a century of undisturbed development. Immigrants from Europe poured into England and America; most were willing to work in one form or another, if not wholly legally. In 1912 it was reported that New York detectives found that Hungarians had replaced British and Italian tricksters working the pocketbook scam on passengers waiting at piers for ships to sail.[5]

It was a time of change from a rural to an urban society, although in places the change was a long time in coming. One of the last recorded cases of old-fashioned highway robbery in Britain seems to have occurred in 1866 at Dollar on the southern fringe of the Highlands when Joseph Bell, an impoverished poacher, turned his hand to the sport. His effort was a far cry from the exploits of such gallants as Claude Duval, but it had the same result. He had pawned his shotgun and so he borrowed one from a local farmer before setting out to waylay Alexander McEwan, a banker's vanman. The day after McEwan was killed, with a bullet wound to the head, Bell paid £5 10/- – the exact amount stolen – for goods from local shops. The police tracked footprints from the body to a bridge under which they found the borrowed shotgun. Bell was quite unable to account for his possession of the money and a witness gave evidence to the effect that Bell had asked him to take part in another robbery. The jury retired for a bare 25 minutes before returning a 'guilty' verdict, but despite exhortations from the local clergy and an apparent rediscovery of the Christian faith, Bell refused to admit his guilt. He was hanged at Perth prison by the London executioner William Chalcraft, on gallows which had been borrowed for the occasion from Aberdeen. For many years the site of the killing was something of a tourist attraction, with the locals making money from driving the inquisitive to the spot where many carved their initials in the trunk of a tree.[6]

There were enormous developments in science and what we now call technology; the invention of the wireless telegraph is just one example. When Edward Sherwell, a clerk with the Capital and Counties Bank, walked off one morning with jewellery and £940, he was caught the same evening in Liverpool boarding the White Star liner bound for New York.[7] By the same token when two

[5] *New York Times*, 7 January 1912.
[6] George Forbes, 'The Last Highwayman' in *Scottish Memories*, February 2001.
[7] *Empire News*, 20 August 1910.

Croatians, Milovar Kovovich and Milovar Patrovich, blew up Samuel T. Ferguson and his book-keeper in Pittsburgh and made off with the payroll of $2,600 as revenge for being sacked, they fled to England. It only needed a cable to the police in Southampton to begin the extradition proceedings which would lead to the execution of Kovovich (who actually threw the bomb) and a 20-year sentence for Patrovich.

It was the use of the telegraph which retrieved the American Harvey Hawley Crippen, escaping back home with his girlfriend Ethel Le Neve after he had murdered his wife, the music-hall artiste Belle Elmore, in 1911. The whole of Britain followed the bulletins as Inspector Walter Dew, sailing in a faster liner, gradually overtook the pair as they headed for New York and safety. More importantly in the investigation of crime and the identification of criminals came fingerprinting, and some progress was made in the then infant study of ballistics as well.

There were also developments in criminology and the elementary profiling of criminals. The Italian Cesare Lombroso produced a theory that criminals had differently shaped heads from the remainder of the population, and the engaging supposition that women with excessive pubic hair were more inclined to prostitution and theft than their less endowed sisters. A study of cadets at Sandhurst tended to disprove the first half of the theory, but it was one which held good until well into the 1900s and, indeed, has been revived in one form or another over the last 100 years.

As time has passed Lombroso's theories may have become discredited, but the police of the period did not dismiss them out of hand:

> There could be no mistaking the character of such burglars as Evans, Hurley and Smith. All three bear the stamp of the hardened criminal so plainly on their faces that any masquerade on their part as respectable citizens would not impose on the verdant criminal. Even a child who met with one of them in a lonely lane would scamper off with trembling legs.[8]

---

[8] Benjamin P. Eldridge and William B. Watts, *Our Rival the Rascal*, p. 111.

There was also great interest in criminals' brains; in 1910 a pathologist examined the brains of four guillotined murderers and was able to say they showed no signs of abnormality. The next year it was reported that a French scientist had discovered that criminals tended to have shorter arms than average men.[9]

It was similarly of scientific interest to see if there was life after death and in April 1879 the murderer Knox Martin, in return for a new black suit in which he was hanged, willed his body to the doctor who purchased the clothes for him. As was the fashion, the doctor tried to resuscitate the body and reported that the corpse had shown 'pain, fear, anxiety, hope, delight, anger and disgust. Had the surroundings been more favourable much more could have been achieved.'[10] Only two months earlier a series of experiments was carried out on the body of the wife-murderer Merrick by the Professor of Physiology and Anatomy at the Medical College of Indiana in Indianapolis. This time the corpse had apparently been made to breathe, cough and roll its eyes. The whole experiment had been conducted:

> . . . with decorum and skill; there was, in fact, little conversation and no levity. As our reporter passed out of the room he was shown a barrel which contained the remains of Mrs Merrick.[11]

This was also the time when the great New York lawyer William J. Howe endeavoured to introduce a rudimentary psychiatric defence. In 1870 he appeared for Jack Reynolds without a fee but, when it came to it, his younger partner Abe Hummel wrote up the case as an advertising pamphlet: 'Lawyer Howe had evidently made extensive preparations to prove his client *non compus*.' And, in fairness, he clearly had.

The facts were simple. In the evening of 29 January, Townsend, a small-time shopkeeper, was sitting at home with his young daughters at 192 Hudson Street when Reynolds, who a few minutes earlier had stolen a knife from the shoe repairer who worked next door,

---

[9] *New York Times*, 24 January 1909; 3 November 1910.
[10] *National Police Gazette*, 12 April 1879.
[11] *National Police Gazette*, 22 February 1879.

came into the basement and sat down saying, 'I'm your brother.' Townsend told him that he was not and must leave. The man went outside; when Townsend followed him and placed a hand on his shoulder, he was stabbed in the heart. Passers-by tackled Reynolds and the police were called. The only defence open to Howe was one of insanity.

Reynolds had a depressed left frontal eminence onto which Howe latched in support of his theories. Psychiatry was than in its early stages and Howe had the idea of raising the defence that his client had suffered an epileptic fit which resulted in either what he called volitional insanity – which meant he had no control over his will – or impulsive insanity, which meant he could not resist the impulse. To this end he quoted the doctor Trousseau who cited the case of a judge who would leave the bench, urinate on the carpet of his chambers and return to the courtroom without any recollection of what he had just done.

At the end of the case Howe called Reynolds to the witness box to be questioned not by himself or Samuel B. Galvin, who pros-ecuted, but by the jurors themselves, something they did with enthusiasm but without any success in eliciting more than 'I can't remember' to their questions. No doubt Reynolds had been well schooled by his attorneys.

All the books on Howe say that his forte was his closing speech to the jury, and his efforts for Reynolds were a good example of the rhetoric he favoured. Here he is at the beginning:

> . . . for some good reason, known only to HIM 'through whom we live and move and have our being', it is left to you by your verdict to say whether this poor wretched animated piece of ruined nature, one certainly of the poorest of God's creatures is, upon testimony, such as has been introduced, to be strangled by the cord of the hangman when an indication is there, defying science . . .

It is clear that Howe managed to instil some doubt because the jury retired for over two hours and twice asked if alternative verdicts could be introduced, but the judge's rulings went against him. The next day Reynolds was sentenced to be hanged. Abe

Hummel, who went on to write two Broadway plays, set out his stall as an author:

> At this announcement the doors of the court were ordered to be barred to prevent the egress of the vast audience and the condemned man who seemed in no perceptible manner affected by the sentence, was conveyed to an adjoining room and from there thence to the streets, but before gaining the Tombs the crowd again flocked around him and, amidst the hootings and yelling of the gamin, he was lodged in his dark cell on the lower tier of the prison, moody and dejected, to receive such spiritual comfort as would prepare him for the next world.[12]

As for sources, American criminals tended to write their memoirs, proving that the seeming phenomenon of such as 'Mad' Frankie Fraser, Lenny McLean and the others putting pen to paper today is no such thing but merely a continuation of a centuries-old tradition. Sophie Lyons, 'Chicago May' Sharpe and Eddie Guerin all wrote their memoirs in book form, with varying degrees of truth and frankness, as did the bank robber Langdon Moore and both the Bidwell brothers who nearly succeeded in robbing the Bank of England.

As a rule English criminals did not do so, although in the first three decades of the twentieth century their memoirs crowded the Sunday newspapers, notably the *Empire News*, on a very regular basis. It is possible to find the memoirs of three different criminals in the same issues of that paper in April 1926. Those who contributed included Harry Grimshaw, the crooked jockey turned jewel thief, and another Harry, this time Harry 'The Valet' Thomas, who stole the Duchess of Sutherland's jewels in Paris. Also writing in the issue was the American Annie Gleason, one of whose numerous talents was to pose as the daughter of General Ulysses S. Grant. She told of her rehabilitation following a long stretch in Aylesbury. Sadly, this lasted barely the time it took her to cross the Atlantic.

[12] Abraham Hummel, *The Trial and Conviction of Jack Reynolds for the horrible murder of William Townsend.*

Because the criminals of the time worked under a variety of names and aliases, certainly until the 1900s and the coming of a workable fingerprint system it was impossible for the police always to identify them correctly. One example is 'Chicago May' Sharpe or Churchill. During her career she worked as May Wilson, May Avery, Lilian White, Rose Wilson, Mary Brown, Margaret Smith, May Latimer and no doubt many others. Now at this distance in time it is impossible to match them all to their misdeeds and nicknames, but I hope I have managed to do so at least in respect of the first rank.

I have concentrated on criminals from London, New York, Chicago and to a lesser extent Paris, but that does not mean those cities had an exclusivity of the talent then operating. By the turn of the century Australia had already had Ned Kelly and Frederick Ward, known as Captain Thunderbolt, and very soon afterwards Leslie 'Squizzy' Taylor made his impressive mark. It was not until 1916 that he really began to flourish and so he rather falls outside the scope of this book. Those interested in the career of this larrikin who became the darling of the Australian press and public, and whose life ended in a shootout with another gangster – a case which has never been satisfactorily solved – might care to read my *Gangland International*. South Africa provided one set of major robbers towards the end of the period, the Foster Gang led by Robert William Foster which operated out of Johannesburg from 1909 to September 1914. Then, holed up in a cave after killing a detective and a police sergeant, they committed suicide.

Of much sterner stuff was the German-born Carl Ludwig Kurtze, better known as von Veltheim, who plagued South Africa and England as well as his home country. As a general rule confidence tricksters are not killers, but he was a notable exception. He was born in Brunswick on 4 December 1857 where his father was a forester's clerk. At the age of 12 he was on his way, stealing his father's watch and some silver spoons. This was forgiven, but when his father died he was sent to the Gymnasium at Blakenburg. At 13 he stole a master's pistol and contrived to shoot himself in the face, which marked him for life. From there it was to an orphanage and then to sea as a cabin boy. In 1872 he deserted and, now as

Louis Weder, came to London. In 1880 he was in the German Navy, but he stole Freiherr von Veltheim's gold chain, diamond ring and a seal engraved with the von Veltheim arms. This was to be his future identity.

Many women, very often to their cost, were attracted to him. In Australia on 19 November 1886 he married Mary Laura Yearsley from Perth. He lived with her until in early 1887 he left for South Africa before coming once more to England. But it seems that Mary Laura was his equal. Now she sailed for England, met a man on the way and after somehow meeting again with von Veltheim worked the badger game with him. A payment of £2,000 for the deceived husband was negotiated down to £750 by the victim. Then it was to Belgium and on to Germany where he relieved a woman of a considerable sum, met up yet again with Mary and it was off to New York for a spell of high living.

In 1894 he was back again in Europe, with Mary left in America. He then managed to obtain an appointment as the U.S. consular agent for Santa Marta from where he advertised for a wife in the German newspapers. Now he was contacted by a Paula Schiffer.

In the meantime Mary had turned up in London and he told her he was penniless and had to return to Germany. There he collected Paula Schiffer, as well as £500 from her. Then it was back to London where he married her at St Giles Register Office and collected another £1,000 from her to start a business in America. She went home to Germany. He stayed in London spending much of his time in schemes against the South African millionaires Barney Barnato and his nephews, Solly and Woolf, the Joel brothers.

Meanwhile von Veltheim had married again. This time the lucky woman was Marie Mavrigordato and he was Franz Ludwig Platen. He obtained £300 in cash, but was refused more by her trustees. It was then that he let slip that the marriage was bigamous and went into hiding. In April that year he sailed for South Africa and enlisted in the Cape Mounted Police.

Then came a curious incident, presumably designed to thwart any possibility of bigamy proceedings. In August 1897 Mary Laura identified a naked body bound in ship's line and found in the Thames near Wapping as von Veltheim. Subsequently she decided, quite correctly, that it wasn't her husband. In 1900 he was deported from South Africa back to England. From there it was to Trieste for a splendid fraud where, in an outrageous version of the Spanish Prisoner Swindle, he represented himself as the last survivor of men who had been entrusted with the burial of £1 million belonging to ex-President Kruger. He only needed funds and the opportunity to return to the Transvaal to retrieve it and to this end he raised a considerable amount, giving bills of exchange as security. Acclaimed a public benefactor, a bust was executed in his honour.[13]

When he had milked the good burghers of Trieste he was off to Nervi where he seduced Henrietta Crodel away from her husband and then back to Capri. She did not last long. At the Hotel Pagano he met Maria Carrie Hulse and they began living together in Naples and Sorrento before he persuaded her to go to New York with him where he married her. June 1905 saw a 'marriage' to Ernestine Gauthier on board a transatlantic liner, with a friend posing as the priest, and in August 1905 he could be found in Neustadt in the Black Forest where he was Captain Oliver Jackson and took up with an old flame Clara Ketterer whom he promised to marry and from whom he obtained a substantial sum. Two years later she committed suicide. By now he had at least 20 identifiable aliases.[14]

However, his greatest long-term campaign was directed against Barnato and the Joels. It is difficult to know how much of von Veltheim's version of events is true – all of it was challenged by Solly Joel – but his story ran to the effect that in August 1896 in the smoking room of the Hotel Metropole, he had been introduced to Barnato who apparently wished to see the overthrow of President Kruger.

Von Veltheim proposed a plan to cause a split amongst the Boers, when he would then head a force of Uitlanders to join a rival leader. All very much *Boys' Own Paper* stuff. He reckoned the capital needed

---

[13] After von Veltheim's conviction in 1908 at the Old Bailey, the Trieste authorities offered to sell the bust to Solly Joel who understandably did not reply.
[14] They are listed by Sir William Nott-Bower in *Fifty-Two Years a Policeman*. See PRO Crim 10 98; the *Morning Leader* carried long and detailed reports of the trial, 11, 12, 13 February 1908.

would be less than half a million and he would expect that if successful he would receive between £30,000 and £50,000. Cheap at the price, said Barnato. Meanwhile von Veltheim received £500 as initial expenses and was put on the payroll at £1,000 a month. In April 1897 he left for Cape Town and met Barnato there on 7 May. It was arranged that he should try to find out what he could about the Transvaal government and have everything in place for the arrival of Woolf Joel. Meanwhile he was to say nothing about these matters to Solly.

What is certain is that Solly Joel took Barnato, whom he described as a very sick man, to England and during the voyage on 14 June Barnato, clearly disturbed, eluded his nurses and jumped overboard. The next year on 12 February von Veltheim sent the first of a series of letters signed 'Kismet' to Woolf Joel demanding £12,000. The diamond merchant was to put an advertisement in the Johannesburg *Star* by way of reply. Fifteen more letters to the brothers followed, including one signed 'Baron von Veltheim' seeking a meeting with Woolf Joel in the President Tea Rooms.

According to Woolf Joel's manager, a man called Strange, on 14 March 1898 von Veltheim called at his office and demanded £2,000. When this was refused he said, 'If that is your final decision, you two know too much to live and neither of you will leave this room alive.' He pulled out a revolver and shot at Joel. Strange produced a Derringer and shot at von Veltheim, who in turn shot him and then shot Woolf twice more.

Von Veltheim' s version was that Joel had fired first and hit him in the face, and he had then seen Strange with a pistol. He had only acted in self-defence and had immediately gone to an outer office to have the police called. The story was frankly incredible. The wounds to von Veltheim's face were over 25 years old and Woolf's revolver was found unused in his pocket. But Barnato and the Joels were not popular. Von Veltheim appeared before a Dutch jury on 20 July, when to the fury of the trial judge he was acquitted, but was immediately arrested and charged with blackmailing Solly Joel. A month later on 28 August the charge was adjourned *sine die* and von Veltheim was deported as a public danger to Johannesburg, which was then Portuguese East Africa.

He was not done for yet, however. From Delagoa Bay he wrote demanding more money from Solly Joel, who sought police protection in London in case von Veltheim should turn up there. Turn up he did via the Transvaal, where he served 4 months for breach of the expulsion order, and Natal to which he was then deported. Thrown out of Natal and sent to Lourenço Marques, he was arrested there as a vagabond and sent to the Cape. In September 1899 his wanderings temporarily ended with the outbreak of the Boer War. He offered his services as a secret agent to the Boer government which promptly had him arrested and jailed in Pretoria, where he remained for a year until the British released him and he was sent to Cape Town and then on to England. On the day of his arrival in London, Solly Joel sought police protection again, but von Veltheim was on his way to Trieste to work the Kruger scam. It was not until 6 June 1907 that he wrote again, this time from Odessa, saying Joel would not 'quite have forgotten the writer of these lines, and the unsettled account between us'. He continued:

> Let me see now if you have learned anything from the past or not, or again regret when too late. There will be no threats made, no further letters etc.; only a bill drawn against you, and presented for payment, which you can refuse to honour if you choose. I only assure you that you will have the sure opportunity to tell me personally your reason why you have refused.

Von Veltheim was arrested in Paris and extradited to London, where he stood trial on 8 February 1908 charged with demanding money with menaces. He was defended by Vachell K.C. and Artemus Jones, claiming that 'the letters were only to frighten Solly Joel and the scare came off. Indeed it did.' The jury was out a bare 20 minutes. His convictions and activities were read to the court, during which time this bull of a man frothed and shouted, 'They are a tissue of lies.' He received 20 years penal servitude, reduced on appeal, and was released on licence and deported during the First World War.

Meanwhile there had been another curious incident when, on 10 March 1906, a woman named as Marie Derval died of poison in Liffen's Hotel, Pimlico. A Mrs Young came forward to say that the body was in fact that of Mary von Veltheim who had been living in Cap Rocbrune with her 9-year-old son. It was generally regarded as a hoax.[15]

Obviously those such as von Veltheim did not fold their tents with the outbreak of the War and I have ended with a résumé of the subsequent careers of major players like him, and others whose careers are not concluded in their own chapters.

It is difficult to verify some of the stories. For a start, detectives in particular who wrote their memoirs used pseudonyms for those they arrested. Some of the memoirs were written 25 years after the events and, in the case of the criminals, these would be without diaries or contemporaneous records so it is not surprising that many are wildly inaccurate. There were also scores to be settled by the Sharpes, Lyonses and Guerins of this world.

One of the most interesting tales is that of Jean Cavaillac, written by H. Ashton Wolfe who claimed to have been an interpreter for the Sûreté and a general secret agent of sorts.[16] His books were hugely popular but it is impossible to verify many of the stories, in some of which he plays a major part. For example he claims that the French gangster, Jules Bonnot, was once his chauffeur and that he was present at the final siege in which the man was killed. The first may be true because in one of his books there is a photograph of Wolfe in his electric brougham, apparently with Bonnot at the steering wheel. The latter is certainly possible because half Paris seems to have travelled to the farmhouse to watch the shootout in which Bonnot was killed.

According to Wolfe, Cavaillac started life by being left in the tent of trapeze artists who brought him up. They are given only the names Auguste and Jeanne C. Then when Cavaillac was 18, Jeanne fell and was killed and her grief-stricken husband threw himself down to the sawdust after her. By this time Cavaillac was in the Army, but he deserted and took up with a Juliette Vendage. She deceived him and, with him tied to a chair, had sex with a rival in front of him. Later he cut her face with a broken bottle and was

---

[15] *The Umpire*, 25 March 1905.
[16] H. Ashton Wolfe, *Outlaws of Modern Days*.

sent to Biribi. On his release he killed her in Paris, where she was living as Mme Chataignier. The killing was conveniently written down to the Apaches.

He then killed a well-known prostitute, Régine de Montille, and a Marie Gremeret and her daughter. He robbed Eugénie Fougère at Aix-les-Bains and stole £20,000 from the Marchesa Malatesa on a sleeping car on the Paris–Genoa Express between Toulon and Monte Carlo. Now he teamed up in another killing with Marius Cabouet and Charles Fourrier who on their conviction were sentenced to death; he received 20 years. Having escaped from the King René prison in Tarascon after attacking a warder, he then occupied the Château d'If and killed a policeman before his recapture.

He was declared mentally unbalanced and sent to Noumea where apparently he became a model prisoner, but this was a ruse because he killed the warder and tried to seize an Australian trading schooner. Put on a boat back to France he jumped overboard, making his way by stages to Peru where he murdered a *haciendero* and his wife before being shot by soldiers. Unfortunately I have been unable to verify one single detail of the story, but it would make a good novel.

In these days of violent crime, with fortunes made through the sale of drugs, it is impossible not to have a sneaking regard for the ingenuity and resourcefulness of some of the men and women who worked throughout the period. Anyone such as the receiver 'Cammi' (also known as 'Kemmi') Grizzard, who had the quickness of mind and sheer nerve to drop a valuable pearl necklace in a plate of pea soup during a police raid, must have had something going for him. Regard must also be given to those who, sometimes successfully and often with limited resources, laboured to keep them in check. This, then, is the history of them all.

My thanks are due to Jane Adler, Tish Armstrong, Jeremy Beadle, J. P. Bean, Barbara Boote, Tracey Booth, Mary Croft, Marie and Clifford Elmer, Nan Ernst, George Forbes, Tony Gee, Jonathan Goodman, James Hogg, P. Hall of the Sunderland Local History Library, Gwen Kissock of D.C. Thomson & Co., Barbara Levy, Jean Maund, Judith Rollestone, John Sellers, Sarah Shrubb, Linda

Silverman, Matthew Spicer, Joe Swickard, Marie Swillo, Richard Whittington-Egan, Linda Wright, the staff at the Burton Historical Collection, Detroit, the Library of Congress, Washington DC, and the staff of many other public libraries and collections but in particular those in New York as well as the staff of the Public Record Office, Kew and the British Library in London and Colindale. As always any mistakes are mine alone.

Once more, this book could never have been completed without the unfailing help and support of Dock Bateson.

EARLY YEARS

1

Early Times in England

With peace in Europe following the end of the Crimean War in 1856 came the discharge of unwanted British soldiers. Many who were unable to find work in civilian lives turned to street crime to provide a livelihood. This was now the time of the garrotter, a trade which continued until the beginning of the twentieth century. It was not the Spanish form of execution involving a mask with a metal pin slowly tightened, but a neck hold which, properly applied, brought about unconsciousness. 'Properly applied' was the key phrase. Too much force and the victim died.

> You would come up to a man from behind, put your arms round his throat, with your fists on his throttle. If it went on for more than a few seconds he would choke, so you had to be skilled.[1]

A convicted garrotter could expect a heavy sentence: 5 years and, worse, a 'bashing', 18 strokes with the cat-o'-nine tails. A flogging in those days was not to be recommended. The former detective Tom Divall recalled Little Tim:

> . . . who had received two long terms of penal servitude as well as two floggings of fifty lashes. I saw this man's back after he had

---

[1] Arthur Harding. See Samuels, R., *East End Underworld*, p. 112.

served his times and it was similar to large pieces of cat-gut sewn together, and he had not the slightest feeling in his skin.[2]

The so-called High Rip Gang may or may not have flourished in Liverpool in the mid-1880s, but without doubt there was a considerable amount of violence in the Scotland Road area where the police patrolled in pairs. Here the legend of the gang grew up, much to the annoyance of the Chief Constable William Nott-Bower who denied its existence.[3]

Certainly there were a great many robberies with violence and woundings in the list for the November Assizes of 1886 presided over by Mr Justice Day. He dealt with the defendants sternly. After each verdict of guilty, and there seem to have been about twenty of them, the defendant was put back to await sentence at the end of the Assize. On the last day he was brought up and sentenced to a term of imprisonment coupled with 20–30 lashes of the cat. As a reminder, this was to be administered in two instalments, the second just before the man's release from prison. Crimes of violence in Liverpool, High Rip Gang or not, decreased sharply for a time after that.[4]

---

[2] Tom Divall, *Scoundrels and Scallywags*, p. 47.

[3] W. Nott-Bower, *Fifty-Two Years a Policeman*, p. 148.

[4] Certainly the *Daily Telegraph* thought there were High Rips. As part of Mr Justice Day's swingeing sentencing two lads of 19 said to be High Rips received 15 years penal servitude for stabbing a member of the Logwood gang. One man, said the newspaper, had to have police protection because he would not allow the High Rips to use a goods shed of the Lancashire and Yorkshire Railway Company, the keys to which had been entrusted to him. *Daily Telegraph*, 15 November 1886. There is some oral evidence that there was such a gang. In an interview in the *Liverpool Echo and Express* on 19 October 1960, Elizabeth O'Brien (then aged 86) recalled that, 'There were women in the High Rippers who identified themselves with a flower or plume in their hair. They were more vicious than the men.' She also said that the only control of the High Rippers came from a policeman known as Pins. When he approached, the gang scattered, calling, 'Pins is coming.' She would have been nine at the time when Mr Justice Day dealt with the gang.

Day also dealt severely with a small South East London team led by John Milligan who at the age of 22 had amassed 19 convictions while his brother three years younger had acquired nine. They were regarded as the terror of the neighbourhood, blackmailing shopkeepers and publicans. In the early hours of 4 January 1892 they were found trying to break open the safe at Maze Hill Railway station in Greenwich. The police arrived and a fight broke out in which PC Henry Smeeth was very badly beaten, with head injuries penetrating to the bone. The men were eventually caught and Day received 15 years and his brother seven. A third man George Martin maintained he had been wrongly identified. He was said to resemble a man Toomey who at the time of the burglary was on the

The Manchester detective Jerome Caminada approved of the cat:

> We hear occasionally about the brutality of the lash, and I am prepared to admit it is brutal. Still desperate diseases need desperate cures and the lash was the desperate cure that put an end to garrotting.[5]

Of course not all robbers were garrotters, and a temporary end of robbery with violence in London came with the hanging of the Reubens brothers.

On 15 March 1909 the steamer *Dorset* berthed at the Victoria Docks and that night two officers, William Sproull the second engineer and McEachern the second mate, went off on what was to be a drunken spree. They were not complete innocents; they expected to be tapped for money and, since they considered it insulting to give beggars bronze coins, they carried with them a supply of silver threepenny-pieces.

Around 2.30 the next morning the body of Sproull was found in Rupert Street just behind Leman Street. A policeman, called by the night watchman who found the body, saw McEachern leaning against a wall in the Whitechapel Road. His almost incoherent story was that the pair had eaten somewhere in Aldgate and had then toured the public houses. They met two girls, Emily Stevens and Ellen Charge, and agreed to go home with them to 3 Rupert Street. While they were with them the door burst open and in came the Reubens brothers, Morris and Marks.

Questioned by Inspector Frederick Wensley who was called to the scene, the constable remembered that two rough-looking men had been looking through the shutters of a house in Rupert Street earlier in the night. From the place where Sproull's body was found a trail of silver coins led back to 3 Rupert Street. Marks Reubens was arrested in the house, and Emily Stevens in Room 13 admitted that she had brought a man back to the room. As the police searched the remaining

---

run from Canterbury Prison where he had been awaiting trial on a burglary charge. Despite the judge's strictures that no one had called Toomey so that the jury could see what he looked like, Martin was acquitted. The police officers were highly praised and a public meeting was held at which presentations were made to them.

[5] *Thomson's Weekly News*, 6 January 1906.

rooms Morris Reubens was found and admitted that two girls had brought back Sproull and McEachern. When the men refused to hand over the rest of their money the brothers had attacked them.

When Morris Reubens was searched a constable found that sewn into his trouserleg were a series of hooks on which swung Sproull's watch and chain. It appeared that after having sex with the girls, McEachern had decided to return to the ship rather than to stay the night, taking Sproull with him. The Reubens brothers had known the girls had gone back to Room 13 and probably one of them had signalled to the brothers who were listening outside the room. Instead of rolling the sailors while asleep, as would have been the normal practice, if they wanted the remainder of their money – about £5 each – well, they were forced to attack them as they left. McEachern may have been hopelessly drunk, something which probably saved him, but Sproull put up serious resistance. Morris Reubens had a stick of hippopotamus hide and this was broken in the fight. Now Marks used a pocket-knife. Sproull was stabbed twice in the face and in the wrist as well as the body. They managed to get Sproull to the door and pushed him out on to the street saying, for the benefit of a passer-by, 'Get out! You don't live here.'

At the Old Bailey trial Morris claimed he did not know his brother had a knife. Both said it was the sailors who had attacked them; they were unable to explain the watch and chain. The defence was not one which appealed to the jury, who convicted them both after a bare 12 minutes. Morris began to call out 'Mercy! Mercy!' while Marks fought with the warders before they were led away screaming. They were hanged at Pentonville on 20 May by Henry and Thomas Pierrepoint. Marks is said to have apologised to Sproull's relatives and said, 'Goodbye, Morris, I am sorry.'

According to Inspector Wensley:

> From that date, robbery with violence grew unfashionable in East London and few unaccountable dead bodies were found in the streets.[6]

*   *   *

---

[6] See PRO Crim 1 112/4; F. Wensley, *Detective Days*, p. 92.

Inner-city poverty was rife throughout the second half of the nine-teenth century. During the winter of 1886–87 some 70 per cent of dock labourers, building craftsmen, tailors and bootmakers were unemployed, many for over two months. Unemployment in the three preceding years was the worst continuous sequence of any prior to the First World War.[7]

By 1887 it was estimated that one-third of Tower Hamlets fami-lies lived on or below the poverty line, and 55 per cent of East End children died before they attained five years as compared with 18 per cent of children from other parts of London. Plenty of other areas in cities throughout Great Britain were similarly affected.

Throughout much of the period up to the First World War, despite the attempts of social reformers mainly concerned with saving the working classes from sin while preserving the social *status quo*, there was no great financial incentive amongst the poor them-selves to lead an honest life. By 1904 in East End sweatshops a blouse with 'elaborately finished lace insertions and divers compli-cated frilleries' fetched 2½d for its maker. Bundles of firewood were assembled for a farthing each, and a pair of baby's shoes fetched 4d for the maker. Matches were made at 2¼d a gross, and bristles inserted into brushes made between ½d and 2d a hundred knots depending on complications.[8]

As a result incomes, such as there were, were supplemented by other means. In 1906 when Ernest Miller was sentenced to 18 months with hard labour at Clerkenwell for the theft of a watch and chain, the court was told that he worked in the popular music hall act of Dr Walford Brodie who pretended to cure the disabled. Miller would be brought on stage each night and hop about after being cured. The next night he would be carried on again. Each night he became worse. His case was reported in the same month that a young boy was killed trying to ride an unride-able mule; he and his colleagues were given a shilling each a night. The jury added a rider that they did not think the act was a safe one, something which must have consoled the boy's

[7] See W. W. Roston, *British Economy of the Nineteenth Century*, p. 49.
[8] *Morning Leader*, 6 May 1904.

parents.[9] Miller and his like may have been habitual criminals but they were minor players on a bigger stage.

At the other end of the scale, in 1864 and 1865 there was a series of major robberies in the City of London and eventually eleven people appeared in the dock at the Mansion House Justice Room before the Lord Mayor.[10] The principals were a fine quartet of men. The leader William Brown, also known as Scotty Brown or (his real name) Miller, had in the past served 10 years penal servitude and two sentences of 18 and 12 months. With him were Thomas Brewerton known as Velvet Ned, William Jeffrey also known as William Barrett, and Edward Wilkinson known as Carroty Ned.

The allegation was that in December 1864 they had robbed Bowen Sons & Co., bullion dealers of Lombard Street. The job, it was said by Brown, had been put up for them by an Inspector Potter. They had also been charged with a big jewel robbery at Walker and Johnson in Threadneedle Street as well as a silk robbery. In 1865 Waller's in Cornhill was burgled and the safe broken open by Brewerton who, along with Scotty Brown and Jeffrey, removed £6,000. Later an action was brought against the patentees of the safe who had claimed it would take a minimum of 11½ hours to open. Velvet Ned said that he had taken a mere 2 hours, and that was the time he would expect to use on any safe.

One of the witnesses was the 9-year-old Alfred Evershed whose

---

[9] *Morning Leader*, 22 May 1906. Samuel Murphy Brodie, who claimed to be a doctor from Chicago and FRMS, a Fellow of the Royal Metereological Society, advertised that he would 'give advice free to the helpless and paralysed. God Save the King!' He was in a civil case himself the next month. He offered 10 shillings per half-minute to anyone who could sit in an electrically wired chair. This feat was accomplished at the Palace Theatre, Blackburn, by a James Wright who with the help of friends had bound himself in copper. He sat in the chair until the irate Brodie had him bundled off stage and taken to the dressing room where he was stripped and searched. He was then brought back on stage and exposed as a trickster. Wright, who claimed damages for false imprisonment, was awarded £3. *Thomson's Weekly News*, 23 June 1906. Three years later he was in much more serious trouble when he was sued by Charles Henry Irving, a young man who paid him £1,000 to teach him the 'science of hypnosis and medical electricity'. Despite calling a number of people who said they had been cured after doctors failed to help them, Brodie lost the action after the student had given evidence as to how the tricks were worked. The next night he was pelted by university students on the stage of the Glasgow Coliseum and his shows were cancelled both there and in London. *Illustrated Police Budget*, 13 November 1909.

[10] Until the Criminal Justice Act 1967 Aldermen of the City of London were allowed to sit as single justices.

father had been involved with the quartet when they stole some 11,000 yards of silk worth about £500. Brown asked him when they had met and little Alfred helpfully replied, 'I've seen you long before you did the silk job.'

Also in the witness box was Brown's mistress, Susan Jane Price, and she was no help to him. The report in *The Times* indicated that he had questioned her 'at some length and with a strong vindictive flavour but without eliciting any circumstances in his favour'. Nor had Brown learned from this ineffectual cross-examination of his mistress. Asking questions of the Inspector Potter whom he had accused of putting up the robbery in the first place, he inquired how long Potter had known him:

> *Potter:* I knew you five years ago as a thief when you lived at the house of Blind Charley in Golden Lane and I have seen you dressed as a labourer.
> *Brown:* What was I doing when I first went to Blind Charley's?
> *Potter:* Thieving, which you have done for years.[11]

At the Old Bailey the women in the case were acquitted and Brown and Jeffrey received 20 years penal servitude while Wilkinson and Brewerton went down for 14.

Five years later came an early warning that travel in Europe could be dangerous for the wealthy. On 11 April 1870 the Greek bandit Takos, along with his gang of around 40 men, kidnapped Lord and Lady Muncaster and their family while they were visiting the site of the battle of Marathon. The women, along with Lord Muncaster, were allowed to return to Athens to arrange the demanded ransom of one million drachmas. The rescue operation was no great success; four of the remainder of the party were killed near the town of Dilessi before the survivors were released.

Back home the year 1875 produced a series of large country-house burglaries, mostly in and around Windsor. The Count and Countess Morella were robbed while the family was at dinner; thieves broke into the Countess's bedroom and stole jewellery. The

---

[11] *The Times*, 1 April 1865.

Belgian ambassador's home at New Lodge and Lord Ellenborough's home at Bracknall were also looted, as was Battle Abbey.

Then as now, the police tended to make a case against known suspects and stick with it in the face of other evidence. A prime example was the so-called Edlingham Burglary on 7 February 1879. There the vicar, Buckle, was awakened by his daughter at 1 a.m. and going downstairs found two men in the drawing room. He thrust at one with the sword he was carrying, and one shot him and his daughter with a spread shotgun. Neither was seriously injured. Superintendent Harkes arrested Michael Brannagan and Peter Murphy, both known poachers, who had certainly been out that night. Neither had injuries, nor were their clothes damaged by the sword thrust. The Buckles failed to identify them at first, but later the vicar did so. There was no evidence that they ever carried a gun on their poaching expeditions, preferring to rely on nets and snares. Although it was well known in the village and, it was said, amongst the police that they were not the culprits, they received penal servitude for life.

Seven years later a local solicitor discovered that an unsuccessful poacher named George Edgell had been out and about on the night of the burglary, and the vicar of St Paul's, Alnwick found that Edgell's companion had been a Charles Richardson. Edgell confessed to the vicar and the men received 5 years, sentences in sharp contrast to the unfortunate Brannagan and Murphy who were now pardoned and given £800 which they put to good use. Unusually, both had learned trades in prison and they took these up on their release. A prosecution was brought against some of the junior officers in the case but they were acquitted.[12]

Then at 6.30 p.m. on Tuesday 20 January 1885 Inspector Simmons, aged 37 with 20 years' service, and PC Marden, of the Essex Constabulary, the latter in plain clothes, were driving in a trap near Romford investigating a burglary. Approaching a railway line, they saw three men who appeared suspicious and challenged them. Marden spoke with David Dredge, whom Simmons knew and recognised, while the inspector apparently drove off for help.

[12] Arthur Griffiths, *Mysteries of Police and Crime.*

When he returned Dredge and Marden were to one side and the officers approached the others. Shots were fired and Simmons was killed. Dredge was arrested at the scene and James Lee was arrested some time later when he tried to pawn his revolver at a shop near Euston Square. The third man John (known as Jack) Martin, who described himself as a cigar maker with racing connections, was not caught for nearly a year.

Because of the hostility towards the men, the case was moved from Essex to the Old Bailey where it was heard in April that year. The defence was something of a cut-throat one. Simmons had made a dying declaration saying that Dredge was not with the others when he was shot. Lee called no evidence but, through his counsel, claimed he had not fired. The implication was that it was Dredge, whose defence was that he had been in the area on perfectly lawful business and was in the company of the others because he had asked them the way. In any event, in an early example of Craig and Bentley, he was talking to Marden when the shot was fired. He called several witnesses and was acquitted, though later he was brought up on a charge of assaulting Marden and received 12 months with hard labour.[13] Lee was not pleased at being found guilty. At a late stage he had asked to be allowed to call witnesses and was told he'd been defended perfectly well. When Mr Justice Hawkins ended the death sentence with the words, 'May God have mercy on your soul', Lee broke in, 'I've had none from either judge or police.'[14]

Lee, whose real name was James Menson, had joined Martin's Somers Town Gang after receiving two terms of penal servitude. He had changed his name after hearing of John 'Babbacombe' Lee who had survived three attempts to hang him. 'They couldn't hang him no more can they hang me', he is reputed to have said. If he did, he was wrong. On the way to the scaffold he is said to have told the clergyman, 'Stop your damned preaching.' His last words under the hood were reported to be, 'My poor wife.'

[13] PRO Crim 10 75. The volume merely reports the result of the case, giving no details at all.
[14] *Morning Post*, 28 April 1885; *The Times*, 30 July 1885; *Illustrated Police News*, 14 November 1885, 30 January, 27 February 1886.

The sequel to the killing was the raid made on Netherby Hall in Cumberland on 28 October 1885, one of the most sensational of Victorian robbery-murders. It has been suggested that the robbers were visiting Americans but they were Martin's gang. Before the raid there had been an attempt to arrest Martin in the Commercial Road outside the Theatre of Varieties but he had threatened an unarmed policeman, a Sergeant Roff, with his gun and escaped.

Sir Frederick and Lady Graham lived at the mansion surrounded by a park. He was a wealthy man who liked seeing his wife display the jewellery he had given her. She, despite the abundance of jewel thieves operating at the time, liked wearing them and – instead of putting them in the bank to be trundled out on formal occasions – kept them in a dressing-room which opened off her bedroom. That night she appeared at the dinner table and after discovering she had not brought her handkerchief, she sent a maid to fetch one.

When the girl went to the bedroom door she found it locked and went down to report the matter to her mistress. Sir Frederick, realising what was happening, sent his footmen to break down the door.

The bedroom had been wrecked, with drawers and contents thrown on the floor. A window was open and there was a ladder against the outside wall. It was painfully obvious that there had been a burglary. In fact jewellery worth about £400 had been stolen. The haul included a pair of diamond earrings, but because of the maid's interruption the thieves had not ransacked the dressing-room.

A servant was sent to the local police station and, in turn, the officer in charge there sent a message to the police in Carlisle. He also sent two officers to set up a road-block between Netherby Hall and Carlisle. Some hours later Sergeant Roche and PC Johnston saw four men coming down the road. Their orders were to stop and question everyone on the highway but when they called on the men to halt, two shots were fired and both were injured. Continuing on their way to pick up the railway line to Carlisle, the men were then seen by a PC Fortune who chased and challenged them and for his pains was badly beaten. They were then seen running into a goods yard and their pursuers lost sight of them. It was here that one of the four – Jimmy 'One-Armed Jimmy' Smith – split away from his companions.

By the end of the next day the trio of Rudge, Martin and Baker had reached Plumpton, near Penrith, and asked about a train to London. Since the last one had gone, they decided to stay in the village and two walked to the inn while one remained outside it as lookout. Presumably they thought that news of the burglary and the injuries to the police would not have reached the village because there were no telegraph wires, but it had been brought by carrier and there was a local officer, PC Byrnes, who seems to have been a man of some resource. He realised that with only his truncheon he could not tackle the three thieves alone and arranged for half a dozen men from the village to arm themselves with whatever they could find – hatchets, mallets and any shotgun they might have to hand. Unfortunately, by now the thieves had become suspicious of the hostile villagers and were on their way again when they encountered Byrnes on his own. He was shot in the head and died two hours later.

Now it was clear that there was no chance of their getting on the morning train to London and they set out again, this time to find a goods train. They walked north and arrived in Penrith about 10.30 that night. Their luck was in and they found a train facing south, but were spotted getting into a wagon by the guard Geddes who, with the train gathering speed, started to try to signal for help. His first effort at waving at a signalman was interpreted as a greeting and the man waved back. When the train neared Shap station Geddes wrote a note and threw it to a man working the points who did not see it. The next stop was at Tebay some miles away, so he decided to write another note asking for a telegram to be sent to the police there to meet the train fully armed. But of course he had to do this without warning the thieves.

Displaying great ingenuity, Geddes took his billy-can and put a note inside. Then – having applied the brakes gently to slow rather than stop his train – he showed his red lantern to signal to an approaching train to slow and as the engine passed he threw his billy-can to the driver. It was brilliantly conceived, but unfortunately the driver was going to a siding and that was his first priority. On the way there were no stations which had telegraphs, and the train came first. After that he would go to Penrith with the message.

When Geddes' train reached Tebay he was surprised to find no police on the platform, but he got off and spoke to the station staff as well as his driver and fireman, telling them of the situation. He too was a servant of the railway; there was no way he could delay his train until a message was sent to the police and they arrived. Reckoning on the men being asleep, he determined that the staff armed with iron bars and shovels should attack them. His move was a partial success. When he called on the men to come out, they fired but missed and the station staff then attacked, disarming two of them. The third escaped in the confusion. The two captured men were lashed to a telegraph pole to await the police and off went the train, barely delayed.

The men caught by Geddes were Anthony Benjamin Rudds or Rudge – also known as Fennell and Walsh, who called himself a dog trainer – and John Martin. The third man, James Baker, who had previously served 5 years in 1877 for a robbery in Greenwich, reached Lancaster before he was found hiding on another goods train. Baker had already served 18 months following the theft of the Duchess of Montrose's jewels.

One evidential problem, however, was to link the three men to the robbery at Netherby Hall. None of them had any of the jewellery on them when they were arrested. It was only after an earring was discovered at the station and later a pouch containing all the stolen gems was found by a river – which, it was presumed, Baker had swum in his escape from the goods train – that a link was made. A bullet taken from one of the injured constables matched the ball cartridges in a leather pouch which fitted Rudge's revolver.

Chief Inspector Abberline, who would go on to be prominent in the hunt for Jack the Ripper, travelled north to identify Martin as one of the men who had shot Inspector Simmons at Romford the previous year. Martin was also suspected of involvement in a robbery in Crookstown, Glasgow, the weekend before the Netherby Hall robbery. When pronouncing the death sentence the judge charitably warned them, 'not to busy themselves with any hope of pardon in this world'.

The three were hanged at Carlisle on 8 February 1886 by James Berry with a new assistant hangman, Charles Maldon. In fact Maldon was the Essex magistrate and Under-Sheriff Sir Claude de Crespigny, who paid Berry £10 for the privilege of assisting him. When his identity was discovered, something of a furore arose and questions were asked in the House of Commons about the propriety of taking work away from the working classes. De Crespigny said he had assisted because he wanted to be able to do the work himself if Berry was ever unavailable. He had spent one night in the prison, a second in a local hotel and had been the one to pinion Baker. He had seen many executions in India, had been present when Lee was hanged the previous year and the whole experience had affected him 'very little'. The Home Secretary replied that a baronet was as much entitled as anyone else to be a hangman's assistant provided he carried out his duties properly. There had been no complaints about the quality of Sir Claude's work. The role of hangman, like that of a guest at the Ritz Hotel, was open to rich and poor alike.[15]

Much to the annoyance of the police, local women had sent the prisoners flowers and food during their time awaiting execution. In his memoirs Berry recalled that the three men seemed indifferent to life once their sentences had been passed, something he found common amongst habitual criminals. Rudge spent some time writing to the Home Office setting out his views on the system of penal servitude. The others spent most of the time in bed. Baker was troubled about his companion Nellie and spent part of his last night writing her a long letter. Apparently on the gallows the three men shook hands. Martin told the clergyman that he had fired the shot which killed the officer. Baker called, 'Keep straight, Nellie' and they died, 'without a word of fear or even a quiver or a pallid cheek amongst them'.[16]

Afterwards there were, of course, congratulations and rewards all round and Geddes, who did so much to capture the men, received

---

[15] When the English multiple murderer and confidence trickster Frederick 'Mad Fred' Deeming was executed in Melbourne on 23 May 1892 it is said that the hangman, under a false white beard, was 'a person interested in one of Deeming's victims'. *Empire News*, 22 February 1920. For an account of Deeming's career see Colin Wilson and Patricia Pitman, *Encyclopaedia of Murder*.
[16] James Berry, *My Experiences as an Executioner*, pp. 73–4.

£50. As for 'One-Armed Jimmy' Smith, he managed to make his way to London and soon after the execution of Martin and the others he was informed on by his wife when he left her for another woman. She went to the police and told them that they would find him in Beak Street at 2 p.m. He was duly arrested and a wire was sent to Carlisle, but by then the police in Northumbria had lost interest. 'Man not wanted – am writing' was the telegraphed reply. It seems the only evidence against Smith would have been identification evidence, and the surviving officer was too ill to be troubled.

It is not recorded what Smith said to his wife, if indeed he discovered his betrayer. He was seen the following July at Wood Green Races, where he had a drink with Roff who had earlier failed to arrest Martin. By chance they were joined by the hangman Berry. Smith disappeared from sight shortly afterwards.[17]

[17] Henry Sutton, *From Constable to Commissioner.*

2

Charlie Peace

Despite claims in the rather dubious memoirs of Darkie Hutton, Charles Frederick Peace almost certainly never formally belonged to a gang.[1] Indeed, when he was hanged by William Marwood, he had been what could reasonably be described as a one-man crime-wave. Even though he mostly worked alone he undoubtedly had contacts with organised criminals here and abroad to whom he sold the proceeds from his numerous burglaries.

Peace was born on 14 May 1832 in Angel Court on the corner of Nursery Street and Lady's Bridge, Sheffield. His father had been a collier before becoming an animal trainer, and Peace himself later trained parrots and pigeons. He also learned the violin to a good standard and was a frequent pub entertainer.

At the age of 14 he was working at Millsands Rolling Mills when a piece of red-hot steel pierced the back of his left leg, coming out just under the kneecap. Peace spent the next 18 months in hospital before being released as incurable. Nevertheless, not only did he walk again but he also managed to learn to hide his limp. Nor did the injury in any way hinder his later career as a very high-class burglar.

[1] 'Darkie Hutton's Remarkable Life Story' in *Thomson's Weekly News*, 12 March 1910 *et seq.*

He started his criminal life as a pickpocket, when his speciality was a false collapse in the street. Afterwards, the samaritans who had picked him up would discover that their watches and jewellery were gone.

It is a measure of Peace's ability that his first conviction did not come until the age of 19 when he and a man named Campbell broke into Mount View, the home of a Mrs Catherine Ward, and stole jewellery and two pistols. He sold one and pawned the other, which was traced, and he received a month in the House of Correction. Campbell was acquitted.

It was the pawnshop which caused his second and more serious spell of imprisonment. In 1854, already an experienced cat burglar – or portico thief as it was known at the time – he broke into the house of a local magistrate and stole, along with jewellery, some seven pairs of boots. His sister and another were caught trying to pawn a pair and when Peace's mother's home in Bailey Field was searched a considerable amount of stolen property was found. This time it was 4 years penal servitude.

During his sentence he tried to escape, and when that failed he made a second attempt. After this there was no question of a ticket-of-leave and he was not released until he had served his full sentence in 1858. Now effectively he became a mobile criminal moving from town to town, staying only a few weeks in each. That year he met Hannah Ward, a widow with a six-month-old son named Willie, and began living with her. Soon afterwards he was arrested in Manchester. He and an Alfred Newton had hidden the proceeds of a burglary in a sewer, and when they returned to collect the jewellery the police were waiting for them. A fight broke out and Peace was overpowered. His mother gave him an alibi saying he had been home all week, but this time it was 6 years penal servitude. His daughter Jane was born shortly afterwards.

In Chatham prison Peace was involved in a mutiny and was flogged and transferred to a convict settlement in Gibraltar, but in 1864 he was given a ticket-of-leave and returned to Sheffield. It may just be that he intended to reform. Now he started a picture-framing business, which collapsed when he became seriously ill with rheumatic fever. So it was back to the houses, and he was arrested in August 1866 burgling a house in Manchester. He had been unusually careless because instead of taking the jewellery and leaving he had been punishing the master's whisky and was easily overpowered by servants. Charged as George Parker, alias Alexander Mann, he received a 7-year sentence.

He was released in 1872 and moved out of Sheffield to Britannia Road, Darnall, where he lived two doors away from an Arthur Dyson and his wife Katherine. The extremely ugly Peace had a considerable effect on women and he set his mind to seducing Mrs Dyson. Later he maintained they had had an affair, something she denied. Certainly he was able to establish that they had been to a music hall and a fair together, and he also produced letters which he claimed she had sent him. Whatever is correct they started off as friends, with Peace showing her son the tricks he had trained his parrots and pigeons to perform. There is no doubt either that the relationship, however shallow or deep, did sour. The Dysons moved to the Ecclesall Road but found to their horror that Peace had followed them.

He left them alone for a month and then on 29 November 1876 paid a visit to the Vicar of Ecclesall to tell him that the couple were wicked and they had ruined his business. He stalked about the neighbourhood, telling one woman that Mrs Dyson was a bloody whore and that before morning he would shoot them both.

At 8 p.m. Mrs Dyson saw Peace at the back of their cottage and screamed for her husband. He came running and Peace shot at him twice. The first bullet hit the wall and the second struck Dyson in the temple; he died within three hours. A coroner's jury held that Dyson's death was wilful murder by Peace, and £100 reward was offered for his conviction.

It was here that Peace's career as a burglar really took off. He and Hannah had been living in Hull, but he now took separate lodgings and worked his way around England on a spree – Birmingham, Bath, Bristol, and Nottingham where he lodged with a noted receiver. There he met Susan Bailey, separated from her husband, and again was able to seduce her. He is described thus: 'In spite of being as ugly as a monkey, Peace was a lion among the ladies.'

They began living together as Mr and Mrs John Thompson and moved to Hull where, with great daring, he rented rooms from a police sergeant who thought he was a commercial traveller. As for Hannah Ward, she thought he was on the run. The burglaries continued.

Finally the Thompsons moved to London where he took a lease on a large house and set up a *ménage à trois* with Hannah who brought Willie and Peace's daughter Jane with her. There they maintained an outwardly respectable façade, attending the local church, and Peace played his violin at musical evenings. He had stained his face with walnut juice and shaved his hair at the front.

For the rest of the time he continued his business as a professional burglar. He was quick and careful and would rob several houses a night. Carrying his tools in his violin case, outwardly he appeared a perfectly respectable middle-aged to elderly man. Diamonds, gold and silver plate were his speciality and he carried them in a large pocket sewn inside his coat.

On 10 October 1878 he was leaving a house in Blackheath through the drawing-room windows when he found the police waiting. He shot at them hitting one officer, PC Edward Robinson, in the arm; but the constable managed to hold on to Peace and he was arrested. He gave the name John Ward and his age as 60 years. On 19 November at the Old Bailey he was sentenced to penal servitude for life for the attempted murder of Robinson.[2]

Unable to keep up with the staining while in prison, the walnut colouring on Peace's face now began to fade. But before any serious inquiry was made into his identity he wrote what proved a fatal letter to a former Peckham neighbour, signing it 'John Ward' and asking him to come to visit him. When the man did so he was astounded to find that Ward was in fact his friend John Thompson. He went to the police; the police went to the Thompson house and

---

[2] Hannah Ward died at New Year 1892. She had been living with her married daughter who kept a shop at Burnall near Sheffield. *Illustrated Police News*, 7 January 1892. Robinson lived until May 1926, dying at what was thought to be the age of 78. For some years he had been an inmate of the Greenwich Poor Law Institution, for the last six or seven of them in Greenwich and Deptford Hospital. *Illustrated Police News*, 27 May 1926.

discovered a cache of burglar's tools. Of Mrs Thompson, Mrs Ward and the children there was no sign. Little was found in the way of stolen property.

Mrs Thompson was soon found and when she discovered that the £100 reward was still on offer for the murder of Dyson she confirmed Peace's identity. Somewhat unsportingly she also disclosed that Mrs Ward was back in Darnall, from where she was retrieved and prosecuted for receiving at the Old Bailey, but she was acquitted on the grounds that she had been under Peace's influence. Again little in the way of stolen property had been found. Peace almost certainly had professional contacts in Hamburg where he was sending the property for sale.

Things never recovered for Peace. Katherine Dyson, who after the death of her husband had emigrated to America, indicated that she would return to give evidence against Peace and on 17 January 1879 he was taken by train from London for committal on the murder charge. The case was part heard and Peace was remanded for a week. He was not lodged in a local prison, however, but taken back to London and Pentonville prison. He had behaved badly during the proceedings, interrupting witnesses, complaining that a sketch was being made of him and accusing the prosecuting solicitor of putting words into the mouth of a witness. Crowds came to see him at the station and police and porters had to make a tunnel through which he and the prison officers could pass.

On the way back to Sheffield the following week although handcuffed to a warder he managed to throw himself out of the carriage. The handcuffs came off as he did so and Peace landed beside the railway track dazed and bleeding, but he was quickly recaptured after the warders had stopped the train. News had reached Sheffield by the time of his late arrival, and thousands came to the station and the court. When committed he asked if he could sit by the fire for a little before he was returned to London but the sensible stipendiary, Mr E.M.E. Welby, no doubt fearing another escape, declined.

Peace was tried at Leeds Town Hall on 4 February 1879 and was defended by Frank Lockwood, who would later become the Solicitor

General. The only witness when the shots were fired had been Mrs Dyson, and Lockwood did what he could to discredit her over the supposed affair. The jury retired for a mere ten minutes. In the condemned cell Peace turned to religion and admitted that he, rather than a young Irishman Aaron Habron, had shot and killed a PC Nicholas Cook in Manchester in 1876. Habron, who had been heard making threats against the officer, had been sentenced to death but reprieved. He received £800 compensation for his 2½ year stay in prison. Peace had watched the proceedings from the public gallery.

Peace was hanged by William Marwood at Armley Jail, Leeds, on 25 February where he made a pretty if sanctimonious speech to the reporters:

> Tell all my friends that I feel sure they have sincerely forgiven me, and that I am going into the Kingdom of Heaven, or else to that place prepared for us to rest in until the great Judgment Day. I have no enemies that I feel to have on earth. I wish all my enemies, or those would-be enemies I wish them well and I wish them to come to the Kingdom of Heaven at last. And now to one and all I say good-bye. Good-bye, Heaven bless you and may you come to the Kingdom of Heaven at last . . .

And much more. He then asked for a drink and complained that the straps were too tight. Marwood is said to have remarked soothingly, 'Keep still. I won't hurt you a bit.' And he pulled the string.[3]

But Peace lived on to become one of the immortals of British crime, taking his place in the pantheon along with his contemporary Jack the Ripper. Edgar Wallace wrote a novel *The Devil Man* about his exploits and before that on 12 December 1927, nearly 40 years after Peace's death, the retired executioner James Ellis, playing William Marwood, hanged the actor William Morris as Peace on stage before a full house at the Grand Theatre, Gravesend. Echoing Marwood, he told a reporter that he was feeling nervous

---

[3] See Horace Bleackley, *Hangmen of England*, p. 240; *The Times*, the *Daily Telegraph*, 26 February 1879; *Notable British Trials*; J.P. Bean, *Crime in Sheffield*.

and, 'If Mr Morris complains afterwards he will be the first one I have handled who has ever done so.'

Questions about the propriety of the production were asked in Parliament and the Executive Committee of the Variety Artists Federation passed a resolution:

Deprecating the attempt to pander to the morbid taste of morbid-minded people by the appearance of a man who has held the position of public executioner and the enacting by him of a representation of his gruesome occupation.

However, the theatre manager commented that:

The hangman scene takes only three minutes and it is carried out quite decently. There is plenty of clean humour in the show which our audience enjoys and up to now we have received no complaints on any score whatsoever.

The piece was withdrawn after a week. Ellis had apparently invested some of his own money in the production.[4]

Actually, as a hangman Ellis had undergone an unhappy time with women. As an assistant he helped Henry Pierrepoint hang Emily Swann, who was hanged back to back with her lover John Gallagher on 29 December 1903. On the morning of her execution she was found on the floor of the condemned cell and had to be revived with brandy. After that, quite understandably Ellis was never keen on hanging women. Having conducted the execution of the terrified Emily Thompson on 9 January 1923 in the celebrated Thompson–Bywaters case, and of Susan Newell on 23 October that year, convicted of the motiveless killing of a newspaper boy in Glasgow, his nerve gave and he retired to become a publican. This career did not last and he returned to his initial trade of barber. Later he toured seaside towns giving exhibitions at 6d a time with a working model gallows. On 24 August 1924 he tried to commit suicide, then a criminal offence, and was discharged by the bench on his promise never to try again. But he

[4] *The Performer*, 21 December 1927.

broke that promise on 20 September 1932 when, after threatening to kill his wife, he cut his throat with a razor. Ellis was 58, and the verdict was of suicide while of unsound mind. He is credited with hanging 203 people.[5]

[5] See John Ellis, *Diary of a Hangman*. Ellis also wrote a series of articles for *Thomson's Weekly News* beginning 22 March 1924 in which he explained that while he was unable to bring himself to drown a kitten he had always wanted to be a hangman.

3

Jack in New York,
Chicago and London?

The Jack the Ripper murders gave Americans the same *frisson* as those in London outside his area of operations. Opinions abounded and the *New York Herald* sought out the celebrated lawyer William Howe to comment on the likelihood of the man being caught.[1] Chief of New York Detectives Thomas Byrnes was quite sure that should the Ripper dare to set foot in New York there would be no question of anything but an immediate arrest as opposed to the shilly-shallying which was going on in London. Thirty-six hours was the maximum it would take. He had the chance to put his theory to the test when a prostitute who went by a variety of names including Carrie Brown, but was better known as 'Old Shakespeare' because of her ability to recite bleeding slabs of the Bard when drunk, was murdered. Overall it was not Byrnes' finest hour.

Her body was found on 24 April 1891 in Room 31 of the East River Hotel off the Bowery; there had been some slashing of the stomach. It is possible the killer might have been attempting to disembowel her, and likely she had been strangled before the cutting began. Byrnes had to live up to his reputation and an arrest had

[1] For details of the life and times of William Howe, see Chapter 5.

to be made. The unfortunate was a French-speaking Algerian, Ameer Ben Ali, known unsurprisingly as Frenchy.

He had rented the room directly across the hall of the doss-house and the police said that bloodstains had been found on both sides of the door of his room. Convicted of second-degree murder and sentenced to life imprisonment, he was relatively fortunate in that a number of people were unhappy with the verdict. There were witnesses who said that there were no bloodstains on his door until well after the time of the murder. Carrie Brown's door was locked, but the key was not found in Frenchy's possession. She was known to have taken a client back to her room on the night she was killed, but no attempt to locate that man was made by the police. In fact the client had been recognised through descriptions in the newspapers and it was found that he had disappeared from a New Jersey boarding house, leaving behind a bloodstained shirt and the key to Room 31.

The Algerian was unfortunate in that it took eleven years to clear him. On his release he booked a passage home, but the man from the New Jersey boarding house was never traced.

That Jack the Ripper ever went to New York is highly doubtful. The story was nothing more than a bit of journalism which along with the boastful Byrnes had seriously unfortunate consequences for Ben Ali. But there were two career-criminal candidates from North America around whom passable cases can be made. The first is the extremely curious quack and patent medicine man, Dr Francis Tumblety, a late entry into contention for the title.

Tumblety was born in Canada about 1833, one of 11 children. His family came to Rochester, New York, when he was a child. There he sold pornographic prints on the canal boats and worked for the dubious Dr W. C. Lispenard who purported to specialise in venereal diseases. Tumblety disappeared from view in about 1850. He returned very grandly to Toronto ten years later, by which time he was calling himself a doctor, and he was arrested for manslaughter there after a patient died from what was described as 'atrocious treatment' – or what we would call a botched abortion. Now he went to Boston and, from then on, dealt in the much safer art of herbal cures. He was fêted by the press for having devised a cure for pimples.

He was in trouble again, this time only partly of his own making, when in 1866 he was arrested in Cincinnati and charged with some knowledge of or complicity in the assassination of President Lincoln. He maintained that he had been mistaken for a Dr J. H. Blackburn and was released after three weeks. The reason for the mistake was that Blackburn was the name he had been using at the time.

Now he published a book which in reality is little more than an advertising puff in which he described his ordeal. He walked the streets dressed as an English sportsman with tremendous spurs fastened to his boots and accompanied by a pair of greyhounds lashed together, and sued for libel over a music-hall sketch *Dr Tumblety's First Patient*. He claimed to have made a good deal of money and in 1875 he was urged to stand for the Colonial Parliament against Thomas Darcy McGee.

Tumblety first came to England in 1869, staying at the Langham Hotel in London, and he set up business in Liverpool in 1874 and from then on commuted between England and New York. He was certainly in London on 31 August 1888, the night of the murder of Mary Nicholls.

That day he had been arrested under Labouchere's Act, the Criminal Law Amendment Act 1885 which made homosexual conduct between males, falling short of buggery, punishable by two years' imprisonment. His partner on this occasion was an Arthur Brice. Accused on two further occasions on 14 October and 7 November, on 16 November he was bailed with two sureties and, being rather wiser than Oscar Wilde some half-dozen years later, fled to Boulogne before continuing on to America.

He had already quarrelled with the editor of *Frank Leslie's Weekly* and had been exposed as being 'involved in a modern Babylon' by W.T. Stead in the *Pall Mall Gazette*. Tumblety turned up again in New York in December 1888. The *New York Times* said the 'doctor' had been arrested over the Whitechapel murders, but the newspaper was wrong.[2]

A Scotland Yard officer was sent to New York, where Detective

[2] *New York Times*, 19 November 1888; *New York Herald*, 4 December 1888; *Pall Mall Gazette*, 31 December 1888.

Byrnes called at his lodgings just to see where he was and what he was up to, but then he dropped out of the picture. There are suggestions that Tumblety might have gone to Jamaica and Nicaragua at the end of the month, for two well-publicised murders took place there. He was also vaguely suspected of the Carrie Brown, 'Old Shakespeare' murder. The New Jersey lodger in the case was said to have sported a large black moustache, as Tumblety did. From the early 1890s he lived with his niece back in Rochester, and then with the Sisters of Mercy in St Louis where he died in their hospital under the name Townsend on 23 May 1903.

He is one of the many possible suspects for Jack the Ripper against whom there is very little in the way of hard evidence. Certainly he disliked women but so did, and do, many men. At one dinner party he had said he would sooner poison his guests than put them in the company of women whom he described as 'cattle'. He can be traced to Whitechapel at the time of the murders, where he was probably living in Batty Street. There is also some evidence that he was trying to obtain body parts of women. Chief Inspector John Littlechild wrote to the journalist G.R. Sims, saying he had never heard of a Dr D. as a suspect:

> . . . but amongst the suspects and to my mind a very likely one, was a Dr T. (which sounds very much like D). He was an American quack named Tumblety and was at one time a frequent visitor to London and on these occasions constantly brought under the notice of the police, there being a large dossier concerning him at Scotland Yard. Although a 'Sycopatia Sexualis' he was not known as a 'Sadist' [which the murderer undoubtedly was] but his feelings towards women were remarkable and bitter in the extreme.

Littlechild went on to write that Tumblety had got away to Boulogne after his arrest for unnatural offences, and he thought he had committed suicide, '. . . but certain it is from this time the "Ripper" murders came to an end'.[3]

---

[3] Detective Inspector Littlechild to G.R. Sims, 23 September 1913. Sims was a journalist who covered the criminal courts. Perhaps his best-remembered work is the often parodied, 'It was Christmas Day in the Workhouse'.

That Tumblety was Jack the Ripper is doubtful and certainly is unlikely to be proved. His name does not appear in the Ripper files at the Public Record Office and the dossier of which Littlechild wrote has disappeared. What is certain is that the doctor who hated prostitutes made a will in Baltimore two years before his death leaving $1,000 to that city's Home for the Fallen Women of Baltimore.

The second American candidate is another doctor, Neill Cream, who was at least convicted of murdering prostitutes in London. His claim to a position in the pantheon is that when he was being hanged for the murder of Matilda Clover, just as he swung he called out, 'I am Jack . . .' Unfortunately, by then it was too late to cut him down and question him.

Thomas Neill Cream was born in Scotland in May 1850, the eldest of eight, and went to Canada when he was four. At the age of 22 he entered McGill College, Montreal, to study medicine and he graduated with merit on 31 March 1876. He became involved with a Flora Brooks (whose father owned a hotel), impregnated and then aborted her. This latter was not the success it might have been and she nearly died as a result. Forced to marry her on 11 September that year, he walked out the following day and sailed to England where he enrolled for a post-graduate studentship at St Thomas's Hospital. He followed this with a qualification from the Royal College of Physicians and Surgeons in Edinburgh.

Returning to Canada to continue his career as an abortionist, he narrowly avoided a prosecution following the death of Kate Gardener, a young chambermaid who was known to have been seeking an abortion and who was found dead in a lavatory near Cream's rooms. He then moved to Chicago where he opened a surgery at 434 Madison Avenue and again was fortunate to avoid a conviction when Julia Faulkener died. By now he was peddling a remedy for epilepsy.

Despite a very pronounced squint, Cream must have been a man of some charm because a railway agent and epileptic Daniel Stott sent his young and pretty wife, Julia, to Cream to collect his pills. It was not long before Stott became an encumbrance to the pair and he died in agony on 14 June 1881. This time Cream was not so fortunate. In fact he was the author of his own misfortune, since he sent a message to the Boone County Coroner blaming the pharmacist for supplying the wrong pills. An exhumation and prosecution having followed, Cream was sentenced to life imprisonment in Joliet.

In this case 'life' meant 10 years and Cream was released for good behaviour on 31 July 1891. He went to Canada to collect an inheritance of $16,000 and sailed for England on the *Teutonic*. On 7 October that year he took up lodgings at 103 Lambeth Palace Road. Two days after settling in he met a young prostitute named Matilda Clover and then purchased a quantity of *nux vomica* of which strychnine is a component.

However, Matilda Clover was not his first victim. On 13 October Ellen Donworth had collapsed outside the Wellington public house in the Waterloo Road. She was taken to hospital but died before reaching it. Questioned, she managed to say she had met 'a tall gentleman with cross eyes, a silk hat and bushy whiskers'. He had a bottle of white stuff from which he had persuaded her to drink.

A week later Matilda Clover had the misfortune to meet with Cream again. This time she brought her client, whom she called Fred, back to her lodgings at 27 Lambeth Road. Although she died in agony, her death was ascribed to *delirium tremens* as a result of alcoholism. She was buried in a pauper's grave in Tooting.

On 26 October Cream picked up a Louise Harvey at the Alhambra Theatre and spent the night with her in an hotel in Berwick Street. The next evening he met her again and gave her some pills to take, but she threw these over the Embankment into the Thames. He had also given her five shillings to meet him at the Oxford Music Hall, but he never arrived. She described him:

> He wore gold-rimmed glasses . . . he had a dress suit on . . . spoke with a foreign twang . . . I noticed he was a very hairy man.

Later in court she would also describe him as being cross-eyed.

Next he sent letters to a Dr Broadbent who practised in Portman Square, accusing him of the Clover murder and asking for £2,500. He also sent a letter to the Countess Russell, then staying at the Savoy, accusing her husband.

Then came a lull. First, he fell in love with the unfortunate if ultimately lucky woman, the perfectly respectable Laura Sabbatini, who lived with her mother in Berkhamsted. Then on 7 January 1892 he sailed for Canada, returning on 2 April.

Ten days later he poisoned a pair of young prostitutes from Brighton who were then lodging at 118 Stamford Street. A passing policeman, PC Cumley, recalled seeing a man being shown out of the door at around 1.45 a.m., and two hours later the girls died from strychnine poisoning.

Cream then set in train a series of actions which brought about his downfall. First he suggested to his landlady, Miss Sleaper, that another of the tenants at 103 Lambeth Palace Road, a medical student Walter Harper, was the murderer of the two young girls. She thought he must be mad and disregarded the allegations. Then he wrote to Harper's father claiming to have incontrovertible proof that his son had murdered Marsh and Shrivell, the Brighton prostitutes. He took the opportunity of enclosing a copy of a report of the death of Ellen Donworth. If, however, Dr Harper cared to send him £1,500 he would keep his information to himself. Harper took no notice and Cream did not persist.

Then Cream began to behave even more irrationally. He told an acquaintance John Haynes of the murder spots, and discussed the cases in some detail. He also spoke at length to another man, McIntyre, who turned out to be a Police Sergeant. On 12 May Cream was identified by PC Cumley as the man seen leaving Stamford Street on the night the girls died.

Cream was arrested on 3 June 1892 and told the police, 'You have got the wrong man, but fire away.' The body of Matilda Clover had been exhumed and a jury brought in a verdict that she had been killed by Cream.[4] He was tried at the Old Bailey before the hanging judge Mr Justice Hawkins and sentenced to death on 20 October. On 15 November he was hanged at Newgate, when he

---

[4] There have been suggestions that the dishonest William Hobbs, who was later sentenced to imprisonment for blackmail and again for fraud, acted for Neill Cream. If so it must have been a clerk with the firm which practised from 13 Temple Chambers, Temple Avenue, because John Waters appeared for Cream at Bow Street Magistrates' Court and endeavoured to obtain a reprieve for him. For an account of Hobbs' interesting career see James Morton, *Gangland, The Lawyers*.

uttered the words which have immortalised him to those seeking the identity of Jack the Ripper.

Could it have been a confession? Possibly, but another theory is that since strangulation is known to produce an erection and emission amongst men, as a medical gent he may have simply been calling out, 'I'm ejaculating.'

Could he have been Jack the Ripper? His detractors, of whom there are many, suggest that the change in his *modus operandi* tells against him. If so that would rule out another suspect, George Chapman, who certainly took to poisoning a series of common-law wives. More telling is the fact that during the Whitechapel murders Cream should have been safely in the penitentiary in Illinois. Donald Bell circumvents this by suggesting that given the combination of undoubted corruption and lack of accurate records Cream may not have been in Joliet at all. Donald Rumbelow counters this with an affidavit from a clerk in the Montreal law firm which administered Cream's estate, which was sent to the Home Secretary. The affidavit, sent in support of an application for a reprieve, recounted the efforts made to have Cream released after the death of his father and the fact that when he called at the law firm in the early summer of 1891 they regarded him as unmistakably insane.[5]

There is a further theory which was advanced by Edward Marjoribanks, the clerk to Sir Edward Marshall Hall. Some years prior to the murders Marshall Hall had defended Cream for bigamy and now at his trial he recognised him. In the earlier case, despite advice Cream had refused to plead guilty, maintaining he had been in prison in Australia at the time. A check on the records there suggested that this was correct. Hall's theory was that Cream had a *doppelgänger* who had in fact committed the Whitechapel murders and as a repayment for the bigamy alibi Cream claimed the Whitechapel murders, so clearing his double.

In any event, two days after Cream's death a letter to the *Daily Telegraph* suggested that his undoubted insanity was the result of defective eyesight, something which the writer could have easily cured.

[5] See Donald Bell, 'Jack the Ripper – The Final Solution?' in *The Criminologist*, Vol. 8. No.33, 1974; Donald Rumbelow, *The Complete Jack the Ripper: Notable British Trials*; Edward Marjoribanks, *The Life of Sir Edward Marshall Hall*.

A third, if most improbable, transatlantic candidate was the Chicagoan serial murderer and career criminal Herman Webster Mudgett, better known as H.H. Holmes, who is said to have confessed to being the Ripper on the gallows at Moyamensing prison, Philadelphia. He also had the necessary medical qualifications. However doubtful his claim to be the Ripper, he is well worth including in a history of organised crime. He seems to have turned his hand to just about every conceivable type of criminal activity from bigamy through long-firm frauds to abortion, and killings both contract and serial.

Holmes was born into a respectable family in Gilmanton, New Hampshire, no later than 1860 and in 1879 he married Clara Lovering. For a time he taught in school and then went to Ann Arbor to study medicine at the University of Michigan. It is said that he paid for his tuition by using a corpse stolen from the school to swindle an insurance company. He may also have had an infant son whom he killed and dissected.

By 1887 he was working in a drugstore in Chicago owned by a widow, Mrs E.S. Holden, who then disappeared. Holmes said she had gone West without leaving a forwarding address. He may have been doing well in business, but he was having matrimonial troubles and his divorce suit against Clara dragged on until 1891 when it was dismissed after Holmes failed to appear in court. In more recent years his marriage had not troubled him greatly and on 28 January 1887 he had married Myrtle Belnap, daughter of a Wilmette businessman. They certainly had a daughter, but lived separate lives. Unfortunately he decided to forge his father-in-law's name on some deeds and, so Belnap said, tried to poison him. The bigamous marriage effectively ended in 1889.

By now Holmes was expanding into other forms of crime. The drugstore was also selling stolen jewellery and he was involved in an insurance swindle with Benjamin Pitezel who went to prison for his trouble. Holmes stayed outside, planning to build himself a castle at 701 W 63rd Street. In 1890 he purchased an interest in the ABC Copier Company, promptly swindled his partner, and ran the business as a long-firm fraud. He also made use of such medical knowledge as he had when he set up the Silver Ash Institute, selling patent medicines including a guaranteed cure for alcoholism. The building work on his castle was being paid for by his victims and he nearly collected $25,000 from the local gas company when he announced that he had a device which turned tap water into natural gas. This claim failed when it was discovered that Holmes had tapped a natural gas main in his home. However, he did manage to sell the scheme to a Canadian businessman, if only for $2,000, and meanwhile was selling bottled water to locals telling them it was pure artesian well water.

If a number of his enterprises failed, the store was doing well and now he hired a salesman, Ned Connor from Iowa, at a salary of $12 a week. Connor and his wife Julia, together with their daughter Pearl, moved into a flat over the store. Holmes transferred the business to Connor, at the same time suggesting he take out insurance policies on the lives of Pearl and also Julia who seems to have had some history of threatening suicide. Now he hired Julia, sacking his book-keeper to make a place available. Connor, no doubt correctly suspecting that his wife had become Holmes' mistress, left the business and Julia and her daughter moved into one of Holmes' houses. By now he had become a one-man crimewave. In August 1890 he incorporated the store, naming Julia as a director. The business was promptly mortgaged to pay for the building of the castle.

It had something over 60 rooms, with 51 doors cut in the walls. Holmes acted as his own architect, hiring and firing the builders at will. There were trapdoors, secret passages, and most sinisterly a series of *oubliettes*. One staircase opened onto a 30-foot drop over the alley behind the house. He planned to let out rooms to visitors to the 1891 Columbian Exposition to be held in the city.

Holmes was obviously proud of his work and in November 1894 showed a reporter from the *Chicago Tribune* around:

> Its staircases do not end anywhere in particular. It has winding passages that bring the rash intruder back to where he started from, and altogether it's a very mysterious building.[6]

[6] *Chicago Tribune*, 25 November 1894.

When the crash came and the police began their lengthy investigations into Holmes and the building, they could find no evidence that any guests had died there but plenty of evidence that a series of women had done so.

In 1893 Holmes had met Minnie Williams, a woman hoping to make her way as an elocutionist, at a recital she was giving. She was indeed the heiress to some prime sites in Fort Worth, and he had temporarily become Harry Gordon, a wealthy inventor. They became engaged and Holmes persuaded Minnie's sister, Nannie, to come to Chicago for the wedding. Julia was less than pleased and suddenly both she and her daughter Pearl disappeared. Later Holmes would say that Julia died from a bungled abortion and he had poisoned Pearl.

Then in April 1893 Minnie's Fort Worth property was deeded to Benton T. Lyman, an alias of the now released Ben Pitezel. Five months later Minnie's brother Baldwin Williams died in an 'accident' in Leadville, Colorado, said to have been arranged by Holmes. Minnie had assigned a $1,000 insurance policy on her brother to Holmes and when the insurance company made inquiries prior to paying out, Holmes and Minnie left for Denver. Sadly, Nannie could not go with them since she was already dead – killed, so Holmes would later say, when in a fit of temper Minnie had hit her sister over the head with a chair. To protect his wife, he had disposed of the body in Lake Michigan.

Holmes and Minnie were joined on the road to Colorado by the shadowy Georgianna Yoke. Holmes told her that Minnie was his cousin and married Georgianna on 17 January 1894, with Minnie as a witness, at the Vendome Hotel in Denver. It is almost certain that Minnie was a willing participant in the bigamy and frauds. Georgianna was thought to have a fortune of $3,000. The three travelled to Fort Worth where Holmes worked a horse swindle, buying them under a false name and shipping them to St Louis. Sadly, Minnie did not live long after the trip home. Holmes killed her on their return to Chicago.

Helping out in the Silver Ash Institute for reforming alcoholics was Emmeline Cigrand who perished, along with her fiancé Robert Phelps, when she decided to return to Indiana to marry. She had been introduced to Holmes by the ever-helpful Pitezel who met her when he was drying out at the Keeley Institute in Dwight, Illinois, where she had been working. She was only one of a number of the young women Holmes killed in his castle. Phelps had, admitted Holmes, been tortured before his death; he had been the unwilling participant in a 'stretching' experiment.

However, things were starting to unravel. In July 1894 Holmes was arrested for selling mortgaged land and was bailed out by Georgianna. Unfortunately she did not get there soon enough and while he was in jail he met Marion Hedgepeth, then coming to the end of a 25-year sentence for train robbery. Having devised a plan to cheat the Fidelity Mutual Insurance Company of Philadelphia by taking out a policy on Pitezel, Holmes was offering $500 to Hedgepeth for the name of a lawyer who could be trusted in the scheme, and he came up with Colonel Jeptha Howe.

This time the long-suffering Pitezel was set up in a store selling patents in Philadelphia. The plan was that he should drink a potion which would make him unconscious; there would be an explosion, afterwards his face would be doctored by Holmes to make it look badly burned and a genuine doctor would be called. Pitezel would be sent to hospital and on the way a corpse would be substituted. The Fidelity Mutual would be told that Pitezel had died of burns. Colonel Howe pronounced the scheme foolproof.

The explosion at the shop took place on 4 September and the next morning a severely burned dead man was found. No one claimed the body and then 11 days later Jeptha Howe filed the insurance claim. Carrie Pitezel, who knew of the plan, thought her husband was safely in New York. The insurance company paid up, but foolishly Holmes did not pay the $500 to Hedgepeth who told the police. They in turn informed the insurance company, who in their turn contacted the Pinkertons and Detective Frank P. Geyer was sent to investigate.

And investigate he did. Holmes was seen first in Cincinnati with Yoke, Carrie Pitezel and her children Howard, Nellie and Alice. They were next spotted on 1 October in Indianapolis and Carrie was sent East. It was then that Holmes killed the boy Howard. The remainder of the troupe went to Detroit and then into Canada where they lived for a time at 16 St Vincent Street, Toronto. It was there that he locked the girls in a trunk and asphyxiated them . . . which left Holmes and Georgianna Yoke.

They travelled to Boston where Holmes took time out to visit Clara, still the real Mrs Holmes, in Tilton, New Hampshire. He told her he had been seriously injured in an accident and had been nursed back to health by Georgianna. Unfortunately he had suffered from amnesia and, temporarily forgetting Clara, had married his nurse. Now he hoped for a reconciliation. There must have been something hypnotic about Holmes for Clara agreed. Meanwhile Holmes took the opportunity to borrow $300 from his brother.

Back in Boston on 17 November he was arrested for the Texan horse deal, a crime which carried with it the possibility of a lynching. He preferred to admit to the insurance fraud and in turn Carrie Pitezel and the good Colonel Howe were arrested. On 3 June 1895 Holmes pleaded guilty to a charge of fraud and Detective Geyer, who had been sifting through the lies told by Holmes – which included Minnie Williams taking the children to London where she was to open a massage parlour – now organised a search of the castle. There Ned Connor was able to identify some clothing of his wife, Julia. Minnie Williams' watch was found along with buttons from her dress, and there was a ball of woman's hair wrapped in a cloth along with the bones of a child.

The bodies of the Pitezel girls were found in Toronto on 15 July and Howard's remains on 27 August just over a week after an explosion destroyed the castle. It was never fully established who caused the explosion and suggestions ranged from arson, a safe-blowing expedition which had gone severely wrong, possibly viligantes and possibly Holmes' associates who wanted to destroy any traces of a connection with him.

Holmes' trial lasted five days and the jury returned a verdict of guilty of the murder of Benjamin Pitezel and his children, something he denied to the end. It was then that he admitted – a confession he withdrew within 24 hours – to 28 murders. Pearl Connor had been poisoned, as had Minnie Williams. Emmeline Cigrand and the Pitezel children had been suffocated. He also included in his confession some crimes he certainly did not commit. For instance, it was never satisfactorily established that Cigrand's fiancé Robert Phelps had ever existed.

At his hanging he, like Cream, is said to have called out, 'I am Jack . . .' It is also said that at the time of his execution a lightning bolt struck at the exact moment when Holmes' neck was broken.[7] His legend lived on with suggestions that he was controlling things from the grave, and certainly a number of people with whom he had been involved met unfortunate ends. Emmeline Cigrand's father died in a gas explosion; a fire at Fidelity Mutual nearly bankrupted the company; the jury foreman, Linford Biles, was accidentally electrocuted some weeks after Holmes was hanged; the priest who gave Holmes communion was murdered in a robbery in his churchyard. The janitor of Holmes' castle, Patrick Quinlan, who had helped to build a number of the tunnels and passageways, swallowed strychnine at his home in Portland, Michigan, on 6 March 1914. Dying, he said he could no longer sleep at night and wanted to die.

More prosaically Holmes' lawyer at his trial, William A. Shoemaker, was merely disbarred.

---

[7] See Richard Lindberg, *Chicago by Gaslight*; Robert L. Corbitt, *The Holmes Castle*. The lightning-bolt story also occurs in the hanging of John Herbert Bennett, convicted on not wholly convincing evidence of the murder of his wife. He was hanged at Norwich prison in a botched execution by the Billington brothers on 21 March 1901. The prison flagstaff was struck by lightning at the moment when the black flag was raised to announce the death. This was taken by his supporters as a sign that Bennett was innocent.

MARM MANDELBAUM
AND HER FRIENDS

4

Fredericka Mandelbaum

Since, as many a judge has said, 'If there were no receivers there would be no burglars', perhaps as good a place to start in America and with whom to set the stage is the Lower East Side, New York and the greatest receiver of the day, Fredericka Mandelbaum. From the middle of the 1860s the seriously overweight 'Marm' Mandelbaum, described as a 'bustling Israelite' and 'as adept in her business as the best stockbroker in his', was undoubtedly the queen. Her office was her home at 79 Clinton Street in what was known as Little Deutschland and she maintained representatives along the eastern seaboard, Chicago, Mexico and Europe.[1] She graduated from being a small-time receiver to the queen of criminal society, holding

[1] The district known as Little Germany was around 2nd Avenue and 6th. On 15 June 1904 the *General Slocum*, an excursion vessel, was chartered to take the congregation of the St Mark's German Lutheran Church for a boat trip. It left the East and 3rd Street pier at 9.40 a.m. and within 20 minutes a fire was discovered under the door of a forward cabin. By the time the captain, William Van Schaik learned of the fire the boat was in the treacherous Hell's Gate waters and he was trapped by rocks. The safety equipment in place since 1891 had rotted and had never been replaced. The intense heat prevented rescue vehicles nearing the boat, which burned out in 15 minutes. 1,021 people, if not more, died. The funerals lasted over a week and one involved 156 hearses stretching a mile on the way to the Lutheran cemetery in Queens. Van Schaik, then aged 68, received 10 years for manslaughter but was pardoned after serving 3½ by President Taft. He lived to the age of 90. The year before the tragedy he had received an award for safely transporting 35 million passengers. The district did not survive the tragedy. The German community moved to Yorkville on the Upper East Side and now Jewish families moved in. The church became an orthodox synagogue.

splendid dinners at which her favourite thieves, such as George Leonidas Leslie, 'Western George' the bank robber, sat at her right hand. 'As a handler of stolen goods Marm Mandelbaum had no peer in the United States.'[2]

Born Fredericka Goldberg, she came to America from Germany and took a position as cook to the dyspeptic Wolfe Mandelbaum, a pawnshop owner and harberdasher at 79 Clinton Street in Little Germany on the Lower East Side of Manhattan. A little good home cooking goes down well and, following the maxim, the way to Wolfe's heart was through his stomach. Given that she had by far the stronger personality of the two, it is fair to say she married him rather than the other way about. On his death she took over the business. Pledging stolen goods was a standard receiving practice, with the clients never intending to redeem their pledges. The receiver had the rudiments of a defence if charged. The scope of her dealings was immense. Sophie Lyons, one of her protégés, thought she herself might have had up to five hundred transactions with her, big and small.[3]

Marm took care never to have the goods initially brought to her home. Instead a messenger would call and she would send a trusted representative to examine the stolen articles and report back to her. Her integrity was described as absolute. She also established what was referred to as a Bureau for the Prevention of Conviction and would lend money to those who needed defending, but woe betide those who could not or would not repay her the fees advanced.

> Suppose you are a burglar and last night's efforts have resulted mostly in jewellery and silverware, you would have neither the time nor the plant to melt the silver and disguise or unset the stones. 'Mother' Mandelbaum would attend to all that for you on about 5 per cent commission.[4]

Although Lyons wrote that Marm never stole anything herself she was a regular visitor to Tiffany's to examine their collections of

---

[2] George W. Walling, *Recollections of a New York Chief of Police*, Chapter XX.
[3] Sophie Lyons-Burke, *Why Crime Does Not Pay*.
[4] Ibid. p. 193.

diamonds, her own preference. It was there that the idea occurred to her to set up a robbery and to this end she employed a Chicago shoplifter, Mary Wallenstein, and a pickpocket called 'Swell' Robinson. The man was the first into Tiffany's to examine diamonds and reject a number of them. Before he left one was found to be missing. Robinson was also a con-man and angrily rejected suggestions that he had the stone; he demanded to be searched and when no diamond was found, he was released. Next, in comes Wallenstein who looks at a few diamonds, rejects them and goes out.

The next morning chewing-gum with the print of a diamond was found on the underside of the rim of the counter. If Lyons is correct, this was the first recorded example of what was known as pennyweighting. She says that the trick was not worked again because jewellers' associations alerted their members, but she is wrong. It was certainly worked in 1905 by the highly talented Annie Gleason, posing as the daughter of Ulysses S. Grant, in London.

Marm was also credited with running the Grand Street School, one of the numerous schools of crime in New York towards the end of the nineteenth century at which small boys and girls were taught the art of pickpocketing and sneak theft. Older and more talented pupils learned safe-breaking and burglary as well as (for women pupils) the very skilled art of blackmail.[5]

Over the years Marm's weight bulged to more than 200 lbs and she was described in the Pinkerton files as 'a gargantuan caricature of Queen Victoria with her black hair in a roll and a small bun hat with drooping feathers'. Apparently, however, she was not vain enough to wear corsets.[6]

Not all her vendors were as faithful to her as she to them and one Mike Kurtz, known as Sheeny Mike and Mike Sheehan, was a good example. On 2 March 1877 he was arrested in Baltimore and taken to Boston charged with robbing Scott & Co. of bundles of silk. On

[5] Other thieves' schools were run on the East Side by Meyer Lewis, 'Cockeye Meyer', Joseph Monkey and Fitch. Children were dressed up and sent up to the Fifth Avenue stores. Those who worked downtown were dressed as schoolchildren and often carried books. Herman Doritz claimed he was taught in Teddy Gaunt's school of crime. There were 40 pupils in the school and after graduation they were sent out to steal property and pocket-books. They brought them back to Gaunt who gave them to men to peddle at half price.
[6] George W. Walling, *Recollections of a New York Chief of Police*, Chapter XX.

29 March that year he received 12 years imprisonment. Now it was a question of devising his release, which took him a year and a half.

During that time he drank soap-water and as a result lost weight by the stone. He also cut his side and, it appeared, pus began to flow. Now, with his wasting coupled with the wound, the prison doctors believed he would not live a month and there was a discussion about his pardon. Then, as now, rehabilitation cannot occur without a confession of past sins and Kurtz told the authorities that he had indeed stolen the silk and sold the whole parcel to Marm Mandelbaum.

Now Kurtz's rehabilitation was complete and he was pardoned by Governor Butler on 19 October 1880. The wound healed, he began to put on weight and was well enough to travel to New York where the good Mother M. seems to have forgiven him his lapse of conduct – if indeed she ever knew he was her betrayer. To add to her troubles she, poor woman, was sued in the civil courts and was ordered to pay $6,666 by Judge Van Vorst for acting as a receiver when James Scott, a Boston dry goods merchant, brought an action over 2,000 yards of material stolen by Kurtz in 1877.

Kurtz was again arrested on 30 January 1881 and sent to Washington, where he had robbed another silk business of over $5,000 of goods, but his luck was still running and he was discharged. This luck continued through the spring of 1882 when he was charged and acquitted on 17 May of possessing burglary equipment in Pittsburgh.

Superintendent George Walling, who later became Police Commissioner, said after the case, in which he described Marm as having grown 'greasy, fat and opulent':

> . . . we even hired rooms on the opposite side of the street from her store for the purpose of obtaining such evidence as would lead to her arrest and conviction as a receiver of stolen goods. Mrs Mandelbaum is a very sharp woman, however, and is not often caught napping. Whenever she buys goods off thieves she appoints a place of meeting where she can confer without suspicion. She will not allow them to come to her store under any consideration. Whenever any of the men from whom she buys stolen goods is arrested, she advances money for their defence

and compels them to pay a good round sum for her trouble and the use of her money. I am glad that for once the old lady has been outwitted and made to suffer for her violation of the law.[7]

Worse, in the July of 1884 she was very badly betrayed. There are a number of differing accounts of her downfall but it was almost certainly Mary Holbrook, aka Mollie Hoey, who did the deed. At the time Holbrook was working as Lizzie Wiggins. Marm Mandelbaum would not provide the services of her retained lawyers, Howe and Hummel, and when Hoey went to prison for 5 years she squealed.

Mollie Hoey had an interesting career. She had lived with George 'Buck' Holbrook, a gambler and thief who had run a sporting house in Chicago as well as a road-house in Randolph Street. He was arrested for a bank robbery in Illinois in 1871 and was sent to State prison from where he tunnelled out with two colleagues. As soon as he put his head above ground he was shot. Sensibly, his fellow-escapers backed down the tunnel.

What was a girl to do in the circumstances? The now common-law widow was arrested in Chicago in January 1872 charged with stealing $40 from her landlady, but she was able to put up $1,200 bail and fled to New York where she met and then married Jimmy Hoey. Wanted for the badger game in Chicago in 1874, where she had relieved a man of $25,000, she was taken back to that city for some reason via Canada where she managed to persuade a passing policeman that she had been kidnapped and had her escorting officer arrested. Taken before a magistrate, she was discharged and was not rearrested until two years later. From then on it was in and out of prison, very often in Boston, and it was to obtain her release in March 1884 that she peached on Marm Mandelbaum.[8]

On Hoey's information, Marm was finally entrapped by Detective Frank over some silks coming from a burglary on W 14th. The *grande dame* was not pleased and said to Frank, 'So you are the

---

[7] *National Police Gazette*, 7 February 1884. Marm Mandelbaum was not the only criminal of the time who erected a series of defensive barriers. No one knew where Eddie Goodie, known also as Muller, Goodrich, and Red Gearing, lived. The only way a thief could make contact was to leave a letter at an intermediary's address asking for an interview.

[8] See Benjamin Eldridge, *Our Rival the Rascal* and Thomas Byrnes, *Rogues' Gallery*.

one who is at the bottom of this, you wretch you.' She had hit him on her arrest and he wanted to prefer an assault charge but was told to wait. On 23 July she was produced in the court in Harlem, much to the protest of Howe who had wanted the case heard in one of the more sympathetic regions of Manhattan.[9]

The courts may not have been sympathetic, but the *New York Herald* was:

> When a man who has lost a $50 watch went to the police station and offered '$25 and no questions asked' for its recovery what could be more profitable for the time consumed than for a detective to go to 'Mother Baum' and buy for $15 an identical ticker for which the shrewd woman had paid no more than $10?
>
> To now have to run about among a lot of minor fences in search of stolen property that once could be confidently looked for at the Mandelbaum place will be very annoying to detectives whose habits have become fixed. It is no wonder that Mother Baum had never before been troubled by detectives. Shall a man quarrel with his own bread and butter, particularly when the person who provides it gives him occasionally a new dress for his wife and diamond studs to illuminate his own official front?[10]

In July 1884 a Grand Jury returned a bill against her and her son Julius along with Herbert Stroub, described as a clerk but possibly an unofficial replacement for the now deceased Herr Mandelbaum. She had trouble raising bail of $100,000 and three sureties were turned down before she was eventually released. A date in December was fixed for her reappearance:

> Rows and rows of stiff-backed, rusty seats were crowded with people who had come to see Mother Mandelbaum, the protectress of thieves, brought to the bar of justice. There were bankers and bank burglars elbowing each other in the eager chattering throng. Bewhiskered policemen and dusty old-court loungers were jammed together. Lawyers, actors, pickpockets, clergymen,

[9] Howe could see no reason, except to cause inconvenience, why she should not have been produced in say Essex Market Police Court on the Lower East Side. Harlem was at that time an area in which many Italians lived and worked.
[10] *New York Herald*, 26 July 1884.

merchants and clerks by the score strained and jostled and whispered in the most democratic fashion.

And in the midst of it all sat lawyer Howe with his legs crossed and a look of peace in his eyes.

There were only three empty chairs in the courtroom and when one man tried to take one he was smartly told it was for one of the defendants. Detectives Frank and Pinkerton lolled sleepily in their chairs. The District Attorney and his assistants were brimming with enthusiasm.

But yet the lawyer with the sparkling diamonds looked happy. Nor could all the detectives and District Attorneys disturb the beautiful serenity of his rosy countenance.

The case was called:

> Lawyer Howe arose and looked around the court carefully. His eyebrows went higher and higher up his peaceful brow as his gaze wandered back to the troubled visage of the District Attorney. Then a very red hand that glimmered and shone with jewelled gold was swung on high. 'I am forced to confess that the defendants are not here,' he said. 'No, they are not.'[11]

The authorities were right to have been wary of letting the woman out of their sight. Despite being under watch by Pinkerton agents who rented a house opposite hers, she had escaped. The neighbours who had let out the house to the Pinkertons were also telling Marm when the detectives were on the premises. She sent out a servant about the same build and heavily veiled and, while the agent was decoyed away, she and the others left the house and were driven to New Rochelle, where they boarded a train to Chatham Five Corners and from there rode to Canada.[12]

When she fled she took with her jewels said to have been stolen in Troy by two of her best clients, Billy Porter and the redeemed Kurtz. She was arrested and held in Montreal, from where the New York District Attorney prophesied the speedy return of her and the jewellery. But Howe did not think so and, as was so often the case,

---

[11] *New York Herald.* 5 December 1884.
[12] Ibid. Howe gave an interview to the paper the next day.

he was proved correct. Abe Hummel, the junior partner, was immediately dispatched to deal with matters, something he did completely successfully. Marm remained unmolested north of the 48th parallel.

It might be supposed that the authorities would at least pick up the $100,000 forfeited bail, but that would be wrong. Hummel had arranged a string of interlocking sales and mortgages so that the poor bondsmen were quite unable to pay the court and, better still, because of the complexity of the deals no further action was taken against them. Overall it was an outstanding triumph for Howe and Little Abe Hummel.[13]

Safe in Canada, Marm Mandelbaum opened a ladies' and children's wear shop and also bought a handsome house in Victoria Avenue North where she lived with her daughter, Mrs Sarah Weill. She seems to have pined for New York and through Hummel attempted to settle the charge against her. But she failed, although her son Julius eventually returned to New York in June 1888 where Moss, one of Hummel's staff, confidently predicted an acquittal. Despite all the earlier problems he was once more given bail. She was generally resentful of her situation; that or the newspapers made up their own copy – which is by no means impossible. She told a reporter, 'The *World* drove me out of New York and I'll have nothing to say to its reporters.'

Before she left for Canada, Howe had described her as: 'A lady the peaceful rectitude of whose life has been broken in upon by the rude acrimony of official strife.'

Marm may have pined in Canada, and the shop may not have been an unqualified success, but she was still making a decent living buying and selling stolen silk and diamonds. In October 1886 an undercover police officer nearly lured her across the border claiming he was looking for a bargain in diamonds, but her antennae still twitched. She gave the officer a stone, telling him to take it home and send her the price agreed upon. The next day he discovered

---

[13] It was not a good period for Marm Mandelbaum's team. On 10 December a Mrs Mitchell, described as one of a number of London thieves, was arrested in Chicago along with Mrs Martin, the wife of Ed Miller the safe-breaker who was then serving 10 years in Sing Sing. Mrs Martin was one of Marm's most faithful clients, *New York Herald*, 11 December 1884.

he had been given paste. During her time in Canada she was twice acquitted of smuggling lace and jewellery.

Marm did once return to New York. Her other daughter, the teenage Anna, had remained in Clinton Street and in November 1885 she contracted typho-pneumonia. Mrs Mandelbaum was reported both to have visited her – with the connivance of the authorities turning a blind eye – before she died, and to have watched her funeral at a distance. The route she travelled in disguise to the funeral was arduous – Montreal to Rouse's Point, Rome, Watertown, Ogdensburg on to Utica, then the Erie Road to New York. When questioned on the subject, Hummel was evasive.[14]

Mother Mandelbaum died in Hamilton on 27 February 1894, having been suffering from Bright's disease. Her body was returned to New York for burial. Like so many figures – Robin Hood, Lord Lucan, Elvis, J.F.K. and Robert Maxwell amongst them – people were not prepared to accept her death and six months after her burial there were reports that another body had been buried. It was thought that with the bribes paid and Howe and Hummel's fees her escape cost her $125,000. Overall this was probably not a heavy price.[15]

As for Mollie Hoey, after her piece of bad behaviour she was pardoned, but such credibility as she had in the Underworld was gone. She was arrested again in Canada and once more in Chicago, and took to visiting Detroit to see her husband. Hoey himself never amounted to much, contenting himself with fencing some of the property his wife stole. Mollie was a woman of undoubted courage. In 1886 she was jailed in Cleveland but dug her way out of jail with a pair of shears; her face and hands were badly bruised and scarred by the effort and when questioned by a cab-driver she told him she had been beaten by her husband. Later, in a house-to-house search, she was almost arrested, but disguised as a man she

[14] Readers were told that the shop was opposite the post office, and that she had begun attending the Anshe Synagogue to which she made substantial bequests but had not been allowed her own pew. 'Life in Hamilton' in *New York World*, 22 March 1885. See also *New York World*, 16 April, 12 October 1887; *New York Herald*, 11, 12, 13 November 1885; 12 January 1887; 23 June 1888; 27 February, 30 March, 31 March 1894; *New York Times*, 12 November 1885.
[15] George W. Walling, *Recollections of a New York Chief of Police*, Chapter XX.

took a boat to Detroit. She was thought to have eventually made her way to London.

Marm Mandelbaum probably had no rival worthy of the name, but there were several other women who were major receivers. The foremost was, perhaps, Lena, 'Black Lena', Kleinschmidt who, along with her sisters Amelia Levy and Mary Anderson, known as Mother Weir, visited nearly every prominent city east of the Missouri. Mother Weir was another of those who ran a pickpocketing school and was also the head of one of the larger organised gangs of thieves. It was a family business because one of Mary's sons would act as coachman. Lena (or Adelaide) Kleinschmidt built a huge house in Hackensack, New Jersey, paying workmen what was regarded as an overly generous $1.25 an hour. Claiming to be the grand-daughter of an English merchant and described as a sensuous brunette of 30 years, she kept a team of milk-white horses and half-a-dozen lapdogs. What interested her neighbours were her twice-weekly trips to New York. She also interested a man only named by the former detective Phil Farley as 'Blank'. According to the highly colourful account 'Mrs Blank', suspecting infidelity by her husband, took to following him disguised as a boy. It was then she discovered that the elegant Lena was a pickpocket working 34th Street and allowed herself to be relieved of an emerald ring. Back home in Hackensack she denounced her rival in front of Farley, brought in for the purpose. It then emerged that Ms Kleinschmidt was also the much more prosaic Lizzie Johnson, alias Rice alias Smith.

In 1883, only two months after a prison sentence, Lena Kleinschmidt and Mary Anderson were arrested in Chicago with large bunches of ostrich feathers under their cloaks. When their room was searched Saratoga trunks filled with goods were discovered. For this 'Black Lena' received 8 years in Joliet. She was discharged in June 1889 and went straight back to work in Chicago, but her skill was passing and in 1894 she could be found in the workhouse in St Louis.[16]

---

[16] B.P. Eldridge, *Our Rival the Rascal*. Another version is that 'Black Lena' Kleinschmidt also had a penchant for the upper echelons of society and she too gave dinner parties. These came to an end when one of her guests saw her own ring now adorning 'Black Lena's' finger.

Sophie Lyons believed that Marm's male counterpart was John D. Grady, who was known as 'Supers and Slangs' and who specialised in diamonds. It was in his offices that the failed robbery of the Manhattan Bank was planned. Grady also traded out of a satchel, visiting thieves at night. It seems that he was only once sandbagged and robbed of around $7,000 of diamonds, something which he good-humouredly put down to his own foolishness. The story of his death is in a contorted way rather romantic. He fell in love with the widow of a socialite and together they worked a series of confidence tricks and robberies. She apparently despised him but could not live without the work he provided. When it came to the pass, under increasing pressure, it was agreed that they would go away together. At the rendezvous to which he had brought his collection of diamonds, she tried to poison him. Although he saw her eyes flicker at the wrong moment and suspected her, he nevertheless drank the poison and died on the spot. She fled, leaving the diamonds behind.

Grady did not have that much luck with women. Earlier he had fallen foul of the highly talented swindler Ellen Peck, who persuaded him to hand over cash against a compartment in a safe full of imaginary diamonds.

Others believed that the best was William Brandon, '. . . a fine looking man with long silky auburn beard, clear complexion, a clear eye and regular features. He was dressed with all the elegance that ample means and good taste can command.' Edward Crapsey thought that Brandon, who operated from Eighth Street and Broadway, was Marm's superior, certainly in the early days. Although he had a number of run-ins with the police and courts he seems to have avoided any conviction. Once when gambling equipment was stolen from 720 Broadway the judge conveniently ruled that such articles were not property. On another occasion there were no identifying marks, and again when he was arrested over the theft of $3,000 of kid gloves, there was a defect in the evidence.[17]

Another of the great receivers was Marm's friend, 'General' Abe Greenthal, who in his younger days had been an expert pickpocket

---

[17] Edward Crapsey, *The Nether Side of New York*, pp. 86–7.

and was known throughout the States as the man who led the Sheeny Mob.

The General was born Abraham Lester in Prussia in 1831 shortly before his father began a 15-year sentence for robbery. He received 2 years for theft of a gold watch at the age of 18 and on his release teamed up with his father and another man who was later replaced by Lesler's brother in a nationwide series of thefts. It resulted in a 7-year sentence for both. The General escaped with the help of his wife while being transferred between prisons; she had been allowed to walk part of the way with him and they took the opportunity to make off. It was on to Berlin where he bought papers that enabled him to get to Liverpool. On the day his wife arrived in England they left for New York, where they again took up pickpocketing. A passionate gambler, he served a 3-year sentence, again for theft, in 1864 and then became a high-class receiver.

He lived in the 10th Ward and had been a receiver for the better part of 30 years. Unlike Brandon, however, he had been in and out of prison. On 19 April 1877, with his brother Harris and Samuel Casper his son-in-law also in the dock, the General had received 20 years for robbery in Rochester but had been pardoned in the spring of 1884. The General was arrested again – this time with Bendick Gaetz, known as The Cockroach – for pickpocketing on a cross-town horse-car in Williamsburg and received 5 years. On his release and on the disappearance of Marm, he took over a large part of her business.

5

'Here's Howe, Here's Hummel'

In 1851 a young man gave evidence at the celebrated Stanfield Hall murder trial when James Bloomfield Rush, who had been disguised in a red and black mask and a long wig, was accused of killing his landlord Isaac Jermy, the Recorder of Norwich, and injuring his wife and maid. Rush, who lived with his mistress-cum-servant Emily Sandford and nine children, had farmed at Potash Farm. He had been made bankrupt and was due to be evicted within the next forty-eight hours.

Rush was the only suspect and, the worse for him, was recognised through his disguise. He denied everything, produced a certificate cancelling the mortgage and claimed he had not left Potash Farm that night. However, Emily Sandford would not support the alibi, the wig and mask were found at Potash, and the certificate was shown to be a clumsy forgery. It was such a simple case.

Nevertheless it was a trial followed with interest throughout the country from Queen Victoria downwards. The weekly Norfolk papers ran daily editions for the duration of the proceedings, and there were special excursion trains to Norwich. The jury retired for a bare six minutes and Rush was publicly hanged outside Norwich Castle by Chalcraft to great acclaim on 21 April 1849. His effigy was made for Madame Tussaud's and, as was the custom, was dressed in his own clothes. A set of Staffordshire pottery flatback figures of

Jermy, Rush, Emily Sandford, the Hall and Potash Farm were cast and became highly collectable items.[1]

The young man who gave evidence was William F. Howe, who would go on to become the greatest advocate of his day in New York and probably one of the greatest, if crookedest, criminal lawyers of all time. Howe's modest part in the trial was confined to producing some mortgage documents, but overall his career spanned more than half a century.

It is said that the word shyster is a corruption of Scheuster, pronounced shoister, an unscrupulous lawyer in the Essex Street court on the Lower East Side in the 1840s. 'Don't let's have these Scheuster practices in this court,' Justice Osborne is alleged to have said. The story has been denounced on the grounds that records show no lawyer of that name on the rolls of the court, but the name has stuck. Whether it is true or whether Scheuster is an apocryphal character, he could not have lived with the misdeeds of Howe and his protégé, later his partner, Abraham Hummel.[2]

Howe was primarily a great advocate; unscrupulous in his court appearances but probably far less venal than the more astute and businesslike Hummel who made a practice out of blackmail and dishonesty.[3] It is sometimes said that they were the real brains behind crime in New York of the period. This may be an exaggeration but it is certainly not a major one. The roll-call of their clients produces the great names of crime of all hues – General Abe Greenthal's Sheeny Mob of thieves; Chester McLaughlin's gang of

[1] The night before his execution on 21 April 1849, Rush told the Governor of Norwich prison that he wanted 'roast pig and plenty of plum sauce' for his dinner. On the scaffold he instructed William Chalcraft, the hangman, to 'put the noose a little higher'. For an account of the case and Howe's small part, see the *Notable British Trials* series. Other accounts include Leonard Gribble, *Famous Judges and their Trials*.

[2] Of course there were many other crooked lawyers. In one case, on 10 February 1909 the District Attorney Travers Jerome foiled a plot to free Harry Rimington Mercer from the Tombs. Lawyer Joseph A. Shay was picked up in the sweep, along with Walter Peck who obtained accident work for Shay on a contingency basis. Mercer had also been an accident chaser for Shay and had obtained a $4,000 settlement for the little daughter of William Helter who received no money. The escape was to be a simple switch of identity with eyeglasses and a coat at the time of the 4 p.m. changeover for warders. It was thought that Shay had gone along with the plan rather than have his conduct in a previous case revealed.

[3] Not everyone agrees that Howe was the less dishonest. Richard Rovere describes him as a 'very queer tick indeed. He was a man with a past which he found prudent to conceal . . .' *Howe and Hummel*, p. 35.

forgers; the Whyos, the toughest and most political of the street gangs of the time; Joe Douglas, kidnapper of little Charley Ross; Charles O. Brockway, whose forgeries of treasury bills were such that for a time the $100 note had to be withdrawn; and George Leonidas Leslie, the most accomplished safe-breaker of the period. At least 74 brothel keepers who were rounded up in one of the periodic purity drives of the 1880s named Howe and Hummel as their legal counsel. They also represented the notorious Clafin sisters, swindlers and charlatans who went on to become pillars of London society – one married into the peerage – in their fight against Anthony Comstock and the New York Society for the Suppression of Vice. The claim was over an alleged libel in a magazine they had published libelling friends of 'the Divine,' Beecher Ward. But the *crème de la crème* of their criminal clientele was the celebrated receiver, Fredericka 'Marm' Mandelbaum who was said to pay them a $5,000 annual retainer. Backed by the *New York Herald* they were constant sources of copy. What did Howe think of Jack the Ripper? What did Hummel think of the new play on Broadway?

Amongst their regular clients were politicians, judges, jurors, police officers, society men and women, thieves, prostitutes and almost every murderer who could raise the money for their fees. At one time, out of 25 murderers in the Tombs prison awaiting trial 23 were represented by Howe and Hummel and the pair had what might be described as an interest in one of the others. Howe put it about that he had 'been invited to assist in the defence of Stokes, but for reasons which cannot now be made public I declined'.

In fact it was more than an interest. The murder by Edward S. Stokes of Colonel James Fisk on 6 January 1872 on the steps of the Broadway Central Hotel garnered the most attention since the murder of Lincoln by John Wilkes Booth. Both Stokes and Fisk were rich men. Fisk was the financial wrecker of the Erie Railroad, while Stokes came from a wealthy Brooklyn family. Business rivals, they had recently been involved in a libel action and were also rivals for the affections of the beautiful actress Josie Mansfield. Although there was substantial evidence of Stokes' guilt, after three trials and, it was said, a great deal of tampering by Howe, Stokes

was given a 4-year sentence for manslaughter. In fact, the reason
why Howe had declined to appear at the trial was the sensible one
that there might have been, even for them, an insuperable conflict
of interests. Howe and Hummel had got to the only eye-witness to
the shooting. They had paid the man, probably a doctor, a huge
sum of money to leave the country with an undertaking never to
return or let them know where he had gone.[4]

Howe maintained he was born on 7 July 1828 at Shawmut Street,
Boston, the son of the Rev. Samuel Howe M.A., and then went to
England. He said he attended King's College, London, and entered
the office of George Waugh, the noted barrister. He then moved to
the offices of E.H. Seeley. Unfortunately records to support this
claim do not exist.

Another, less generous, version of Howe's life before arrival in
New York was that he was a ticket-of-leave man. It is also said that
at times he spoke with a cockney accent. It is almost certain that
he had some sort of criminal record in England and when he was
sued over his fees in 1874 by a pair of white slavers, William and
Adelaide Beaumont, he was asked about his early life. A. Oakey
Hall of the Tweed Ring appeared for him and objected to the question on the grounds of its relevance. The objection was sustained,
as was a question whether he had lost his licence to practise medicine. He was also asked if he was the same William Frederick Howe
wanted for murder in England and the same W.F.H. convicted of
forgery in Brooklyn a few years earlier. He denied both allegations
and – unlike the situation in an English court, where the accuser
would have been required to offer some proof of the allegation –
there is no record of the judge ordering this.

Howe clearly had financial troubles in the middle part of his
career and he went into voluntary bankruptcy in October 1885.
This was seen as a ruse because 18 months later in May 1887 a
Joseph E. Redmond petitioned the court to vacate the order on the
grounds that Howe had acted deliberately to impede his creditors.
It was estimated that his debts had been in the region of $20,000.
Redmond said that Howe had enough money to pay everybody,

[4] Edgar Salinger, letter to *The New Yorker*, 28 December 1946.

and on 25 May a creditors' meeting showed debts of only $8,700 which he paid. His behaviour does not appear to have impeded his practice in any way. In any event all his financial problems were ironed out the next year when he received a fee of $90,000 for representing Leslie's interests in the Manhattan Savings Bank case.

Howe weighed nearly 300 lbs, and in later life had closely cropped curly white hair and a moustache. Arthur Train, who practised law shortly after Howe's heyday, maintained that his fortune was not in his face but in his clothing:

> In imitation, it was said, of Commodore Gerry, he always wore a blue yachting cap, sometimes a navigator's blue coat and white trousers but more often a loudly checked brown suit, with a low-cut vest, displaying the starched bosom of a bright pink shirt and a pink collar innocent of tie, in place of which he sported a gigantic diamond stud, with others of equal size adorning his chest. These he changed on occasion to pearls in the afternoon. Diamonds glittered upon his fingers; on his feet were either yachting shoes or dinky patent leathers with cloth uppers; in his lapel a rose or carnation; in his breast pocket a huge silk handkerchief into which he shed, with enormous effect, showers of crocodile tears when defending his clients.[5]

New cases meant more jewellery and, in October 1887, Howe wore an entirely new set of diamonds when successfully defending policeman Edward Hann for the murder of 'Captain' Jack Hussey.[6]

Towards the end of his life Howe was asked about his jewellery:

> When I was a young lawyer it was necessary to show signs of prosperity. All the young lawyers who were getting a good fee wore diamonds. The size of a lawyer's fees were then somewhat regulated by the size of the diamonds he wore. If I had given

---

[5] Arthur Train, *My Day in Court*, p. 27. Howe was not the only flamboyant dresser amongst the New York lawyers of the period. Counsellor Tom Nolan wore a Prince Albert coat with low-cut sateen evening waistcoat, and sported in lieu of a tie a diamond collar-button and three jewelled breast pins; the top one was an emerald shamrock, in the middle came the United States flag in rubies and at the bottom was a flapping American eagle also in rubies.
[6] *New York Herald*, 11 October 1887.

up wearing those diamonds the word would have gone all over the city, 'Bill Howe is broke.' I hate those diamonds but, you see, I have to keep wearing them so that people won't think I'm broke.[7]

He was certainly one of the great old-fashioned barnstorming advocates, but he must also have been a considerable lawyer. The Conscription Act 1863 was aimed at family men. No longer could a family man claim exemption from the Union forces on the grounds that he was the sole support of his wife and children, but he could furnish $300 or provide a substitute for himself. There was great resentment, particularly amongst the Irish in the Hell's Kitchen district of 8th and 9th Avenues, and the consequent Draft Riots ran from 13 to 17 July 1863. Howe was responsible for the successful argument that the Draft Laws in the American Civil War were unlawful because they discriminated against the poor. For a time he was known as Habeas Corpus Howe because of the number of soldiers he managed to get out of the Army on the grounds that they had signed their enlistment papers when drunk.

He also persuaded the authorities to accept a plea of attempted arson on behalf of the professional arsonist Owen Reilly. The prosecution had not noticed that there was no set penalty for attempted arson, only one half of the maximum for the completed offence, in this case life. Howe was at his most biblical:

Scripture tells us that we knoweth not the day nor the hour of our departure. Can this court sentence the prisoner at the bar to half of his natural life? Will it then sentence him to half a minute or half the days of Methuselah?[8]

Reilly walked free but the law was swiftly changed.

On another occasion, perhaps with even less merit, Howe argued that his client could not be hanged because the State had passed a Bill ruling that all future executions should be by electrocution.

[7] Quoted in 'Decadence of New York's Criminal Bar' in *New York Times*, 7 September 1902.
[8] Quoted in Richard H. Rovere, *Howe and Hummel*, p. 52.

Since this was not yet in force, it followed that his client must go free.

On the night of 28 October 1888 Harry Carleton, known to his friends as Handsome Harry, shot and killed Patrolman James Brennan. He was regarded as the leader of an East Side gang which included his brother-in-law Thomas 'Boss' McKenna, Edward Ahearne and William Burke. Carleton, Ahearne and Burke had had their eyes on a somewhat drunken German waiter, Julius Roesler, or at least on his silver-handled umbrella, and had been trying to buy him drinks in Tuckers at Third and 33rd where he had left the umbrella for safe-keeping. He had turned down the offer and they followed him home. When he asked the help of Patrolman Brennan, he was told to go on home. As he arrived on his doorstep Carleton and the others reappeared. He called for help, and Brennan answered the call only to be shot in the face at point-blank range by Carleton. To his credit Roesler chased after Carleton, who shouted, 'Go back, you Dutch pig, or I'll shoot you', but by this time two other plainclothes police officers had joined in and arrested him. Ahearne and Burke escaped.

It was just a lucky night for 'Boss' McKenna; he was already in custody on a robbery charge on which the victim, James Scotty, failed to identify him. But it was not a good night for Scotty. Apart from being relieved of his watch, the court took $10 off him the following day for drunkenness.

The next day, unsurprisingly, the press was not at all keen on Handsome Harry. The *New York Herald* described him as having a weak face and vicious lines 'abated by a mustache'. In keeping with the times they gave a list of his previous appearances in court. His first had been at the age of 16 for till tapping, and on 27 November 1882 he had been convicted of robbery at Corcorna's Roost at First and 40th. He had tried to shoot a policeman on this occasion as well and had received 5 years.

On his arraignment, 'Handsome Harry's Ugly Day', it appeared that drunkenness would be his only defence; but with the arrival of 'Little Abe Hummel and his belligerent partner, the redoubtable William F. Howe', things took a different course. Prosecution counsel ex-Judge Gunning S. Bedford for one was impressed – or was his tongue wedged in cement?

His counsel it is usually admitted stand the first among their peers for unsurpassed ability, great legal acumen and eloquence, which it is indeed difficult to resist. But gentlemen [of the jury] even these high and ennobling attributes of mind must occasionally give way and yield to the majesty of truth.[9]

Whatever is said about the methods of Howe and Hummel, they worked hard for their clients. The junior partner, Joseph Moss, handled the empanelling and challenging of the jury but the great man, Howe, was there himself to challenge the way the trial judge was making him object to each juror one by one rather than wait until all twelve were in the box. An attempt to get the prosecution to use their 30 challenges failed. Howe's objection was overruled and he asked for an exception to be noted; this was the standard way of setting out an appeal case. In all, by the end of the three-day trial he would have 35 exceptions noted. As for the jurors, 9 of the 18 stood down were excused on the basis that they opposed capital punishment.

The case would seem to have been overwhelming, but Howe was not done for. Drunkenness would no longer be the issue except insofar as it concerned the unfortunate Roesler whom the newspaper reported as saying, when an attempt was made to challenge his recollection, 'Of course I was not sober like dem temperance beople vot drink nodings, but I vas not drunk' (sic).

Now Howe was going for a verdict of murder in the second degree, which did not carry the death penalty. It would be a question of self-defence. New York policemen were noted for their use of the nightstick and Howe was able to show that Brennan did in fact have two charges of clubbing against him. He claimed that Carleton had only shot the officer after he himself had been hit, but unfortunately there was only Carleton to support this theory. Despite the initial belief of the police that they would soon have the others in custody, they had failed to find them.

The jury was sent out at 7 p.m. on the evening of 14 December and returned in 40 minutes with a guilty verdict.

[9] *New York Herald*, 29, 30 October, 10–15 December 1888.

Did Carleton quail? No; he stood up with one hand on the desk before him, with one leg crossed carelessly over the other, and his face was as if carved in stone and as if some sculptor had placed two cruel glittering orbs in the spot where the windows of the soul are found.[10]

Sentencing was postponed for a week and now Howe produced one of his great coups, maintaining that Carleton could not be sentenced in any way. The previous spring the Assembly, in the Electrical Death Penalty Law, had abolished death by hanging, substituting electrocution. Howe discovered that death by hanging was to be abolished as from 4 June. Prisoners convicted after 4 June were to be kept alive until 1 January 1889 when they could be electrocuted. At least that was the intention, but according to Howe:

> He [Carleton] says that Your Honor cannot now pass any sentence of death upon him. He says that the Legislature by its enactment of Chapter 499 of the laws of 1888, a statute passed, approved, and signed by the Governor . . .

The judge agreed and, while the prosecution appealed, unsurprisingly panic followed. If Howe was right, then not only had all murderers to be released but also the logical extension was that until 1 January 1889 they could kill with impunity. Chief of Police Thomas Byrnes and the District Attorney released statements assuring the public that measures would be taken to ensure public safety over the Christmas period.

Howe, with Hummel supporting him, was adamant that Carleton could not be punished 'because of the slipshod drafting of the bill', but other lawyers were not convinced. Of course, in practice Howe's reading of the law could not be allowed to stand and the appeal court held that while it was strictly correct, a mere slip of syntax should not permit the guilty to go free.

But Howe and his firm did not give up and Carleton was still alive the following October when his application for re-trial was

---

[10] *New York Herald*, 15 December 1888.

dismissed. Howe now produced affidavits from Ahearne and Burke supporting the clubbing theory. Surely Governor Hill would grant a reprieve? No, Governor Hill would not.

In all Howe defended in 600 murder cases, more than twice the number of all other practising lawyers in New York at the time. These included Edward Unger, who killed a lodger Bolles for a bank-book. The body was cut up and the head thrown in the East River; the legs and arms were sent to Baltimore in a box. Inspector Byrnes, confident of a conviction, said that, 'Unger's grave is dug and his coffin is made.' Howe blamed it all on the golden-haired daughter sitting throughout the trial by her father. Acquitted.[11]

Howe had taken on Hummel as an office boy in his offices at the corner of Leonard and Center Street at $2 a week in 1863, where he worked putting coal on the fires. There was still no formal Bar examination. Lawyers were attached to other lawyers for their training and simply took over work from their employers. In May 1869 Hummel became his partner. In 1900 they moved to the New York Life Building on Broadway.

Bald, diminutive and almost always dressed in black, Abe Hummel was also said to have been born in Boston – some say New York – this time on 27 July 1847, and attended Public School No. 15 on E 5th Street. He was, without doubt, the more astute and venal of the pair, but he maintained standards. When he organised the blackmailing of young men who had so forgotten themselves at the sight of the underwear of chorines that they proposed marriage and wrote confirmatory letters, he would invite the lawyer acting for the man round to his office when brandy would be drunk, cigars smoked and the lawyer could see the foolish letters destroyed. Nor did he allow one girl more than one bite at the same man. Fees were split equally between the girl and the partnership.

Hummel had style and better still the support of the newspapers. In one of his civil cases he appeared successfully for Mme Emi

---

[11] Amongst his non-gangland clients, Howe defended William Chambers who was accused of shooting Commodore Vorlis of the Brooklyn Yacht Club. Chambers had insulted the American flag and told the Commodore to take it down. The Commodore refused and Chambers went home, found a gun and shot Vorlis. Howe ran a plea of insanity and during the hearing Chambers sat with his head bandaged. When Chambers was acquitted he snatched the bandage from his head, proclaiming his sanity.

Fursch-Madi who had been employed by the American School of Opera. She had not been paid for her second year and the School was accusing her of soliciting their pupils. The *New York Herald* described her:

> The witness stand is occupied by a divine creature who is fairer, fatter and fortier than most women of her general appearance, size and age.

And after the case:

> Her rosy lips pucker and she plants a smacking kiss upon his left cheek. It pops like a champagne cork. It takes a good deal to disconcert Mr H. He calmly turns the other cheek and she, still hugging him places a warm lingering kiss upon it. He rearranges his coat collar and remarks as he leaves the building. 'They all do it.'[12]

On the credit side of his activities, he became an expert on theatrical contracts and the firm's legitimate clients included P.T. Barnum, Sir Henry Irving, John Barrymore and Lillie Langtry. They also represented Olga Nethersole who, when playing the title role in Daudet's *Sappho*, was arrested for publicly demonstrating the embrace known as 'the Nethersole Kiss'. They argued that the actress had given art a new dimension and the court agreed.

The pair were also keen sporting gents. Bare-knuckle fighting had long been illegal and they appeared for the promoters in the unsuccessful prosecution following the Sullivan–Greenfield contest on 17 November 1884 at Madison Square Garden. Captain Walling had stepped in when Greenfield was helpless on the ropes in the second round. This may have been a case where there was some nobbling of the police witnesses because when Walling gave evidence, much to his disgust and dismay he found there were no other officers there to support him and the case was dismissed.

Howe was never afraid to stand up to a judge. He also defended in the murder case of Harris W. Horner and Harry N. Braden. It

---

[12] 'Yum! Yum! What a lucky dog!!!' in *New York Herald*, 20 March 1889.

was hardly a glorious affair, merely a fight in which the aggressor, said Howe, had died. The quarrel with the judge arose over the question of bail. Howe was well dressed for the application:

> . . . a bright red tie was set off by a huge horseshoe pin of sparkling green emeralds and scintillating diamonds.

Howe suggested that bail should be granted but Judge Duffy, known as the Little Judge because of his diminutive size, said he was not sure he had the power and believed it was a matter for the coroner. Howe puffed himself up to his full 300 lbs. The exchange was short if not sweet:

> —If you refuse to take bail you do not know your duty.
> —Motion denied.
> —Then you are quite wrong. I ask for their discharge.
> —I'm very sorry to hear you say that.

For that little exchange Duffy fined Howe $10.

> —I shalln't pay it.
> —Then you'll stay here until you do, I have fined you $10 for disorderly conduct and if you don't pay, I'll lock you up.

Howe half backed down and half threatened the Little Judge:

> —Judge, I think you'll find it a very dear $10. I did not insult the court.

What he had in mind was impeachment proceedings. He believed, or at least was prepared to allege, that Duffy was drunk. Certainly Duffy had been behaving rather oddly earlier in the afternoon because he had dismissed a civil case when the plaintiff said 'Mother of God' in reply to a question. He told her if that was how she felt she should seek her remedy in the court above. In any event he was quite willing to meet Howe halfway. He remitted the fine and committed the men for trial but again he refused bail.

Afterwards Howe gave a press conference to the always listening

Herald reporter, saying that he was 'going to make it warm for Duffy' and that he regretted the fine had been remitted. He continued the next day when the *Herald* called on him at his home on the old Boston Road, Brooklyn. There was no question in his mind; he meant to impeach Duffy who had been drunk in court the previous day, and it was by no means the first time. He reminded the *Herald* and its readers of the wise words of Elbridge T. Gerry who had said that 'Mr Duffy is the one police magistrate on the Bench who is totally unfit for his duty.' Nor was this the first time Howe had had impeachment in mind for the unfortunate judge:

> A few years ago when articles of impeachment were preferred against Duffy in the Court of Common Pleas, he came cringing to me and begged me to help him. I advised and helped him and he came out all right.

The paper very properly adopted the Latin and legal tag of *audi alterem partem* and went to hear what the judge had to say about things. In the comfort of his chambers he was equally forthright:

> Howe is a coward, a cur and a liar and if I was half his size I would break him in two. I fear him not. Before I am impeached he may be disbarred . . . I locked him up once in the 57th St Police Court and he cried 'Peccavi'. He is like a big blustering schoolboy who tries to cow the small boys at school; but when anybody shows fight Howe shows the white feather.

By the following day the weight of legal opinion, or at least those sought by the *Herald,* was against Howe. Most thought Duffy a decent little man and that Howe's threats were pure bluff. Indeed, some independent witnesses marvelled at the judge's self-control that afternoon. One judge, Justice Gorman, while saying he had never seen Duffy drunk, did however add a few curious words:

> Duffy drinks, of course. He has a very nervous temperament and, I dare say, he always takes a stimulant after each sitting in the court. He probably would not be equal to the strain upon his nerves if he did not.

The matter was resolved the following week when the intrepid *Herald* visited the great lawyer again. This time it was all smiles and bonhomie. But was this through the influence of Hugh J. Grant of Tammany? No, said Howe. Well then, what about the man Hewitt? Had he persuaded Howe to back off? That might be, but Howe was sure he would have succeeded. He had some 15 separate instances. Was it correct that last time Algernon S. Sullivan had intervened? That was as maybe, but everything was hunky-dory now.

The previous incident showed Howe to have been on much firmer ground. Again he had 'drifted in with Counsellor Abe Hummel in tow' for the afternoon session and, in the time-honoured tradition of lawyers, wanted his case heard there and then because he was supposed to be in two places at once. He had found Duffy in an unhelpful mood. When he asked for his case – another bail application – to be called, Duffy had replied:

—You seem to have come up here to hector the court.
—If your Honour says that you are wrong.

That was all it took.

—Put that man down, officer. I can't tolerate this contempt of court. I fine him $10.
—I protest. I refuse to pay the fine.

And with that Howe was taken to the cells. Hummel then took over, saying he was representing Howe, who had not intended discourtesy and in any case he couldn't understand what the contempt was. Duffy was backtracking and said he wanted to hear this from Howe's own lips. Brought up to purge his contempt, the great man was in no conciliatory mood. The allegation against him was false and unfounded. He was taken down again. As he left he produced a gesture worthy of Sidney Carton:

Officers, stenographers, citizens, I call upon you to witness that I am committed without a hearing and have the meanest offender's rights denied me.

By now other barristers had joined in. After all, what was happening to Howe today could happen to them tomorrow. Now Duffy had Howe brought up once more and released him on parole to appear at 3 p.m. Whatever the outcome, the afternoon was ruined for him. Howe had clearly not wasted his time in the cells because his first task was to lodge a petition at the Supreme Court setting out Duffy's felonies and calling on him to explain himself and, while he was doing so, pay $50,000 damages.

The next day, up came Howe with his whole flotilla in tow before Justice Donohue. Now Howe had Edmund Blackman on his side, who said that never in his 30 years' experience at the Bar and in all his studies of the textbooks had he come across a more glaring outrage on a lawyer. Howe added his twopennyworth, saying that Duffy's conduct was 'one of the most high-handed outrages'. Whether by design or accident, Duffy had in fact not made up his mind whether Howe's conduct was a contempt and the lawyer was discharged before an admiring throng. Now he arranged for one of his junior partners, Steinhardt, to serve Duffy with the papers claiming damages. The press must have been alerted because the following dialogue is reported:

—Ain't this a bit premature?
—I should think not. Mr Howe is honorably discharged.
—By whom?
—Justice Donohue.
—How long have I to answer this summons?
—Twenty days.
—All right.

And the judge retired 'to consult with his assistants'.

It all blew over, but if nothing else the incidents show how close Howe and Hummel were to the benign influences of Tammany.[13]

On what could be described as the white-collar side of his practice, Howe represented Policy Number organisers who were always

[13] *New York Herald*, 24, 25, 26 November, 3 December 1888. Algernon Sydney Sullivan and William Nelson Cromwell formed their mainly commercial law firm in 1879, acting for industrialists such as John H. Flagler, the railroad king, and J.P. Morgan, and having serious Tammany Hall connections. The firm still flourishes today as one of the most prestigious in the United States.

keen to ensnare people with spare cash, their own or others. What the firm could do was to give the impression that they had judges and city officials in their pockets, and undoubtedly in many cases they did:

> The 'vulture like' Hummel was also the more literate and inventive of the pair. He kept an unconnected telephone in his office and if a client asked whether he knew a judge there would come the reply that he had lunch with him practically every day. Hummel would then reach for the telephone and hold an imaginary conversation arranging a meeting with the named judge.
>
> The client by virtue of such an auricular demonstration of intimacy would be convinced that his success or liberty was 'in the bag' and that Howe & Hummel were cheap at any retainer they might choose to name.[14]

Some stories were embellished over the years, often to Howe's advantage. One very popular one, recounted by Arthur Train as told to him by Francis Wellman, is of the girl prosecuted for the murder of her lover. At the end of his speech to the jury Howe pushed his long fingernails into her cheeks so that she screamed. He then continued:

> Look, gentlemen! Look into this poor creature's face! Does she look like a guilty woman? No, a thousand times no! Those are the tears of innocence and shame! Send her back to her aged father to comfort his old age. Let him clasp her and press his trembling lips to her hollow eyes! Let him wipe away her tears and bid her sin no more!

The girl in question was Ella Nelson and another version is that she had been hiding her face in her hands when Howe prised them apart. The language is certainly florid enough for the great man. Having offered to plead to manslaughter – a plea which Wellman, then an assistant district attorney, had rejected – she was wholly acquitted.

---

[14] Arthur Train, *My Day in Court*, pp. 29–30. Arthur Train also wrote *The Confessions of Artemus Quibble* based on Abe Hummel. It was enormously popular and there sprang up a number of Artemus Quibble clubs one of which, based in Harvard, lasted for many years.

Howe's tricks did not always go unnoticed by the judge, however. On another occasion, with the lawyer on his knees and weeping as he made his final speech, he moved closer to his client and her child. At once the child began to yell and then stopped. Howe wept more.

> *Recorder Hackett:* 'Mr Howe, you had better give the baby another jab with the pin.'

Howe was a great believer in publicity. Here he is explaining for the benefit of his adoring public how he chased away burglars:

> Yes, I shot at 'em. There were two and I think I hit one of them but he got away. No, I shalln't report it to the police. I've got a revolver in every room and I'm a good shot. I don't object to burglars as clients – they're pretty good clients – but I seriously object to their operating on my house.[15]

His last great case was in 1897 when at the age of 69 he defended not a gangland figure but the matronly Augusta Nack, described as a woman of operatic proportions, in the notorious Nack–Guldensuppe murder. It was a case which he believed he was well on the way to winning until a touch of religious intervention caused him insuperable problems.

The story was one of the usual domestic triangles so loved by the press and public. All participants were good-looking German immigrants. Augusta was a midwife by trade and lived with Herman Nack, the owner of a sausage shop on Tenth Avenue. He also kept a boarding-house, one of whose tenants was Willie Guldensuppe, who sported a still-life tattoo on his chest and was what we would now call a masseur but was then described as a 'rubber' in a Turkish bath. Soon Nack was supplanted in Augusta's affections and this went well until she fell in love with Martin Thorn, a barber. Willie was not as compliant as Nack and the pair planned to dispose of him.

They leased a cottage in Woodside, and one day in May 1897

---

[15] *New York Tribune*, 23 November 1901.

they killed him. They had left nothing to chance because Thorn was armed with a revolver, rope, dagger, poison, a knife and a bottle of carbolic acid. Willie was shot, stabbed with the poisoned dagger and an attempt was made at decapitation. Augusta Nack then cut up the rubber, putting him in a bathtub and leaving the water running while Thorn took the head to drop in the East River.

Unfortunately for the pair, the water and blood burst the drain-pipe outside the cottage and instead of disappearing into the sewage system formed a puddle in the yard in which a duck took a bath. The disappearance of Willie had already been reported and had caused considerable interest, so when the duck waddled home with its feathers covered in blood its owners told the police. It was only a matter of time before two and two were added together.

The defence was a blanket denial. The pair did not know of Willie's life or death nor, until it was proved that they did, had they known each other or rented a cottage. The dissection had been a fine one and there were still a significant number of pieces of the body missing, including the head and the tattoo. For Howe, Willie simply did not exist. He argued that the assembled parts could have come from half a dozen mortuaries and he had a fine time making up a string of names including Gildersleeve, Goldylocks, Gludensup and, since the jury was well educated, about 'a creature as imaginary as Rosencrantz's friend Guildenstern'. Observers regarded him as being well on his way to another spectacular acquittal.

Then, unfortunately, a local Presbyterian vicar started visiting Augusta Nack in prison and, worse for Howe, brought his simpering, curly-headed 4-year-old son with him. According to the story, the child climbed on her knee and lispingly asked her in the name of the heavenly and earthly Father to tell the truth. As a result, Thorn received life imprisonment and Augusta a modest 9 years.

Howe wrote to his partner:

> I had the prettiest case, and here is all my work shattered. I can still prove they couldn't identify Willie's body and that it wasn't cut up in the Woodside cottage. Now all my roses are frosted in a night and my grapes withered on the vine.

Always a high liver and a heavy drinker, his health began to fail and although he continued to defend a number of murder cases, including Michael Considine who had been accused of shooting a man in the Metropole Hotel on Broadway,[16] the Nack case was effectively his legal swan song. He died on 2 September 1902.

Howe married three times, leaving a widow, Lottie A. Howe. He had one daughter Emma Smith, two grand-daughters and a great-grand-daughter. He was buried at Greenwood Cemetery after a funeral attended by his family and Hummel, Moss and Kaffenburgh, as well as a former Assistant District Attorney Frank Oliver and former Police Magistrate Charles Simms. The rest of the New York bar was conspicuous by its absence.

As an advocate Hummel was never in Howe's class, but that does not mean to say he did not have his moments. One of the firm's great opponents was humbug in the human form of the vice reformer, Anthony Comstock, 'the Roundsman of the Lord'. Comstock had been dealt an earlier blow when the forces of evil were represented by Howe and Hummel in a vice case in New York, and he lost another brush with Abe over the aggravating spectacle of a *Danse du Ventre* by three Philadelphian Egyptians named Zora, Fatima and Zelika.

Hummel had argued that the dance was part of an ancient religious ceremony which devout Moslems, such as these girls, were bound by their faith to perform at regular intervals. The second point was that the dance was not as Comstock had said 'a lewd and lascivious contortion of the stomach'. Hummel explained that the stomach was a small sac whose contortions, if any – which was not admitted – could only be seen from inside the body.

The girls gave evidence, swearing on a copy of the Koran which Hummel had thoughtfully provided. During his speeches, when he regularly mentioned Allah, the girls looked appropriately and 'reverently toward the East as is the custom with members of their faith'. The case was dismissed and Comstock reprimanded as an interfering busybody.

[16] The Metropole, which was near Times Square, was immortalised in Cole Porter's 'Ace in the Hole'.

Continuing to display his literary talents in addition to his work on theatrical law, Hummel wrote *In Danger*, a highly readable book which amounted to in-house advertising and explained the firm's services to clients and potential clients.

Hummel's downfall was the Morse–Dodge case, one of almost infinite complexities. His efforts to evade the finality of the process were regarded in American legal circles as almost a triumph in themselves. Indeed, even while District Attorney Travers Jerome was prosecuting him as being a suborner of evidence, he was still quite prepared to have Hummel as a witness in the celebrated Stanford White murder trial.[17]

Essentially, in June 1901 Charles W. Morse, the dubious Maine financier, had married the divorced wife of Charles Foster Dodge. At one time Dodge had been a conductor on the Southern Railroad, but had fallen further in society so that he was now managing cheap hotels on a fairly irregular basis. The divorce had taken place in New York after a perfectly reputable lawyer, William A. Sweetzer, swore that he had personally served the papers on Dodge who had employed another lawyer, Mortimer A. Ruger, to act for him.

The new marriage was not a success and members of the Morse family, notably 'Uncle Jim' Morse, spent a good deal of time and money with Hummel – a figure of $60,000 is suggested – trying to dissolve it. Fortunately Ruger had died in the meantime and for the small matter of $5,000 Dodge was persuaded to sign an affidavit saying that he had never received the original papers.

In October 1903 Hummel obtained an order requiring Mrs Morse to show why her new marriage should not be declared invalid. At the hearing he produced a Dodge lookalike, named Herpich, and snared Sweetzer into saying to him, 'How do you do, Mr Dodge?' The divorce was annulled. Sweetzer was not pleased and managed to obtain possession of Ruger's papers which showed he had acted for Charles Dodge.

[17] On 25 June 1906 Harry Thaw, a millionaire playboy, was accused of killing the architect Stanford White whom he shot dead on the Madison Square Garden Roof. He believed that some years previously White had debauched his wife Evelyn, a Gibson girl in the hit show *Floradora*. She was known as 'The Girl on the Red Velvet Swing'. Jerome wanted evidence from Hummel about visits by Evelyn Thaw to his office. See Gerald Langford, *The Murder of Stanford White*.

Travers Jerome had long been unsympathetic to Hummel's behaviour and now he tried to use Dodge to impeach his lawyer. Dodge was arrested in Atlanta and brought to New York. Hummel obtained $10,000 from 'Uncle Jim' and bailed out Dodge who then, surprisingly, disappeared. In fact Hummel had sent him with ample funds to drink and whore himself to death in New Orleans. There then followed something approaching a farce. Jerome's detective traced the drunken Dodge and put him in the hands of the Texas Rangers. Hummel tried one last rearguard action by enlisting an armed posse to free him, but Dodge had been spirited out of Texas before battle could be joined.

On 27 June 1905 Hummel was finally tried. With his enemy in his pocket Jerome seems to have been extremely generous and offered Hummel a plea bargain which he foolishly declined. Dodge, assisted by a new set of $40 teeth, gave evidence and Hummel sensibly declined to go into the witness box. The generosity of Jerome may have stemmed from the fact that he wanted Hummel as a prosecution witness in the Stanford White case.[18]

Hummel was found guilty on 20 December and sentenced to 2 years' imprisonment. The appellate court found against him on 10 May 1907. On 16 May his conviction was affirmed and when Judge Edgar M. Cullen, the Chief Judge of the Court of Appeals, declined to give a certificate of reasonable doubt and to stay the proceedings, Hummel took the news well. To conform to prison regulations of the time he had his hair cut and his drooping moustache shaved off. He then gave a party for his friends, to which the press was not invited, and on Monday 20 May a crowd gathered in front of his brownstone at 52 E 73rd to see him off. At 4 p.m., escorted by his nephew Abe Kaffenburgh, he surrendered to the warden at Blackwell's Island where he was given cell 23. He was to be allowed daily visitors except on Saturdays and Sundays. Almost immediately there were rumours of his ill health and he was admitted to the prison hospital. According to the reports, he suffered a complete nervous breakdown and his life was despaired of.

Would his sentence be remitted so that he could die in peace?

---

[18] For a full account of the Morse–Dodge case see Richard Rovere, *Howe and Hummel*.

That was one of the questions which kept readers buying the papers. Would he survive? Would he be pardoned? The New York papers kept a daily bulletin. No, yes and no were the respective answers. He survived and was released on 19 March 1908 after which he left New York, returning only once when his cruise ship landed and he took time out to have a chat with reporters.

6

George Leonidas Leslie: 'Western George'

In the days when the James brothers were still robbing the railroads, a very much more sophisticated criminal with a genuine claim to the title of 'King of the Bank Robbers' was working the cities. Marm Mandelbaum's pet dinner guest George Leonidas Leslie, 'Western George', operated at a time when robberies were not just over-the-counter snatches but also encompassed his specialities of safe-breaking and burglary.[1]

Leslie was a somewhat unusual criminal of that or indeed any time. Born in 1838, the son of a wealthy Toledo brewer, he graduated with honours at the University of Cincinnati as an architect. In 1865 both his parents died and, regarded as a war-slacker, he left for New York where he began his highly successful criminal career. In short order he assembled a team of some of the highest quality criminals of the time including Johnny Dobbs, Jimmy Hope and Shang Draper.[2] In

---

[1] Edward Crapsey thought there were a maximum of 75 safe-blowers working in New York at the time. *The Nether Side of New York.*

[2] Draper, who was a partner in the banks of the policy king Albert Adams, was also from time to time a brothel keeper playing both the panel and badger games using under-age girls. It was estimated that up to 100 men a month were shaken down when the irate father and mother burst into the room. It is thought the most successful of the badger-game workers in the Tenderloin area was Kate Phillips, whose short romance with a tea dealer from St Louis was interrupted by a 'policeman' who hauled the man before a 'judge' who fined him $15,000 cash. See Luc Sante, *Low Life*, p.186.

the meantime he practised his trade on a safe made by Valentine and Butler.

In 1869 Leslie organised the robbery of the Ocean National Bank at Greenwich and Fulton Streets, removing $786,869. The take would have been considerably higher had not the team left some $2 million in cash and securities on the bank's floor. The robbery had been planned in William J. Sharkey's billiard parlour on Broadway; three years later Sharkey would escape from the Tombs and vanish.[3] The job had not been without difficulties and Charles King, an English expert sneak-thief, had been brought to New York on a fee paid rather than profit-sharing basis to examine the premises and advise. King himself nearly came to grief when he was surprised in the bank president's offices and was forced to jump from the window to escape. After that the tactics were changed.[4]

Leslie's work was by no means confined to New York. In succession he also organised robberies of the South Kensington National Bank in Philadelphia, the Wellsboro Bank in the same city, the Third National Bank of Baltimore and the Saratoga County Bank of Waterford in New York State, as well as a bank in Macon, Georgia, in 1873.

The North Hampton Bank was robbed on 27 January 1876 by his team which now included Shang Draper, John 'Red' Leary, Billy Connors, James Burns, Thomas Dunlap and William Scott. The job had been fingered by a traveller for Herring & Co., William D. Edson, an expert in locks and safes, and Leslie probably supervised the planning. In all $1.5 million cash and securities were taken. The cashier Whittlesy, his wife, children and servants were tied up and he was later released and forced to unlock the bank.

Efforts to obtain the return of the money took a year and finally Scott and Dunlap were arrested in Philadelphia. Edson was arrested and squealed. Scott and Dunlap were tried initially with entering

---

[3] See Chapter 22.
[4] Other sources, including Thomas Byrnes, attribute the Ocean National Bank robbery to George Miles Bliss and Mark Shinburn who, with the assistance of corrupt detectives, blamed it on the Leslie team. See Luc Sante, *Low Life*, p. 209.

the cashier's home and threatening lives, something which carried life imprisonment. The prosecution having failed, they were then tried for simple robbery and sentenced to 20 years apiece, which they were serving in Massachusetts State prison in Charlestown when Scott died.

Shang Draper was arrested in 1877 and Billy Connors was held in Ludlow Street prison from which he escaped; he was arrested on 4 February 1888 in Philadelphia. Leary was also arrested and he too broke out of Ludlow Street when he escaped on 17 May 1879. A German family, along with Mrs Leary, had rented the tenement backing on to the jail. Leary had then dug through to a closet in the building. He was generally regarded as a great jail-breaker who had escaped from the Paris galleys. Leary, who was English, received 5 years in Paris for pickpocketing at the first World's Fair. Leary had rather daringly escaped from a Detective Folk of Brooklyn. The unfortunate officer having gone to arrest him at his home, Leary asked his wife to fetch him an overcoat and, when he put it on, produced a revolver from the pocket and pointed it at the officer's head. He then made his way into the backyard and escaped. After the Ludlow Street breakout Leary stayed away until he was arrested in Brooklyn on 4 February 1881. He and John 'Butch' McCarthy had fled after the robbery.[5]

However, it was after the Manhattan Savings Institution robbery at Bleeker Street and Broadway in September 1878 that Leslie paid the lawyers Howe and Hummel $90,000 for his defence; the highest sum paid to Bill Howe during his long and illustrious career. It was money well spent. Leslie was acquitted, as was Jimmy Hope. Others, including Jimmy's son Johnny, were not so fortunate; he received 20 years. There is a suggestion that as a part of the price for his discharge Leslie was less than careful in what he said to the police.

The raid on the savings bank, which had been jointly financed by Marm Mandelbaum and John D. Grady, was another carefully organised one with – said the police and the Pinkerton Detective

---

[5] 'Red' Leary killed himself accidentally. He threw a brick in the air, saying, 'What goes up must go down.' It did – on his head, fracturing his skull. In later life he had kept a tavern at Fort Hamilton on Long Island.

Agency – some inside help. It was said to have been on offer for three years. The bank's trustees had been extremely lax. The janitor, Louis Westall, had the combination to the safe and when a number of armed men burst into his room, handcuffed him and his wife and pointed a pistol at the forehead of his mother-in-law, he passed both combination and the keys over.

Arrests took place on 13 December that year when Inspector Byrnes and three colleagues staked out a saloon on 92nd and 7th Avenue. Into the bag went John 'Red' Leary and John 'Butch' McCarthy who were known to have left New York immediately after the robbery. 'Red' Leary had been regarded as a principal along with Bill Connors in the robbery in North Hampton in 1876. Connors had escaped from Ludlow Street jail and was still at large. The arrest of Leary meant that the whole of the North Hampton team with the exception of the fugitive Mr Connors were now inside.

The robbery which seems to have soured Leslie took place in Dexter, Maine, on Washington's birthday in 1878. He had done the planning but the raid went badly wrong. James W. Barron, the elderly cashier, put up resistance and was badly beaten. He had always said to his friends, 'If bank funds have to go I prefer to go with them', and his stubbornness cost him his life. He was beaten and later tortured when he fought the robbers in the early afternoon. His body was found with his hands cuffed behind him. The robbers – said to have been a team made up of Worcester Sam Perris, Johnny Dobbs, Jimmy Hope, Abe Coakley and Leslie – escaped with $100,000, but no one was prosecuted. Leslie was said to have been very unhappy about the way the cashier had been treated and although he continued to be in great demand for some years as an adviser on raids all over the country, he seems to have lost some of his appetite for the game.[6]

In 1880 Leslie travelled to San Francisco to assist the Ace Martin

---

[6] Langdon Moore says that Detective Al Dearborn put it about that Barron, the clerk in the Dexter Bank case, had tied himself up to make it look like robbery when in fact he committed suicide over defalcations. Moore said that this allegation was disgraceful. Langdon W. Moore, *His Own Story*, chapter XLII, p.523. In her memoirs *Why Crime Does Not Pay*, Moore is supported by Sophie Lyons who goes on to say that the bank sued Barron's widow for the money allegedly stolen by him.

gang in plundering a bank there. He regarded Martin, an all-purpose criminal, with some contempt, believing him to be little better than an amateur. The only initiative which met with his favour was that the robbery should be carried out over a weekend, something which has been imitated worldwide over the years since then. The aspects of which Leslie disapproved were the lack of any arrangement with the local police and also the employment of an inexperienced safe-blower whose quantity of gelignite might well have destroyed both themselves and half San Francisco. Leslie assumed control of the preparations and he devised a scheme which meant that two separate entries would have to be made into the bank.

He, Martin and six others including a locksmith forced the lock on the bank's side door which was immediately replaced with a duplicate. Leslie then took the lock from the safe and inserted a piece of thin steel wire before replacing the lock. The wire would cut out grooves every time the dial was turned and the deepest cuts would be those of the combination.

He returned to New York, leaving the second break-in and actual robbery to Martin and the others. The break-in duly took place, but Leslie was not pleased with the results. Martin's men had taken about $173,000 from the safe, a figure some $30,000 shy of the estimated haul. Leslie believed that Martin should have waited until nearer Christmas when deposits would have swelled the total, if necessary being in and out of the bank several times until there was a satisfactory amount in the safe.

In May 1884 Leslie returned to Philadelphia and his wife with the apparent intention of getting out of crime. Over the years he had led a double life. First, he had persuaded his wife, Mary Henrietta Croath – his one-time landlady's daughter – that he was an Internal Revenue detective. Now he was regarded as an expert bibliophile and a man about-town. He was a member of several well-known clubs and, with his lawyers Howe and Hummel, was a regular attender at opening nights and art exhibitions. He seldom mixed with criminals, apart from Marm Mandelbaum at whose right hand he would be seated at her celebrated Underworld dinners. He was, however, a ladies' man. Two of his conquests were Babe Irving

– sister of the Johnny Irving later killed in Shang Draper's saloon – and, rather more dangerously, the wife of Draper himself. Towards the end of May Leslie returned to New York.

On 29 May 1884 he disappeared. He had stopped at Murphy's Saloon on Grand Street where he was given a letter in a woman's handwriting, and had spoken of an appointment or business 'over the water', which meant in Brooklyn. On 4 June his body was found by a police patrolman at the base of Tramps' Rock near the dividing line of Westchester and New York counties. The body was in an advanced state of decomposition but it was clear that he had been shot in the head. The useful Herbert Stroub was sent by Mother Mandelbaum to identify the body.

The probability is that he had been shot while naked and dressed after his death, for there were no bloodstains on his clothing. If this is correct, then it can be assumed that the letter was one of assignation designed to decoy him. The best theory is that Shang Draper's wife was forced to write Leslie the luring letter and that he was killed in Williamsburg by a permutation of Draper, Johnny Dobbs, Worcester Sam Perris and Billy Porter, all of whom lived there. It is likely that the body was transported in a cart to the Astoria ferry by another of the Mandelbaum team, Ed Goodie, whose sorrel horse was recognised.[7]

Billy Porter, whose real name was William O'Brien, was one of the more sinister figures of the period. A member of what was known as the Patcham Street Gang – he lived at 152 – without a doubt on 16 October 1883 he killed John Walsh, 'John the Mick', in revenge for the death of his partner John Irving who was shot in Draper's saloon. Quite what the quarrel was about is not clear. The police detective George Walling thought it was because they were at odds over the division of the profits of a series of burglaries, coupled with Irving's belief that Walsh knew too much about his involvement in the death of Leslie for his own good. Eddie Guerin, admittedly writing some 40 years after the incident, rather

[7] Ed Goodie or Gearing was regarded by Inspector Byrnes as one of the smartest of American thieves. He was an expert driver and one of the most talented of the butcher's cart robbers. On 21 February 1884 he received 20 years for robbery with violence in New York.

romantically believed it was over an insult made by Irving about Walsh's convent-educated daughter.[8]

It seems that Walsh came into the saloon and simply opened fire. Harry Hope, son of Jimmy, was behind the bar and sensibly rushed off to tell Draper who was next door in Kane's Oyster Bar. By the time the case came to court the evidence was muddled and it was never quite clear whether Irving or Porter shot back and killed Walsh, but in any event Abe Hummel obtained an acquittal which really was all that mattered.[9]

On 1 June 1879 Porter and Irving had escaped from Raymond Street jail in Brooklyn, where they had been for 12 months. A $2,500 reward for information was never claimed and Porter lasted some four months on the outside. After the escape the pair made straight for Boston and then to Providence, R.I., where they took $15,000 worth of silver and watches from another jeweller. An attempt was made to arrest them in New York three days later, but they escaped and also survived another attempt to arrest them towards the end of July. Porter was finally caught on 28 September and received 5 years.

At the end of his sentence in February 1884 he went to England, where he posed as Leslie L. Langdon along with 'Sheeny Mike' Kurtz as Henry C. Appleton. They left under suspicion of blowing a number of safes in London, Paris and Berlin which were said to have netted them $25,000 each. Porter should have stayed abroad. He was arrested in New York on 19 January 1885 and charged with a jewel robbery in Troy which he had executed with Kurtz just before they left for Europe. After a long fight against his extradition Kurtz was brought from Florida to Troy where he received 18

---

[8] George W. Walling, *Recollections of a New York Chief of Police*; Eddie Guerin, *Crime: The Autobiography of a Crook*. James Hope had more or less retired by the 1890s. He was reported as spending his evenings in a well-known saloon on 29th Street near Broadway. He had taken up the Green Goods speculation which he regarded as strictly legitimate. Described as short and stout with a reddish-brown beard that had grown very long in recent years, apart from a long scar on his right cheek 'one would rather take him for some inoffensive countryman than for the most successful bank robber and all-around desperate criminal this country has yet produced.' John Hope was by then a barman in a Bowery saloon. *The Illustrated American*, 20 July 1895.

[9] For those interested in gangsters' graves, Irving was buried on 17 October at Evergreen Cemetery and Walsh the next day at Cypress.

years, only to have the conviction quashed on appeal. Porter was
back in London with Adam Worth in 1888.

Leslie was buried in a plot in Cypress Hill Cemetery in a funeral
financed by Marm Mandelbaum, who told Leslie's wife of his death
and arranged for her to stay with her for the funeral. Marm also
gave money to the widow, who visited Billy Porter and John Irving
in the Tombs. They had been arrested as 'usual suspects'. Apparently
they both treated her with contempt. When she returned once more
to New York, again staying with Marm Mandelbaum, Porter – now
released – openly sneered at her, and his wife 'treated her as though
pitying yet dreading her'. On this occasion Marm was 'economi-
cally generous' to the widow. It was thought that Leslie's fortune
was between $40,000 and $70,000 but none of it surfaced.[10]

It was estimated by George W. Walling, the Superintendent of
Police from 1874 to 1885, that during Leslie's working career he
and his team were responsible for 80 per cent of all bank thefts in
America and that they had stolen a conservative minimum of $7
million, possibly as much as $12 million.[11]

---

[10] Another less likely theory but one advanced by the police is that he committed
suicide. George W. Walling, *Recollections of a New York Chief of Police.* A third is that
Michael Kurtz, 'Sheeny Mike', was involved. Inspector Thomas Byrnes is quite clear
that Leslie was shot by his associates. *Rogues' Gallery*, p. 118.
[11] George W. Walling, ibid.

7

Adam Worth: 'The Emperor'

Another of Marm's dinner guests was Adam Worth, or Harry Raymond as he was later and better known, said to have been a model for the evil Professor Moriarty in the Sherlock Holmes stories. He is often cited as 'the Emperor of Crime', or sometimes 'the Napoleon'. Probably, given his circumstances at the end of his life, he does not fully justify the titles, but there is little doubt that during his long career he was a major thorn in the flesh of the police in New York, London and most of the other capital cities of Europe. However, stealing a known work of art, for which Worth is most celebrated, is rarely the way to riches. There are very few rogue collectors who have cellarsful of paintings, and Worth was one of a number to learn the hard way that stealing paintings such as Gainsborough's portrait of the Duchess of Devonshire can lead to years of frustration and misery.[1]

Worth was born in eastern Germany in 1844 and came to the States with his parents when he was five. His father then opened

---

[1] Pinkerton Archives Drawer 3, The Adam Worth Gang. Worth took the name Raymond from that of the former *New York Times* editor Henry Jarvis Raymond, a family man of the utmost probity, who died aged 49 of a heart attack following a visit to an actress.

The celebrated London receiver 'Little' Stan Davies told me he had been looking for a rogue collector for over fifty years but had failed. When he bought the sword of the Duke of Wellington, stolen by the burglar George 'Taters' Chatham, he had failed to find a buyer and been reduced to prising the jewels from the hilt.

a tailor's shop in Cambridge, Massachusetts where, like so many, they subsisted on the breadline for a number of years. Worth never grew beyond 5' 5" and consequently was known as 'Little Adam'. He had thick eyebrows, a mass of hair and eyes which bulged when he was annoyed.

He was in New York working, for once legitimately, as a clerk before the Civil War in which he enlisted in the 34th New York Light Artillery and for which he was paid a $1,000 bounty. One of the practices of the time was desertion after the payment of the bounty, followed by re-enlistment under another name and in another regiment, and Worth became relatively proficient at this. It was a dangerous game and, when he was identified on his third time round, he was sent to the front. He survived the Battle of Bull Run and promptly deserted again to collect a $30 bounty from the Confederates, but he was not obliged to enlist with them and then made his way back north.

By the end of the war he was just another small-time criminal working as a pickpocket on the New York circuit. Sophie Lyons, who knew and admired – some say she was in love with – Worth, wrote of him:

> Like myself and other criminals who later achieved notoriety in broader fields, he first tried picking pockets. He had good teachers and was an apt pupil. His long slender fingers seemed just made for the delicate task of slipping watches out of men's pockets and purses out of women's handbags.[2]

Now Worth put together enough capital to bankroll a team of pickpockets and the admiring Ms Lyons wrote that it was, 'the first manifestation of the executive ability which was one day to make him a power in the Underworld'. However, 'the Napoleon' was shortly due for a chastening experience when he was arrested for stealing a package from an Adams Express truck and received 3 years in Sing Sing on the Hudson. It was there he learned the art of using nitroglycerine which was employed for blasting in the prison. He escaped within a matter of weeks, made his way back

[2] Sophie Lyons-Burke, *Why Crime Does Not Pay*.

to New York by hiding on a tug-boat and reassembled his team of pickpockets who met morning and evening in a café near Canal Street. It was now that he approached Ned Lyons, Sophie's husband and one of the most highly regarded thieves of his day, with a view to breaking into bank work. According to Sophie, her husband was not interested.

So it was with his brother John, whom he later described as a 'damn fool for a crook', that in 1866 he broke into the Atlantic Transportation Company on Liberty Street but failed to blow the safe. However, there was more success when he stole $20,000 of bonds from an insurance company in Cambridge. He fenced them through Marm Mandelbaum and now began the career which would see him described as the 'Prince of Safemen', even though by the late 1880s several of his pupils were regarded as being his superior.[3]

Raymond's later career was entwined with those of two more of Marm Mandelbaum's favourites, 'Piano' Charley Bullard and the very impressive Mark Shinburn, alias The Dutchman, Henry Moebus and a host of other *noms de crime*, whose real name was Maximilian Schaenbein. Shinburn was born in Germany in 1836 and described as very erect with broad shoulders; he was 5' 8" tall and weighed around 170 lbs. A keen duellist in his youth, in addition to scars and bullet wounds he was distinguished by a very deep dimple in a small chin and by two tattoos of rings on the first and third fingers of his left hand. Apart from German he spoke English with a slight accent and also French. He had at one time worked for the Lilly Safe Company, which experience stood him in good stead, and he had perfect hearing which enabled him to count the safe tumblers. There was also another story that he had developed a machine which, when placed under the safe dial, would then puncture a piece of paper when the dial stopped, a device which has also been attributed to George Leslie. He purported to hate criminals and, posing as a banker, would happily converse with lawyers' wives at the Mandelbaum trough.

Shinburn's was a genuinely remarkable career. Once when trying

---

[3] Thomas Byrnes, *Professional Criminals of America*, p. 327.

to escape after a job in St Catherine's, Ontario, all routes to the safety of the United States were blocked by the Canadian police. The only possible way was via a half-constructed suspension bridge over the Niagara Falls. Shinburn and his colleague tied ropes around their waists and to a girder. They agreed that if one fell there was no question of the other hauling him back; he was to be cut loose, so letting him drop into the Falls rather than freeze to death. They both survived the crossing.[4]

When Shinburn first arrived in New York in 1861 he stayed at the Metropolitan and as the associate of sporting men he was under observation from the start. On 21 April 1865, along with George Bliss and Dave Cummins, he robbed the Walpole Savings Bank in New Hampshire.[5] He was arrested in Saratoga three months later with seven $1,000 bonds. Convicted at Keene, New Hampshire, he received 10 years hard labour at Concord State prison.

Shinburn was also a high-class hotel creeper, someone who could enter a bedroom and, instead of stealing the sleeping victim's property, take wax impressions of the bank and safe keys the man had with him. On 2 November 1865, the night after his conviction, he escaped and stayed away until May the following year when he had the most unfortunate piece of luck. Trying to rob the St Albans Bank in Franklin County, Vermont, he had been seen by the watchman who opened fire. He and his colleagues escaped and Shinburn caught a train, but one of the passengers had been a juryman at the original trial and he alerted the police. Shinburn was returned to Concord where he lasted another nine months before escaping again.

He was next seen at Wilkesbarre, Pa., where he was arrested for another robbery. It was late at night and a room was taken in the

---

[4] Some give Shinburn's birth as 1842. The St Catherine's escape is retold in Carl Sifakis, *The Encyclopedia of American Crime*. The ratchet device is explained in Edward J. Gallagher's *Robber Baron*.

[5] Cummins, known as Hogan and 'Little Dave', was a Chicago-born high-class hotel and bank thief. He had worked the riverboats in Chicago as a waiter and had been betrayed by another thief, Johnny O'Brien. His first jobs of importance were with Frank Dean, 'Dago Frank', and Billy Forrester in 1868 when they carried out a series of skilled robberies in New Orleans. In the spring of 1873 he worked with George Leslie and Pete 'Banjo Pete' Emmerson, robbing a bank in Macon, Ga., of some $50,000. Over the years he worked with many of the top men. He was regarded as skilful and daring but, when it came to it, he was willing to sacrifice everyone to save himself.

Valley Hotel with Shinburn handcuffed to the bed. When the officer awoke the next morning Shinburn was gone – and so was the man's wallet and watch.

As for 'Piano' Charley Bullard, he was a brilliant pianist whose touch of the keys was equalled by his touch on safes, at least in his early days. He spoke French and German fluently and was one of the few burglars who could open a combination safe with his hands alone.[6] His grandfather was said to have been a burglar but, that apart, he came from a respectable family. He tried his hand at the butcher's business but soon found crime more profitable.

In early 1869 Worth, Shinburn and Bullard, along with Isaac Marsh and Robert Cochran, blew the vaults of the Ocean Bank. This was followed by a raid on the Merchants' Union Express between New York and Buffalo. The train was boarded, the messenger bound and gagged and $100,000 stolen from the safe. Bullard and Marsh fled to Canada where they were arrested and extradited. The pair were lodged in White Plains jail and Recorder Smith was instructed, for a $1,000 fee, to defend them. Smith lost his money in short order; his pocket was picked on the train back to New York. Now it was decided that rather than rely on the courts and lawyers an escape was necessary. In later life Shinburn would claim that it gave him more pleasure than many of his thefts, but in fact it was not particularly difficult. Marm Mandelbaum, Billy Forrester and others were consulted and, when it came to it, to dig through the crumbling walls was a relatively easy matter.

Then came what really was a coup. Under the name of William A. Judson, Charley Bullard rented the house next door to the Boylston Bank, Boston, and set up a shop, theoretically selling Grey's Oriental Tonic with which the window was piled high. This had a double purpose. First, it gave the impression of a genuine business; second it blocked the interior of the shop from view. After that it was a question of night-time tunnelling. As Byrnes puts it, 'From that day out the bank was doomed . . .' Its actual demise was on 21 November 1869 when, again following the Leslie precept of weekend break-ins, the tunnel was completed. Bullard, Worth, his

[6] John Cornish to George D. Bangs, 23 November 1886, Box 182.

brother John, Marsh and Cochran cut through the walls and took out $450,000. Amongst the debris were two hundred bottles of the tonic.[7]

Now for Worth and Bullard, the principals, there was some problem with disposing of the bonds which formed part of the haul. Staying in New York was not a serious option and the securities were sent to lawyers there, almost certainly Howe and Hummel, with instructions to sell the bonds back to the bank for a percentage. This has long been a tried and tested method of disposing of otherwise unsaleable stolen property, and the money was to be remitted to England. With the remaining money in their trunks they sailed from England on the SS *Indiana*.[8] Shinburn had already left for Europe with an estimated several million dollars from his thefts. There he took an interest in a silk mill, purchased a title and bought an estate in Belgium. Now he was, more or less genuinely, Baron Shinburn.

Worth and Bullard turned up in the Washington Hotel in Liverpool in January 1870 where they both fell in love with the 21-year-old blonde, vivacious Dublin-born barmaid, the 'unusually beautiful' Catherine Louisa Flynn who apparently resembled the actress Lillian Russell.[9] It was to be a forerunner of the celebrated *ménage à trois* which Butch Cassidy and 'The Sundance Kid', Harry Longbaugh, had with Etta Place. Both men sought and obtained Kitty's favours, but it was Bullard she married on 22 February at St Francis Xavier's Church, Everton. If, as the story goes, Worth was the best man he did not sign the register. Bullard had now become Wells and so it was Kitty Wells from now on. However, she continued to sleep with Worth.

Why did Bullard allow this relationship? Ben Macintyre takes a

[7] *Boston Post*, 23 November 1869.
[8] Marsh, not regarded as the brightest of criminals, went to what he announced would be retirement in Tipperary where a homecoming parade was held for him. He gambled and drank away his fortune and returned to America for yet another last big job. In 1888 Marsh was said to be a broken man serving 17 years for robbing the Wellsboro Bank, Pa. He died in poverty shortly after his release.
[9] Sophie Lyons, *Why Crime Does Not Pay*, p. 44. The Washington Hotel stood on Lime Street until it was pulled down in a redevelopment plan after the Second World War; it is now the site of the St George's Hotel. The celebrated actress and singer Lillian Russell died as Mrs Alexander P. Moore in June 1922. In her theatrical days she was also a client of Howe and Hummel.

generous view of Worth and his conduct. Bullard, who had described himself as a 34-year-old bachelor and commission agent, was already married with two children and at this stage Kitty certainly did not know of the real Mrs B. It is possible, therefore, that Worth was exercising a certain amount of pressure on him. Macintyre suggests it was not his style and that this was a simple free-spirited arrangement. In any event, while the happy pair went on honeymoon Worth stole £25,000 of jewellery from a Liverpool pawnbrokers. It was the well-tried and tested technique of cosying up to the man and then obtaining a wax impression of his keys.

After the honeymoon the trio were reunited and went to Paris where they opened the American Bar at 2 rue Scribe. The refurbishment of the premises had cost, it was estimated, something in the region of $75,000. Bullard played piano, Worth was mine host and Kitty helped the rich and foolish to lose their money at the completely illegal gaming tables upstairs. It became one of the most popular places for businessmen and criminals alike. One patron was a director of the Merchant's Express Co. which had in part financed the bar.

On the criminal side, Edward Crapsey estimated that about that time there were no more than 100 bank cracksmen working in New York. Sophie Lyons, who was a frequent visitor to Europe and the American Bar, wrote, 'I could name a hundred men who got a good living at it [bank robbery] and then came over to Europe to try their luck.' Many of them found their way to the bar, known as a good and discreet place to conduct business. Other habituées of the bar included Eddie Guerin and, to the annoyance of Worth since he made overtures to Kitty Wells, the newly created Baron Shinburn.

It all came to an end when the detective William Pinkerton, son of the founder of the Agency, came looking for the team of forgers which included Charles Becker, Little Joe Elliott and Joe Chapman. Worth helped Little Joe out of a window during a raid to arrest him, but it was clear that the bar's days were numbered. Pinkerton gave the French police details of the careers of Worth, Lyons, Becker and Bullard and it was inevitable that a full raid would take place. Worth, who did not help matters by the opportunist theft of a bag of diamonds left by a gaming table and stolen by Little Joe, was arrested and released, but the resulting publicity was damaging in the extreme. Bullard was the only one of the trio left when the raid took place. Granted bail, he fled to London leaving Kitty and Worth to sell the place. They disposed of the premises to an English book-maker, Jack Ballentine, and followed the deceived husband.[10]

Now began Worth's purple patch in which he was without dispute the head of the most substantial pre-twentieth-century criminal empire 'to whom all the American thieves go on their arrival for points'.[11] It covered the spectrum of commercial criminal enterprise – burglary both residential and office, banks, post offices, diamond robbery, armed robbery, fraud of all kinds and forgery. Socially he set himself up in the West Lodge, Clapham Common, with Bullard and Kitty and their mutual daughters, Lucy Adeline born in October 1870 and Katherine Louise in 1871. The criminal fraternity regarded Worth as the father rather than the bigamous Bullard, but it will now never be clear. William Pinkerton certainly believed they were Worth's, principally on the basis that Bullard, now well into drink and depression, could no longer cut the mustard. As for the house, it had a shooting gallery, tennis court and bowling greens. Now Worth accumulated the cream of American and many fewer British criminals around him. Later he would say, 'There were some men among the Englishmen who were really staunch, loyal fellows and could do good work and take a chance, but the majority of them were sticks.'[12]

There were other lodgings for members of the entourage both in South London and elsewhere. The forger Charles Becker was now living with Joseph Chapman in Stoke Newington. Another of the notorious women in London was Carrie (or Ray) Hamilton, the divorced wife of 'Stoney' Montgomery, President of the Memphis Jockey Club. Described as being rather stout but with brilliant dark eyes and dressing very stylishly, she had been the mistress of many prominent men in New York and was regarded as wealthy in her

---

[10] Ballentine ran the bar for another two years and then finally closed its doors. The ground floor is now a part of the chain of gentleman's outfitters, Old England; the upper rooms are part of the Hotel Intercontinental.

[11] Thomas Byrnes, *Professional Criminals of America*, p. 243.

[12] Adam Worth, alias 'Little Adam' – Theft and Recovery of Gainsborough's Duchess of Devonshire', p. 13 (pamphlet in the Pinkerton Archives).

own right. She was also known as Burstein and Case and was a friend of Charley Becker. Said at one time to have been sentenced to two years in America and pardoned, from time to time she was used as a courier for the stolen jewellery.

There was also a flat at 198 Piccadilly where Worth threw dinner parties à la Mandelbaum, a string of racehorses, a pair for his carriage which cost £750, a bodyguard named Jack 'Junka' Phillips, a 6' 4" wrestler who conveniently could carry a safe on his back – and, best of all, a 110-foot yacht the *Shamrock*, named for Kitty, with a crew of 25 which was used to transport his colleagues. In 1874 it outran a British gunboat after a successful £10,000 raid on a warehouse in Kingston, Jamaica.[13]

In many of the operations Worth did not participate personally. He simply organised, advised, financed and took the lion's share from the proceeds. If his men, or women, were in trouble, again like his teacher Marm he arranged their defences, bribed their guards to obtain better conditions and, where he could, organised their escapes. All the time he was watched by his implacable foe, the New Scotland Yard officer Detective Inspector John Shore.

But then things started to fall apart and one of the problems arose through the gang of forgers he had assembled and who had been operating on his behalf in the principal cities in Europe. Little Joe Elliott, Joe Chapman, Carlo Siscovitch and Charley Becker were arrested in Turkey.

[13] For a biography of Adam Worth see Ben Macintyre, *The Napoleon of Crime*.

8

Charles Becker: 'The Scratch'

Charles Becker, known as 'The Scratch', was perhaps the greatest forger of bonds and banknotes of his generation. Born in Württemberg, Germany, in 1848, he came to New York at the age of nine. As a teenager he forged a cheque to provide money for his fiancée who promptly dumped him.[1] He then fell under the tutelage of a team which included Henry Wade Wilkes, alias George Wilkes Willis, said to be the American equivalent of Moriarty, Old William Brockway, Joseph 'Little Joe' Chapman – who had been a bank clerk and therefore had intimate and extremely useful knowledge of how a banking system worked – and Joe Reilly who was known as 'Little Joe the Second'.

Over the years he associated with the great English forgers such as Oscar Decker, alias Deneker, George Johnson known as 'Pretty George' and a Captain Bevan alias Smith who committed suicide in Cairo after being caught passing a large amount of forged paper in the city.

[1] There is a story that Becker was planning on going straight when he bumped into Clara Bechtel in the Louvre. By then she was married to a jeweller. He began seeing her and they went to Florence together and stayed as a couple until his imprisonment in Turkey. She was described as 'a realization of the Italian artist's conception of Margaretta'. See A.E. Costello, *Our Police*, pp. 436 *et seq.*

Over the years there have been a number of forgers capable of free-hand drawing. One was the Englishman William Reynolds who drew 7 years in 1917, 10 in 1938 and a further 10 in 1937, by which time he was aged 67 and although crippled with arthritis was still able to draw.

In August 1872, along with 'Little Joe' Chapman, 'Little Joe' Reilly and Worth, Becker robbed the Third National Bank, Baltimore, after which the team went to Europe and squandered the profits. It was then that he transformed his team from a gang of burglars to one of forgers and after a little practice was regarded as the best in the business.

> His ability was such that given a piece of naked white paper, Becker could copy a news story, including headlines, column rules, ten point or even smaller type through the body of the item and turn out what anyone might have unhesitatingly accepted as a 'clipping' from a newspaper. For ghastly accuracy this feat has never been reproduced.[2]

Unfortunately, Becker was a chancer. The layer of the forged notes who goes to the cashier does not know who did the artwork he is offering at a bank window. In general the forger received 40 per cent of the money while the layer and the middleman received 30 per cent each. Instead of staying in his workshop turning out the forgeries, Becker liked to tour with the layers to see how his work was received and bask in the reflection of a bill well pushed. He did not drink because he feared the effect it would have on his eye and hands, but he would later say that whisky had ruined him. While he was watching the money being passed a $100 bill of his was laid on the bar of the Hoffman House and unfortunately whisky was spilled on it, causing the inks to run. Technically Becker had not yet offered it, but he still received a year in the penitentiary on the general ground that he was a professional crook.

On his release and after a series of successful operations in Minneapolis, Boston, Cincinnati and New Orleans, leavened by a side trip to London, they were chased out of Milwaukee by the police. Now he, Joe Elliott, Siscovitch and Joe Chapman went back to Europe where, under the organisation of Worth, they became the scourge of European banks operating in London, Paris, Berlin, Vienna and every other northern city of note. As fast as money was

[2] 'The Dutchman' in Chicago *Sunday Tribune*, 19 January 1919.

obtained it was sent to Lydia Chapman, the beautiful, blackmailing wife of Little Joe who was living in some style in Chelsea.

Lydia Chapman had an interesting career. Born in London, she had started as a child pickpocket and shoplifter as well as being a stall for sneak thieves. She had first married an English burglar known as 'Two to One', but after he was convicted and transported she fell in love with Jack 'Junka' Phillips who for a period was Worth's errant bodyguard. For some time Phillips made a good deal of money from Becker, but 'The Scratch' was always afraid that he was in fact liable to squeal when arrested. Lydia's husbands seem to have had a bit of bad luck because Phillips too received a sentence and now she married Chapman.[3]

Becker, Elliott and Chapman then went to Turkey where they obtained $20,000 from the forgeries and where Carlo Siscovitch was working independently. Inspector Thomas Byrnes notes that they did not counterfeit Turkish money, 'because it isn't worth counterfeiting', instead passing false letters of credit. But through a mistake by Chapman they were all arrested in July in Smyrna and sentenced to 3½ years. Curiously, Siscovitch also came a tumble quite independently and they all wound up in the same jail in Constantinople to where they were transferred. According to Becker, escape from Smyrna would have been no trouble because the prison only had mud walls. Escape from Constantinople was a different proposition: the walls were four feet in thickness, the cell doors were solid and there were cast steel grate bars an inch and a half square.

The escape took a month to organise and, again according to Becker, they were betrayed by Little Joe Chapman on three occasions. The cells had top and bottom locks but there was a general key and an impression had to be taken. They managed this when the prison marshal put down his keys in order to sign some papers.

---

[3] One man they left behind in England was Robert Bowman, who married and went into the licensing trade. The Pinkertons introduced him to Scotland Yard and he became a stool-pigeon. Evidently he crossed the brothers after they had helped him over the Fritzy Deihn diamond robbery. On 22 June 1889 he wrote asking for the name of their London agent, something he said he had forgotten, and it provoked a burst of wrath. 'I hope that they [the English] will give him a good long sentence if they get him. I have got a thorough dislike for the man.' WAP to RAP, 6 July 1899. Bowman eventually returned to America, going to Detroit.

The impression, either in soap or bread – Becker did not say – was smuggled out to the soi-disant Mrs Siscovitch who brought back blanks, files, Turkish caps and lanterns.

Over the wall, they took a cab to the English cemetery where they were recognised as they sat in a café. Fortunately it was by a man who was sympathetic and he hid them out for two months. Elliott was sent to England to bring back money Becker had left there, and it was then to London. Mrs Siscovitch was arrested and held for some time before returning to America with her husband; he and Joe Elliott had gone to stay with Lydia Chapman.

Everyone wanted some credit for the escape. One story is that word was sent to Mrs Siscovitch in Paris and she – and according to one version, Lydia Chapman – went to rescue the team. Adam Worth maintained that he had financed the escape by bribing the jailers. It is likely that as a prisoner's wife, or rather mistress, Mrs Siscovitch obtained a visit and was told to produce wax and rope. An impression of the keys was taken and sent to Worth who made keys. The three climbed down the 50-foot wall where they were met by Worth. Chapman had been left behind either because he was thought to be a squealer or because it was his initial blunder which had caused their arrest. Becker and the others said it was because he was ill.[4]

Another variation of the story is that Chapman, furious at being left behind, sent a message to his wife not to hand over any of the money until his release. If so, it must have been a measure of their collective charm that they talked Lydia Chapman into letting them take rooms with her.

One version of what happened next is that they then demanded their share, telling her they needed it to go to Australia but, obeying the still incarcerated Little Joe's orders, she refused. She would have

[4] There are numerous other conflicting accounts of the escape. The tale that Lydia Chapman went with Mrs Siscovitch to Turkey was denied by Becker in an interview on 19 March 1889 in King County Penitentiary, New York. Another is that the three were held to ransom by bandits, and a third story is that they hid out with Mrs Siscovitch in Constantinople disguised as women until danger passed. For one detailed account of the escape, see A.E. Costello, *Our Police*, and for a different version, Becker's account of the escape and the death of Lydia Chapman in Thomas Byrnes' *Professional Criminals of America*.

done well to display her independence. They then decided she must be drugged and the house searched, so on 13 April 1876 they drugged her drink and ransacked the house. Unfortunately she had some heart trouble and died.

They left with the money and her collection of diamonds. Becker would later maintain that she had died from a heart attack and it was Siscovitch who, after her death, had pillaged the house. He also claimed that by the time Siscovitch and his wife turned up Elliott had gone and he left shortly afterwards. Whichever is true, Siscovitch did at least put his share to some temporary good; he opened a bar under Booths Theater in New York which became a home from home for forgers. He was later arrested and questioned about Lydia Chapman's death, but it was thought there was insufficient evidence to try to have him extradited to England.[5]

The actual story seems to have been slightly different. Lydia certainly died at her home at 46 Maude Grove, Chelsea, on the night of Thursday 15 April 1876. An inquest was convened at the Weatherley Arms in King's Road, Chelsea, with Dr Diplock sitting as the coroner with a jury of 15 men. They heard that William and Louise Wallace (the Siscovitches) – she was said to be stout and with a foreign accent – had taken two furnished rooms with Lydia, paying rent of a guinea a week. On the night of Lydia's death her seven-year-old boy saw Wallace 'romping on the bed with mama'. From the other evidence it appears that he was chloroforming her and then stripping her of her jewellery. She had, said the doctor, as poor a heart as he had ever seen. The Wallaces left that night in a cab for Charing Cross Station. There was also evidence that her jewellery had been insured for £1,500 and some had already been sold for £750. The officer in the case was Meiklejohn and the solicitor 'instructed by friends of her husband in prison' was the corrupt Edward Froggatt. The next year that pair would be in the dock of the Old Bailey together. In the Chapman case the jury returned a

---

[5] As for poor Chapman, he was flogged after the escape and according to one story his health deteriorated sharply. He was not released until 1881. He died in New York, but not before he had approached Reilly who knocked him down with a silver-topped cane. Also according to this version Reilly had a brief affair with Lydia Chapman while staying with her in Paris. See Jack Lait, 'Lydia's Joe' in *Buffalo Courier*, 9 October 1919.

verdict of wilful murder and warrants were issued for Mr and Mrs Wallace. The children were packed off to Canada with the Emigration Home for Destitute Little Girls.

Whichever is the true version of the death of Lydia Chapman, after his return to America Becker, along with Reilly and Henry Wade Wilkes, devised a plan to defraud the Union Trust Co. of New York, borrowing a cancelled cheque from a dishonest clerk. An account was opened and a counterfeit cheque for $64,000 was successfully cleared. He, his father-in-law Clement Hearing and Reilly were arrested in April 1877. Now Becker behaved badly; he turned State's evidence and was freed. Reilly went to prison until the autumn of 1892 when he was pardoned by Governor Flower.[6] He died the following year in Boston of typhoid fever. Perhaps the most unfortunate of them all was Pontex, the clerk who had been persuaded to pass over the note to be forged in return for the cancellation of a debt. He died in prison awaiting trial.

Four years later Becker was back in King's County and this time, on 16 September 1881, again with his father-in-law he began to serve 6½ years of a 10-year sentence for the forgery of a 1,000 French franc note. An attempt to escape was thwarted when one of the prisoners informed on him.

At some point in his career he seems to have married Carrie Kline, widow of the original 'Gentleman Burglar' ('Needles') Kline who was hanged in Tennessee for the murder of a night-watchman. The story is that Becker met her when, after 'Needles'' death, she had teamed up with the notorious Ellen Peck to work the badger game in Detroit. At the time Becker was posing as a German exporter who had just sold a deal of machinery and had money to spend. Word of a potential sucker reached Ellen Peck and Becker was duly enticed into a dinner at Carrie Kline's apartment. A moment after

[6] On one of his trips to England Joe Elliott married the well-known music-hall artiste Kate Castleton. After his conviction over the Union Trust Co. she divorced him. Byrnes believes they met when she was playing in the San Francisco Minstrels in New York. The marriage had broken up because of his increasing jealousy. In any event she later married Harry Phillips, the manager of the show *Crazy Patch*. Another account of Elliott has him joining up with Henry Wade Wilkes and serving 10 years for a forgery on the Flour City Bank, Rochester. An unsigned Pinkerton memorandum records that his health was broken by this sentence and he died in Bellevue Hospital in about 1894. Wilkes was found dead in the street about the same time (Case Binder 1).

she began to disarrange her clothing and scream in ran Ellen Peck, in standard badger game practice. 'Mother.' 'My daughter.' 'Seducer.' Peck then demanded $1,000 from the amused Becker who paid with his own forgeries. He later warned Carrie Kline against passing the note and married her within a week.[7]

At one time he had a saloon on Atlantic Avenue which he sold in April 1891. Certainly he was later arrested with Nathan Marks, an English forgery middleman, and sent to King's County Penitentiary for a year. Later still he had great success with another Englishman James Cregan or Joe Howard, who acted as the financier, putting up the money for expenses and sometimes acting as the middleman. Their forgeries, aimed at American banks and in big sums, caused considerable problems for the Pinkerton-guarded American Bankers' Association. They were also fortunate that the actual layers of the money, when caught, would accept terms of imprisonment rather than inform on them. There was no *quid pro quo*, Becker and Cregan being quite prepared to leave the layers to face the music on their own.

The end came on the West Coast when, along with Frank L. Seaver (alias A.H. Dean), they extracted $20,000 in gold from the Nevada Bank of San Francisco on a draft worth $12. This time the pair were not so fortunate; they were finally tracked by the Pinkertons and arrested in Philadelphia as they were planning to leave for Guatemala. Released on the grounds of insufficient evidence, they made their way to Newark where they were again arrested; at that time they were trying to retrieve $1,200 left behind with the Philadelphia police. They were then transferred to California where Seaver was finally persuaded to turn State's evidence. In August 1896 the pair originally received life sentences, but these were whittled down to 8 years for Becker and 4 for Cregan. The Pinkertons were jubilant:

[7] That is one story. According to Note 4835 in the Pinkerton files his wife was the former Annie Herring, 5' 6" with light blue eyes, a thin face and a thin nose inclined to be a little long and Roman-shaped. Far from having the red tresses of Carrie, her hair was said to have been light brown. She was the one-time mistress of a detective James Murphy and was also arrested over the Bank of France case.

Their conviction breaks up the last of the bands of professional criminals who were operating against banks prior to 1894 and since, and completes a promise made by Mr Pinkerton to the American Bankers' Association when they were appointed their agents . . .[8]

All was not unalloyed joy however. There were suggestions that certain German societies which Becker had joined believed in his innocence and were planning to produce an alibi for him. Nor, had he known about it, would Becker have been that happy regarding a note from Robert Pinkerton which inquired of the activities of Mrs Becker and her 'close relationship' with Captain French.[9]

Becker was released on 28 September 1903 after serving just over 5 years of his sentence. Some accounts have him a broken old man, but according to a contemporary report he seems to have been sprightly enough. He was quite prepared to have a few words with a local reporter but not to have his photograph taken, smashing the camera of *The Bulletin* photographer Charles V. Estey:

'You wouldn't smash me the way you did the camera?' asked the reporter timidly.
    'No, you're right. But I'm going to get a permit to carry a gun and then I'll plug every —— camera that comes around me.'
    'Let's have a drink,' said the reporter.[10]

Before they both went to what was described as a 'fashionable' breakfast at the Russ House, a man who had been released with Becker said:

When a man has paid the price the State demands and done it fair and square, it's not right to ask him to stand for that. It's as much as saying he's going back to his old tricks.

Becker returned to his home at 117 Bradford Street, Brooklyn. Later he moved to 292 Etna Street, New York, where he died; he had

[8] Unsigned Pinkerton memorandum, 29 August 1896.
[9] RAP to GDB, 23 June 1896. Captain Harry French was in fact the Commanding Officer of the Twenty-Third Precinct who for some years boarded with the Beckers.
[10] 'Charles Becker, Prince of Forgers, steps out of prison a free man' in *The Bulletin*, 28 September 1903.

been suffering from diabetes. In accordance with Pinkerton policy towards elderly and hopefully reformed crooks who might help them, they had been employing him as a guard at various race-courses they supervised. There is also a suggestion that he was being paid a pension by various banks to keep him from forging their drafts. Earlier Robert Pinkerton had written suggesting that when William was on the West Coast he might visit Becker in San Quentin.

> There was never any personal feeling between Charlie Becker and ourselves. He never did anything against us. It was purely a matter of business as you know, and if we can favor him any way, I should be pleased to do so.[11]

Becker was buried in Evergreen Cemetery. He was 68.

Just as there were many conflicting stories of his life and escapades, so there were a number of versions of his death including the inaccurate and sanctimonious:

> . . . never profiting much from the many thousands he stole, more than one-third of his years spent miserably in prison, dying at last in the most abject poverty, friendless and his body going to Potter's Field. His life was an utter failure and proved again that crime does not pay. The 'easy way' is always the hardest way, after all.[12]

[11] Robert Pinkerton to William A. Pinkerton, 2 May 1900.
[12] *Kansas City Times*, 23 September 1916.

9

The Empire Declines

At the time of the Turkish fiasco there were two other clouds in Worth's sky. The first was light grey. Charley Bullard had returned to America where, unable to survive without advice and help, he had been arrested and sentenced to 20 years in Concord jail for his part in the old Boylston Bank robbery. One version of the story is that he had returned to try to find Kitty in New York and while he was living on E 13th in the home of a noted burglar, Dutch Dan, he was betrayed. His drinking was now such that he had a hard time opening the bottles, let alone playing the piano or opening safes. However, Charley was not completely gone, and he fooled his guards.

> His conduct as a prisoner was uniformly docile and good for many months, until one day he surprised his keepers by a seemingly inexplicable outbreak of insolence and riotous disturbance. For this offence against discipline he was confined overnight with five other rioters in the cells for refractory prisoners. The next morning it was discovered that the birds had flown. Bullard had somehow fitted keys to the locks of the cells, released his confederates and found a way to escape.[1]

[1] Eldridge and Watts, *Our Rival the Rascal*, p.34.

Chicago-born Jim Dunlap, a member of the powerful Scott–Dunlap team of robbers and a friend of Little Dave Cummings, declined to join in because he did not think they could make it.[2]

There is a story that after Bullard escaped Kitty Wells met him in Stuyvesant Park, Philadelphia, and gave him money and clothes to get to Canada. In any event it was back to drunken rioting in New York from where he sent what is described as an insulting postcard to the Warden of the prison.[3] It was only a matter of time before he was gathered in once more, and now it was for penny-weighting in Toronto. Sentenced to 5 years in Kingston, it was while there that he received notice of his divorce, if that was indeed necessary, from Kitty Flynn.

So that she could marry Adam Worth? No, the far darker cloud for Worth was that she also had packed her bags and the children and taken them back to America. Perhaps she had brilliant antennae which indicated that the great London days were closing about her lover. She opened what was described as a high-class gentlemen's boarding house, but this may have been a synonym for a house of assignation, and she was said to have been the mistress of the police magistrate Justice Ottoward. She also travelled with George Mason the counterfeiter and the Lord brothers. In any event her criminal associations did not hold her back in her aim to be a society figure, maintaining that Bullard had deceived her by telling her he was a millionaire. As for the two children by Worth, there was no mention of their parentage.

It was then that she met Juan Pedro Terry, heir to vast estates in Cuba and the brother of the Baroness Blanc, and she married him in March 1881. Once Terry inherited, the pair went through the money in short order. Her husband died of consumption at Menton on 17 October 1886 when she was seven months pregnant. She returned to New York where she pursued a society and litigious career, suing and being sued with equal abandon. Both of these pleasures cost a fortune.

[2] On 7 December 1903 the Illinois State Board finally pardoned Jimmy Dunlap. They also pardoned Michael Burke who was said to have stolen over half a million dollars during his career as a sneak-thief and pickpocket.
[3] *Illustrated Police News*, 22 September 1888.

She died of Bright's disease at 102 W 74th on 13 March 1894. Despite an estimate by Sophie Lyons that she was worth $6 million, her estate came to a paltry $5,000. Much of her family did not survive her long. Her daughters Juanita and Katherine Louise were killed in an accident at Seabright, New Jersey, when their car was hit by a train. Her other daughter Lucy Adeline – who had married Charles Trippe – survived with her young son, Juan. In the twentieth century Juan Trippe went on to create Pan American Airways.[4]

Worth was now short of money. His empire needed constant financing and the Pinkertons were advising Inspector Shore in London on how to clamp down on his activities. Forgery was still an option and Becker and Little Joe Elliott were passing relatively small amounts which did not create too much suspicion. Then in April 1876 Becker forged and Elliott cashed a counterfeit cheque for £3,500. In these cases it was essential to get the money changed again before the counterfeit was discovered and notice circulated over the notes paid out. Worth's brother John was sent to Paris to do the business at a currency exchange on the Grand Boulevard, the idea being that since this would be a busy *bureau de change* little notice would be taken of the notes. Wrong . . .

Well, it might not have been wrong if John Worth had gone to the bureau, but instead he went to Meyer & Co. in the rue St-Honoré who had already been touched by Becker. Shore had warned them to beware of large-denomination English notes and Worth was arrested. Returned to England, John Worth had (if possible) to be granted bail and to leave the country. Fortunately he had provided a false name and there was nothing to link him to his brother. It was clear that Adam Worth as Harry Raymond could not stand bail – someone had to do it for him.

On 26 May 1876 Adam Worth and 'Junka' Phillips saw the crowd at Agnew's at 39b Old Bond Street where the portrait of the Duchess of Devonshire by Gainsborough was on view prior to auction.

---

[4] WAP to RAP, 12 February 1902; *New York World*, 4 March 1894; *New York Evening Journal*, 25 August 1899. Ben Macintyre recalls her career in *The Napoleon of Crime*. That of the Terry family appears in Francisco Xavier de Santa Cruz y Mallen, *Historia de familias Cubanas*.

William Agnew had himself bought it at auction for 10,000 guineas and was selling tickets priced at a shilling before it was again sold. There had also been a limited edition engraving made and this was selling well. Worth's idea, born of desperation for his brother and hopelessly thought out, was that if he could kidnap (rather than steal) the Duchess, Agnew could in effect be blackmailed into standing bail for John who would then skip.

The picture was stolen by Worth, who had cut the canvas from its frame, with Little Joe Elliott and 'Junka' Phillips in attendance, around midnight on 26 May. It was then taken a short way down Old Bond Street to Worth's Piccadilly flat.

In charge of the recovery of the painting was Superintendent Frederick Adolphus 'Dolly' Williamson of the Yard, and *The Times* was sure it would not take him long.[5] For some curious reason no one seems to have suspected Worth. Here was the great master criminal of Victorian England in town, apparently hounded by Inspector John Shore, and no one even looked at him.

Then, suddenly, the whole exercise became valueless. Beasley, acting for John Worth, persuaded the court that his extradition had been based on the wrong premise. He had been extradited as a principal in the forgery when in fact he had only been an accessory after the fact. Beasley obtained a writ of *habeas corpus* and John Worth was free. He was hustled onto a boat and sent back to America. However, it would be 30 years before the Duchess returned to her owner. During that time Worth, apart from a few abortive attempts to sell back the painting, travelled with the Duchess throughout Europe and America, sleeping with her under the mattress. Ben Macintyre believes the painting was a constant reminder of Kitty Flynn, Worth's lost love.

Over the years Worth was unhappy at the treatment he had received from Shore, who suggested that he was a laughing-stock and knew nobody except three-card-monte men and pickpockets. In turn he had berated Shore, saying that without the Pinkertons he would never have risen above being a street pickpocket detective. Worth had also devised a scheme to catch out Shore.

[5] *The Times*, 27 May 1876.

Nellie Coffey, wife of the burglar Big Jack Casey who was killed by Tom McCormick of Troy,[6] was keeping a brothel in the Borough. She and Shore were very close and it was known that he was taking girls to the house. Pinkerton had in fact introduced Shore to Nellie Coffey back in around 1874. At the time her brother Mickey was in custody for stealing paper from a mill which printed the Bank of England paper. Shore kept up with her and would meet her in the Rising Sun in Fleet Street where there were private dining rooms. She had not known he was a police officer until he saw her one day picking pockets at a racecourse, but apparently he continued to use her as an informant.

The scheme was that Worth had found an old swell down on his luck and had started paying his hotel bills; the idea being that he would be given a piece of jewellery which he would accuse a girl employed by Nellie Coffey of stealing. The girl would be traced to the house and when the arrest was made there would be Shore. The deviser of the scheme was apparently the dishonest detective, Meiklejohn,[7] but it fell apart because at the time Shore was at the brothel they found the old man had abandoned his post and gone on a drinking spree, and was therefore unable to press the charge. The Pinkertons thought there was some truth in the story of Shore being involved with women and also that he was drinking heavily. Worth seems to have taken the failure of his little plot in good spirit and allowed the old swell to keep the suit he had provided.

It is probably fair to say that although there were many successes still to come, the theft of the painting was an almost imperceptible turning point in Worth's career. Becker was becoming less and less reliable. Joe Elliott had been arrested in New York and while in Sing Sing told Robert Pinkerton that Worth had stolen the Duchess. 'Junka' Phillips wanted payment for his part. Worth told him he had sold the picture for £50, but even though his intelligence was limited Phillips was sufficiently bright not to believe him. In turn Phillips went to Scotland Yard. According to Worth a trap was set

[6] McCormick's wife lost a leg in the New York riots.
[7] See Chapter 19 for details of Meiklejohn's career.

for him in the Criterion Bar in Piccadilly where, with disguised Scotland Yard officers listening, Phillips would lure him into damaging admissions. Instead Worth spotted Inspector Greenham and hit Phillips. The former wrestler slipped and Worth gave him a good kicking. That was the last time Worth saw his bodyguard.[8]

It was after the marriage of Kitty Wells that Worth may also have married. At one time he had taken lodgings in Bayswater and afterwards supported the widowed landlady and paid for the education of her two daughters. Now he possibly married one of the daughters, whose name may have been Florence.[9] There were said to be two children, but accounts vary as to their sex. It is likely there was a son, Henry L. Raymond, born possibly in 1886 (although some say it was in 1888) and a daughter in 1891. Some accounts have the union producing two sons.

There were still successes for Worth and in 1880 he went to South Africa where he set up a front business as an ostrich-feather dealer. He had taken with him Charlie King, the English thief recruited years earlier to spy out a New York bank for him. This time Worth planned an old-fashioned stagecoach robbery, holding up the coach in which diamonds were transported from the mines to the coast. It was not a success. The trip-wire installed to bring down the horses worked well enough, but so did the Boer guard armed with a Winchester repeating rifle who drove Worth and his friends away. King, who was after all a bank sneak and not an armed robber, was thoroughly put off. Worth was made of sterner stuff and wanted a second go, so Charlie King was sent back to England with specific instructions that when he read of a big diamond raid he was to send Worth £200 in Brindisi, Italy.

This time things went better. There was no armed hold-up; instead he cultivated the assistant postmaster and obtained a wax impression of the man's keys. Next, he cut the wire rope on the ferry which hauled the coach across a river. By the time the coach,

---

[8] Phillips was later arrested in 1886 in Quebec over some forged Bank of Scotland notes and received 10 years' imprisonment.

[9] The only evidence for this is Sophie Lyons, *Crime Does Not Pay*, p. 58. She does not name Worth's wife but describes her as beautiful but weak-willed. There is no record of any marriage or indeed the birth of Henry L. Raymond in the Family Registry in London.

delayed for eight hours, reached Cape Town the boat had sailed for England. Worth took £500,000 in diamonds and the wholly innocent assistant postmaster received 5 years. Meanwhile King had not sent the money to Brindisi; he had taken himself there. But the pair missed each other and Worth was obliged to sell some diamonds to pay his way back to England.

There was a successful raid on the post office in Hatton Garden when on 16 November 1881 two registered mailbags were snatched. It was thought that some £30,000 was realised. About 5 p.m. Worth's accomplice turned off the gas at the mains, which shut down all lighting, and Worth leaped over the counter. There was also a profitable foray onto the West Coast where, working with a new team plus Little Joe Elliott, some $4,000 was taken from a Sacramento bank.

On 13 March 1888 Worth and Billy Porter, aka Walsh and Morton, fought in London and fell out of a cab in St Martin's Lane while doing so. They then continued fighting on the pavement and were arrested. Worth had fallen asleep and on waking he gave Porter 'one from the shoulder'. He must have been having a nightmare, recalling the incident three days earlier when he had escaped being hit by police bullets at the Mitchell–Sullivan fight at Chantilly. Porter had come to England at the invitation of Worth, who had lined up a tour of Europe for him; also he had been due to meet the burglar and shoplifter Johnny Curtin. Unfortunately Porter had been in difficulties trying to put together bail money following his arrest in Troy, and had been delayed. Curtin, under the name of Colton, had taken the opportunity for a bit of freelance work to keep up his funds and had stolen a small pack of diamonds worth around £60 from a jewellers at Grand Hotel Buildings, Charing Cross. He received 18 months with hard labour at Middlesex Sessions.[10]

The day after the scuffle the pair appeared at Bow Street in front of Vaughan the magistrate. In the dock Worth again attacked Billy

---

[10] Johnny Curtin, born in America in 1850, was a highly regarded shoplifter and burglar who often worked with Eddie McGee. He had already served a 2-year sentence in Paris in 1884. He also made a number of celebrated escapes from courthouses and prisons in California, Ohio, New Jersey, Philadelphia and Chicago.

Porter and denounced him in strong words while he waited for someone to pay the £1 fine. Porter, who was said to be living at 24 Maddox Street, Regent Street, was ordered to find a surety of £5. Worth's address was still West Lodge, Clapham Common.[11]

Two months later West Lodge was under constant police observation. Worth was still there with a man named Sunter, known as an expert toolmaker, appearing at the house daily. They were reported to have brought in an anvil which enabled them to make any tool they required.

Meanwhile there was the news that 'Piano' Charley Bullard, released after his spell in Kingston jail, had rejoined Worth's enemy the Baron Shinburn. Despite his enormous fortune the Baron had managed to run through his capital at the tables and on the Bourse, on both of which he was a consistent loser. It was in 1883 that the pair were arrested before they were able to rob a bank in the small Belgian town of Verviers. By then, Shinburn and Bullard had stolen and spent a fortune in Europe.[12]

In straitened circumstances, they decided that the provincial bank in the town was a good target. According to Thomas Byrnes, who wrote a long account of the failed attempt, Shinburn expected to collect $100,000 and was prepared to offer Bullard $6,000 for his help. During a preliminary reconnoitre Shinburn removed the keyhole plate over the lock on an old-fashioned oak and iron door. After that it was an easy matter to pick the lock and get into the bank. Unfortunately for them a night-watchman came to try the gate during the course of his rounds and saw the two pairs of shoes that Bullard and Shinburn had left outside. He contacted the police and the bank was surrounded. Now Shinburn found that they had lost one of the screws to the lock, so he quickly made a wax screw and gave it a head by drawing his thumbnail across. As they left

---

[11] John L. Sullivan and 'Little' Charlie Mitchell had fought 39 rounds in driving rain before the bout was declared a draw when the police arrested both boxers. They later fought at Madison Square Garden, New York, when Mitchell, despite being only a middleweight, knocked Sullivan down before himself being knocked out of the ring by the heavyweight.

[12] *New York Herald*, 18 July 1879. One of the jobs attributed, incorrectly, to Shinburn was the Belgian mail robbery on 27 November 1886. The train left Ostend at 3.30 a.m. and by the time it reached Verviers the safe had been rifled.

they were surrounded. Bullard opened fire but was chased and caught.

For a time it looked as though they would get away with things. There was nothing except a piece of wax found on Shinburn. Nothing had been disturbed in the bank. Then shortly before they were to be discharged another examination of the bank locks was made and the wax was taken for comparison. In it was the missing screw. Shinburn received 17 years and 6 months and Bullard a year less. Bullard died in prison after serving 7 years of the sentence; he had been talking about a reconciliation with the widowed Kitty Terry when he was released.

In fact Worth had gone to see him, combining business with friendship. In 1892 he went to Switzerland to meet with Oscar Klein and went on to Liège. In the meantime he had arranged to have some bespoke burglars' tools made for him. Undaunted by the South African experience, he decided to go in for another robbery.

He found that once money had been delivered to the railway station at Liège it was distributed by express van with an armed driver who had only a young boy as an assistant. Worth could see that from time to time both the driver (who delivered the boxes) and the boy (who delivered other parcels) left the van at the same time. He reasoned that if he had a package for delivery at a point near a bank, both would be gone for the necessary minutes.

Now he recruited John Curtin, again currently on the run in England. He was a good friend of the Worth family, a one-time partner of Billy Porter with whom had served sentences in Chicago, Sing Sing and Pennsylvania. Byrnes wrote that he was 'one of the most notorious burglars and shoplifters in America'. One of Curtin's claims to fame was that he had swallowed a forged cheque rather than allow the police to have it as evidence.

Worth also brought in 'Dutch' Alonzo. The handsome 'Dutch' Alonzo Henne, said by some to have been born in good circumstances, had made his way in the Underworld as Sir or sometimes Lord John, or George, Grey – turning his hand to any form of crime which paid sufficiently well. Apart from his reputation as having picked more pockets than any other man in America, he was particularly adept at land frauds and racing swindles. Posing as Sir George or Lord John Grey, he would form associations with wealthy men and was always going to visit his cattle ranches in the South West. His friends would appear and he would introduce them as men who had made major sums by having advance knowledge of racing results. Also known as 'Paper Collar Joe', he later had an interest in the faro bank at Lou Ludlum's New York house until it was closed. He was not always regarded as reliable. Worth considered him as big a coward as anyone who ever lived.

The idea was that Worth would fill the bag and hand it to Curtin who would run. He would also be a lookout. On the day of the robbery, 5 October 1892, at 9.30 the driver got off the box to make a delivery to a M. Comblen at 31 Boulevard Frère. The boy also left to deliver Worth's parcel, whereupon Worth was on the box in a trice and tore the lock off. The contents went into a small sack.

Now came the problems. Worth should have gone while he was ahead, but greed did for him. He decided to take as many packages with him as he could, and when he looked up he found to his horror that the only person in sight was a railway employee. Now the driver returned and began to chase after Worth who was making for rue St-Véronique where he hoped he could lose himself. Off he went, dropping parcels as he did so, but he was now nearly 50 years old and had lost his pace. He was caught by a policeman and handcuffed. Curtin and 'Dutch' Alonzo faded away.

When questioned Worth started making half boasts but maintained he was acting alone. The Belgian police knew they had somebody special but they did not know who. Then details of Worth's teeth, or rather the lack of them because he had no regard for dentistry, were circulated and recognised by Scotland Yard. Shinburn in his cell also saw the opportunity to help himself and he provided a full account of Worth's career. The people who did not help were the Pinkertons, who were contacted but chose not to reply. But it did not matter. Worth received 7 years solitary confinement with hard labour, wearing the mask required of convicts in Belgium.[13] By the time he was released in 1897 his health was gone and he was a broken man:

> In October 1892 Adam Worth was in custody in Liège. He was beginning to look very old and was by no means the dapper chap he was when I saw him in London 18 or 19 years ago.[14]

According to Worth, Curtin proved no friend. Back in England he sold off Worth's horses and houses and seduced his wife. The *Shamrock* was sold to Lord Lonsdale.[15] Then having pillaged home and family, Curtin disappeared. Worth's wife was committed to a lunatic asylum and the two children were sent to Boston to their Uncle John. Having served 5 years at Portland following the theft of £1,212 from a Manchester bank in 1888, Curtin was reportedly released in April 1892, but was a ticket-of-leave man until April 1896. Arrested for failing to report under the Prevention of Crimes Act in May 1893, he had been living in Woburn Place under a false name. He was discharged on the failing to report matter and immediately re-arrested over a theft from a Frankfurt bank in which 137,000 marks had been stolen.

What with debauching the unfortunate Mrs Raymond and disposing of the proceeds of Worth's fortune, Curtin had been a busy man because his name cropped up again in June that year when James White, described as a betting man, was acquitted of the theft of the Countess of Flanders' jewels from a safe in the Palace at Brussels on 1 February. White maintained that he had been attacked by Curtin in Monte Carlo on 23 January and had

---

[13] The wearing of masks was not uncommon in continental prisons. It had been tried in England, but abandoned when it was realised prisoners recognised one another's voices. In September 1925 'a crook of quality' who baffled police of two continents died at Clairvaux prison. Count de Salles, swell mobsman and soldier of fortune, had in 15 years allegedly committed more burglaries than any other single man; he died at the age of 45. He was said to be the chief of a powerful gang of about 60 who operated in London and New York. He was kept in solitary confinement and had to wear a mask when other prisoners were present. *Thomson's Weekly News*, 26 September 1925.

[14] WAP to John Shore, CID, NSY, 3 November 1892.

[15] The Lonsdale archives show no record of the *Shamrock* being owned or leased by them. In fact the *Shamrock* was the name of the yacht owned by the tea magnate Sir Thomas Lipton, so it is highly unlikely they would have one of the same name. Worth may well have been spinning the Pinkertons a yarn.

immediately left for England; he had not been well on his arrival and had not sent for his bags at Victoria Station until 2 February. The prosecution's case was that he had arrived at tea-time on the afternoon train on that day. Discharging White, the magistrate said there was a good deal of suspicion but no evidence.[16]

As for 'Dutch' Alonzo, he was probably a peculiar choice in the first place. In the autumn of 1887 there had been a quarrel between him and Sophie Lyons' later husband, Billy Burke, and Westley (Charles) Allen. They had all been involved in the robbery of a bank messenger in Geneva. Allen and Burke were convicted there and Alonzo was meant to have taken Burke's property back to his mother. Instead he had kept it himself when he returned to work in Montreal. Retribution seems to have been in the form of a stabbing, after which all was forgiven.

In October 1896 Billy Miller and 'Dutch' Alonzo were said to have each received 5 years in Bruges under the names of Bowers and Alexander respectively. There followed a short sentence in Hamburg. Alonzo next turned up in New York in November 1901 where he met a Pinkerton operative at the Hotel Metropole. He had promised the police captain Titus not to work in New York any more.[17] He may have kept his promise, for in March 1903 he was reported as operating a series of jewel thefts in Nice with the help of a young woman and 'a Jew named Winter'.[18]

By the autumn he had begun to work with the great British bank thief 'Fearless' Frederick Smith, known as 'Long Almond', and they both received 4 years in Paris in 1904. Smith had long been a police target and it was noted that he passed through Paris and took the express train to Bordeaux in early October 1903. There he was joined in what was described as a 'swagger hotel' by a number of policemen as well as, on 30 October, by Alonzo (under the name of Howard), the 65-year-old George Ward Thomas and John Mahon. It was in and out of banks until the next day Thomas had his hand on a customer's bag and a detective had his hands on Thomas. The others escaped back on the Bordeaux Express, but it was a simple

[16] *Daily Telegraph*, 11 May 1893.
[17] Ass. Supt. Beutler to RAP and WAP, 7 November 1901.
[18] Donald Swanson, NSY to RAP, 4 March 1903.

matter to watch for them when they arrived at the Gare d'Orléans. Again it was a question of in and out of banks and they were arrested when they tried to take 70,000 francs from the Comptoir d'Escompte. The authorities also took the opportunity to charge them with the theft of 450,000 francs at the Gare du Nord in November 1900. At the hearing before the investigating magistrate, Mahon protested that they were all honourable men with substantial properties in London. Speaking for himself, he had two well-known metropolitan magistrates and a solicitor amongst his tenants. The police agreed that they were men of property. It was however 'undoubtedly the most important capture made by any detective force for many years'.[19]

On 17 June 1913 Alonzo died of opium poisoning in a rooming house on W 43rd at the age of 55. Addicted for many years, he was now thought to be a drug dealer. He had been arrested the previous autumn following allegations of wire-tapping swindles.[20]

On his release Shinburn, ever the opportunist, circulated the news of his own death. He had not behaved well to other prisoners while in Belgium and, fearful of reprisals, he now had an operation on his cleft chin. It did him little good. He returned to America where he was soon in trouble again, serving a 4-year sentence followed by another 9 years for an old robbery over which he continued to maintain his innocence. One account relates that having purchased real-estate holdings in Chicago, on his release in 1908 he retired to live off the rents. Here, in theory, was a rare example of the truly successful criminal who lives out his old age in comfort.

In fact it was not quite like that. Certainly Shinburn had financed a man named Tomason who blew up a number of ships with a clockwork device for insurance purposes, but there was no money and he became yet another Pinkerton informer, to an extent living off their charity. At their instance he wrote a history of Victorian safe-cracking, *Safe Burglary – Its Beginning and Progress*. It was such a detailed manual that it was never published.

---

[19] *Morning Leader*, 5, 6 November 1903.
[20] *New York Herald*, 17 June 1913.

William Pinkerton felt sorry for Shinburn in his later life:

> I am sorry you told him I was in the city, as he writes the life
> out of me with long letters and it is a continual touch for money.
> I have been very good to the old man in the last few years, and
> am still willing to help the old fellow along, but I think he is a
> bit off his head in some things.[21]

He changed his mind three months later after Shinburn gave the
Boston Herald completely false information about Worth in connection with the South African diamond robbery and other thefts:

> His story of the Gainsborough portrait was just as big a fake as
> the story of the Kimberley diamonds. The old fellow is not as
> foolish as we thought he was in the way of getting money.[22]

Mark Shinburn died on 14 March 1916 in Detroit.[23] He had spent
his last days in a home for reformed prisoners.

> In spite of his many viscissitudes (sic) he lived to a ripe old age.
> I always feared he might take part in the present war. I may have
> been wrong about it but I always feared he would be in some
> explosion or other as he was very tricky. However, he is now out
> of our way for all time to come.[24]

After Worth's release from prison in Belgium there were still some
raids which helped to pay for the children in America, but the last
big task was to return the Duchess and if possible to obtain some
money for her. He considered the Pinkertons had behaved well to
him after his arrest in Liège, as indeed they had, and now he
approached William Pinkerton who advised against using the
lawyers Howe and Hummel since they were likely to keep the whole
proceeds of the matter or possibly tip him off to the police.[25] On

---

[21] WAP to George Leith, Boston, 20 January 1913.
[22] WAP to Allan Pinkerton jnr, 23 April 1912. Apparently Shinburn received $120 for
the series of 10 articles. Leith to George Bangs, 25 April 1913.
[23] A slight variation is 13 February 1916 in Boston.
[24] WAP to AP, 25 February 1916.
[25] WAP to RAP, 16 January 1899.

18 July 1899 Worth became a paid informant for the Pinkertons under the ironic name Jewstone.

In the end it was the Pinkertons who delicately opened negotiations which were completed by their informant Prieststone the gambler, and general man-about-town Doc Sheedy. The Duchess was finally ransomed by William Agnew for $3,000 and probably delivered to his hotel by Worth in disguise.

Worth clearly had a little money left because in 1901 the two children returned to the house at 2 Park Village East where he was renting rooms.[26] He died the next year on 8 January. Harry L. Raymond wrote a note which at first was thought to be a possible hoax, and then a longer letter to the agency about his father's death:

> My father's death was sudden and he told me little or nothing about his affairs before his death; he was sick for several weeks, but would consult no doctor, and it was not until after his death that we knew he had died of liver trouble. I left his room to go down to my supper and he seemed to be in the best of spirits but when I came back to his room he was as I thought sleeping; several hours afterwards the landlady when (sic) into the room and came out to me and said she did not like the looks of my father and requested me to go in and I did so but my father had quietly passed away without a struggle.[27]

A coroner's inquest was held and the death certificate notes that Worth, described as 'of independent means', died 'from chronic habits of intemperance'. He is buried in an unmarked grave at Highgate Cemetery in North London. The register for the plot number 34281 is in the name of Henry Judson Raymond.

The Pinkertons sent his son, Harry, a cheque for $700 on the pretext that it was a debt owed by a man in the city to his father. It is suggested that at some time later Harry L. Raymond joined the firm which for so long had helped and hindered his father, but there is no material in the Pinkerton files to confirm this rather

---

[26] Neither he nor his family appears on the April 1901 census as living at the address. The householder was a Mrs Jane Burrows who lived there with her daughter and a maidservant.

[27] Henry L. Raymond to WAP, undated.

romantic story. The biographer James Horan appears to have had some papers which never found their way into the archive and quotes:

> One would like to know whether the boy ever really knew his name was Worth. Certainly not from the hard-boiled Pinkerton who shortly afterward gave him a small job in their New York office. His employment record still exists and states that no investigation is to be made as the boy is known to both Mr Pinkertons.
>
> He certainly must have his father's name because it was he who wrote to the Pinkertons in the first place and the newspapers were full of the Raymond–Worth connection.

As to the employment Robert Pinkerton wrote to William:

> He writes like an intelligent boy, but I doubt the advisability of taking him away from his present position. He appears to be with a good firm, and if he is smart, eventually, he will come out all right.[28]

Like so much of Worth's story, his family is shrouded in the mist of romance, much of his own telling. Such accounts as there are come in a letter from William Pinkerton to his brother George, the contents of which are based on two interviews with Worth in the Chicago offices. The pair seem to have sat down and reminisced. How much of Worth's recollections are accurate and not self-serving it is difficult to establish.[29]

[28] RAP to WAP, 25 February 1902.
[29] WAP to RAP, 16 January 1899.

MARM'S GIRLS

10

Sophie Lyons

The finest protégée of Marm Mandelbaum was, without doubt, the formidable Sophie Lyons who may genuinely be described as a Queen of the Underworld.[1] Not everyone liked her, however. In contrast to her unbounded admiration for Annie Gleason, Chicago May Sharpe may have respected the talents of Lyons but she did not really like her. It was an animosity which dated back to the time when she first met her at the Savoy Hotel around the turn of the century. Lyons had fallen out with Eddie Guerin who wanted Sharpe to plant some jewellery on her and have her arrested. She refused, but was always wary of Lyons. Nor did Sharpe approve of the way Lyons, the grand lady, spoke disapprovingly of Annie Gleason.[2]

According to her whole self-serving memoir written at the time when she briefly became a gossip columnist for the *New York World*, Lyons first stole at the age of six, receiving the approbation of her stepmother 'who patted my curly hair, gave me a bag of candy and said I was a good girl'. She maintained that her good father who was fighting for President Lincoln never knew of his second wife's proclivities.[3]

[1] Sophie Lyons, Case Binder 33.
[2] May Churchill Sharpe, *Chicago May – Her Story*, Chapter XXVI.
[3] Sophie Lyons-Burke, *Why Crime Does Not Pay*, p. 11.

The reality was very different. Born in 1850 as Sophie Elkins alias Levy – the daughter of Sophie Elkins, herself a shoplifter,[4] and a housebreaker father – Sophie Lyons became one of Marm Mandelbaum's team of shoplifters and pickpockets. Her first husband was the noted burglar, Ned Lyons.[5]

Ned Lyons was born in Manchester in 1839 and arrived in America in 1850 when the family lived at W 19th Street. Here he came under the patronage of Jimmy Hope and became his partner, carrying out a number of very successful bank robberies with him. In the middle 1860s he married Sophie, but the marriage was not without its teething problems.

Inspector Byrnes describes Sophie Lyons' mania for stealing as so strong that:

> When in Ned's company in public she plied her vocation unknown to him, and would surprise him with watches, etc., which she had stolen. Ned expostulated, pleaded with and threatened her, but without avail; and after the birth of her first child, George, Ned purchased a farm on Long Island, and furnished a house with everything a woman could wish for, thinking her maternal instinct would restrain her monomania; yet within six months she returned to New York, placed her child out to nurse and began her operations again.[6]

The result was inevitable and on 9 October 1871, after she had served a term on Blackwell's Island, she was sent to prison for 5 years. By now she had four children. Ned Lyons had preceded her to the penitentiary.

In the early summer of 1870 Ned Lyons came to Perry and stayed at the Walker house. He was later described as a cultured gentleman in appearance, educated and apparently refined, dressed in good taste and representing himself as being a travelling agent for a New

[4] As late as 22 November 1876 the elder Sophie Elkins, under the name of Julia Keller, received 4 years in the New York State prison for shoplifting.
[5] Some accounts give her first husband as Maury Harris, a professional pickpocket whom she married at the age of 16. If this is so, it would account for her skill and possibly her apparent kleptomania. B.P. Eldridge and W.B. Watts, *Our Rival the Rascal*.
[6] Thomas Byrnes, *Professional Criminals of America*, p. 140.

York or Boston carpet manufacturing company. He was certainly sufficiently regarded to be allowed to mix with the town's young gentlemen, notably with a Dr Patchin. During the three weeks when he was in town, they went to baseball games together in nearby Genesco.

At the time the only bank in town was Smith's Bank, which later became the First National Bank of Perry. Shortly before Lyons arrived a new Herring-Hall-Marvin safe had been installed which, said the manufacturers, was burglar-proof. When Lyons had laid out the land he sent for two colleagues, Hayes and Watson, who arrived with a team of fast horses and a set of tools.

About 1 a.m. they broke into the bank but the safe, constructed of overlapping layers of heavy steel, was all its manufacturers had cracked it up to be. It took until 3 a.m. to reach the last layer, and then the charge they used was so great that it awakened the neighbours. The three abandoned their efforts and made for the horses with the townsfolk now in hot pursuit. It was reasoned that Lyons and Co. would make for Livonia to catch an early morning train for Corning and New York, which was a correct assessment; the three men were on the platform. Shots were fired and the men were chased off the station, with villagers joining in throwing stones and sticks at them. Lyons is said to have remarked, 'I'll surrender to the fellow with the guns, but I'll be hanged if we'll submit to being stoned to death like a dog.' The trio were taken to the township of Warsaw where they were held in the county jail.

Enter the 'educated and cultured', apparently genteel woman Sophie Lyons who 'by her attractive personality won the admiration of a considerable number of people there, gaining their sympathy by her refinement, being presented with flowers and other testimonials of regard'. She was there to persuade them that there was no possible way in which her husband, 'no common crook', could have been involved. She fixed her attention on one of the pursuers, M.H. Olin, to whom she offered $5,000 and a trip to Europe if he would not give evidence. When that failed, threats followed: he would 'never see daylight afterward'. Olin is said to have replied heroically that everyone had to see their finish sometime and so far as he was concerned it might as well be 'one time as another'.

Lyons received 10 years, as did the others. Watson, who came from a good family, was pardoned but Hayes died in prison. As for the heroic safe, it was sent to New York and exhibited in a store window in Broadway with a placard stating it had withstood the efforts of the notorious Ned Lyons.

The safe remained there until about the time when Lyons escaped from Sing Sing on 4 December 1872.[7] It was, said Sophie, she who had planned the escape with the assistance of the celebrated 'Red' Leary who, posing as a lawyer, seemingly mislaid his pass. He was warned about his carelessness and allowed to leave. In fact the pass was behind his back teeth and a fresh one was forged in New York. This was smuggled into the prison and when the warden and senior staff were absent, Lyons simply walked out and stepped into a waiting buggy.

A fortnight later he drove a sleigh to the female prison, which was then on the hill at Ossining, under the pretext of delivering a basket of fruit to a sick prisoner. Sophie Lyons had managed to insinuate herself into a position of favour with the prison doctor as well as the warden and his family, and had obtained work as an assistant nurse in the prison hospital and as a helpmate with the warden's children. She obtained an impression of the key to the warden's home which she smuggled to 'Red' Leary's wife Kate. A new one was made and at suppertime she was by the door. In her memoirs she recalls one of the warden's children asking when Sophie was bringing her supper. When Lyons arrived and opened the door she ran out, jumped onto the sleigh and the pair fled to Canada. As for the Lyons children, George – who later became a relatively successful burglar in his own right – was sent to a private school. Once in Canada Ned Lyons robbed a pawnbroker of some $200,000 in money and diamonds. Now the girls, who had been placed in an orphanage, were retrieved and sent to a convent.

It might have been thought that this haul was sufficient to last

[7] *Perry Record*, 29 December 1921.

them their lifetime, but they were soon back in America where they evaded arrest until they were caught picking pockets at a fair in Suffolk County, Long Island. Lyons received 3 years and 7 months, and Sophie was discharged only to be rearrested and taken back to Sing Sing.

After she had served her time she immediately transferred the scene of her operations to Boston where she worked the badger game with Kate Leary. It was here that they became involved in the celebrated Room Eleven, Revere House case when they tried to obtain $10,000 from a prominent Boston merchant after having taken his clothing. Since there were insufficient funds available to meet the cheque when Lyons presented it to the bank, unwisely she told the clerk where to find the drawer of the cheque and both she and Kate Leary were arrested. The man – whose family life was now in ruins – declining further exposure, refused to appear at court and the pair were discharged.

Lyons continued working the badger game for the next three years, moving to Detroit. There she met her match. For some weeks she would go each day to the home of a prominent businessman and sit on the horse-block outside his house. He retaliated by turning a hose on her and beating a theatrical agent who came to her rescue.

On 6 February 1883 she was arrested and sentenced to 3 years in the Detroit House of Correction after a conviction in Ann Arbor, Michigan, for theft. Then it was back to New York where she received 6 months on 2 June 1886 for stealing silk – and off she went again, this time to Blackwell's Island.

On her release it was over to London where in 1890 she was back in business shoplifting and pickpocketing, working again with Kate Leary. Both were said to have hooks fastened to their shoulders to help them.[8] In Europe she also worked with Helen Gardner who, operating in Nice as Lady Temple – the widow of Sir Charles, the well-known doctor – sold options on his practice many times over. Lyons also opened a bank with the celebrated Carrie Morse and for a time worked with Ellen Peck whose

[8] See *Police News*, 14 June 1890.

great delight was to con other criminals. Lyons lost a $500 shawl to her. Carrie Morse, also known as Marian Dow and Marian la Touche, had the great idea of the Ladies' Investment Bureau which she opened in 1883 and which closed with a total loss for the investors. Morse received 2 years but, undeterred, she was immediately back in business offering women $50 a month for every $300 invested.

Ned Lyons was out of the scene in 1892 because by then his wife had become involved with Hamilton Brock from Boston. When Lyons was released he went to shoot Brock, but on 24 October 1884 was himself shot in the jaw and the body in a quarrel at the Star and Garter saloon on 6th Avenue. Later Brock informed on him and the unlucky Lyons was shot again when attempting to rob a store in South Windham, Connecticut. He went to hospital and then prison. Lyons was something of an unfortunate; he had already lost the upper part of an ear in a street fight in 1869. Now Sophie went off with Brock. But the affair did not last long because by 1892 she had teamed up with her future husband, the handsome and much younger Billy Burke (also known as Jem Brady), who in December that year went down for 3 years for stealing $4,000 in Mount Sterling, Kentucky.

Sophie Lyons was acquitted.[9] As for Ned Lyons, he survived his shootings and imprisonment but he was on the way down. On 21 January 1906 he was arrested in Toronto for swindling James Tierney of Brooklyn of £500 by means of the Green Goods trick, passing counterfeit notes as real.

At that time Sophie possibly did not write too well, because a letter to the Pinkertons dated 3 March 1897 was dictated by her to her daughter. The next year came another letter to the Bureau regarding Billy Burke.[10] She wrote saying that she was seriously ill and needed money. She had been locked up with him in Kansas and had mortgaged her house to pay the defence:

[9] *The Sun*, 2 December 1892. Four years later Billy Burke aka Jem Brady was described as the handsomest crook alive and the take was upped to $45,000. *New York World*, 20 January 1895.
[10] Sophie Lyons Brady to John Ryne, 13 June 1898. The Pinkerton brothers were hugely amused that 'Little Billy . . . has given Sophie the shake'. WAP to RAP, 15 June 1898.

He seems to feel that he is perfectly justified in having used me as a tool for his work and that there is no obligation on his part.

The idea was that the Pinkerton operative John Ryne would try to get Burke to assist her. The postscript was particularly touching:

> Mr Ryne, God Knows, there was no sacrifice I did not make for this fellow. All the written contracts, sealed, signed by any Priest minister in the Land could not have possibly strengthened the ties that bounded me to this person. No suffering, no hardship I did not endure for him. A public sneer he made of me, I endured all. Since his release from Alleghaney he refused to come near me. Believing you to realise the obligation which he owes to me, I have presumed to address you with the hope that you will speak to him before 'tis too late. Sophia.

But true love eventually found its way and Lyons was happy to go to Sweden to try to help Burke when he received 5 years for a bank robbery in Stockholm in 1906. Refused entry after the Pinkertons had wired the authorities there, she now began her painstaking drive to reform and respectability.

One of her targets was to keep Billy Burke out of trouble. After her death Detroit Police Inspector Thomas W. Lally recalled:

> I well remember once some years ago when Billy Burke, her second husband, was alive. I met her and she told me that Harry Schindler who was sent up for his part in a robbery of the *Pittsburgh Gazette* payroll had been to visit her.
>
> 'I don't want him coming over the house and leading Billy off into trouble,' she said. 'I don't trust him. The dirty little pup stole my gold-handled umbrella, and if I catch him, I'm going to prosecute him.' She was just trying to shield Billy who had also been in the Pittsburgh hold-up and to make me think he was going straight.[11]

---

[11] Quoted in 'Sophie Lyons No Piker' in the *Detroit News*, 10 May 1924. Umbrellas had long been highly prized. When Porter Bennett, a hotel sneak, took $25,000 jewellery from Henry Ward, the Pontiac millionaire, it was a $25 gold-headed umbrella which caught the fancy of reporters. *Detroit Journal*, 10 August 1908.

Lally recalled some of her other friends including Bill Stedson, known as 'English Bill' or 'Bill the Brute', who died in Los Angeles under the name of Parker, and particularly 'Stone Wall' DeFrance who would not look at a job which would net less than five figures. His particular claim to fame was that he robbed a St Paul bank in the morning, netting $35,000, and took the same figure out of a Minnesota bank in the afternoon. Kalamazoo was his downfall; he received 11 years after a hold-up there.

The Inspector believed that Sophie did actually love Billy Burke and that it was he who spent a good deal of her money:

> He was 'the prince of crooks' if ever there was one. He looked and dressed like an English gentleman and was the smoothest article I ever saw. He was another who worked on big jobs only. Billy hired out in San Francisco as a labourer once, and got himself assigned to the task of helping a bank to move to its new building on the opposite side of the street. Billy directed the moving of the gold and if the president of the bank had not happened to look out of the side window just in time, Billy probably would have got away with half a dozen boxes of gold. He was moving it by the cartload, but not to the place it was supposed to go. He did time at San Quentin for that.

Apart from a conviction in New York in 1896, the year she allegedly 'saw the Light', from then on Sophie worked the North West and Europe. She certainly had not seen the light, or if she did it was only faintly because she was working in London with Guerin and Adam Worth in 1900. In 1906 she was in prison with Annie Gleason at Aylesbury, having been convicted of cheating an English milord out of £700.

In 1913 she wrote her best-selling autobiography *Why Crime Does Not Pay*. Apart from a few cautionary lines at the end of each chapter, the real design was to show exactly what fun crime was and how it *did* pay. There is no mention of Billy Burke amongst all the characters who flood the pages, but by then Sophie had certainly retired and was in the process of reinventing herself.

As the years went by and she became a *grande dame*, her ancestry changed. Her father, the brutal Levy who had once seared her arms as a punishment, became a Dutch Jew, Van Elkan. Her grandfather, who had in fact been a safe-breaker 'to whom Scotland Yard doffed their caps', was in time elevated to a rabbi.

In fairness to Sophie, she put some of her money to good use. In 1909 she tried to establish an orphanage in Detroit for African-American children. The neighbours objected and she commented that she could not see how there could be any commotion in a neighbourhood which already included a garbage plant and a dog pound and which had a saloon on every corner. In 1916, when she offered a large plot of land in Detroit for a Home for the Reclamation of Children with Criminal Tendencies, she asserted, 'It is more than 20 years ago that I heard a voice calling me and I saw the error of crime.' Well, perhaps it was a little less time than that.

Over the years she campaigned for prison reform and put her money towards prisoners' welfare. In 1922 she furnished the Christmas dinner, complete with trimmings, for the Wayne County jail. Never known to turn down an appeal from a released prisoner when that appeal was made personally, she also argued against capital punishment before the Michigan legislature.

On 6 May 1924 she died in Detroit. One story was that she was attacked at her home by three men who had come apparently to view with the intent of leasing it. Her last words before she lapsed into a coma were, 'Quit, don't do it.'[12] It was suggested that the beating might have been in revenge for her informing on them and their colleagues, or to steal her jewellery. For years there had been tales that there was a king's ransom concealed in the house where she lived at 908 23rd Street. However, the story of her death was probably just another one about Sophie Lyons because there was nothing in the Detroit papers at the time about such an attack.

She had become a complete eccentric, taking her dogs with her to eat the same food as she did at her table. Undoubtedly, three weeks before her death the diner run by Arshag Andonian at 3350 West Fort Street where she was eating was held up and – stories

[12] *New York Times*, 8, 9, 11, 18 May 1924.

differ – she either fainted and was pushed under a table or deliberately hid there to avoid a search of her belongings. Certainly it
was well-reported:

> These poor deluded boys. I pity them so much. If I could talk
> to them for five minutes I know I could make them see crime
> will never pay. It's a mistake: any act against society and law is
> a mistake. I've proved it in my own life.

She added, however, that she was taking her diamonds to the safe
the next day.

On the day of her death she had been talking to real-estate
salesman Aaron Kurland and two prospective tenants – which given
that someone supplied his name rather argues against the robbery
theory – when she said she was feeling faint and collapsed. This
time her last words were said to be, 'Lay me in white.'

It was never really clear quite how many children she had. When
her strong-box was opened there was a tiny American flag wrapped
in paper with a note, 'God bless this flag. My dear father, brother
and only son died for it. That is why it is so precious to Sophie
Lyons-Burke.' However, she seems to have had two sons: George,
the burglar who died in prison and whom she named in her will,
and Carlton O. Mason, who had died two years earlier and who
may also have been in prison. He had certainly changed his name
and become a clerk in Seattle. She was said to have loved only him,
and indeed her ashes were scattered at his grave in Woodmere
Cemetery, Detroit. Hundreds attended her funeral at which the
hymns 'Beautiful Isle of Somewhere' and 'Sometime we'll understand' were sung.

As for her daughters, she was said to have taken against Florence
who had been born in 1874 and who, when she discovered her
mother was a notorious thief, had asked her not to visit the convent.
The story went that she had been reduced to penury and pushing
a barrel organ and playing the penny whistle around Detroit,
receiving no help from her mother. Sophie was rumoured to have
referred to her as 'a perfumed vagrant'. When Florence appeared
at the funeral of Carlton and was pointed out to Sophie Lyons she

replied, 'I see no daughter of mine.' Stories abounded, for either she or another of her daughters was said to have taken the veil on hearing of her mother's career.

In the event Sophie had, said the newspapers, provided for all three – Florence Bower, Charlotte 'Lottie' Lyons-Burke of Switzerland and Madeleine Brady Belmont of London. Her fortune was estimated as being between $150,000 and $300,000.[13] Provision was probably not the right word, because the girls were only to receive $2,000 each. The remainder of the money was to be used in a number of ways for prisoners – $100 a year to provide comforts for sick prisoners and those on Death Row; a subscription to the *Saturday Evening Post* for prisoners in Michigan; and a sum not exceeding $1,000 to buy a piano for the Detroit House of Correction. The rest was to go to a quasi-orphanage for children with one or more parents in prison; they were to receive four trips a year to Belle Isle and there were to be plenty of toys and a tree at Christmas.

It was not long, however, before lawyers and her daughters, including the 'perfumed vagrant', started to make inroads into the estate. Both she and lawyers acting for Madeleine – who was in the Horton, a mental hospital near Epsom, Surrey – sued. Madeleine had, stated her claim, been left to fend for herself as a stenographer and had been a nurse in the First World War, following which she had a breakdown. The third daughter Lottie, born in 1881, was said to have become an opera singer in Europe and had disappeared in France some years prior to her mother's death. Her legacy was never claimed.

Of course, once the lawyers had their hands on the estate there was never going to be an orphans' home, particularly since the locals resented the proposal. Nor in the ten years after her death were there any trips for orphans to Belle Isle as she had wished, nor had the children had their Christmas trees or parties. Those ideas had soon been scuppered, and now came healthy payouts to both Florence and Madeleine. What was left by the time things were finally settled in April 1938 was put into a trust fund for the

[13] *New York Times*, 8, 11, 18 May 1924.

children. It was then that the story of her murder was again mooted.[14]

What was indisputable in all this was that she had never thought very well of the robber Eddie Guerin, and perhaps his later career showed she was correct.

[14] See *inter alia Detroit Free Press*, 23, 26 March, 10 May 1924; 21 January 1929; *Daily News*, 8 May 1924; 13 January 1936; 24 June, 4 October 1927; 13 April 1938.

11

Annie Gleason:
A Princess of Thieves

Annie Grant – or Ferguson, or Lillie Latteral – who married Mickey
Gleason at the age of 14, described herself as an actress or comedy
artiste and in fairness she possibly appeared in some of the lesser
Chicago music halls. Born in 1873, she was barely five feet tall (or
5' 2" or 5' 3" depending on the police report and who did the
bertillonage measurements), had brown hair, blue eyes and a sallow
complexion. She had been born in Union Street, Aberdeen, and
when she was young her father had emigrated, working as a cab-
driver in Detroit and prospering sufficiently to have his own livery
stable on 12 Street, Michigan Avenue. For some reason, when she
was 8 he sold up and moved to Chicago.

Some accounts say that she started life in the badger game but,
taught by her husband, she quickly became an expert pickpocket,
shoplifter and confidence woman.[1] Her version is that as a blushing
virgin of 16 she eloped with the handsome Gleason to Milwaukee,
completely unaware that his trade in life was that of bank robber;

[1] The simple version of the game which has been worked over the centuries all over
the world involves a woman taking a man to her room and when he is almost completely
undressed and she is partly clothed in bursts her uncle, father, brother, probation officer
etc. The role played will depend upon the apparent age of the girl. Money is then
extorted from the man to assuage the husband's feelings or, if the girl is seemingly young,
to pay for a period in a hospital to allow her to recover from her terrible experience.

he had told her that he was a traveller for a firm of dry goods merchants. He was arrested in Shelville and, after he had been on remand in custody for some months, she persuaded the judge to give him probation.[2]

Back in Chicago with an Irish girl, May Croman, and a man she calls Chancy Frank, Annie and her husband were in the Owl Restaurant on 33rd Street when the men decided to rob it, holding up the waiters and rifling the safe. Later that night she and May went to a ball at the Swedish Hall and were arrested in the middle of a quadrille. She spent some time in custody and eventually was given probation. From then on it was downhill all the way. She and her husband robbed a jeweller in New York of $10,000, and then returned to Chicago. Gleason then decided to go with Charlie Williams to Europe where they robbed the American Express van in Paris, money which he gambled away with Pat 'Doc' Sheedy in Chicago.

Meanwhile she had teamed up with Sophie Lyons who gave her an attaché case with a concealed spring, ideal for stealing lace. She was arrested in May 1904 with Josie Cherry and taken to Jefferson Market jail from where she escaped with the help of Dan Carney. Recaptured, she too was given probation and promptly fainted; she had thought she would be given 3 years. Now she travelled to Europe where she worked successfully posing as the daughter of General Ulysses S. Grant.

On 10 July 1905 Annie received 3 years penal servitude for grand larceny in London. In a robbery planned between Joe Killoran[3] (working in England as Joe Howard) and Baby Thompson (the one-time *inamorato* of 'Chicago May' Sharpe), in her role as the daughter

---

[2] In her memoirs 'My Life as the Queen of Crooks' in *Empire News*, beginning 15 August 1925, she calls Gleason, John Anderson. An early English woman jewel thief was Emily Lawrence who operated between 1850 and 1870 during which period she served two sentences of 7 years each. There was a legend amongst criminals that she had managed to take with her into Millbank prison a quantity of loose diamonds which she had stolen in Paris and which she cached in her cell. Women prisoners would try to get her old cell so that they could search for the treasure. If anyone found the jewels they never said, because none were discovered when in 1895 Millbank was pulled down to make way for what is now the Tate Gallery. Arthur Griffiths, *Mysteries of Police and Crime.*

[3] 'Chicago May' Sharpe gives the name of the planner as Harry Bennett, but the Pinkerton records must be preferred.

of General Grant she had switched a worthless necklace for a diamond and pearl one valued at £1,700 at Christie's, St James's, on 29 June. She was caught not because she had failed to match the colours of the stones exactly but through extremely bad luck. A jeweller who happened to be in Christie's saw her examine the jewels and went over to look at the pearls she had decided not to buy. He noticed that the cheap £5 necklace had a white tag when it should have carried a yellow one, and gave the alarm. In true thespian tradition, at first she braved it out when stopped but on the way to the police station she threw the stolen necklace in a doorway. Howard escaped.

Now she claimed that the necklace had only been stolen to raise a passage back to America to see her children. Not so, said Detective Inspector 'Tricky' Drew. She had been working in London with Howard, who in his absence from the dock would no doubt have been pleased to be described by his title of a Prince of Thieves. She had already absconded from $1,500 bail in America on a theft of jewellery charge with May Porris. This time the pair had had some $5,000 worth of gems for which they could not account. Since then she had been working with top quality English and continental thieves. She was also known as a pennyweighter.

> The Recorder—A what?
> Inspector Drew—A pennyweighter, my Lord; that is a person who goes into a jeweller's shop, inspects jewellery, and with some sticky substance on the fingers palms an article and deposits it beneath the counter for a confederate to pick up.
> The Recorder—Well, we are always learning something new (Laughter).[4]

Released on licence, she was seen about town with Eddie Guerin, but she failed to report a change of address to the police and where she went was not entirely clear.

But at some time she certainly returned to England because on 6 September 1911, giving the name of Mary Ferguson, she began a spell of 5 years. This time she had been caught with Alexander

[4] *Morning Post*, 6 July 1905; *Inter Ocean*, 16 July 1905.

Ivanovitch or 'Prince Makaieff' and her crime was, on the face of things, very much down market. She pleaded guilty to stealing a total of eight pairs of stockings from London shops. The Prince had also pocketed a 3-guinea Panama hat. Apparently he had asked for a 10-guinea hat, but being told the most expensive was 5 guineas he took the cheapest one (Laughter in Court). He certainly did not behave in a princely or even gentlemanly fashion, saying when he was arrested, 'The woman is a devil. She is a thief and made me a thief. It is very hard on me.'[5]

But she had made him quite a successful one because he had £58 in gold and over £300 worth of jewellery on him. The pair had also been seen at a Brighton jewellers from where a ring disappeared, but there had not been enough evidence to prosecute.[6] This had proved her downfall. The Brighton police contacted Inspector Gough in London, she was seen with the Prince coming out of the York Café in Jermyn Street and the pair were followed for some four hours.

But Ms Gleason's crimes apparently did not stop at penny-weighting and shoplifting. Bigamy was also on the agenda. She had been living at 34 Little Newport Street in Soho with an American music-hall artist, Theodore Albert Gillespie, who had seemingly married her in the rather appropriate name of Anna Chisel at Camden Town Register Office in January 1909. He had been on the boards as half of Ferguson & Mack, Comedians.

Now she was gratifyingly described as the Princess of Crooks.

> Annie Gleason is the best-dressed woman thief in the world. She wears hats that cost $125 and $300 gowns, but she never over-dresses. Patrons of the Grand Prix in Paris and London have known her for her style and engaging manners.[7]

---

[5] In fact the Prince was being economical with the truth because he had already been convicted in January 1902 at the North London Sessions when he received 9 months, and again in April the following year when he received 21 months with hard labour. He had also picked up a 15-month sentence *in absentia* in Paris. His letters from prison had been stopped when it was discovered he was in communication with a well-known jewel thief then in Wormwood Scrubs. *Illustrated Police News*, 2 May 1903.

[6] *Star*, 6 September 1911.

[7] *New York Press*, 7 September 1911; see also *New York Sun*, 7 September 1911; *Chicago Daily Tribune*, 7 September 1911. Meanwhile husband Mickey was serving his sentence in Munich.

According to her memoirs Makaieff was hissed by the public gallery when he tried to put the blame on the Princess who was appearing under her alter ego, Mary Ferguson. Gillespie had been following the case and obtained permission to see her in the cells. He died a fortnight later of, she says, a broken heart.

William Pinkerton had seen her on the promenade at the Alhambra, 'where all the fast women walk', shortly before her first conviction in England and he was not impressed: 'The newspapers make a great handle out of her, but she does not amount to very much. She has just been a badger and shoplifter.'[8]

On 23 April 1915 she was back at the Old Bailey as Ferguson along with Charley Allen, under the name of Williams who, years earlier along with Killoran, had escaped from Ludlow Street jail on Thanksgiving Day 1895. Her previous sentence had been only recently commuted because she still had one year and 243 days to work off her ticket-of-leave from the 1911 troubles.

This time it was not simply switching but robbery with violence of a jeweller named Wladyslaw Gutowski when they stole some £1,600 worth of gems. As Mrs Ferguson, she had again been working with Russians and she told the jeweller, who had a shop in Percy Street, Tottenham Court Road, that she was being kept in style by an English milord who wanted to buy her some valuable diamonds. She had already dealt with the jeweller, having bought a small diamond ring from him for £27 as part of the come-on. She was staying at the Savoy Mansions, where the actress Billie Carleton would kill herself with a drug overdose some years later on the night of the Victory Ball.

On 10 February Gutowski dutifully appeared for the appointment, bringing some £20,000 with him. He was sandbagged and then chloroformed by one of the Russians posing as a page. Allen was the look-out man. When the police searched the flat they found a lady's silk handkerchief in a drawer and she was traced through the laundry mark. None of the gems were recovered. Gutowski lost his hearing following the attack.

At least in court she and Allen were given their due when they

[8] William Pinkerton to Allan Pinkerton, 9 September 1911.

were described as 'two of the most dangerous thieves in the world', and in her case as 'looked upon as one of the most successful American thieves we have here today'. Allen had received 4 years at North London Sessions in 1900 and had then been taken back to America to serve out the 3 years he was doing when he escaped from Ludlow Street. Now he received 12 years and 12 strokes of the cat. Defended by Purcell who had earlier represented Chicago May Sharpe, Annie was sentenced to 10 years and, as she left the dock, 'looked reproachfully' at Mr Justice Lawrence.[9] Allen died in prison. She was released on licence on 27 January 1923.[10]

On 18 November 1925, now known as English Annie, Gleason was back in New York, accused of grand larceny along with Harry 'The Phony Kid' Campbell. The pair had stolen a $150 jade ring from an Upper East Side jeweller. Having posed as a surgeon and special nurse buying a present for the head of the hospital, they were seen coming out of a jewellery store at 22 W 88th Street and were promptly arrested. Again Gleason tried to brazen things out, saying they were on a week's visit from London and were horrified that the American police should do such a thing to them. Unfortunately they were then put on an identification parade and two detectives said they had been seen at an art store on 40 E 57th. When the stock was checked it was found that a jade ring was missing. It was retrieved from Gleason's finger. Campbell received a 15–30 months sentence in Sing Sing, and she was given 15 months in Auburn.

Now she may have been on the slide, or it may have been a cover story but she told detectives that she had worked in London after her release but then returned to New York where she became a chambermaid at a hotel on 44th Street. She remained there for three months until being laid off; then she met Campbell and they had stolen the jewellery and a fur necktie. But her story belied her appearance: she resembled 'a fashionably-gowned, refined woman in court yesterday'.[11] She was released in October 1926.

[9] *Illustrated Police News*, 29 April 1915.
[10] PRO PCom 6 28.
[11] *New York Herald Tribune*, 18 December 1925.

Annie next surfaced in Chicago in the spring of 1933 where a Grand Jury was investigating a series of substantial jewel thefts. They thought photographs showed these had been carried out by Harry Campbell, still using his medical guise, probably along with his wife Hattie Campbell – now out of prison where she had been when her husband and Annie Gleason stole the jade ring – and possibly Annie too.

Hotels were watched and on 4 May 1933 it was learned that 'The Phony Kid', who had been living under the name of Dr Clayton, had committed suicide at the Park Manor Apartment Hotel. He had served another 5 years when he pleaded guilty to grand larceny in the second degree on 7 May 1929. Poor Hattie, only recently released from the previous sentence, had been with him, and this time she went down for 2½–5 years. Campbell left a note citing ill health – he had long been a morphine addict – and stating that 'The Eye' was closing in and another pinch meant 25–50 years.

On 9 May 1933 Annie Gleason was arrested at the Paradise Arms Hotel where she was identified as one of the women who had been with Campbell. This time, much to Pinkerton disappointment, she was discharged when the judge held there was no positive evidence that she had stolen the jewellery. She had told the police on her arrest, 'I have blown safes in Baltimore, stolen pearls in London and lifted fur coats in Berlin.'

She died two years later in November 1935 in Mercy Hospital, Chicago, aged 63 and still a beautiful woman. She was buried in St Mary's cemetery.

Her husband Mickey Gleason, 'The Plutocrat of Pickpockets', had an entertaining career. Born in Bridgeport, Chicago, in 1873, he came from what was described as a good family. His father, John, had a saloon on the corner of 31st and Emerald Avenue and was looked on as a man of property. Earlier he had worked with the Sherlin Gang and had been taught the art of safe-blowing by Eddie Fay. On 21 June 1897 he went down for his first conviction for taking $1,300 from the pocket of R. W. Headly while travelling on a tram.

Gleason was estimated to have been arrested 100 times and

to have stolen thousands, but when in difficulties he usually managed to square his victims or enter into some sort of deal with the authorities. Regarded as one of Chicago's most expert thieves, on one occasion he was released from 22nd Street Station where the police were holding him while awaiting other officers who were coming to have a look at him. At the time he was wanted for shooting Kid Burgess, with whom he had quarrelled in a Halstead Street saloon. On another occasion he negotiated his way out of an arrest for pickpocketing at the racetrack in Memphis on the understanding that he would secure the return of a stud stolen by Will Hawkes in that city. His talent was such that he could pick out money from the stocking tops of the women with whom he was dancing.[12] He also worked in Pittsburgh with James Thornton, who had the distinction of removing a diamond stud from Governor Upham of Wisconsin at his inauguration ceremony. It took William Pinkerton some trouble to retrieve it.[13]

At the end of March 1900 Gleason was working in Paris with Jerry Daly and Kid Morris, where they relieved a bank messenger of $80,000 and were back in Chicago by the May.[14] By 26 April 1900 he was on the Pinkerton books as Cimstone. In July that year he was arrested in Cleveland and jumped $500 bail. He had been working with Sid Yennie and Charles Diehm, 'The Phenomenal Kid'.[15] He was arrested in Baltimore on 30 March 1901 and on 24 April received 10 years, later reduced to 8, for pickpocketing.

The sentence which he served in Sing Sing expired on 24 December 1907 and he was in Munich with the English crook, John Anderson, on 13 July 1908 when the pair robbed the Bavarian Mortgage and Exchange Bank. Caught before they left the building, they were found to have a collection of false beards and, perhaps

[12] *Daily Tribune*, 22 June 1897; *Chicago Herald and Examiner*, 22 June 1919.
[13] WAP to Roger O'Mara, Chief of Police, Pittsburgh.
[14] *New York Sun*, 9 May 1900.
[15] Diehm did what he could to live up to his nickname. In 1908 he stole $15,000 from the counter of the Park National Bank and was only captured after 'a desperate struggle'. He received 4 years.

even more interestingly, a quantity of what appeared to be Kansas Central and South-West Railroad Company stock. They had done a 'Cook's Tour' of the Continent, robbing banks in London, Copenhagen, Paris, Berlin, Vienna and Frankfurt. Anderson had also robbed the Compagnie des Métaux in Paris a few years previously. When arrested for the Munich robbery Gleason first pretended to be a deaf mute. He was described as being amongst the 12 top bank sneaks in the country.[16] At the end of that 10-year sentence he went to London, where he died in Pentonville on 19 April 1919; he was serving 5 years after trying to pick the pocket of an MP.[17]

As for Charles Allen, he came from a well-thought-of family. The Allen brothers were long-standing criminals. One, Mart Allen, was sentenced with Steve Raymond on 1 November 1883. Raymond, convicted of uttering Union Pacific Railroad Bonds with altered numbers, seems to have minded the pontifications of Recorder Smythe – telling him 'Cut your lecture short, please' – more than the 'natural life' he received. The Recorder for his part does not seem to have minded being interrupted. If Raymond behaved he would, he said, endeavour to have the sentence commuted.

Mart Allen – who was said to have often been recruited to lead teams – had already gone down for 10 years for burglary. In October 1866 Allen, along with Edward McGuire, 'Gily' McGloin and Gus Tristam known as 'Sleepy Gus', robbed an Adams Express car on the New Haven Railroad. Allen had been acquitted three times and convicted three times. Brother Theodore was said to have spent $100,000 trying to extricate Mart and his other brother, Westley, from their own activities, but had now given up on them. Possibly Theodore was not quite the white sheep he may have seemed. He was known as The. Allen and had a saloon in New York. Of the other brothers, John was a jeweller and Jesse had before his death

---

[16] *Pittsburgh Dispatch*, 7 August 1908.
[17] John Mahon, an Englishman, also received 5 years. *Chicago Herald and Examiner*, 22 June 1919. However, a note in the Pinkerton file suggests that in 1922 Gleason had received a 1–14-year sentence in Peoria.

been a burglar. But it is Wesley who is the most interesting of the family.

Byrnes regarded Wesley Allen as 'probably the most notorious criminal in America' and 'a saucy treacherous fellow, and requires to be watched closely, as he will use a pistol if an opportunity presents itself'. At some point he had lost his left eye and wore a glass one, sometimes a green patch and sometimes green goggles. Born probably in 1846 in New York, by the mid-1880s he was described as having a sallow complexion, dark hair going grey and a black moustache. He had a scar on the left of his face and 'W.A', an anchor and dots of India ink tattooed on his left forearm.

As with the Sabinis in England in the first half of the twentieth century, the brothers exchanged names to suit themselves. On 7 July 1873 under the name of Charles Allen, Wesley received 5 years in Sing Sing after being found trying to break into a silk warehouse. He was released in 1877 and from that time on Byrnes noted ruefully that he had been arrested in almost every city in America but had always escaped conviction. Part of his time was spent picking pockets, and he was arrested in New Haven, Connecticut, in January 1880 and in Reading, Pennsylvania, three months later. On both occasions he was discharged. On 23 December 1880 he ran an alibi defence at the King's County Court of Sessions in Brooklyn, where he had been charged with stealing a watch. Again he was acquitted, as he was also in August 1883 when he was back in New Haven, and again at Jefferson Market Police Court. This time, unusually, the charge was assault and the complainant was a bar-keep in Theodore's saloon.

On 13 September he was arrested at the funeral of his wife, Amelia, on a warrant alleging grand larceny in Syracuse, but again his luck held. In November 1883 in Alleghany City, Pennsylvania, using the name Fisher, along with a man giving his name as Grimes he ordered suits of clothing valued at a little under $150. They were to be sent COD to West Jefferson, Ohio, and were duly shipped; but on the night they arrived the Adams Express office was the subject of a burglary and the suits were found some days later at the home of Allen's father-in-law Martin Fisher who, along with his wife, was promptly charged with receiving. The old man was over 70; his wife was not much younger and they were discharged. As for Allen, he had left for England where he would end his career.[18]

[18] *National Police Gazette*, 14 November 1883.

12

'Chicago May' Sharpe

At the end of the nineteenth century and during the early years of the twentieth, a genuine transatlantic example of an independent was May Sharpe. Born in Dublin in 1876, she spent six years in a convent school before running off to New York at the age of 13 with £60 of her father's savings. She seems to have been a genuine operator on her own account. Of course she was obliged to rely on male help, but by her late teens she was clearly the dominant and financially successful partner in any relationship. In New York she met and married Dal Churchill, 'robber, highwayman, safe-cracker and rustler', who rode with the Daltons and was hanged near Phoenix, Arizona, in 1891. May, now 15, went to Chicago where she became Queen of the Badger Game. During her career she called herself Churchill by which name Eddie Guerin, the safe-breaker, knew her.

At the age of 17 she had apparently accumulated the astonishing sum of $300,000. Travelling to New York she is said to have teamed up with Charlie Becker, the corrupt police officer, before – via a number of other men – she moved on to Guerin in 1901. It does seem highly likely that she was under the protection of Becker because although while in New York and Detroit she was convicted in 14 cases, including dealing in revolvers and larceny as well as the more mundane prostitution and disorderly conduct, she 'seems to have escaped so lightly as to have suffered practically no punishment at all'.[1]

The convict Jim Phelan remembered her as:

> . . . a beautiful woman, very resourceful and courageous, what Hollywood would nowadays describe as a gunman's moll . . . [She] was no mere ornament of the alliance, but took her share of the planning and execution in many capacities. Seducing a bank-manager – to get impressions of his keys – or standing guard with a revolver while a safe was blown or 'taking the dairy' [diverting suspicion] in a counting house, all came equal to Chicago May.[2]

However, the man with whom she is inextricably linked in the annals of criminal folkore is Eddie Guerin, who was born in 1860 either in Soho or in Chicago where he certainly grew up. In February 1887 he shot a police officer before escaping to England where he immediately picked up a three-month sentence at Mansion House court after being found on enclosed premises with intent to commit a felony, in this case to rob a post office. He was working under the name of George McCaull. In July 1888 he was reported as having been shot and captured in London. The shooting part was not accurate, but captured he had been. Next year he was back inside for burglary and he then attempted to escape from Holloway prison. He had a reputation for peaching in a tight spot and at the time was regarded as much less celebrated than his brother Paddy who served a 6-year sentence in Kentucky for his part in a $20,000 jewel robbery. Both of them

---

[1] Lieutenant Charles Becker (1869–1915) followed in the great tradition of corrupt New York policemen such as Inspector Alexander 'Clubber' Williams. After a re-trial he was convicted of complicity in the murder of the gambler Herman Rosenthal who refused to pay protection money and was believed to be about to blow the story to Herbert Swope of the *New York World*. There is little doubt that the District Attorney Whitman bribed witnesses to secure the conviction but a second jury convicted. Becker was electrocuted in the most clumsy manner at Sing Sing on 7 July 1915. His wife attached a silver plate on the top of his coffin: *Charles Becker Murdered July 7 1915 by Governor Whitman*. She was persuaded to have it unscrewed when it was pointed out that she might be prosecuted for criminal libel.
[2] J. Phelan, *The Underworld*, p. 111–12.

had worked for Jimmy Carroll, a thieves' ponce in Chicago.[3] Carroll's practice was to demand 10 per cent of the take or he would report the theft to the police. As the years went by Eddie Guerin, on the back of his escape from Devil's Island, supplanted his brother in the legends.

Before that, however, he had fallen foul of the celebrated Sophie Lyons who was queening it in Paris with Billy Burke, then still her fancy man rather than husband. Guerin believed Lyons, for whom he had no time at all – a feeling which was mutual – to have been another thieves' ponce, and that she had her eyes on him both as an additional beau and as a worker. Once he had rejected her overtures she became his enemy. He wrote:

> Sophie Lyons was a pimp; she battened on crooks, sucked their life's blood and then bartered away their liberty to the police.[4]

In 1888 he took part in a snatch in Lyons when a bank messenger was relieved of something in the region of a quarter of a million francs. This was the work of Billy Burke, 'Dago Frank' Denin and Guerin, with Guerin making the grab and Denin being the stall to hinder any chasers. Guerin buried the money in woods some miles out of the city. At first three Italians were arrested, but on his return to Paris Guerin could not keep his mouth shut and word was soon around London and Paris. He and Burke retrieved the money – Denin had already launched an unsuccessful retrieval mission on his own behalf – and Guerin was next approached by Bill Stedson, 'Bill the Brute', another friend of Sophie Lyons, who demanded a share. When Guerin refused Stedson shot him in the shoulder in the St Petersburg Hotel in Paris and retreated to London.[5] Denin was arrested in France and Guerin, who always maintained Lyons

---

[3] *New York Times*, 24, 25 July 1888. The report added, half admiringly, that if Guerin had himself been armed he would have used his gun to escape.
[4] Eddie Guerin, *Crime: The Autobiography of a Crook*.
[5] Stedson died some years later in Boston, leaving his money to a niece. Guerin says that he was offered £1,000 to give evidence on behalf of Crédit Lyonnais who were suing Stedson's estate. He also maintains that it was after his raid that bank messengers in France were obliged to have their bags chained to them. Eddie Guerin, *Crime: The Autobiography of a Crook*.

had shopped him, was captured in London by Detective Sergeant Leach.

This was the first time he tried to avoid extradition, claiming that he was English-born. He was represented by the celebrated Charles Gill, but an officer was brought over from Chicago to say that he had known him since infancy.[6] He was duly extradited and, along with Denin, received 10 years in Rion prison in Vichy. Although Denin paid for Guerin's defence, they fell out during their sentences.

Throughout his sentence Guerin had been in touch with the celebrated Alderman Mike 'Hinky Dink' Kenna, gambler, saloon owner and political fixer who sent him money from Chicago, and on his release he made his way to London.[7] Kenna also arranged for Guerin to meet Doc Sheedy at the Hotel Metropole there, and the latter financed Guerin's temporary return to America. In 1900 he was back in London.

It is difficult to know exactly how Guerin and May Churchill met. In her book she says it was at the funeral of the thief Walter Finch, accidentally killed in a fight in London, but wherever they first met there is no doubt that within weeks if not days they were working and living together. The funeral itself had a high turnout of both English and American crooks including Jimmy Lockett, and the receiver, panel worker and police informer Tim Oates.[8]

On 26 April 1901 she, Guerin, George Miller (known as 'Dutch

[6] The case *The Queen v Eddy Guerin, aka Call and George Graham* was heard before Baron Pollock and Mr Justice Mauristy. PRO DPP 4/22.
[7] Kenna, who flourished from the 1880s to the 1930s, was an alderman of the Fourth Ward where he perfected the system of graft payoffs and collection. He is also credited with being the man who first recognised and employed the talents of Big Jim Colosimo, Al Capone's mentor in Chicago.
[8] For an account of Lockett's career see Chapter 18. On 10 September 1886 Tim Oates was arrested in New York under the name of Charles Wilson, along with Bernard Corcoran alias Barney Rose and Mary Morton, for robbing two people at 16 Clinton Place working the panel game. As was often the case, the complainants decided not to prosecute and all three were discharged.
   In France the panel game was known as *entolage* and the trick was not merely to take the man's wallet but to remove the money from it and substitute newspaper or counterfeit notes. There the proprietress of an *entolage* house would expect 5 per cent of the take. *Morning Leader*, 10 January 1904.

Gus')[9] and another man Kid McManus removed £50,000 in francs and cheques from the Paris branch of the American Express Company next to the old Garnier Opera House where they blew the safe. The janitor had locked up for the night and was awoken by two men pointing guns at him. Miller was captured at the Gare du Nord just as he was catching a boat train. On investigation by the magistrate Leydel, he was found to be in possession of a number of cheques stolen from the safe in the rue Scribe offices and 6,000 francs from the burglary. In a small casket inside a leather bag were found dynamite cartridges, as well as jemmies, saws and boring tools all made of the finest steel and bearing the name of a New York manufacturer. The day before the robbery the thieves had purchased some thick cord, which was identified as the cord used to bind the caretaker.

Miller, who said he was from Chicago, made a full confession but exonerated Seager, the young coloured porter at the American Express Company. The police were still searching for Guerin, who was then going under the name of Tom Edwards.

When contacted, the Chicago police believed that George Miller was not known to them; they knew plenty of Millers, but not a noted cracksman. The New York police didn't recognise his photograph, but one officer thought he might be Charles Marks alias 'Jew Sam', particularly because of a scar on his cheek. 'Jew Sam' had apparently been cut in a fight in a bar-room opposite the Hopkins Theater on Clarke Street. The officer was wrong, for Miller was in fact August Henry Brake, alias Bailey, alias Paxton. The Pinkertons thought that the third man was not Kid McManus as at first suspected but more likely Richard Harris, known as Little Dick.[10]

Miller, also confusingly additionally known as Ed Blake and Gus King, was a Scotsman by birth but had lived in Chicago for some years. William Pinkerton was dismissive of him:

---

[9] In newspaper reports Miller's name is often spelled with a single 'l'.
[10] *New York Herald*, 2 May 1901. It was thought he might also be Fred Searles alias Fred Young who, in around 1882 or 1883, had sued the Edinburgh *Scotsman* for libel.

He has no standing as a thief and in Europe has simply been a 'badger puller', or a man who worked with a woman.[11]

He was probably being unkind. Further research showed that Miller was also known as John Sweeney and had served a 3-year spell after the burglary of a clothing store in Iowa.

Chicago May and Emily Skinner, also a mistress of Guerin, now went back to France to see what they could do to help and both were arrested. Skinner was released after a week; Churchill received 5 years, but did not serve out the sentence and was released early. Both Guerin and Miller were sentenced to life imprisonment. The theory as to why Miller implicated Guerin is that it was jealousy after being supplanted in Chicago May's affections.

Guerin and Miller were sent to Devil's Island from which Guerin with three others made his famous escape in 1905.[12] There have been a number of accounts of this escape, but it is generally accepted that the men made a raft out of a fallen tree and after paddling 200 miles they landed on the mainland of Dutch Guiana. Actually, only three landed because one had been eaten by sharks, said Guerin. Once on land the survivors separated. The other two were eaten by wolves; one was torn to pieces and the other climbed a tree and died from starvation and exhaustion while the wolves 'watched cynically from below'. How anyone knew that is not clear, unless they were extremely educated wolves.[13]

Guerin alone was picked up by a steamer near what was then British Guiana. He was exhausted but fairly well nourished. Unfortunately, later in his criminal career he let slip that on the voyage he, and not the sharks or wolves, had eaten his companions. From then until he died he was regarded as an outcast in the Underworld.

---

[11] William Pinkerton to John Cornish, New York Police, 31 January 1902.
[12] In fact the escape was rather more prosaically from Maroni on the mainland.
[13] Jim Phelan, *The Underworld*, p. 107 *et seq*; PRO MEPO 3/346; *Morning Leader*, 1 May 1906, 10 June 1918.

His escape was probably financed in part by the shadowy Pat 'Doc' Sheedy – something he did not exactly deny, saying somewhat sanctimoniously:

> Did I assist Eddie Guerin to regain his liberty? Well, now I will answer that in this way. If you expose the roots of a beautiful rosebush to the sun all its fragrance dies and the leaves wither. So it is in life. If a man does a good deed for another and then advertises and exposes that good act it takes all the good out of it.[14]

Guerin and Sharpe met again in England, quarrelled at Aix-la-Chapelle – although Guerin was wanted in France he seems to have skipped across the Channel with impunity – and met yet again on this side of the water. It seems that she was now blackmailing him, threatening that if he did not look after her she would inform on him to the French authorities. It would certainly be her stock in trade. The officer in the attempted murder case which would follow, Inspector Stockley, described her as 'one of the most notorious women in London, whose chief business is to compromise and blackmail men'. She was said to have worked out of Northumberland Avenue for a team known as the Northumberland Avenue Gang specialising in panel work and blackmail, and was also believed to have run an opium den.[15] 'She has driven men to suicide by these means,' said Stockley. In her book Sharpe certainly admits blackmail and gives The Hon Archibald W., an English barrister of 3 Stone Buildings, as one of her victims.[16]

Guerin went to prison to await extradition to France to serve the remainder of his sentence. It was there that he met Charles Smith, apparently Irish, a tinsmith by trade and, wrote May, a

---

[14] Newspaper cutting, 'Guerin had no help' in Pinkerton Box 110. There is no date, nor identification as to the paper.
[15] Percy J. Smith, *Plutocrats of Crime*.
[16] Sharpe, more than most others, was good about giving the correct identities of those mentioned in her book. One member of Lincoln's Inn was Archibald Willis, called in 1896, who practised from those chambers, which would fit.

'good prowler by vocation who reminded me of my first husband'. He had been thrown out of Cape Town the previous year. He was also known as Cubine Smith and Clarence Coldwell and clearly had known May Churchill at some earlier time in their lives.

Smith was also capable of mixing things up. According to him, Guerin had wanted him to throw vitriol over Mrs Churchill and had told him to go to Pat Sheedy, 'a well known sporting man who lived in New York' – in fact he owned a gaming house and was the one-time manager of the prize fighter John L. Sullivan – who would give him $200 and then he could blind her. According to Guerin, it was Smith who wanted to throw the acid of his own volition. He was apparently complaining that Mrs Churchill had not done enough for him while he was in prison.

Sir Richard Muir, for once acting on behalf of the defence, and in the finest tradition of the Bar apparently without fee, obtained Guerin's release from the extradition proceedings on 14 June 1907. His argument had been helped by the fact that the French maintained they had shut Devil's Island well before Guerin escaped from the colony.[17] Guerin spent the night with Emily Skinner, and next day he had to see his lawyers and then the newspapers in Carmelite Street who were after his story. May had clearly patched things up with Smith – if indeed they needed patching – and was now living with her new companion.

There is little doubt that Guerin was a violent man and May Churchill had every reason to be afraid of him. Now she and Smith took matters into their own hands and went looking for him. On 16 June they went to the Hotel Provence in Leicester Square where Guerin and Emily Skinner had been within the hour. An acquaintance there said it was just as well Guerin had

---

[17] Another who escaped from Devil's Island but who was not as fortunate as Guerin was Adrian Demerian, born Fortune Roger Roques at Foix in 1878. Sentenced to life imprisonment for attempted murder at the age of 19, he escaped three times and on the last occasion managed to stay out for six years before he was arrested as the *Mauretania* docked at Liverpool. He pleaded with the Bow Street magistrate to allow him to go and live in South America, but an order for his extradition was made on 15 April 1910. *The Times*, 1, 8, 12, 16 April 1910.

left. May said she was afraid Guerin might throw acid over her. Smith boasted that if Guerin was a bad man, he could be one too. Having learned that the pair had gone to Bernard Street near Russell Square tube station, they went after them in a hansom cab.

The whole episode was a blunder from start to finish. At the corner of Marchmont Street May called out, 'There he is!' Smith got out and fired six shots at Guerin at almost point-blank range, managing to hit him once in the foot. He hadn't finished firing before a police constable arrived and arrested Churchill. Guerin said, 'When you could not succeed in sending me back to Devil's Island you stoop to murder.' 'Yes,' she replied, 'and I am sorry we did not succeed.' Smith managed to get only a short distance before he was surrounded by police and civilians. He tried to shoot again, but the gun was now empty and he merely threw it at one of the bystanders. At the trial he alleged that Guerin had fired at him first and had then tried to throw vitriol over Churchill, but there was absolutely no evidence to support this. Churchill, arrested by the solitary constable, was taken to the police station followed by a rough crowd, some of them kicking the officer. During the mêlée she dropped her handbag and Robert Ward – a witness who picked it up – noticed there was an open knife sticking through the side. 'I carry it for my own protection,' she replied when questioned about it. Smith tried to do the decent thing by her; when charged he replied, 'She has done nothing wrong. I don't see how you can charge her.'

While in Holloway prison awaiting trial, she did her cause no good. She wrote a letter to Edward 'Baby' Thompson who was then (or had been in the recent past) another of her lovers. It was intercepted by the authorities:

> Dear Ted,
> I wish you to retain Purcell, otherwise I am done. They will not let me have bail everything has been kept back. As far as you are conserned (sic), those letters of yours would help me where you warn me of this man, will I use them, as your name would not appear. Good bye you might never see me again. This fellow

Smith was the one Eddy got to throw the vitriol so you see I lost
no time, turn the tables.

Yours as ever,
May

You can hear all from Arthur Newton. Help me.[18]

At the committal proceedings of Churchill and Charles Smith on a
charge of attempting to murder him, Guerin gave evidence that she
had said, 'You dirty bastard. If you don't take care of me I will send
you back to Devil's Island where you will die like a dog. If I can't
do you that way I will do you another.'

Smith received 20 years and Chicago May had 15 for her pains.
She appears to have been a model prisoner and was released from
Aylesbury when she had served a little over 10 years; then she was
deported back to the United States where she was a source of trouble
to the police until her death. Clearly she held no hard feelings
towards them, for she dedicated her book *Chicago May* to the great
reforming Californian police officer August Vollmer, 'who first
showed me a practical way to go straight'.

For part of the time she ran a small house, which translated
means brothel, in Philadelphia and then, before her death in 1929
in a hospital there, she announced that at long last she was going
to marry Charles Smith. She was 53 at the time of her death.[19]

It seems that Smith's name was actually Robert Cubine and he
remained in prison until 1921 before, according to May Churchill's
book, he was released early following the efforts of Lady Astor –
there was some sort of suggestion that he was a distant relation.
The file at the Public Record Office on Charles Smith contains an
application for the parole that year of Robert Coldwell Cubine.

---

[18] Arthur Newton was a very fashionable if dishonest lawyer of the time. He defended
the murderer Crippen, Robert Ward in the Camden Town murder case, and Samuel
Douglas, the Moat Farm murderer. He later went to prison for fraud; he had already
served a spell for perverting the course of justice. PRO Crim 1 108/2. For an account
of his career see James Morton, *Gangland: The Lawyers*.
[19] C. Sifakis, *The Encyclopedia of American Crime*, p. 144. Some accounts incorrectly
have her arrested for soliciting in Detroit in the early 1930s when she was said to be
charging $2, and give the year of her death as 1935.

The application was submitted by Cubine's brothers, saying that Robert was born in King's Mill, Virginia, on 12 August 1881. According to the papers submitted, his father W.J.B. Cubine, who died that year, had been a farmer, contractor, mason and carpenter, and a Freemason of 32nd degree. His mother Anna, born in Tennessee, had died in 1913.

The application also stated that Robert Cubine had gone to Kansas City at the age of 16 where he became a sheet-metal worker. In 1899 he left Missouri and went to South Africa as a circus rider with Hall's Circus, and remained there until 1907. At the time of the shooting of Guerin, Smith/Cubine was living at 107 Gower Street with Mary Churchill. In 1904 they had been convicted of attempting to blow up and rob the American Express Company in the rue Scribe. In 1908 Guerin escaped from Devil's Island. Churchill served 3 years.

In fact Cubine had been convicted in England on 23 July 1907, so clearly the dates in the application are wrong. But does it mean that he was the missing robber Miller? Probably not, because Guerin if not May would surely have named him.

The brothers said that the only reason Robert gave the name Charles Smith was to avoid the disgrace to his family. He had (they said) no previous convictions. What he did have was $400 coming to him from his mother's estate, and this could be used to repatriate him.

The story about his being a man of impeccable character was wrong, thought the Home Office. Smith had in fact committed a crime in the Cape Colony where he served 4 years penal servitude, and while being deported to America he had escaped en route at Southampton. The application also omitted the conviction he had acquired in England when he was arrested while trying to burgle a house in Regent's Park and subsequently defended by Arthur Newton. He had been remanded in custody for a week and curiously enough was in the same prison as Guerin who was then fighting extradition proceedings. No one was able to trace a conviction to Cubine and he was discharged.[20]

---

[20] 'Mexican Smith's Own Story: Secret History of Amazing Romance of the Underworld' in *Thomson's Weekly News*, 20 December 1924.

It was with Home Office approval that arrangements were made for his return to the States: 'He is a desperate criminal. We should be well rid of him.' Just as she had interceded for Chicago May Churchill so Lady Astor intervened for Smith, using the very fashionable firm of solicitors, Lewis & Lewis.[21]

However, yet another version of Smith's story was published a few years later. He had apparently been speaking to Cornelius de Rysback who recounted:

> 'Mexican' Smith who told me the whole story was a typical American gunman who had no regard for human life and who during a fight did his best to kill another convict with whom he had a row in Dartmoor, for which he lost 87 days remission. He told me that his family were large-scale fruit growers in Virginia.

Apparently Chicago May had spent the proceeds of the American Express robbery, believing that Guerin would die on the Island. Once he escaped, she wanted Smith to kill him to protect her. According to Smith or de Rysback or, most probably, the journalist who wrote the article:

> Chicago May had a fascination over men. In her hands they were clay in the hands of a potter.[22]

The now balding Charles Smith aka Robert Cubine, aka Nigger Smith, returned to America on the *Majestic* on 16 May 1922. He said that Chicago May was now in a convent. If this was in fact accurate, in her case it would be another euphemism for brothel. His release had come about, he said, because he had defended a warder attacked by another inmate.[23] After his release Cubine seems to have eschewed the family fruit business, and continued

---

[21] PRO HO 45 24541.
[22] *Thomson's Weekly News*, 11 April 1925. Cornelius de Rysback was a British subject born in Berlin who joined the German Secret Service. Arrested as a German spy and sentenced to life imprisonment, he served 10 years. The 'Mexican' Smith story is a small part of his memoirs of prison life.
[23] *Chicago Herald and Examiner*, 23 July 1922; see also *Chicago Evening Post*, 10 May 1922.

to work in America notably with the Englishwoman 'Blonde' Alice Smith. In September 1924 there were reports that he had been arrested under the name Robert Considine in South America, and again in California where he was said to have received 30 years following a series of burglaries in the Los Angeles area. Charged with a young man named Ruoff, he is said to have asked the court to 'Give the kid a chance'. He was arrested following the death of a night-watchman in a robbery in New York and received 14 years. The reports that he died in Sing Sing in 1928 are inaccurate.

In 1928 there was an announcement that Chicago May was to marry the much younger English conman turned writer, Netley Lucas. When asked about the disparity in age he replied, 'Well, she's a blonde and a man in the toils of a beautiful, fascinating and unscrupulous woman has no power to control his own actions.' It is likely that she never knew of the engagement because it was Lucas who announced it in *Reynold's News*. In any event the marriage never took place.[24]

In fact Chicago May Sharpe died in Philadelphia shortly after announcing her engagement to Charles Robert Considine, 'the only man who ever understood me'. Her complexion was sallow, her tawny hair was thin and streaked, and her bubbling vitality had given way to the slackness of age when an abdominal operation was performed at the Philadelphia hospital. She had, it was said, made a will in Considine's favour. Considine called at her lawyer Henry J. Nelson's office and learned of the death there. Quite why

---

[24] Netley Lucas was an interesting man who began his criminal career at the age of 14 when, in 1917, he was expelled from his public school for theft and forging his housemaster's signature. He was in court at the age of 16 for obtaining money by false pretences from the secretary of a London club, and from then on went variously to borstal, prison and Canada where he was jailed for running a crooked employment agency. His first book, *The Autobiography of a Crook*, was published in 1925 and was such a success that not only were there two sequels but he continued to write biographies, including that of the celebrated judge Lord Darling, under a variety of names. In 1930 he forged the signature of Lady Angela Stanley and wrote to a publisher purporting to offer the memoirs of the late Queen Alexandra. For this he received a £225 advance, and later 18 months at the Old Bailey. He died, living as Robert Tracy in rented accommodation near Leatherhead, in a fire in June 1940. See Richard Whittington-Egan, 'The Netley Lucas Story' in *New Law Journal*, 30 June 2000.

he did not go to the hospital is not explained. 'I am sorry,' he said. 'I have loved her for more than twenty years.'[25]

After the jailing of Chicago May, Guerin's career was initially that of safe-breaker and hotel jewel thief. According to police files, January 1908 found him with Matthew Carr, aka Springate, committing what was described as a heavy jewellery larceny at Starlings the pawnbrokers in Great Portland Street. He was never charged. On 9 April that year he was discharged at Guildhall for frequenting banks, and on 24 April he was again discharged at Westminster Police Court when a charge of throwing corrosive fluid in the face of Alice Mahoney was withdrawn – Chicago May was clearly right to fear for her beauty. In Glasgow in January 1912 a charge of frequenting the Central Station Hotel for the purpose of theft was found not proven. He had been loitering in the hotel on 18 October 1910 when several bags were found to have been ripped open and jewellery stolen. When arrested he had 8 skeleton keys and a contrivance for obtaining wax impressions on him. The stipendiary magistrate accepted that Guerin was a known and reputed thief but, despite the equipment he had with him, gave him the benefit of the very little doubt.

For a time Guerin continued to mix with the best. He was a known associate of both the jockey turned thief Harry Grimshaw and his confederate Daniel McCarthy, and it may be that at the time of the Great Pearl Robbery in 1913 he was working for the receiver Cammie Grizzard. Certainly he was interested in the jewel robbery which Grizzard organised and Grimshaw executed at the Café Monico in Regent Street in 1909, which netted the team £40,000 worth of pearls and Grimshaw 4 years.

However, as the years went by he became an increasingly sad figure who degenerated into a pathetic sneak-thief. Every time he appeared in court he was described as the man from Devil's Island, and he blamed his regular appearances on this sobriquet. In his later years he repeatedly appeared before the magistrates' courts up and down the country, usually on charges relating to small-

[25] *Chicago Tribune*, 31 May 1929.

time shoplifting and pickpocketing. On 4 July 1918 under the name of Thomas Garen he received 18 months for an attempted theft at the Hotel Metropole in Brighton, and on his release he had a shop in the Buckingham Palace Road for a time. In 1920 he was working with another gang of pickpockets and blackmailers when on 3 October he received 3 months, with a further month for kicking the arresting officer. Inspector Alfred Grosse wrote:

> The impact would have been the abdominal parts of the officer and I say without fear of contradiction he would have been ruined for life, the venom and spitefulness of the appellant left no doubt in my mind what he intended.

Guerin's appeal, financed by the swindler Horatio Bottomley, was dismissed.[26] He was put on probation in 1935, and again on 6 February 1938 for loitering with intent to steal. In 1936 he was awarded an advance of $3,500, a part of his share in the estate of his half-sister,[27] but in March 1938 he lost his claim against the estate. Now his claim to British citizenship was that he had been born on a British ship.[28]

Guerin's last appearance in court was in February 1940 when he received six weeks' imprisonment for being a suspected person. Now in his eighties, he was living at 11 Ware Street, Vauxhall, but later in the year he was evacuated to Bury, Lancashire, where he died in hospital on 3 December that year; he had suffered a stroke and a cerebral haemorrhage.[29] Guerin is buried at the Bury Cemetery in 1162 J plot, an unmarked public grave.

---

[26] Perhaps the British king of the fraudulent company, Horatio Bottomley was born in the East End in 1860, the son of a tailor. He became a newspaper proprietor and fraudulent share promoter as well as racehorse owner and a Member of Parliament. Imprisoned for share swindles, he died in 1933. For an account of his life see Michael Gilbert, *Fraudsters*.

[27] *Chicago Daily Tribune*, 19 January 1937.

[28] Ibid., 26 March 1938.

[29] Eddie Guerin, *Autobiography of a Crook*. For an account of the Café Monico and Great Pearl Robberies see James Morton, *East End Gangland*. For a detailed account of the Great Pearl Robbery see Christmas Humphreys, *The Great Pearl Robbery of 1913*; PRO MEPO 3 237B; Alice Smith in *Thomson's Weekly News*, 22 May 1925.

Sophie Lyons may not have thought overmuch of him, but the police did. '[Guerin] is one of the cleverest active organisers and undoubtedly one of the most daring and expert criminals,' said Grosse.[30]

30 PRO MEPO 3 435.

THE PROFESSIONALS

13

The Forgers and Coiners

A trawl through the Old Bailey papers of the last half of the nineteenth century shows a high percentage of trials for coining offences. This was regarded by the police and courts as a particularly despicable crime because, apart from the fact that once again it was the small shopkeeper who suffered, it was seen as striking a blow at the stability of the country. Conviction invariably attracted a lengthy sentence. Coiners, as with other criminals, came in all shapes and sizes with, in later years, many justifying their trade by claiming to be anarchists. Sentences could indeed be swingeing. In March 1887 John Coe, described as a bricklayer, received 15 years for counterfeiting. He had already served 15 years. Many offenders, particularly those who had previously served a lengthy term, simply could not face another. When coiner Charles Croney, already a ticket-of-leave man, was found at his home in Margaret Buildings, Bethnal Green, along with Mary Sullivan he tried to drink a saucer containing cyanide. In the event he received a fairly merciful 5 years, added of course to the unserved portion of his sentence. She received 6 months hard labour.[1]

---

[1] *Morning Leader*, 10 March 1887, 19 January 1907. In April 1904 Ralph Appleton, who ran what was known as the Lambeth Mint in Tyler Street, Vauxhall, received 14 years. He was also thought to have carried on a secondary trade as an abortionist. *Morning Leader*, 30 April 1904. Another coiner who killed himself was Edward Heavyside in May 1912. A notorious smasher, he had already served two terms of penal servitude. Deprived of the father, the police arrested his son. *Illustrated Police News*, 31 May 1912.

A coiner would make dud coins from plaster of Paris moulds and fill them with heavy metal poured through a hole in the mould called a 'git'. It took a long time to make the first counterfeit coin, but after that it was easy enough. They were then sold in loads to 'smashers' – men and, more often, women who would make a purchase requiring change from a half-crown in a small shop. There would be a back-up man to keep a look out for emergencies and only one half-crown would be carried at a time. The reason for this was simple. To be in possession of one coined half-crown was a misfortune which could happen to anyone. Two was simply careless. Possession of three was in breach of the Coinage Act. Obviously the deceived shopkeeper would, if possible, get rid of the coin to an unsuspecting customer. Some, however, would nail the dud to the counter as a warning to the smasher, though whether this was a deterrent is open to question. Leeson, in his biography, remarks that he had never heard of a smasher being put off. There was one small general shop in Stepney where there were over a hundred florins and half-crowns nailed to the counter. The coins were often made out of pewter beer mugs, and a publican who lost a mug could expect to find it returned in the form of counterfeit in the next few weeks.

Generally coiners were not looked on as being very high up the criminal social tree. Wensley of the CID wrote that he could not understand why, with the inevitably heavy sentence, people took up coining:

> They are the most wretched of criminals. I have known scarcely any coiner who was not almost penniless and living under the most squalid conditions. At the best there is very little in the business and it is inconceivable why people should take such risks for such little profit. A very curious fact is that nearly all coiners plead guilty when they have been caught.[2]

Well, perhaps not all that curious. It would require a more fertile mind than that of many a coiner found with the moulds to offer a

---

[2] Frederick Wensley, *Detective Days*, pp. 141–2.

reasonable explanation as to what they were doing in his bedroom.

In 1895 Aston Villa won the FA Cup, beating West Bromwich Albion 1–0 at the Crystal Palace ground. On the night of 11 September the cup was stolen from the window of William Shillcock, football and boot manufacturer, in Newton Row, Birmingham. The shop was a lock-up one, and the zinc covering was removed from the roof thus allowing a man to be lowered in.

A £10 reward was offered by Shillcock, who also said that if the cup was returned there would be no questions asked. It was well insured and consequently it was proposed that a new gold cup should be purchased at a cost not exceeding £200, the insurance money. This proposal was defeated and it was agreed that another cup as closely resembling the old one as possible should be purchased. Aston Villa were fined £25, the exact cost of the replica.

Shillcock wrote:

> It was an incident which seemed to me at the time a great and unprecedented calamity. I pictured myself a ruined man. I seemed to see myself a hated individual – to see my business boycotted. Why, I was the man who lost the English Cup. I am not joking when I say that I believed that incident was destined to ruin my connection with football, but happily such has not been the case. But you see that I shall ever be a man with a record unique in the annals of football.[3]

Nothing was heard of the cup for over half a century until in February 1958 the *Sunday Pictorial* carried a scoop that Harry Burge, an 83-year-old Birmingham man, had stolen it. Burge said that he and his two companions had jemmied the back door, stolen the

[3] *The Book of Football*, 1906. Not quite unique because on Mothering Sunday, 26 March 1966, the World Cup was stolen from the Stampex exhibition at Westminster Hall. The thieves removed the screws from the plates of padlocked double doors and the lock from the back of the glass-fronted cabinet. Several days later a demand was received, along with the detachable top of the trophy, and following a telephone call a 47-year-old docker was arrested.

Shortly after, a Dave Corbett was out with his dog Pickles on Beulah Hill, Streatham, when the animal sniffed out the trophy hidden in the bushes. Pickles was given a year's supply of goodies by a dog-food manufacturer and a medal by the National Canine Defence League. Unfortunately, so the story goes, Pickles did not live long to savour the benefits from his triumph. While chasing a cat, he strangled himself with his lead.

cup, plus money from the till and some boots, and had then melted it down and used it to fake half-crowns some of which were passed in a public house belonging to Dennis Hodgetts, the Villa forward. There were a number of discrepancies in his account, but that may be attributed to a recollection of events which had taken place over sixty years earlier. Burge had been in and out of prison for 46 years and two years after the cup was stolen he was convicted of theft himself, so he had the right pedigree for the job.

Another sport frowned upon by the authorities was sweating, for which Isaac Friedman received 3 years in 1906. Sweating required a certain capital outlay because ten or more coins were put in a cloth and shaken and swung so that they rubbed together and a small amount of gold would be rubbed off and stick to the cloth. These scrapings would then be burned in a crucible and the gold sold to a receiver. The process would then be repeated. The term 'sweating' referred to the efforts required of the shaker and swinger of the cloth.

Forgers were in a different class and by no means all of them lived in London.[4] When Edward William Pritchard, the Glasgow doctor who poisoned his wife and mother-in-law, was hanged by Chalcraft on 28 July 1865 in the last public execution in that city, one of the men at the scaffold was the photographer John Henry Greatrex who had spent the time before the execution urging the crowd to repent their sinful ways.

But portrait photography was not the main interest of this splendid hypocrite, whose studio was hung with texts from the scriptures. He specialised in photographing £1 notes, particularly those of the Union Bank of Scotland. When, initially, he found that the results were unsatisfactory, he sought the help of an expert engraver in copper named Sewell Grimshaw. Soon a satisfactory process combining engraving and litho printing had been worked

---

[4] Nor had England a monopoly of coiners in Europe. Italian convicts in Aquilla were found to have become counterfeiters. Employed to make plant for the post office, instead they used the machinery to turn out two-franc pieces. One of the coiners tried to hang himself in his cell. At the prison in Rensburg, Germany, the police broke up a coining ring run by a warder. He was employing an old-time coiner to work at night in his cell producing five-mark pieces which were then distributed by the warder and his wife. *Morning Leader*, 25 February 1908.

out and, financed by Grimshaw's brother Thomas, some £13,000 worth of notes were printed. Meanwhile Greatrex had become enamoured of one of his assistants, Jane Weir.

Notes were passed successfully in small shops in Glasgow, Edinburgh, Stirling and Hamilton; but in September 1866 while Greatrex and Jane Weir were in Aberdeen passing notes they heard of the arrest of the Grimshaw brothers, and so it was off to America. They travelled to London on different trains, staying in Brown's Hotel. Next it was to Southampton where Greatrex took the SS *Hermann*, and a week later Weir followed on the SS *Deutschland*. They then took lodgings in Renwick Street, New York.

Their capture came about as a result of both good detective work and intelligent thinking by Superintendent Alexander McCall. He had traced the pair to New York and now, correctly supposing they would be looking for work, put an advertisement in the papers asking for a female assistant to work in a photographic studio. There was no such thing as race relations in the 1860s and the advertisement ended, 'a Scotch girl preferred'.

Jane Weir replied and McCall went to Renwick Street. The pair were out but the landlady confirmed Weir's description and added that although the man was clean-shaven – Greatrex was known to be bearded – he was fond of quoting the Bible. It was just a question of waiting. Back in Edinburgh, he received 20 years and the Grimshaw brothers 15 apiece.

A man regarded as one of the cleverest of criminals towards the end of the nineteenth century was George Johnson. Another who never let his colleagues know his home address, he spent a good deal of time in disguise trying to shake the police off his tracks. He lived in Beaconsfield Road, Twickenham, and the counterfeiting plant was kept in Kingsland Road, Dalston. Johnson's great aim was an attack on the Dexel Morgan bank and simultaneous forgeries were presented in Liège, Koblenz, Marseilles and Madrid where the continental criminal who passed as Lord Halifax was captured. Johnson and his partner Phillips received a relatively modest 7 years apiece.[5]

---

[5] Harry Cox, 'Some famous cases from my notebook' in *Thomson's Weekly News*, 15 September 1906 and subsequent weeks.

Some could not take the lengthy sentences on offer. Solomon Barmash, the crippled forger who had been carried down to the cells at the Old Bailey when he was sentenced to 15 years imprisonment, shot himself in the head. Some reports, rather romantically but almost certainly inaccurately, suggest the gun had been smuggled to him in a pie. Barmash had previously been convicted along with his son, William, in 1883, when he received 7 years and his son 1 year.

The coroner, when he sat to hold the inquest, was less than pleased with the security in the court cells. Only the month before Kitty Byron, accused of killing her faithless lover, had been found with a hatpin with which it was suggested she was intending to commit suicide.[6]

It was never clear who had actually supplied the gun to Barmash. Apart from the pie suggestion, it was claimed that his 10-year-old daughter had brought in the weapon. A third and rather more realistic solution was that either his elder daughter or William's wife was the culprit. However, one prison officer giving evidence at the inquest said that neither of the adult women was wearing a muff which might have been used to smuggle the gun. Another warder thought one of them had a muff, but both men were adamant that

---

[6] Court security was generally lax. Four months before Barmash killed himself a prisoner had shot himself in the cells at Guildhall Police Court. In November 1903 James Lloyd Davies was found with sufficient prussic acid to kill several people when he arrived at Brixton prison. In 1904 the swindler Whittaker Wright brought a gun into court with him; he poisoned himself in the cells following the imposition of his 7-year sentence. The press was on the whole sympathetic to Wright who was prosecuted over the failure of his company, London and Globe. It was pointed out that the same week a woman 'found guilty of systematic and heartrending cruelty to her own child should have a paltry fine of £50. Brutality to a helpless little girl is nothing compared with the enormity of obtaining money from the wealthy by illicit means.' *Illustrated Police Budget*, 26 January 1905.

In the case of Kitty Byron the jury had tried to bring in a verdict of manslaughter but the coroner refused. Had she not been reprieved it would have been a travesty of justice. Ethel Rollinson and Eva Eastwood, two young maids in Liverpool who had suffocated their elderly employer, were sentenced to death with a recommendation of mercy because of their age and previous good character. Both were reprieved. One had suggested she was pregnant and a jury of matrons had been empanelled and then quickly discharged. *Illustrated Police Budget*, 26 January 1905.

The newspapers were very much on Kitty Byron's side. 'Women sat in especially reserved seats just as though the grim Sessions was a theatre and the trial a spectacular drama. Up in the gallery, too, was another wedge of sordid-minded humanity staring with open-mouthed, sensation-struck intent into the bare dock below them.' *Morning Leader*, 12 December 1902.

there had been no opportunity to pass a gun under the table. The police were never able to trace the purchase of the gun which was of Belgian make.[7]

One result of the Barmash case was a temporary ban on visits to prisoners before and after the hearing, also suspension of permission for food to be sent into them. A suggestion that visitors should be searched before they were allowed to see a prisoner met with no favour. Chief Warder Scott from Brixton prison put the case against searching. 'The public wouldn't stand for it,' he said, adding with not a little significance, 'not only poor people came.'[8]

When the American forgers came to London they often did themselves well. In January 1891 William Griffs, alias 'Big Griffs' and shortly to receive 3½ years in London, and an American S.G. Stirling known as 'Old Sam' were staying at the Savoy Hotel. Stirling was known as a good engraver. Nat Bennett of New York, a financier of swindlers and forgers, visited them and they were said to be in conspiracy with a number of well-known English crooks along with Phil Hargreaves in their efforts to commit an extensive series of forgeries.[9]

Out of prison in 1894 Griffs stayed at the Barrett House, New York, and the Waldorf Hotel where he was visited by Bennett, Stirling, Hargreaves and a man named Ryan known to be in the Green Goods business. Griffs was accompanied by a young woman named Annie English. He also stayed at the Oriental on 39th and Broadway. They were then allegedly engaged in forging letters of credit on Coutts & Co. The forgeries were first to be carried out in the shape of circular letters of credit and then drafts and securities, the idea being to open a genuine business in London and America, to obtain the confidence of the bank and then distribute forged securities and counterfeit US bonds. Griffs, unfortunately short of funds, tried to raise money on his own account and was arrested. By then, some £4,000 had been obtained on 19, 20 and 21 July 1905.

It was, however, the Bidwell brothers, George and Austin, who came within an ace of ruining the Bank of England, and their tutor

[7] *Illustrated Police News*, 17 January 1903.
[8] *Morning Leader*, 8 January 1903.
[9] Undated memo from John Shore, CIS NSY, to Pinkertons.

Walter Sheridan was the originator of the plan. He had run away from his home in Ohio as a boy. Arrested, he escaped from prison and went to work in Chicago with Joe Moran, the very well-known hotel thief. In 1858 at the age of 20 he was caught housebreaking with Moran and sentenced to 5 years imprisonment. By the time Sheridan was released Moran was dead.

Sheridan, who always took the lion's share of the booty, was regarded as 'so exceptionally close-fisted and saving for one of his class that his fortune lasted until near the end of his life'.[10] He was also considered one of the most versatile character actors in terms of impersonation and disguise. In New York he was accused of an 1876 charge of uttering forged bonds of the New York-Buffalo, Erie Railway. To defeat this Sheridan, who usually dressed with a long, full, red beard, had dyed his hair with coffee grounds, started swallowing soap in prison, cut off his beard and changed into tramp's clothing. Nevertheless, he was still convicted on the evidence of William Pinkerton.

In prison it was wrongly thought that Sheridan was dying, and after his early release he took to robbing jewellers and went to Europe where he served 18 months for uttering forged Bank of England notes. He invested his profits in Colorado where he opened a bank, but there was insufficient return and for a time he joined up with little Horace Hovan. Other reports indicate that he lost his complete fortune gambling in mining stocks. Now he was losing his touch and he slid downhill, ending in prison in Montreal where he died in January 1890 while serving a 6-month sentence for vagrancy. He had been working there with 'Dutch' Alonzo.

In 1871 the Bidwells came to England. Along with George Engels,[11] they set up operations in Liverpool and obtained around £6,000. With this capital they came to London, opening a banking and commission house for the discounting and shaving of commerical paper under the name of Warner & Co.

---

[10] B.P. Eldridge and W.B. Watts, *Our Rival the Rascal*.
[11] George Engels was one of the many who worked with the great forger Henry Wade Wilkes. Arrested in Italy shortly before Christmas 1880, Wilkes made a full confession detailing his many activities and companions. His colleague James Joy Julius, known as Pete Burns, was so upset that he swallowed a prayerbook and choked himself to death.

As is often the case, it was the women who brought them down. George Bidwell and a fourth man, McDonald, became infatuated with the women with whom they lived and, naturally, pillow gossip was exchanged. This did not please Engels who, after about £250,000 had been netted, split with his share.

The remaining three continued but came to grief when a forged note was presented without a date. The clerk who discovered the error sent it to the firm by which it was supposed to have been issued. One Bidwell brother went to Scotland where he was arrested; the other was captured in Havana. McDonald tried to make a run for it alone, but his mistress knew his intentions since he had told her he would meet her in the Northern Hotel in Liverpool and they would take the steamer to New York. He never appeared, instead crossing from Folkestone to Calais. She informed the police and McDonald was arrested as the ship entered harbour. He had already served 5 years for a fraud on a jeweller's, and now he and the Bidwells received life imprisonment. Engels was never caught.

George Bidwell refused to work in Dartmoor, where he was sent. He was released on 18 July 1887 on the grounds of his extreme ill-health and because it was believed he had only a few months to live. By then his legs seemed so wasted that he lay in a doubled-up position. It is curious how often the authorities were wrong, and they were so in his case. He survived the crossing back to America from where he began a campaign for the release of his brother, Austin, who was finally licensed after 17 years in 1890. Both wrote books about their experiences.[12]

---

[12] See Austin Bidwell, *From Wall Street to Newgate*; Ernest Bowen, *72 Years at the Bar*; Tom Tullet, *Inside Dartmoor*.

14

The Thieves

According to the Scotland Yard detective Benjamin Leeson, one of the first cat-burglars of the twentieth century in London was the highly skilled Russian-born Mark Goldenberg whose accomplice was a seamstress, Bessie. In that capacity she would call on people and do their sewing. She was highly competent and was referred on, time and again. Attracted to animals, she would invariably make friends with the dogs of the house.

Then a series of burglaries began which involved the deaths of several dogs. A fox terrier was poisoned, keys taken and a safe opened; a Great Dane was drugged and then hanged on some railings until it choked. This time the safe was opened and two patent keys and a police whistle were taken from the householder's trousers.[1]

Leeson traced the route taken by the thief, which had been up a gutter-pipe and then hand-over-hand along the guttering of three houses before coming down another pipe onto a ledge. There he found what was called a bull's-eye waistcoat button. A tailor identified the button and told Leeson that he expected the owner to

[1] On the subject of animals there was a thriving trade in thefts. In January 1903 Henry Fanshaw Jewell and John Skinnerton, a dog clipper, were arrested for conspiracy to steal dogs for insurance purposes. *The Umpire*, 1 February 1903. Horse stealing was also common, both for resale and also for slaughter.

collect a pair of trousers which had been left for repair. The man, Goldenberg, was followed and in his room in the Whitechapel Road was found a waistcoat with a bull's-eye button missing. The bunch of keys and the whistle were also recovered.

Goldenberg appeared at North London Sessions and represented himself; he also gave evidence. Then he produced his bombshell in the form of a waistcoat with the button in place. Bessie had taken a bull's-eye button to him in prison where it had been sewn on in the workshop.

Later she saw Leeson and gave him a long statement in which she admitted being involved in the killing of seven dogs so that Goldenberg could have a clear run for his burglaries. She had, she said, given him up because he had tried to sell her to a White Slaver. Goldenberg went to Liverpool where he was sent to prison after being convicted of another White Slave transaction. It does not appear that Bessie was ever prosecuted.[2]

Even the more minor criminals put in a certain amount of homework, although sometimes it did little good. John Stanley and John Gray, then aged 65 and 67 respectively, collected a fairly merciful 9 months in December 1902. They had been watched as they went to the Lambeth Library to study *Debrett's Peerage*, then followed to Bristol where they were found in possession of jemmies, candles, a saw and a putty knife. They had long been partners and under the names of Martin and Galton had picked up 7 years apiece in 1892 in Liverpool. Stanley had also received 14 years at Brighton, and Gray 2 years for attempted housebreaking.[3]

One of the worst and most formidable gangs of New York house burglars was run by Johnny Dobbs from the corner of Washington and Canal. It lasted for over 20 years with Michael (or Pugsley) Hurley one of its shooting stars, before the gang was broken up in the summer of 1874. Two years later Hurley, now in prison, tried to escape and in 1877 was sent to an asylum. He made another escape attempt and was returned to prison as a cured convict. After several more attempts he got clear in 1882 when he cut through the roof of the prison, and

[2] G. Leeson, *Lost London*, Chapter XVII.
[3] *Morning Leader*, 19 December 1902.

this time he was out for six months. Discharged in 1886, he was promptly arrested in Bennington, Virginia, pickpocketing at the town's centenary celebrations. He was with another jailbreaker and they promptly dug themselves and another prisoner out of the town jail. A year later when he was arrested for piping off a leading jewellery store, the decorative eagle and star tattooed on his left arm was recognised. He was then identified as a member of a team of bank robbers in Springfield and it was off to Bennington for a year. After his release he was repeatedly arrested until his gang blew the post office in Duboistown, Pennsylvania, and he was shot by the townspeople who had given chase.

William Barratt, aka Bassett, was an Englishman who came to the United States at the age of 25 and opened a taxidermy business in Detroit. Tiring of dead animals, he took himself and his handsome wife off to Chicago to work with live ones. He became a horsebreaker while she, a talented horsewoman, would show off the animals. Unfortunately the business was destroyed and he went back to Detroit. He then picked up a substantial legacy from an uncle in England, ran through it and returned to horsebreaking, this time in New York. He also turned his hand to housebreaking, at which he proved an even greater success until, in May 1894, he shot and killed a farmer in Weston, Massachusetts, and received life imprisonment. He had established a second home for himself in Boston, from where he carried out his burglaries – about which, it was thought, his wife knew nothing.

After his arrest nothing much in the way of property was recovered until his agent, James Chaffey, tried to sell some rare postage stamps and when questioned rolled over and gave up most of Barratt's property which he was supposed to have been minding.

The American creator of the home invasion, now beloved by young Asian crime groups, was 'Gentleman' George A. Elwood from Colorado who was shot in one of the first of his raids but survived to improve his technique. Safes were ransacked, shrieking women would be stripped of their jewellery and the terrified householders were 'forced to set a feast for them in the dining room' before Elwood and his partner Joe Whelen, also known as Wilson, went on their way with their team. Between them they cut a swathe through the mid-West, with Detroit householders being particularly victimised.[4]

Then on 13 August 1885 they broke into a house in Toledo, Ohio, and shot at the servants who discovered them. The police were called and an officer asked to see what was in the bag Elwood was carrying. Elwood replied, 'Nothing of much value – take it and see.' While the officer was searching the bag Elwood shot him in the back, but he survived.

Elwood and Whelan were arrested ten days later in New York and, when their rooms at 220 Forsyth Street were searched, a Masonic ring engraved 'Edison W. Baumgarten' was found which was traced back to the Toledo burglary. They were clearly missing the services of Marm Mandelbaum because a good many other identifiable pieces of jewellery were found which were traced back to a robbery in St Paul. Two days later they were back in Toledo where they stood trial on 12 December that year. Elwood, who called no evidence, maintained that the identification was insufficient, but he was found guilty and received 10 years. Wilson was convicted after a retrial. Before he teamed up with Elwood he had specialised in non-violent burglaries, stealing as much silverware as possible and so earning himself the sobriquet 'The Silver King'. He received 5 years on 15 May 1886.

Elwood broke out of the penitentiary, losing two toes to frostbite while on the run. In the winter of 1892 he was shot in a raid in Hartford and when he went to the city hospital he was identified and subsequently received 25 years. This time, when he tried another escape he was shot dead.

It is often difficult to discover which of a set of versions of a jewel theft is true. The retired police officer Charles Leach, who generally gives no dates or names, when describing the theft of the Duchess of Sutherland's jewels says that a jewel thief had followed

---

[4] An even earlier form of home invader, singing and dancing with the victims, was the Australian bushranger Frank Gardiner, born in Tarago in 1830. He was finally arrested in March 1864 with Johnny Gilbert and John O'Meally for the killing of an informer at Burrangong. He received 32 years imprisonment and was released on 8 July 1874 on condition that he left the colony. He went to California where he died in the early 1880s.

a woman to the Continent. He had, it seems, ideas above his social station and had apparently fallen in unreciprocated love with this lady of means rather than simply with her jewellery; but in a stormy scene in Paris the woman had firmly told him to leave her alone. He went to the Gare du Nord station and there saw the Duchess of Sutherland and her maid on the platform. The maid was carrying a jewel-box which she placed in a compartment before rejoining the Duchess. The thief had time to get into the compartment, snatch the case and, concealing it under his coat, make his way down the train and escape.

He then went back to the hotel of his *inamorata* and threw the jewels down in front of her. Now would she have him? No, was the answer. She made an excuse to leave the room and promptly called the police, but he still managed to escape to London where he was arrested.

Chicago May Sharpe, who throughout her book often named names which can be traced, gives a very different but just as entertaining version of basically the same story. She has it that Annie Gleason, 'the most beautiful girl that ever lived', had trailed the Duchess, who was married to Sir Alfred Rollit M.P., to the Holy Land and back waiting for an opportunity, but none came. Then Harry 'The Valet', Henry Thomas or Villiers, stole the case on the spur of the moment.

In this version Thomas was apparently in love with a girl named Maude Richardson who was a police informer, and when he showed her the jewels she demanded to wear them to a ball in Covent Garden. It was at a time when women known as oysters would openly wear stolen jewellery, advertising items for sale. Thomas, taking the view that these were really just too hot, allowed her to keep a diamond ring and sold the remainder to Cammi Grizzard. Richardson, in love with a Scotland Yard detective, then took the ring to him and Thomas was arrested. He called an alibi and a barman in support of his story that he had bought the ring in a public house, but it did him no good and he received 5 years.[5]

---

[5] C.E. Leach, *On Top of the Underworld*, p. 125; M. C. Sharpe, *Chicago May*, pp. 239–40. She believed that most of the jewellery ended up with Grizzard.

Henry Thomas himself might be expected to be able to provide the most accurate account of what happened, and his version is a combination of those of both Leach and Sharpe.

Thomas was, he said, born in the East End on 15 April 1855, the son of a prosperous shopkeeper. He married while young, stole to give his wife money and when after serving a 4-month sentence he found his wife had died, he set out to revenge himself on society. As for the Duchess of Sutherland's jewels, he claimed that he had met a well-known actress Hetty F. at Ascot races and had squired her around town. He thought he was making progress until she told him she was going to Ostend for the season, so he followed her after financing the trip with £500 he received for a ladies' jewel-case. Finding her staying at the Splendide with another young man, they quarrelled on the promenade. She changed hotels to the Palace, where Thomas went and threatened to kill the man; he was arrested and taken to Bruges. If the tale is halfway accurate this frightened off the new love and Hetty arranged for a lawyer for him. Thomas was bailed and together they went to Blankenburghe.

It was there that he saw the detectives Teddy Gough and Tricky Drew together – they were merely holidaying – and thinking they were after him for the jewel-case he absconded to Aix-la-Chapelle. His money finally ran out in Paris and prudently Hetty would not lend him any more against funds supposedly to be sent over by his wealthy family. Quite by chance – and here the story seems to tie up in everyone's version – he saw the English maid and the valet of the Duchess's husband on the platform at the Gare du Nord. He snatched the jewel-case and high-tailed it in a cab to the Magazin du Louvre where he left the jewels in the *fiacre* while he went in and bought a suitcase to conceal them.

Thomas met Hetty at the Folies Bergère where she had been drinking with friends and she abused him. He must have been besotted because he went to her hotel, the Hotel du Nord on the Canal St-Martin, and spread the jewels in front of her saying that he had told her he was rich and these were his family heirlooms. She wanted them all, but he refused and she reported him to the *Préfecture*. It was now only a matter of time before the Paris detectives called

on him. Having asked permission to dress in private, he was out
of the window and back to London via Newhaven. Now he was
working under the name of Williams and trying to fence the
jewellery before Gough and Frank Froest traced him. They found
him living in Cathcart Road after he had received £10,000 from
Grizzard and others. He had quite an enjoyable time on the run
watching Tod Sloan ride Nunsuch for the Prince of Wales at
Newmarket and going to the South London Music Hall to see Dick
Burge spar in an exhibition match with Bill Hatcher. He was
defended by Gerald Geoghegan at the Old Bailey in front of Judge
McConnell and received 10 years.[6]

Once more the real story was a mixture of all versions. Under
the name of William Johnson, and then aged 45, 'The Valet' was
arrested at 5 Cathcart Road, South Kensington, and charged with
stealing the jewellery on 18 October 1898. With him was a Moss
Lipman who was clearly a receiver. 'If I had not been a fool and
got drunk you would not have found me,' Johnson told the police.
At the committal proceedings 'a stylishly dressed woman whose
name was not made public' told the magistrate that she had met
'The Valet' at the Cyprus Hotel, Brighton, and then moved with
him to the Coach and Horses; she had loaned him money and
generally supported him. She had returned to London, and then
gone to Ostend where he had followed her and shot at her. She
agreed that she had told the police and on hearing this piece of
news he had hit her, nearly knocking her eye out.

It was all disappointment at the County of London Sessions held
at Clerkenwell because he pleaded guilty. Richard Muir prosecuted
and told the court that when Harry had produced the jewels, the
woman – whom he said was 'married to a gentleman of blameless
character' and therefore he would not name – had insisted on putting
them all on in bed and letting Harry sleep with her that night. The
next morning 'The Valet' had 'a very hard job to get them back

---

[6] Gerald Geoghegan was one of the top criminal barristers of his day until, like so
many of his colleagues, he succumbed to drink. Because of the likely result of a guilty
verdict he had a particular fear of defending in murder cases. In 1885 he was briefed
to defend Israel Lipski, accused of killing and raping a fellow tenant, but in fact took
no part, leaving the actual defence to a commercial barrister.

from her'. Unfortunately Muir let slip that the woman was in fact Maude Richardson.

'The Valet' had been convicted of the theft of a diamond merchant's pocket-book in 1891, and in 1894 had received 6 months for stealing a ladies' dressing-case at Charing Cross Station. Acquitted over another diamond snatch in December 1895, much to the fury of the judge who promptly sacked the jury, 'The Valet' then received 15 months in Monte Carlo for stealing banknotes. He had been under constant observation at railway stations since his return to England and, said Muir, it was more his skill than that of his watchers that this was his first conviction in that time.

When the judge invited 'The Valet' to explain what had happened to the remainder of the jewels, offering a discount on sentence if he did so, he declined, saying that 55 years wouldn't make any difference. He was remanded until 25 January when, still silent, he received 7 years penal servitude. The £400 or so he had on him when arrested was returned to the Duchess, as was some of the jewellery.[7]

According to his memoirs, on his release he went to France and stole jewellery from a Maharajah in Nice for which he received 5 years, and when he stole a bag in Nîmes 20 days after his subsequent release he collected another 5 years. This time he was arrested by the great French detective, Coquelin. Finally released, he made his way back to London where he approached Cammi Grizzard for money. The great receiver, always reputed to be generous with ex-convicts, gave him two shillings and as a revenge 'The Valet' walked off with £600 of Grizzard's money. When this was gone, he was convicted of stealing a wallet containing stamps worth fivepence. On this occasion he appeared before Sir Ernest Fulton and received another 5 years. When he wrote his memoirs for a newspaper he was 70 years old and, he said, as he was afraid of the detective Teddy Gough, whom he regarded as his nemesis, he retired.[8]

---

[7] *Illustrated Police News*, 10 December 1898, 25 January 1899; *Morning Leader*, 26 January 1899.
[8] Henry Thomas, 'Harry the Valet' in *Thomson's Weekly News*, 27 March 1926 *et seq.*

Another robbery involving a man whom Leach refers to only as Bert, and an Australian con-man whom he calls Long Jim, took place in Dover. It was in fact the attempted theft of jewellery belonging to the American heiress Rubina Wertheimer, whose portrait by Sargent was in the National Gallery. It was known that she carried jewellery worth about £40,000 and, very much like the snatch of the Duchess of Sutherland's jewel-case, it was decided that if possible the theft should take place while she was on a station platform. When she travelled to Dover the porter who was carrying her case put it down, had his attention diverted, and the case was picked up. Leach has it that the men took the case to a local hotel where, to their chagrin, they found only some £230 along with scent and cosmetics. They took the money and left, but were arrested shortly afterwards. By chance, Leach was at the trial when one of them intended to call an alibi witness whom Leach scared off.

'Blonde' Alice Smith was much more forthcoming in her account of the affair. The job had been set up, she said, by a titled acquaintance of hers, a society swell who financed his racehorses through putting up jobs for the Underworld to execute. He suggested that she could burgle Miss Wertheimer's country home, a large rambling place in Norfolk. She went there with Jim L. – possibly James Lockett, although it is late in the day for him – Harry S., who was almost certainly Harry Grimshaw, and an American named Ben K., 'a continental member of the swell mob'.

Jim L. accompanied her to Norfolk as her brother, and Harry acting as a businessman who wanted to buy a substantial property. Leaving the men to go fishing, Alice Smith reconnoitred the house and decided against the job. The nearest station was half a mile from the gates and the house was plumb in the middle of the estate, at best half an hour's walk. They believed they would be 'certain to fall'.

Through the baronet they then discovered that Miss Wertheimer was going to stay in Paris for a few days, taking the boat from Dover. Grimshaw went to Ashford to telephone for a motor car to await them at Dover. The theft took place and, standing on deck with Miss Wertheimer, Alice Smith was delighted to hear that she had lost a case. She travelled on to Paris and then back to England, but it was as Leach said: Miss Wertheimer had sent her jewellery on ahead. The car sent to collect them having broken down, Grimshaw walked three-quarters of a mile through the streets to the Central station. He knew he had to get rid of the case and had booked into an hotel and checked the contents, only to discover the total of their haul was £250.[9]

What is absolutely clear is that over the years a very consider-able amount of jewellery was stolen, partly through the talents of the likes of 'The Valet', Grimshaw, Lockett and Alice Smith – who were of course helped by the maids and manservants who could be bribed or tricked into giving information on the whereabouts of the jewels. It was also in part due to the negligence of the owners. For example, in 1901 Lord Anglesey was robbed of jewellery to the tune of £30,000 from his hotel room in Piccadilly. Apparently he made a practice of keeping it under his bed. The next year Lord Carnarvon's jewellery disappeared somewhere between Calais and Dover, and the Marquess of Anglesey found his jewels to be missing from his room at the Walsingham.

Jewel thieves worked the Paris–London run operating in sections. If those at the Gare du Nord could not manage a snatch, then the operation would be left to those at Calais and so on. In March 1902 it was reported that two British travellers between London and Vienna who had passed through Calais and Brussels had been relieved of jewellery worth £80,000. However, Inspector Drew was said to be on to the thieves:

> It will be a feather in his cap if with the help of the Paris police and his own knowledge of slippery Continental trotters he manages to smash up the gang.[10]

The cap remained featherless.

In May 1903 the jewellery of Mrs Pierre Lorillard, who was staying at the Berkeley in Piccadilly, disappeared somewhere

[9] C.E. Leach, *On Top of the Underworld*, p. 128; 'Blonde' Alice Smith, 'Secret Part I played in Famous Jewel Robberies' in *Thomson's Weekly News*, 29 May 1926.
[10] *Morning Leader*, 7 March 1902.

between Paris and London with the firm belief that it had been taken on the English side of the Channel. When she left Paris at 9.45 for Calais her jewellery had been in a dressing-case in the compartment. It was thought that a Paris-based gang which had pulled off similar coups in Vienna, Berlin and St Petersburg was responsible. This time the value of the jewels was said to be £8,000.[11]

The next year on 2 May a Mrs Conduit, at the Shelbourne Hotel in Dublin for a grand theatrical opening, left her room and her open jewel-case on the dressing-table 'for a few minutes'. Minus £4,000. Just as the deep-sea-diver card-sharps waited until the liner was about to dock before one last game in which the mark was comprehensively fleeced, so jewels tended to disappear on ocean-going liners the night before docking. In early 1904 a Mrs Rann lost her jewel-case on the London to New York voyage on the *Minneapolis*, and that May a Mrs Barnes lost £7,000 of stones on the same run on the sister ship the *Minnetonka*.

Earlier the same year George Marshall, agent to the Duke of Newcastle, lost his lordship's jewellery in the Hotel Metropole. He left the bag in the room while he went for a stroll, and on his return found it had been cut open.[12]

The nobility and middle classes may have been simply careless, but it is impossible not to suspect a degree of co-operation by the losers in the popular sport of stealing from unattended broughams, 'dragging' as it was known. On 5 September 1911 jewels worth £3,000 were left in a brougham at the Nag's Head in Wood Green. The coachman secured a wheel and then went off on a jaunt of his own. Meanwhile a tall man in livery mounted the box and drove off. The brougham was later found abandoned with a window smashed and the jewels gone.[13]

General stealing from vans was common enough, but it was Frederick Day who improved the technique. On 18 December 1902 he stopped a carman named Lewis, saying he thought there was

[11] *The Umpire*, 17 May 1903.
[12] *Morning Leader*, 8 January 1904.
[13] Ibid, 6 September 1911.

something wrong with the man's load of which some of his goods were part. He gave Lewis some money to send a telegram and when the man returned cart, horse and goods were gone. Lewis attributed the loss to Day's authoritarian attitude. One might think that this was a case where the carman had simply dropped his load, but Day and his team tried the ruse again and this time were caught. He and another received 5 years penal servitude, while two subordinates received 4 years.[14]

Some raised dragging almost to an art form. In February 1903 George Smith and Charles Peters, described as huge receivers, were sentenced to penal servitude for 5 and 4 years respectively. Smith had been under observation for some time. In the summer of 1901 he had been seen driving a four-wheel vehicle with four 'well-known criminals inside'. When stopped in heavy traffic, the passengers would try to remove boxes and bundles from other vans. The police watched Smith for several hours before losing him in New Cross. The proceeds of the draggings were sent to Smith's stables in Sydney Grove, off the Goswell Road, where they were winched over the wall. When his premises and those of Peters in Peabody Buildings in the Essex Road were finally raided, two complete Aladdin's caves of silk, clocks, watches and other goods were uncovered.[15]

Back with jewellery, in 1910 the Queen of Siam's jewels were stolen. Perhaps that is putting it a bit grandly; a diamond collar ordered from the Association of Diamond Merchants and Jewellers the previous year went astray. In a way it was almost a pre-run of the Great Pearl Robbery of 1913. The diamond collar was sent to the Straits, but although the package did not appear to have been tampered with it was found to be empty when it arrived. The police were satisfied that the pearls had not been stolen in England and eventually Jules Paul de Boseck was arrested. There was no hard evidence that Cammi Grizzard was involved but de Boseck lived in Bethune Road, Stoke Newington, unhealthily close to the great man. De Boseck had been at Windows Wharf, Bangkok, when the parcel

---

[14] *Illustrated Police News*, 21 March 1903.
[15] Ibid., 14 February 1903.

arrived and was said to have paid off a Singapore bookmaker with one of the stones.

One of the early noted Scots burglars was James Williams, another known as Silver King. He had been thrown out of the Army for stealing a cash-box and from 1898 until 1906 – when with far too large a charge of dynamite he blew himself out of a window and fell 30 feet – his had been an unbridled run of success. On that occasion he picked up 18 months but in August 1909, given up by a pawnbroker, he received 5 years penal servitude in Edinburgh.[16]

Williams' principal contemporary and successor, Scotch Jamie Muirhead, died in June 1922 at the age of 74. With a height of 5' 4" he was regarded as the best burglar and housebreaker of his generation in Scotland. For years he was associated with another great Glasgow burglar, Charles MacDonald, and also with Felix Moran who drowned in the River Leith trying to swim away from the police after an attempted burglary. The first record of Muirhead's career in the twentieth century was on 26 October 1903 when in Edinburgh he received 3 years penal servitude, but there had been plenty of earlier appearances. Between 1906 and 1909 he was in court nine times, either being acquitted or receiving very light sentences. In 1906 he was circulated as wanted in the *Police Gazette* for failing to report; this time his associates were listed as Thomas Rice Reid and George Robertson. On 27 July that year he was circulated as wanted for a safe-breaking in Dundee. Before his arrest he gave an interview to a journalist, saying he had worked in the States and on the Continent and he thought the Pinkertons were the most dangerous opponents, 'the cutest lot of ferrets in the world'. The journalist believed his accent to be Cockney rather than Scots.[17]

Nothing if not resourceful, on his release he tried his hand as a journalist and appeared on the music halls telling of life in Peterhead. Like his English counterpart James Lockett, he invested in a picture house but this time without success. On 21 March

[16] *Illustrated Police News*, 28 August 1909.
[17] *Thomson's Weekly News*, 1 December 1906.

1909 Muirhead was in court again after being found at 3 Bath Street on the second floor of the workshop of a tailor, busily drilling to get into the premises of the Glasgow Pawnbroking Co.

His last court appearance was in January 1918 after he was found attacking yet another pawnbroker's, and this time he received 14 years. He died in Stobhill Hospital, Glasgow, while serving that sentence.[18]

The arrival of the motor car marked the beginning of the era of the country house burglary, brought to something approaching perfection by George Smithson and 'Taters' Chatham in the 1930s.

The earliest of the protagonists was the now largely forgotten Henry Edward Vicars, known in his day as 'Flannelfoot'. He began his career as a criminal in 1909 when he received 9 months imprisonment; then nothing was heard of him in the criminal courts for a quarter of a century during which time – the war years excluded – he committed something over 1,000 crimes.

He was given the name 'Flannelfoot' by the newspapers, possibly coined by Edgar Wallace, because he wore socks or pieces of material over his shoes, and he attributed his long run of successes to the fact that he worked alone, avoiding receivers and criminal company generally, and varied his targets, travelling by train and bicycle. Friday night when pay packets were left carelessly on tables was a favoured working night. Vicars, who had a vaguely military appearance, either forced rear windows or picked locks. He had no trouble with dogs, usually giving them food from the pantries of the houses he was burgling, and was said never to have used violence.

Then in 1932 he left his wife, taking his daughter who 4 years later was found wandering with loss of memory and was admitted to Highgate Hospital. Vicars had eluded the police on a number of occasions, during which time several lesser Flannelfeet had been arrested. Now information came to them from Norfolk where the woman with whom he was living had relatives.

In October 1937 he was arrested in Eastcote near Pinner and was

---

[18] Edinburgh *Times*, 15 March 1909; Glasgow *Herald*, 16 March 1909, 27 June 1922.

found in possession of keys, pliers and gloves. It was his practice to burgle a series of houses in the area and he had already done one that night. On 2 December 1937 he received 5 years at Middlesex Sessions, and died shortly after his release.[19]

[19] George Totterdell, *Country Copper*.

15

The Prince of Thieves

The Pinkerton Detective Agency believed in the reformation of criminals. This may not have been wholly altruistic but the number of
men they helped, or tried to help, was legion. One of the earliest
was Billy Forrester, suspected of one of the most baffling of the
New York murder cases of the early 1870s. It was that of Benjamin
Nathan, discovered by his son, Washington, at 6 a.m. on 28 July
1870 at their home at 12 W 23rd. Washington was, so he said, on
his way to fetch a drink of water.

Benjamin Nathan may not have been quite the richest man in
the world, but his position was such that the New York Stock
Exchange flew its flag at half-mast when his death was announced.
A $47,000 reward was offered. He had been hit over the head a
number of times with a carpenter's tool; the safe had been opened
and there were signs of a struggle. His attacker seems to have
washed his hands in a basin in the room but not bothered about
a handprint on the bedroom wall. There was really no need, since
fingerprints would not be used in America for another thirty years.
As with any good murder there were a number of suspects.
Washington Nathan was known to have financial problems and
had quarrelled with his father over money. He had an alibi for
most of the relevant time, having been with Clara Dale to whom

the newspapers referred coyly as 'a lass of the pavements'.

Another son, Frederick, had been in the house at the time of the fight as had William Kelly, the son of the housekeeper. Neither of them had been disturbed by the noise. Kelly had a number of Underworld friends and acquaintances. One problem was the street door. Everyone said it had been locked at night, but Washington had found it unlocked.

Again, as with any interesting murder, a number of people confessed and one man, John T. Irving, was brought from California but was unable to persuade the police of his guilt. For a time attention fastened on the well-known thief Billy Forrester, whom a jail-house snitch said had told him that he had been surprised during a routine burglary.

Forrester certainly had the right pedigree. He had been acquitted of killing a gambler in Detroit and then, after a trip to Canada, was sentenced to 13 years in Joliet for robbery. He escaped, was recaptured and escaped again. In 1871 he was involved in the burglary of a jewellers on Canal Street, New Orleans, and then helped three robbers to escape from jail in Mobile.

Forrester was identified by witnesses for the Nathan murder, but proved to have an alibi. While in the Tombs, he offered to name the murderer himself if his unexpired sentence in Joliet could be commuted. The offer was declined.

Nine years later Washington Nathan was shot in the neck by his former girlfriend, Fanny Barrett. It was then that the police decided that while Nathan was recovering from anaesthetic when the bullet was removed he should be questioned. In fact the scheme was never put in place because the bullet worked its way out of its own accord. Washington Nathan remained the chief suspect and left America to live in Europe where he died in 1892 at the age of 42. He was probably wrongly suspected.

The Pinkertons certainly believed that Forrester had been made the scapegoat by a blundering New York Police Department and tried to rehabilitate him. Having sent him food and clothing during the time he was in prison, on his release they established him in a shoe-repair business. The effort was not a success, since Forrester soon became bored and took up his old and probably more lucrative trade of burglary. Years later, Harry Raymond (Adam Worth) told the Pinkertons that the murderer had been Troy Dexter.[1]

As for Forrester, he continued his career throughout the 1880s and 1890s, but by 1900 he was 61 years old and was tiring so he finally became a Pinkerton informant. Dressed in old clothes, he lived and hung around in flophouses and third-rate hotels in Toledo and Canton, Ohio, retailing information to the brothers.

The letters in the Pinkerton files show how often the agency would go to some lengths to provide work or money for ex-criminals, but there was of course a return on their investment. First, those they helped might out of a sense of loyalty stay away from Pinkerton-protected properties, and there is some evidence that a few of them did just that. Then there was the favourable publicity which could be used to counter some of the adverse comments on attitudes to the Agency's strike-breaking. Best of all the Pinkertons could expect those whom they assisted to become their informants, and it may be that this was where they obtained most benefit from their admittedly usually quite modest investments. In general the more prominent of their protégés did not reward them by reforming.

Frank Seaver, a member of the Becker forgery gang, was given a railway ticket to Chicago on his release in 1899. Patsy Flannigan was another who was sent clothing during his sentence, and his family was sent money. A sneak-thief, he had stolen from the Pinkerton-protected Yonkers Savings Bank in 1897. Once he discovered it was part of the American Bankers' Association, and fearing being tracked down, he turned himself in expecting a relatively light sentence for a plea of guilty. Instead he received 11 years. The Pinkertons thought he had been harshly treated and started working for his release. One of their senior staff, Seymour Beutler, visited him regularly and managed to have him transferred from working in the laundry to the library. He was pardoned in 1902, promising the Governor and the Pinkertons that crime was

---

[1] The Nathan murder has always been regarded as one of the great unsolved crimes and has featured in numerous anthologies. See e.g. Daniel Cohen, *The Encyclopedia of Unsolved Crimes*. For an account both of the murder including Irving's confession and of the career of Billy Forrester, see Thomas Byrnes, *Rogues' Gallery*.

now behind him, and borrowed the money from William Pinkerton for a ticket to travel to the South West well away from the temptations of the Big Apple. In 1905 he was killed in a failed bank robbery in Texas.

Some years earlier they had experienced a similar lack of success. On 25 January 1876 Robert Scott, William Edson and the Chicago-born James Dunlap robbed the Bank of Northampton, Mass. Eight months later Robert Pinkerton succeeded in arresting them. Edson turned State's evidence and the others received 20 years apiece. Scott died in prison and his widow took against the Agency, writing articles denouncing their conduct and calling for Dunlap's release. In fact they had been sending him a Thanksgiving turkey each year, and after he had served two-thirds of his sentence began pressing for a pardon. It took until December 1892 for him to be released and, in her gratitude, Mrs Scott tried to get Dunlap to appear in a melodrama in which 'the villainy and perfidy of certain private detectives [would] be exposed'. The Pinkertons were appalled and the Governor of New York warned her to abandon the piece on the grounds that it would corrupt the city's youth. She refused.[2]

Dunlap was then taken out of harm's way by the Pinkertons and back to Chicago where he was given $2,000 to open a day saloon, and the police were informed that he was more or less under the Agency's protection. The saloon was not a success. Dunlap wanted to open a gaming house, but William Pinkerton declined and arranged for him to have another saloon. It also failed and now Dunlap teamed up with an ex-police officer Paddy Ryan and other Chicago notables in opening a gaming den in 1893. This time the Pinkertons washed their hands, and in 1899 Dunlap went to prison for burglary.[3]

---

[2] *New York Herald*, 13, 15, 17, 29 January 1893.
[3] In 1873 Dunlap and Scott had been part of a team organised by David Cummings, aka Little Dave Hogan, which had robbed the First National Bank of Illinois in Quincy of $89,000 cash, $100,000 in Government Bonds and $350,000 in railroad securities. It was the first time the air-pump had been successfully used in a safe-breaking. Ryan was in partnership with 'Blind' John Condon running a faro bank and crap game in the Turf Exchange, 128 Clark Street. In turn until his death Condon, who began his career as a barber and ended with a string of racetracks in the mid-West, was a great champion of Mike McDonald.

The talented sneak-thief and burglar Joe Killoran, in his day amongst the very top rank of bank burglars, was another failure over which the Pinkertons did not repine.

Probably all criminals aspire to a sobriquet as a mark of recognition from their peers. Think of the number of Colonels – Ronnie Kray, George Copley, and George Robinson of the Brinks-Mat robbery amongst them – who have graced the annals of British crime in the last few decades. Joseph Killoran made it to the aristocracy when in 1901 the *New York Herald* dubbed him 'The Prince of Thieves'.

Killoran, also known as John Howard, was born in 1841 and came from a respectable family but soon spent his father's estate. Originally he became a pickpocket before joining the team of George White, alias Bliss, Max Shinburn known as Baron Shinburn and Charley, 'Piano Charley' Bullard who spoke English, French and German fluently, and whose talent on the piano gave him his nickname. Others included Ike Marsh, Billy Maher, Jimmy Hope – known as 'Old Man Hope' to distinguish him from his sons – and Langdon W. Moore alias Charlie Adams.[4] Killoran's real tutor may well have been Charley Allen.

Killoran was first arrested with White and Hope over the Hungerford Bank robbery in Jefferson County. At the Criminal Court in Watertown, New Jersey, he received 5 years to be served first in Auburn and then Sing Sing from which he escaped on 26 September 1872.

A year later, along with Old Man Hope (who at the time was also on the run from Sing Sing), Big Frank McCoy or McConnell and Edward Hulbert, he attempted to rob the Delaware National Bank at 6th and Market Streets, Wilmington. It was the prototype of many a bank raid of the 1980s in England. At about 6.30 p.m. on 7 November while the cashier, Samuel Floyd, and his family were eating their supper in a room at the back of the bank, the four men broke in. The raid was thwarted by the presence of mind of the 16-year-old cousin of Floyd, Jenny Kates, who pretended to

---

[4] See Case Binder 2, The Joseph Killoran Gang in the Pinkerton Archives at the Library of Congress, Washington. The quotations, unless otherwise stated, are from Pinkerton operative reports. Albert E. Brager, 'The Pinkertons and the Bank Ghosts' in *True Detective*, 13 February 1945.

faint and in doing so hid under the table. Now, according to the Pinkerton report, followed a piece of dramatic comedy:

> The coloured cook, no doubt at the time believing in the time-worn adage that imitation is the sincerest form of flattery, crawled under another table.

In the diversion Jenny Kates escaped into 6th Street and although chased by one member of the gang made it to a nearby store and gave the alarm. The gang left Floyd handcuffed to the bank door and fled to nearby 9th and Parkwood Streets where they were found in an empty house. Punishment was intended to be condign. On 25 November they were sentenced to a $500 fine, 40 lashes and an hour in the pillory as well as 10 years. Delaware was the only state at the time where punishment included a whipping, which was thought to take the starch out of a man and concentrate his mind on his future behaviour. They were duly whipped and spent an hour in the pillory but, in their case, it seems to have done them no great harm. They escaped 8 months into the sentence at New Castle State prison when Bill Robinson, known as Gopher Bill, smuggled tools in to them. A steam-tug was waiting on the river and they were clear away. No great effort seems to have been made to recapture them.[5]

In fact the whipping proved to be no deterrent at all because two years later, on 6 June 1875, Killoran – along with George White and Pete Curley from Troy, and possibly with Wooster Sam – robbed the bank at Barre, Vermont. The raid was not a success. They tied up the family and took the cashier to the bank before returning him to his family and tying him up with them. However, they managed to take only $10 and $1,300 in bonds and the cashier freed himself all too quickly. Curley was caught the next morning on a train leaving town and White, in the seat ahead of him, jumped through the carriage window to evade capture. Killoran had already made his escape. When White and Killoran were later caught in New York City, Curley turned State's evidence. Given that members

---

[5] See 'Daring Attempt at Burglary: Cashier Seized and his Family Terrorized' in Wilmington *Daily Commercial*, 8 November 1873.

of Troy's criminal fraternity were noted for their staunchness, this lapse caused the bank robber 'Red' Leary to remark somewhat cleverly, 'There is a breach in the walls of Troy.' White received 14 years. Killoran did rather better; he was returned to Sing Sing as an escaped prisoner.

The whipping may not have cured Killoran but the second spell in Sing Sing seems to have done. Though it was not a cure of crime, simply of bank robberies which attracted harsh terms of imprisonment. In future, and for the remainder of his working life, he would turn to the less dangerous but potentially equally remunerative sneak-thieving, an art form which required observation, attention to detail and a developed sense of timing. It also required 'an iron nerve and, for one of the participants, considerable histrionic ability. No producer ever took more pains to select a first class troop of actors as did the leader of a mob of sneak-thieves when assembling the personnel of his particular coterie.'

The requirements of a successful sneak-thief operation were to observe the bank or office to determine when the minimum number of staff would be on the premises. A diversion, but one which would not cause alarm, would have to be staged – coins might be dropped on the floor of the teller's room so requiring a search, plans of buildings might be spread by a customer, a crippled person might need particular help. Violence was to be avoided where possible. A wave of these robberies took place in the early 1880s.

But the best-laid plans of sneak-thieves go astray from time to time and they did so on 1 August 1883 when, along with Wallace Connor and Ed Quinn, Killoran robbed the First National Bank at Coldwater, Michigan, of $10,000. All was going well until Connor made the error of touching the steel door of the vault and, perfectly balanced, it swung open further thus attracting the attention of the cashier William Throckmorton. Connor tried to face it out, asking if Throckmorton had seen a dog about. 'A dog, the devil, you are the dog,' said the cashier and took hold of Connor who broke away. He was caught when he ran into a dead end but never charged; instead he was charged with a robbery in Lewisburg. By now the Pinkerton Agency had a portrait collection of almost every serious thief in the country and identifications were made. Killoran received

5 years in Jackson from which he was released on 23 July 1889. Quinn, who was also charged with a jewel robbery, drew double. Connor was never charged.[6]

Connor and Killoran fell again when in May 1891 the latter persuaded a cashier to come to assist a cleric in a buggy. Once more they were identified by the Pinkertons and Killoran was arrested in New York. For some time the Pinkertons had been following Mrs Killoran to no effect, but on one occasion she was followed as she drove to and stopped outside a saloon. Killoran walked outside and instead of 'receiving the tender salutation he expected' he was promptly arrested by the waiting Pinkerton operatives. This time he drew a little over 26 months. Connor received a sentence of 3–9 years for a bank in Easton, Pa.[7]

With Killoran now released, the autumn of 1894 saw a spate of robberies from post offices in New York City, throughout the state, and in Pennsylvania. The *modus operandi* was identical. When the employees were gone for lunch the inner door of the safe was removed and postage stamps taken. Impressions of the safe keys were obtained in time-honoured and tested ways. It only needed a few seconds, if that, for a skilled operator to make an impression on a pad. On one occasion the manager of an office obligingly offered his key to two men who were having trouble opening a box. It was estimated that over a few months some $20,000 was taken.

On 22 April the next year Killoran, along with Charley Allen, had a major success when they removed $22,000 from the First National Plainfield Bank. Less than six weeks later on 31 May 1895 they were arrested on the corner of Amsterdam and 145th St in New York – Harlem was not yet a predominantly African-American area. Sent off to Ludlow Street jail, they twice unsuccessfully tried to bribe guards to assist them in escaping; on both occasions the guards reported the approaches made to them. It still did not make the Warden take much more care of his charges, however. At a cost

<hr/>

[6] See notes in Additional Data on History of Joseph Killoran in Binder 29, George M. White. In the version given by Thomas Byrnes in his *Professional Criminals of America*, it is Quinn who is caught in the bank and draws a gun threatening the cashier.
[7] 'Cleverly Captured' in *Philadelphia Ledger & Transcript*, 21 November 1891.

of $15 a week each they were allowed to dine at his table and have both male and female friends visit them at all hours of the day and night in total contravention of the rules. It cannot have come as much of a surprise when they celebrated Independence Day 1895 by holding up the guards on the 8 o'clock exercise and locking them in their own jail. One of the keepers gave the alarm, calling out 'Der Chail is Ouid'. The warden and two jailers were dismissed and were regarded as extremely fortunate not to have been prosecuted themselves. As for Allen and Killoran, along with fellow-escapee Harry Russell it was off to London where they lived on the Brixton Road above the Park, followed by a crook's tour of Europe. A reward of $1,000 per escapee was offered by the Post Office department.

Killoran went on to Paris which he found 'a veritable Tom Tiddler's ground' and where bank guards were 'callow youths or feeble old men'.[8] He and Allen had a successful touch in Brussels where they cleared 75,000 francs. Allen escaped and Killoran was discharged for lack of evidence. Harry Russell, under the name of Eames Curtis, was not so successful, netting 5 years in Bruges on 5 June 1896. By the time he returned to the United States no action was taken over the Ludlow Street jail-break.[9]

Then Killoran's luck changed and on 26 April 1899 he received 5 years in Antwerp where he gave his name as Phillipe Gaspard Reed, saying he had been born in Montreal. After his sentence he returned to the States along with his brother John and was arrested for the Plainfield Bank job. He had suffered further misfortune in Europe and had part of his left leg amputated; he was probably suffering from diabetes. This time he received 3 years and, to their credit, the Pinkertons wrote some letters in which they inquired about his health. The Warden wrote back:

> You and I both must agree that Killoran is not even a 32nd cousin to a fool.
> He is at work in the knitting shop at light work more for

---

[8] '"Prince of Crooks" discusses the Ethics of Crime' in *New York Herald*, 10 May 1903.
[9] Robert Pinkerton to Supt. Donald Swanson, Scotland Yard, 6 February 1900 in Volume II, The James Hope Gang, Case Binder 23.

exercise than profit to the State. I do not think he will ever harm anyone again.[10]

Killoran didn't think he had ever harmed anyone at all:

I've been a crook pretty near all my life but I never went in for physical violence and I can say today that I have never really wronged another man.

This gem elicited some surprise from the *New York Herald*, and Killoran went on to clarify it:

I never betrayed a man who had trusted me and I was never faithless to a friend. No sympathy is squandered on us fellows when the cops or the Pinks take us and we don't look for any but for the detected bank cashier there is sympathy and excuses.[11]

Anyone who thought Killoran was finished was wrong. The Pinkertons noted in their files that nothing had been heard of him for some time, but the reason for this was that in 1905 he had been jailed in Vienna for 6 years for stealing £20,000. 'It looks as though he has committed his last robbery and that this crime will end his days in prison.' The Pinkertons received a letter saying he had been using the Reed alias as well as that of James Patrick Howard. He had been known in London as 'Old Brook' and was an associate of the notorious 'Long Almond', Frederick Smith.

But this Prince of Thieves was tougher than people thought and in February 1913 he wrote to the Pinkertons asking if they could help him get a job. 'I want to go straight for the balance of my short existence.'[12] He had tried to get help from the clergy but they had failed him. The Pinkertons did not. They could not place him in work because of the loss of his leg, but he was sent a gross of pipe cleaners so that he could start a small business.

They last heard of him at Christmas that year. He had swallowed

---

[10] Edward Gaylor to Robert Pinkerton, 3 December 1903.
[11] '"Prince of Crooks" discusses the Ethics of Crime' in *New York Herald*, 10 May 1903.
[12] Killoran to Pinkertons, 16 February 1913.

cyanide after being found trying to steal from the Antwerp Credit Bank. The police there thought he was Jasper Reed. He had apparently used the remainder of his savings to join Horace Hovan and 'Big' Ed Rice, but by the time he arrived they were in prison in Munich. The Pinkertons, using their Bertillon methods, identified him correctly. 'Poor Old Joe. He will never bother anybody anymore.' A rather sanctimonious note on the file records, 'Once again was illustrated the fact that millions of crimes speed the road to the pauper's grave.'

16

The Cons – Long and Short

Confidence tricks and tricksters of both sexes came in all shapes, sizes and ages. Take Bertha Heyman, known as Big Bertha, who was regarded by Inspector Thomas Byrnes as one of the smartest confidence women in America. This was despite the fact that she was a somewhat unprepossessing-looking woman weighing 245 lbs and standing only 5' 4", with four prominent moles on her right cheek. Her father had served 5 years in Posen for forgery by the time she arrived in America at the age of 27 in 1878. She then married a Fritz Karko and then, bigamously, a Mr Heyman in Milwaukee who seems to have been dropped from the picture pretty swiftly.

In 1880 she was sued in the New York civil courts over a claim for $1,035, and two criminal trials followed the next year when she was acquitted in London, Ontario and Staten Island. As she left the second court she was rearrested and charged with a string of offences of obtaining money by false pretences for which she received 2 years. Prison does not seem to have had any greater reformatory characteristics then than now. While serving a sentence for false pretences in 1881 she was employed as a servant in the Warden's quarters and there made the acquaintance of a German, Charles Karpe, who took to visiting her. Even while in prison she managed to obtain his life savings of $900. On her release in 1883 she swindled a firm of New York brokers with the old trick of pretending that a sealed package of worthless papers was worth $87,000. She had the effrontery to say she was worth $8 million, and was believed at least until the packet was opened. She was given 5 years on 22 August 1883. Byrnes considered that she possessed 'a wonderful knowledge of human nature and can deceive those who consider themselves particularly shrewd in business'.

Age does not discriminate against con-women, one of the most talented of whom – Cassie Chadwick – only blossomed in her middle age. She came upon the scene in the 1890s and moved into Cleveland society with the story that she was the illegitimate daughter of Andrew Carnegie. She had with her a number of promissory notes apparently signed by the steel magnate. Her initial trick, which was only a variation of one worked by so many, was to go to Carnegie's house and pretend to be received. The only person she actually saw was the housekeeper. The dupe, this time a lawyer, waited in the carriage outside but he was in a position to give credibility to her story.

Swearing her banker to secrecy, which was of course the best way for her tale to be told, she took out some loans of about $100,000 which she repaid by borrowing from other banks. For a period of some seven years she entertained and was entertained, travelled to Europe and was a major benefactress. Then in 1904 one of her creditors did what perhaps should have been done a decade earlier: he had her background checked. Since she was the Canadian forger Elizabeth Bigley, it was not surprising that the promissory notes signed by Carnegie looked so good. On 26 November her story appeared in the Cleveland press and the game was up.

She was arrested in bed in the New Breslin Hotel, New York, and after a spell in the Tombs was taken back to Cleveland. She received 10 years and died on 10 October 1907 while still in prison. Charles T. Beckwith, president of the Citizens National Bank of Oberlin, predeceased her. His bank was owed $1.25 million by her and, on hearing the news, he promptly had a heart attack. In all it is thought she took in excess of $20 million from a number of banks.

Cassie Chadwick cannot, however, really compete with Ellen Peck who until she was 51 seems to have led a blameless life. Then, tiring of domesticity in Sparkville, New York, she moved to the city itself. By accounts she was physically well preserved and had little difficulty in ensnaring the elderly and lustful B. T. Babbitt who had made his fortune from soap. Invited to his mansion, Ms Peck stole $10,000 in negotiable bonds and then, having already sold them, volunteered to act as his personal detective. In normal circumstances she would not expect any recompense but as she had only her widow's pension . . . The old fool gave her $5,000 to begin the search and later wrote her another cheque for a similar amount. By the time he hired proper detectives she was back in Sparkville. Sentenced to 4 years, she was paroled in a year and now Dr Jason Marks was persuaded to part with $20,000 in cash and jewellery. In 1887 it was the turn of Jay Gould, who as a friend of Thomas Byrnes should have known better.

It was Marks who had her arrested, but she was released in 1892. Two more years in Sparkville and she was bored again so, operating from a Brooklyn hotel she became Mary Hansen, the wife of an Admiral in the Danish Navy, and was able to persuade banks to advance her up to $50,000. Then it was into a house where the 80-year-old Dr Christopher Lott took her to his bed, for which privilege he was taken for $10,000. Lott had clearly thought his money reasonably spent because he said of her, 'She was the last craving of my life.' The roll-call was endless. She took $4,000 from Nellie Shea, a nurse she had installed to look after the exhausted Lott. There were allegations of 'an unnatural and unwholesome liaison'. A former lawyer was yet another of her victims.

She was not averse to helping the police if it suited her and in 1887 her collaboration with Inspector Byrnes led to the arrest of Julius Columbani, a friend of the forger Louis Siscovitch and his brother, the notorious and lethal Carlo.[1]

In 1897 it was 5 years in Auburn, then after a short period of

---

[1] There is a long article on Ellen Peck as well as one on the brothers Siscovitch in Thomas Byrnes, *Rogues' Gallery*, pp. 316–21. See also Robert Nash, *Hustlers and Con Men*.

recuperation up-country she was back to New York where John Grady was persuaded that Ms Peck's kitchen cupboard was a better place than his safe to keep diamonds worth some $21,000. Facing an indictment of 25 counts, this remarkable woman was acquitted.

Swindles on other men followed until in 1907 she was sent away again. An appeal was rejected in 1909, but she was pardoned the following year. She was then 82 years of age, but retirement was never a consideration. In 1913, the year she died, she seduced a Latin American businessman bound for Vera Cruz. So enamoured was he that he signed over at least one plantation to her.[2]

At the end of the nineteenth century one of the more outrageous frauds was attempted by the Liverpool solicitor, John Hollis Yates. It concerned the estate of Helen Sherridan who had come from the West of Ireland and married a young officer, Blake, stationed in Dublin. Her husband subsequently attained the rank of Lieutenant General and died in 1850. She died in 1883 intestate and consequently, unless heirs could be found, the fortune of the then considerable sum of £200,000 would be forfeit to the Crown. The wrangle over the estate continued for over a decade. Yates found a family of the same name in Liverpool and arranged a profit-sharing arrangement: if he could establish their claim they would pay him a percentage of the estate.

He went to Ireland, interviewed many of the 'oldest inhabitants' and sent their statements to counsel to ask what further evidence was required. Advised that birth and marriage certificates were almost essential, he accepted that these would be extremely difficult to forge and so set about preparing a family bible. He found one of the correct age and began the entries, including a note purporting to be by Martin Sherridan's daughter reading, 'my daughter Helen has run away with a young Officer staying in Dublin Castle and has married him privately in Scotland'. It also recorded

---

[2] Cons could also be perpetrated at long range. In 1910 George Osborne suddenly claimed that his fiancée, Gladys Wilson of Philadelphia, was in reality William Barnes, a mechanic. Wilson/Barnes had collected around £1,200 from Osborne over the previous 14 years, during which time Osborne had remained 'faithful to her'. He had always been dissuaded from visiting Philadelphia and had remained at Southington at his business of watch repairer. *Empire News*, 22 October 1910.

the death of old Martin Sherridan and the births of the Liverpool Sherridans. Unfortunately, he had purchased a Protestant bible, an unlikely possession for a poor Catholic family in the first half of the nineteenth century. He also had coffin plates prepared, and a drawing of a tombstone to bolster the claim, but his final coup was his undoing when he purchased a silver watch and had it engraved 'from Helen Blake to her dear nephew Patrick Sherridan, 1886'. Thinking this was wrong, the engraver altered the date to 1896. When Yates took it back the man, now suspicious, contacted the police. A warrant to search Yates' offices uncovered the family bible and the watch as well as the coffin plates. In 1896 at the Assizes, he was sent to penal servitude for life.

The traffic in criminals was by no means all one-way out of New York. In 1908 Gentleman George Barton was sentenced to death for the killing of James P. McCann in St Louis. Nothing he attempted was done clumsily. Nor was prison the great reformer people thought, for Barton remarked, 'Prison gives me a rest. I find time to think out schemes for future adventures. And then – the interest on my hauls accumulates.'

Far from being of noble birth, a role he played throughout his life, he was the son of a cab-driver born in Tunbridge Wells. Sent to a reformatory at the age of 10 for 5 years, this did him no good at all. At the age of 16 he cracked a crib and stole £2,000. This time it was 10 years, but the sentence was reduced by the Home Secretary.

In fact he was helped by the American, Austin Bidwell, who had attempted to rob the Bank of England and who continued his career as a forger while in prison when he created documents for Barton. His pleas for early release had gone unanswered until Bidwell forged two letters informing him that a rich uncle had died and left him £160,000 in cash and 16,000 acres for growing cotton in India; he was needed at once to go to look after the estate. The letters were smuggled out and duly posted back in, whereupon Barton submitted a new petition and was released.[3] He was not out long before he

<hr />

[3] The authorities were often more sympathetic to the rich. When Neill Cream was serving life in Joliet he was released when, genuinely, he inherited a substantial sum from his father who had died in Canada.

did another burglary and received a further 10 years, which was then followed by a 12-year sentence for receiving at Lewes Assizes.

He went to New York in 1891 as Lord Barrington, where he gave fine dinners; his taste in wines was excellent and he had a 'way' with the ladies which was irresistible. He married Celestine Miller, the daughter of a rich widow, robbed her of everything and disappeared.

Next found back in Brighton, where he defrauded everyone in sight and burgled his neighbour's home, 'Oakdene', he took a great interest in helping the police, providing several useful clues until a Scotland Yard detective recognised him as a ticket-of-leave man who had failed to report for several months. The property from the 'Oakdene' burglary was found at his home and he received another 12-year sentence.

Then when he came out he went back to America where he married the daughter of a wealthy coal merchant from Philadelphia, stole £800 from her and abandoned her in Pittsburgh. He married again, this time as Lt. Colonel Frederick Neil Barrington, so-called nephew of the Marquess of Abergavenny. The marriage did not last long because the bride's brother made inquiries about the half-colonel's real status and kicked him down a flight of stairs as a result. For a time he worked in a bar, then he was taken up by the horse dealer James McCann who appointed him his betting commissioner. Later Barton lured him to a lonely spot and beat him to death, then tipped the body into a quarry. The motive was money again. He had persuaded McCann that he had money coming to him from Britain and obtained an advance against it. Now it was easier to kill McCann than repay the loan. He was sentenced to death and was due to hang in the spring, but in fact he was reprieved and sent to Missouri State prison where he had dozens of women visitors and his cell was:

> Like a bride's boudoir, bedecked with floral and photographic emblems of love. Shoals of letters were addressed to him and all of them from women, and many of them contained proposals of their willingness to marry him.[4]

[4] J. Kenneth Ferrier, *Crooks & Crime.*

One of the women he charmed was an English woman, Lilian E. Gates, the wife of Harry Randolph Gates. For many years she laboured under the delusion that he was not Barton at all but a man named Seymour who had been her neighbour in England. In 1913 Barrington applied for parole and Mrs Gates wrote to Scotland Yard seeking their help in correcting this great injustice. She knew full well that Barrington had been sent by the British Government to infiltrate one of the Irish societies in St Louis which was currently feuding with another. Counsel had been retained on his behalf at the parole hearing.

Barrington had also half convinced the authorities that there might be some doubt as to his identity. A letter from L. B. Hurgel of the penitentiary to Scotland Yard said that Barrington claimed the British Government had paid $2,000 to help clear his name and also to try to get parole. At the time of his arrest he had been on a secret mission, but he had refused to say what it was. Would Scotland Yard confirm this to be correct and could they send a copy of Barton's fingerprints and Bertillon measurements?

Meanwhile Barrington was doing what he could on his own account. He was insisting that McCann was alive and a witness, Jack Bennett, was to be called to say he had seen the deceased alive and well in San Francisco a year after his alleged disappearance. It was another of those no body-no crime cases.

The arrival of the fingerprints and measurements settled things as far as the penitentiary was concerned. Thanking Scotland Yard for the documents, Hurgel wrote that Barrington was still denying he had been in prison in England but:

> . . . he is the only one that thinks so and I don't think he will ever have a chance to be paroled out of this Institution unless he acknowledges his part.[5]

Aristocrats such as Barton sprang up worldwide, and one of the most curious pre-dated him by several years. In November 1871 a young

---

[5] See PRO MEPO 3 237A; *Morning Leader*, 14 February 1906. There is a long account of Barrington's career in J. Kenneth Ferrier, *Crooks & Crime*, Chapter 20, in which he calls him Ralph Marrington. See also *Morning Leader*, 22, 24 March 1904.

woman named Kenneaux was arrested in Birmingham, having been obtaining money by impersonating the deceased Lord Arthur Clinton. In the words of the later song, 'I never died, said he' – or rather she. She told the gullible she had had chloroform administered to her as Clinton, and then been lowered into a coffin from which she escaped. Now she had to maintain secrecy until the expiration of an unspecified certain – if that is not an oxymoron – period after which she would reveal himself. Money had poured into her coffers.[6]

Three tricksters came to grief in Paris after sparkling if relatively brief careers. The Marquis de Massa Malaspina, the Baron de Ruelle and the Comtesse de Chatillon worked the South of France. The Marquis had a yacht, the *Sibille*, on which his friends could be found regularly. He, thinking it would be a lovely idea to host a party for the local gentry where they could listen to music as they cruised in the Mediterranean – as paying guests, of course – borrowed some money to defray the advance expenses. Sadly, on the day of the cruise when the invitees arrived at the harbour they found the Marquis, the Baron and the Comtesse had already weighed anchor.

The Comtesse, a handsome woman on the right side of 50 and with two eligible daughters, now moved to an apartment in the Grande Armée and made for the wealthy nobility. One Spaniard was so entranced that he sent home for his sons to come to Paris. He only took fright when the Comtesse began speaking of a safe in the Crédit Lyonnais. After that she took up with a German manufacturer to keep the tradespeople at bay. The house of cards toppled when she was traced along with the Marquis and the Baron to rooms near the Arc de Triomphe. The Comtesse was in fact Anne Simonet, the daughter of a grocer.[7]

At the same time as the trio were flourishing in France, in England the Grand Duke of Mecklenburgh, alias Jacques Roos (or vice versa), was busy ordering jewellery while staying at the Carlton Hotel. He was allowed to return to Holland on condition that he did not set foot in England again.[8]

---

[6] *The Times*, 24 November 1871.
[7] *Morning Leader*, 7 May 1904.
[8] Ibid., 11 May 1904.

Other members of the *soi-disant* aristocracy of the time included Mme La Duchesse Svey Mandas de Villanda – really Mrs Guinness, an Irish lady who rented a house, servants and lived for a summer's worth of credit in Paris before fleeing to the Villa Villanda in San Sebastian. In her absence she received a 2-year sentence. Hard on her heels were a splendid trio, the Comtesse de Mareuil, the Marquise Dampierre and the Abbé Sinquiville. Of the three, the Abbé seems to have been the most resourceful if absent-minded. It was he who collected alms on behalf of the Comtesse's favourite charity, but forgot his station in life when he stole a bicycle. Fortunately for him, on that occasion the church authorities, believing him to be a genuine Abbé, hushed the matter up by compensating the owner for the loss of his bicycle.[9]

They had all followed in the well-trodden path of the Humbert family, led by the redoubtable Thérèse. This lady flourished over three decades, during which time she created a whole family of litigants laying claim and counterclaim to the fortune of the non-existent American millionaire, Robert Henry Crawford, whom she maintained she had nursed back to health and who had, in gratitude, given her a legacy of $20 million.

She created two nephews Robert and Henry – in fact her brothers Emile and Romaine – who obtained a court order sealing a safe in which the Crawford money was being held. Now it is easy to understand why the Spaniard had taken fright when the Comtesse told him of a similar one. The safe stood in the middle of the Humbert salon, during which time Mme Humbert borrowed against its contents. The completely bogus court action she had created spun out Jarndyce-like into a completely impenetrable web of litigation over the years, while Mme Humbert and her family gave the most lavish of parties and balls to *le tout Paris* who were apparently quite under the spell.

Finally, on 9 May 1902 their creditors obtained an order to open the safe while the Humberts were in Madrid. Sadly there was no $20 million, merely about $1,000 along with an empty jewel-case, an Italian coin and some brass buttons. The Humberts were arrested

[9] *Morning Leader*, 22, 29 January 1906.

in Spain and returned in something approaching triumph from the capital, being given a sleeping compartment on an express train. Once in the Conciergerie, Madame H. complained about the cold and a £15 Turkestan carpet was provided for her. As the months went by French opinion, which often carried an unhealthy streak of anti-Semitism, grew in her favour:

> The general public admires Madame Humbert on the whole because she was able to extort so much money from the usually careful and astute Jews.[10]

Perhaps the most curious aspect is that the French aristocracy was quite prepared to bow its knee to a woman described as 'short, stout, yellowed skinned, she looked like a typical French cook'. She was almost completely uneducated and spoke with both a lisp and a thick Provençal accent. Her real name was Dauignac.[11]

Sometimes the French exported their bogus aristocracy, once with fatal effects. Henri Perreau, a man of some considerable charm and talent, was a waiter in Paris when in the summer of 1867 he was befriended by a William Cotton who engaged him to show him the sights of the city, and when this proved to be a success to take him to Constantinople as a guide. One evening the pair left their hotel and neither returned.

Perreau did reappear, this time at the Prince of Wales Hotel in Scarborough where he was no longer a member of staff. He was now Count Henri de Tourville and in this guise he courted Henrietta Bingham, due to receive an inheritance of £30,000 on the death of her mother. The mother must have thought it odd that the Count had to borrow from her to finance the honeymoon, but she did not have to worry for long because on his return he shot her. The coroner's verdict was one of misadventure. A series of complaining letters was sent to the police and a Scotland Yard detective was assigned to investigate. Unfortunately it was the corrupt officer

---

[10] *The Umpire*, 10 May 1903.
[11] They did not fare too well in prison. She sorted feathers and the men addressed envelopes. A hoped-for early release did not materialise, possibly because they had no funds to pay lawyers to petition for them. *The Umpire*, 8 November 1903.

Druscovich and he was bribed by the Count. No further action was taken.

Sadly, Henrietta did not last too long after that. They had a son and afterwards she fell ill and died of natural causes, having taken the precaution of leaving the bulk of her fortune to the child. The infant nearly died in a fire which burned down the house, and was only saved by the bravery of a police constable who defied the flames. The insurance company declined to pay out. De Tourville came to London where he charmed his way into society; he took a houseboat on the river, could be seen at Ascot and Goodwood and read for the Bar. He had taken the trouble to anglicise his first name. By now he was again running out of funds when he met the widow, Madeleine Miller, who had the not inconsiderable income of £7,000 a year. They married in November 1875 but, sadly, she did not survive the honeymoon.

They went on holiday to the Tyrol with her maid, where the happy couple took a coach to the Stelvio Pass. It was such a fine day that they dismissed the coachman and walked back down the Pass. Only de Tourville survived the walk; despite signs that his wife's body had been dragged over the edge, the coroner's verdict was that she had committed suicide. De Tourville may have been home, but he was not free. The Austrian police had not given up and he was arrested at a London dinner party and, despite the spirited efforts of Montagu Williams, he was extradited to Austria. It is not recorded whether Williams was obliged to observe the courtesy of appearing for a fellow barrister without payment. What *is* recorded is that de Tourville was sentenced to death but was reprieved and the sentence was commuted to one of 'perpetual imprisonment'.

Meanwhile Ms Kenneaux, now Frederica Furneaux, reappeared and so far as is known her career came to an end at the Old Bailey in July 1894. She had earlier appeared at Lambeth Magistrates Court on 2 July that year. The charges were obtaining money by false pretences and forgery, and the *modus operandi* just the same as before. Now she was 45 years old and said to come from Leeds. In 1890 she had made the acquaintance of Miles and Ellen Miller who kept a small newsagents in South East London, and she continually borrowed from them on the pretext that she was an heiress due to come into substantial funds. At one time she produced a letter from Nathaniel Cox of Cheyne Gardens, supposedly her trustee, saying he held money on her behalf. Miller may have been gullible, but he did make some effort to protect his vanishing capital and he went with Furneaux to Cheyne Gardens to see Cox. He remained on the pavement while she went inside, returning to say that Cox had gone to London. This apparently satisfied Miller and more money was handed over. She received a 10-year sentence for this and other frauds and was released on licence in November 1900.

This of itself was a good example of a long-term con which must have required a good deal of nerve, but it was her earlier career which had been really quite spectacular. In May 1882 (as Mary Jane Furneaux) she had again been convicted of obtaining £1,400 from Edward Benyon by impersonating the deceased Lord Arthur Clinton. Once more it was a long-term con which had lasted several years.[12]

Having served her sentence in 1872, on her release she went to Birmingham where she met the unfortunate Benyon in around 1875. It was then that she convinced him that she was Lord Arthur Clinton, who had not died as reported the previous year in a village in Hampshire. No, what had happened was that for some unnamed transgression Lord Arthur had been banished from society and forbidden to appear in public in male attire.[13] Over the years she sucked the savings out of Benyon with, the prosecution said, the help of James Gethin. In a much grander variation on her visit to Cheyne Gardens, she even took Benyon to Balmoral to see Queen Victoria. He was left in the guest house where they were lodging while she went to the castle, reporting on her return that the Queen

[12] PRO Crim 10 84; *Birmingham Post*, 22 November 1881; *The Times*, 3, 17 July 1894; Horace Smith, *Crooks of the Waldorf*. Smith has a highly exaggerated account of her swanning in London society, playing the piano with her delicate hands and when dinner was served picking pockets and removing jewellery before getting the night train back to Liverpool where she pawned her spoils.

[13] She was right in one thing. Before his death Lord Arthur Clinton, brother of the Duke of Newcastle, was in disgrace. He had been made bankrupt owing something in the region of £35,000, much of it to jewellers and wine merchants. As to the reason for his bankruptcy, he had told the court it was because he did not have enough income.

had been going into dinner and had been unable to see her. On another occasion she did manage the visit, so she said, and was able to report that the Queen was pleased with the way things were going and if s/he maintained the current rate of progress s/he would be restored to her/his rightful place in society in 18 months time. Meanwhile could she – Frederica, not the Queen – have some more money, please? Benyon obliged.

In fact it all went well until a series of illiterate letters was forged in the name of Lord Coleridge, then the Lord Chief Justice, apparently interceding on Lord Arthur's behalf. These were sent to the police and the game was up.

The trial was the sensation of the Spring Assizes at Warwick. The *Birmingham Post* reported her arrival on the train handcuffed to another woman prisoner and wearing a black hat with a feather and a Newmarket coat. There were three times the number of applications for seats than were available. There was little doubt of her guilt. The real question for the jury, said Mr Justice Fitzjames Stephen, was what role had Gethin actually played. Poor Benyon was subjected to the humiliation the courts hand out to the foolish. Asked if he really believed her to be genuine, he replied that he did: 'I've been shut up in mills all my life.' Lord Coleridge, who was on the bench as well, commented, 'Oh, you need not apologise.' (Laughter). It had earlier been accepted that the letters could not possibly have been written by him.

The jury took a bare 20 minutes to acquit Gethin and convict her. As was her right, she then made a long and rambling speech blaming it all on Gethin who had, she claimed, forced her into the masquerade with threats of the asylum. It did her no good; she received 7 years.[14]

---

[14] The case had produced a great deal of laughter. In his address to the Grand Jury Stevens recounted the earlier case of a woman convicted after claiming that she had the power to bring back a husband over hedges and ditches. He added that he did not know how it had been proved she did not possess the power. (Much more laughter.) *Birmingham Post*, 5, 6, 8 May 1882. Con-men seem to have abounded in Birmingham at the time. One was John Hartwell who as 'the Great English Seer' forecast the possibility of marriage for the gullible (price six stamps). When some newspapers refused to take his advertisements, he too changed sex becoming Anna Ross, 'the Great American Seer'. *Birmingham Post*, 5 May 1882. Of course soothsayers were not exclusively English. There were plenty in America of whom Professor Castrala, 'the Great Spanish Seer',

In December 1902, a Countess married an Austrian prince – in Portsmouth, of all unlikely places. There were reasons for a quiet wedding, for the Countess was the former wife of Earl Russell and had been locked in a decade of litigation over conjugal rights and allegations and counter-allegations of cruelty. It had ended badly for the Earl who served a 3-month sentence for bigamy, one of the last occasions when a peer was tried by his fellow peers in the House of Lords. Now the Countess found happiness with Prince Arthurpold (sometimes Archibald) Stuart de Modena. It should have been a simple question of checking references, since the *Almanac de Gotha* existed for just this sort of thing.

Unfortunately, while described – when he later appeared in court – as being of manly bearing and his occupation noted as that of gentleman, a more accurate description would have been gentleman's valet. William Brown, for that is who he was, had been born the son of a coachman residing in Frimley. Now he received 3 months, but since he had been in custody awaiting his trial he was released after less than a week. Curiously the Countess did not seem to mind the deception – either that, or it spoke volumes for the charm of the groom – because there was a reconciliation. This did not last long, however, for he beat her and was eventually found in Piccadilly with another lady. Now he was a cavalry officer, Captain Stuart. Since she could now prove both cruelty and adultery – the latter alone was not sufficient – as required for petitioning wives, she was granted a decree.[15]

On the same tier in the aristocratic ranks was the Princess

---

was one. He had an almost identical line in patter: 'Send me your age, a lock of hair, the colour of your eyes, 25c and a 3c stamp and I will provide a correct picture of your future husband or wife, the place and time of the first meeting and the date of your marriage.' The Professor turned out to be a man named Harris who had run demi-mondaine balls in Memphis, but being out of funds had taken up soothsaying. *New York Times*, 19 April 1879.

[15] Earl Russell, the elder brother of the philosopher Bertrand, was really rather unlucky. He had contracted a seriously unfortunate marriage to a woman whose sister kept a massage parlour. In 1901, in an endeavour to free himself he obtained a Nevada divorce, something which at the time was not recognised in the English courts. He then remarried in America a month later. The last trial by peers was that of Lord de Clifford, acquitted after an accident on the Kingston bypass. The right of trial by peers was abolished by the Criminal Justice Act 1948. For those interested in the machinations of the Russell divorce see PRO MEPO 3 839. The Countess's hearing was expedited because, it was said, she had a heart condition which would not improve while she was still nominally attached to the Prince. *Morning Leader*, 11 December 1903.

Soltykoff or, rather more prosaically, Margaret Trew-Prebble, who received two sentences for fraud in the early 1900s. Born the fifth child of a joiner in Liverpool on 1 December 1883, she led an adventurous and sometimes courageous life. On 6 February 1906 she appeared, 'entertainingly beautiful', at the Central Criminal Court charged with a variety of offences of obtaining goods by false pretences when it was alleged that, as Lady Muriel Paget, she had been defrauding shops and stores in the West End.

The writer for the *Morning Leader* was clearly half in love with her:

> . . . rich complexion, medium height, commanding presence, mass of beautiful brown hair, elegantly dressed and full of Southern fire, her mouth is the work of an actress and her manner – even in moments of excitement – is quite the manner of the old nobility.

Unfortunately, the case of George Elliott for the prosecution was that she was no more a princess, let alone Lady Muriel, than he was a Mohammedan. She was, he said, the daughter of James McKillem, who lived in Cheshire at Upper Mason Street, Liverpool.

She had first struck by obtaining a miniature from Esmé Collings of Bond Street of 'her cousin the Marquess of Anglesey', and had then conducted operations with addresses such as the fine-sounding Winwick Hall, Haydock (a lunatic asylum), Portslade (where she had been a probationary nurse), Arundel Square (a boarding-house in Barnsbury) and that well-known retreat for swindlers of the day, the Metropole Hotel in Brighton. Apart from Esmé Collings, Debenhams had been amongst her targets. It was alleged that the hat she was so fashionably wearing in court had been obtained by fraud.

Her trial was clearly an entertaining one. Lady Muriel Paget, wearing furs although the court was suffocatingly hot, gave evidence that she was the one and only Lady P. and she had never met the Princess. Then after a sister had given evidence of the Princess's lowly birth, into the witness box went the Princess herself. She looked a tragedy queen in a long red 'wrapper' reaching from neck to feet, and produced a large family bible which she kissed.

Asked her name, she replied Nina Olga Trew-Prebble. Asked where she was born, Judge Rentoul interrupted, 'Surely that is hearsay.' (Laughter.) She said she had been educated at Liverpool College and Windsor College at the expense of Major Paget (the Hon. Alfred).

It was at this point in her evidence that the usher decided that unlike Elliott she was indeed a Mohammedan and therefore had taken the oath incorrectly. Now she had to take off her boots and slippers, place one hand on the Koran and one on her forehead. Would she mind taking off her boots?

'We'll look the other way,' said Elliot. 'I don't mind,' said the Princess. But, reported the *Leader*, no one did look the other way and a 'huge book which looked like a selection from One Hundred Best Books' was produced.

Once correctly sworn, she said she had changed her name in 1892 to Slolterfoht. Who was he? A boy who had made lucky investments for her. The change of name had been talismanic. She had changed her name to Paget two or three years later. By this time Lord Anglesey was, she said, making her an allowance. In 1895 she had become stranded in Paris and when no money was forthcoming, as she believed was her right, she took the name Paget.

In her earlier days she had tried to study medicine and had once run a bakery in Everton. She then went on the stage, which she left to marry Prince Alexis Soltykoff. They had tried to marry in Scotland. When it was pointed out to her that the forge at Gretna Green was not in existence in 1891, she quickly changed her story to having been married in the cottage of the man who used to perform the ceremonies. She had then discovered that they had not stayed for the requisite period and instead had married in St Petersburg. Unfortunately she had given the marriage papers to a woman she had met in a convent, and had never seen them again. She had left the Prince in St Petersburg and returned to England 'under the guardianship of an old gentleman'.

She had then learned that Alexis had died in a Russian prison and, using the name Slolterfoht, she had married a man named Prebble who had been 'at the Varsity' and was studying medicine at Guy's Hospital until funds ran out and he had gone into the Army. The prosecution thought that Mr Prebble was in fact a corporal in the Army. It was never clear whether he had joined up simply to escape the Princess.

—'So you are Mrs Prebble?'
—'No, I-I think I am Princess Soltykoff.'

She had, she said, taken to drink after the death of her sixth child; the other five offspring had passed away during the preceding 18 months. How much was she drinking? Well, this was a bit embarrassing. Two bottles of vodka a day and, worse, she was taking stout as well as morphia and opium pills.

Summing up, Rentoul, acting on the belief that the working classes cannot have intelligent children, was clearly captivated with her as well. 'A person of undoubted ability particularly so when it is considered that she is the daughter of a joiner.' The jury took half an hour to find her guilty.

It was then that the Princess's nemesis Inspector Drew told the court about her. She had left home in 1893 after her mother had made 'an accusation'. Mother was right because the Princess-to-be had given birth to Annette Tarbett McKillem on 10 April 1894 in Liverpool. It was at this point that the Princess had obtained a position as a nurse; it was accepted that she was a good one. She had also been a children's nurse in Wales, and was apparently well thought of and out of trouble before a kindly clergyman did his Christian duty and travelled to Wales to denounce her to the family. On her credit side, she had saved a child trapped in a fire in an upstairs tenement room.

What, the judge wanted to know, was the truth of the marriage? Soltykoff's father had denied any union. 'Couldn't it have been a secret marriage?' asked the judge, and anyway where was Soltykoff *fils*? Dead. So that mystery was never explained.

Any previous? Fifteen months at Suffolk Assizes for fraud in August 1902 in not very dissimilar circumstances.[16] She had, it

---

[16] All in all it was not a good time for the Soltykoffs. In February 1903 the Prince's gamekeeper, Charles Sims, was killed when his dog, scrapping with another over a dead rabbit, accidentally knocked his gun and shot his master. *Illustrated Police News*, 28 February 1903. On 21 November Prince Dimitri died, leaving nothing of his

seems, been dismissed from a nursing position for obtaining goods on credit and had been in Johannesburg for a period of time. She had some of her bills paid by a peer, but unpaid ones included £47 at the Savoy and a further bill at the Hotel Cecil where she had left a worthless packet which she said had contained jewels. In 1901 she had been working at a nurses' home in Ipswich, where a lady had befriended her and taken her to Southwold. There she had posed as the widow of Prince Alexis and the unfortunate Prebble had, without his knowledge, been commissioned and was now a major. That escapade ended when she went to London and ran up another hotel bill. She had been obliged to leave in a hurry because her brother had been badly injured in a gun accident in Southwold. In fact Prince Dimitri Soltykoff, a member of the Jockey Club, had given evidence at the Suffolk Assizes and admitted it was possible that his son had married the adventuress. She had also tried to obtain money from a Liverpool shipowner, pretending she was his daughter.

What about police supervision, would that help? No, said Drew. That would not work. Her barrister then began to mitigate, along the lines that she had got into trouble in the social sense at an early age and everything followed from that. The Princess would not have it. 'That is not true.'

Rentoul thought it was worth 5 years, but instead he sentenced her to 18 months with hard labour, saying, 'She will probably be doing the same thing over again.' But there does not seem to be any further record of her misdemeanours.[17]

She was followed smartly into the dock by Charles Wells, one of the great fraudsmen of his time whose lasting claim to fame is as 'The man who broke the bank at Monte Carlo'.

In fact he did not break the bank, only the pockets of many of his supporters. Wells was born in 1841 and had a remarkable run at the tables in Monte Carlo in July 1891. He had been a small-time con-man who received 2 years for fraud in Paris on 18 December 1885. In the July of his success he turned a stake

£300,000 fortune to the *soi-disant* Princess. The next year thieves, who clearly had inside information, broke into his widow's house in Slough and stole a deed box said to contain some £3–4,000. *The Times*, 3, 4 August 1904.
[17] *Morning Leader*, 4 January; 7, 8, 9 February 1906.

of £50 into something around £100,000. True he wiped out a table a dozen times, but that was far from breaking the bank. He returned later in the year and proceeded to do the same thing. Back in London he raised money to finance another run at the tables. It is a measure of the charm of the con-man that no one asked him why, since he was a winner from the first turn of the wheel, he needed financing, but off he went again – this time with a yacht and his current girlfriend – and lost all his backers' money.

Wells was extradited from France in January 1893. He had been trying to sell his yacht to a Russian in Le Havre for £20,000, something he said he would have been able to do had the arrival of the police not interrupted the sale. Described as a patent agent, he was accused of obtaining £28,000 from various investors. Since 1885 he had filed 192 applications for patents, but had only completed the formalities in 27 of them. His inventions and modifications included saving coal on steam vessels, torpedoes, hot-air engines and more modestly, umbrellas, the preservation of mixed mustards and musical skipping ropes. Only one had been fully completed and sold. Now he received 8 years.

In prison, Wells clearly captivated the experienced governor, Sir Basil Thompson:

> [Wells was] the pleasantest and most unselfish of all the men that passed through my hands.
>
> He believed that he was not simply a swindler but genuinely believed he would make everyone's fortune.
>
> If when I had met him he had been a free man and I had been in possession of money to invest, and Wells had held me with his glittering eye and discoursed fluently on his latest project for making money, he would have defrauded even me who have a fairly large acquaintance amongst fraudulent company promoters, so great is the power of persuasion of the man who believes in himself.[18]

A lengthy term of imprisonment did nothing at all to cure him. In 1905, under the name of William Davenport and working with a

---

[18] Sir Basil Thomson, 'My Years as Governor of Dartmoor' in *Thomson's Weekly News*, 4 February 1922.

bankrupt clergyman, Vyvyan Henry Moyle, he set up the South and South West Coast Steam Trading and Fishing Syndicate, raising mortgage bonds on a fleet worth £4,000. The fleet consisted of two unseaworthy trawlers which might, *just*, have fetched £500. Three years, and 18 months for the 71-year-old vicar.

Wells was released from prison in 1908 and told the police he was leaving the country, possibly to travel on the Continent. In turn they thought he had gone to Canada or the Argentine. In fact he got no further than Lyons, where as Ernest Cuvilier he set up a another fraud, and in July 1910 it was back to Paris where, under the name Lucian Rivier, he set up Chocolite. By the next year the French police were sending telegrams to Scotland Yard asking if by chance they had seen him recently. In fact they had. There he was as Charles de Ville with his current mistress, Josephine-Jeanette Burns, setting up another little fraud; he was then 70. It was back to Paris and prison, but tabs were kept on him and he was reported to be coming to London on 20 December 1915. The French police sent a telegram saying that he had left Dieppe and was staying in the Wilton Hotel, but he must have changed his plans. The waiting police saw nothing of him at Victoria, nor was he in the Wilton Hotel. Nor, for that matter, had any rooms been booked by him.[19] He died in Paris, aged 85, in 1926. By then he had admitted that his roulette winnings were not due to any system but simply to an amazing run of good luck.

It is difficult to categorise the beautiful Anais Chirch from Menilmontant. Of more minor talent but still worth a mention, she flourished at a mixture of the con and the kirkbuzzing game. Chirch, who dressed in black, was something of a professional mourner at Père Lachaise, the Paris cemetery. Attending funerals, she would claim to know the deceased and search for likely prey. In May 1904 she so impressed one widower with her tale of how she knew and treasured his wife that they went off to dinner together and, since that was such a comfort to him in his bereavement, then to the Moulin de la Galette dance hall in Montmartre – shortly after which he found he had lost all his money. When the police raided her

[19] MEPO 3 204; Ernest Nicholls, *Crime within the Square Mile*.

home it was found to be stuffed with prayer books, crucifixes and other religious paraphernalia.

The end of the American Civil War saw a new development in the art of the con-man. Until then most cons had been the short con, which did not mean to say that a con-man or woman would not adopt and maintain an identity for some years, but essentially they worked alone or in a small team and the gulls could be described as the victims of in-and-out raids. Now came a completely new scam, The Big Store, a major confidence game operation.[20] As the name suggests a store, betting shop or office was set up with a number of con-men and women acting in partnership and playing the parts of employees and customers and so forth. It was an essential ingredient that the co-operation of the local police force was obtained.

By 1900 the Gondorff brothers, Fred, Charley and George, had entered The Big Store as had Lou Blonger, a master fraudsman in Denver which was regarded, correctly, as the home of this particular confidence trick. In 1899 the brothers cleared £200,000 from a St Louis businessman, and it was believed they took at least 20 victims annually. As for Blonger, his team operated on the basis that no local person could be fleeced and accordingly in 20 years not one of his workers went to prison.

In 1906 Charley Gondorff opened a more or less permanent Big Store, specialising in the wire fraud, in Manhattan. This was a standard fraud inviting the mark to bet on horse races of which – because of a seeming time delay – the result was previously known. It is amazing to think that people were taken in by this but, given the acting skills and charm of the operators coupled with the greed of the mark, it was not until 1914 that an Englishman, Eugene

---

[20] Carl Sifakis suggests that the first big-time Big Store was opened in 1900 when Buck Boatwright ran a gambling club in Webb City, Mo. One of the sports on offer was faked foot races where the victim's selected runner would apparently drop dead of a heart attack. Since this kind of event was illegal the punter had suddenly become involved as an accessory to murder and would not stay around too long. The final scene of the film *The Sting*, in which Paul Newman is seemingly shot, was a standard ingredient of The Big Store and was based on their Manhattan operation. Sifakis credits Boatwright with inventing the Smack game of matching coins in which two apparent enemies join forces to deceive the mark.

Adams, decided not to take his financial beating lying down and went to the police. Fred Gondorff lasted a year longer before he also went down.

Meanwhile over in Australia some earned their money painfully. Two con-men named Campbell and Henderson travelled the whole of Australia swindling railway companies. Their *modus operandi* was deliberately to fall out of trains and then blame the railway company for leaving the door open. They began with a couple of failures in Victoria and Tasmania, but learned from their lessons well. They first visited South Australia where they picked up £350 and then moved on to Western Australia where the takings amounted to £750. Then they claimed £10,000 in Queensland and this was their undoing. It was really too large an amount even if (as he claimed) Campbell had been paralysed from the feet upwards. He must have had an extraordinary tolerance of pain, for 'extreme electrical appliances were used but he never flinched'. His conduct was regarded as a marvel of endurance by the experts, but he failed the test when it was applied above the seat of the injury and he did not flinch then. Each received 7 years imprisonment.[21]

[21] *Morning Leader*, 30 December 1902.

17

The Robbers – A Changing Breed

Times were changing. The once Wild West was being tamed, but many could or would not accept the fact. Three of the Younger Gang were caught after an unsuccessful raid in Northfield, Minnesota, on 7 September 1876. Bob Younger died in prison in 1889. Jim, released in 1901, killed himself the next year, while Cole Younger toured with Frank James in a Wild West Show for a time, dying in 1916.

Their cousins, the James brothers, had long been hounded by the Pinkertons. Jesse James is credited with being the first daylight bank robber, as we know the term, when in 1866 the brothers carried out a raid on a bank in Liberty, Missouri, taking $58,000 and killing a bystander. From then until his death he led a series of bank and train robberies – not that he seems to have held on to what were undoubtedly spectacular earnings for the period. On 3 April 1882 he was shot in the back by Bob Ford as he stood on a chair to straighten a picture in his home. In the October Frank James surrendered. However, he was such a folk hero that no jury would convict him in either Minnesota, Alabama or Missouri. The last trial was for the killing of passenger Frank McMillan during the hold-up of the Chicago, Rock Island and Pacific train at Winton on 5 July 1881.[1] After his release James also farmed, was a salesman and was a horse-race starter until his death in 1915.

The so-called Last of the Bushrangers, Ned Kelly, had been executed in Melbourne, Victoria, two years before the murder of Jesse James. His father had been transported from Belfast to Tasmania in 1841 where he continued his career as a horse thief.[2] In April 1878 a constable who went to arrest Kelly's brother Daniel was wounded. The Kelly brothers escaped and in the October a police patrol was ambushed. Two constables and a sergeant were killed; a fourth officer escaped. In December 1878 in perhaps the first of the gang's great coups, 20 people were held prisoner and the bank at Euroa was robbed of £2,000. The operation was repeated on 10 February at Jerilderie, when 30 people were held and the bank relieved of over £2,000. On 26 June 1880 Kelly and his gang took another 62 people hostage in their attempt to rob the Glenrowan train. The local schoolmaster escaped and informed the police and the gang was surrounded. Joe Byrne, who had been with Kelly since the April 1878 incident, was shot and killed; Daniel Kelly poisoned himself. At the end of a 7-hour siege Kelly, in the famous tin-can armour he wore, was captured. His legs were unprotected however, and he was brought down by 25 bullets. He was hanged on 11 November 1880.

The phrase 'Ned Kelly was a Gentleman' does not represent the truth, and it is a good example of how a myth is born. It originated shortly after his death and in full ran 'Compared to X, Ned Kelly was a gentleman'. Gradually the first three words were omitted and Kelly was on his way to folk-hero status.

His predecessor Frederick Ward, Captain Thunderbolt, appears in fact to have been more gentlemanly. His worst crime seems to have been shooting a policeman in the hand, but throughout his

---

[1] Lawyer Albert Borowitz in his *Blood & Ink* suggests that the hero-worship may have been mixed with fear. For a revisionist view of James and his gang see T.J. Styles, *Jesse James*. See also Richard E. Nicholls, 'Thoroughly Bad Guy' in the *New York Times Book Review*, 27 October 2002.

[2] There is also a suggestion that he had been a member of the original Irish Molly Maguires who, riding at night in dresses, were in revolt against the land system in the country.

career he committed countless robberies and thefts, often of race-horses, to help in his escapes. Much of the credit for his survival as a bushranger for a little over six years, when the average life expectancy in the profession was less than half that, can be attributed to the resourcefulness of his part-Aboriginal wife, Mary Ann. She rode with him, fed their family and, on 11 September 1863, helped him in his escape from Cockatoo Island, Sydney. From then on it was a life on the run together. She died in 1867 from consumption, but Ward continued his career until it ended in May 1870 when he was followed after yet another theft. He told Alexander Walker – the police officer who had chased him into Kentucky Creek, Uralla – that he would rather die than surrender. Walker replied 'It's you and I for it' and plunged into the water after Ward. Walker's horse stumbled and when Ward tried to pull the bridle to unseat him the officer shot him.[3]

The life of the bushranger does not seem to have been a romantic one. Annie Rixon may have written admiringly of Ward, 'His muscles rippled in the sunlight. Suddenly his splendid body skimmed the air like a swallow', but in truth it was a drab existence, long hours in the saddle and rain, stealing food and enduring the cold from fear of lighting a fire. A police report of the Captain described him as 'his person . . . was found to be dirty like the commonest type of bush labourer'.

Back in Kansas on 5 October 1892 three of the Dalton brothers, Emmett, Bob and Gratton, along with two colleagues, Bill Powers and Dick Broadwell, attempted what was to be a daring feat: they would rob two banks simultaneously in Coffeyville. It would turn out to be a disastrous enterprise.

Four of the brothers, who were cousins of Bob and Cole Younger, had originally been United States marshals serving under Judge Parker. They turned poachers and after a number of successful, if small, hold-ups attempted to rob a train in 1891. It was not a

---

[3] Ward is buried in Uralla cemetery. There is a plaque in commemoration of Walker's bravery, but in 1988 a statue of Captain Thunderbolt was unveiled at the spot. Malcolm Brown (ed.), *Australian Crime*; Annie Rixon, *Captain Thunderbolt*; Roy Mendham, *Dictionary of Australian Bushrangers*.

success and Gratton and Bill were caught, receiving sentences of 25 years. Gratton escaped and with Bob and Emmett went back east to Oklahoma where they joined with Bill Doolin, a far more successful outlaw, forming for a time the Dalton–Doolin Gang. Doolin absented himself from the Coffeyville raid when his horse conveniently went lame.

The raid was an unmitigated disaster. Although from time to time, rather as Butch Cassidy and Harry Longbaugh used Etta Place to research for them, a woman Eugenia Moore was used to reconnoitre, on this occasion there had been no proper preparation. The hitching-posts on the street had been removed and they had to leave their horses in what would become known as Death Alley. They were seen carrying Winchesters by an Alec McKenna who thought he recognised two of the brothers and gave the alarm. However, the brothers were committed to wait until a time lock on a safe opened. By the time they came out through the bank doors the townspeople were armed and in wait for them. Gratton Dalton and Charlie Connelly, the town marshal, shot each other dead. The only one to survive was Emmett who turned and rode back for his brother, an act of courage which gave the Daltons their status in Western history. As he was pulling him into the saddle, Emmett was himself shot in the back. But he lived and was pardoned in 1907, when he became a successful building contractor. In 1931 he wrote a popular if inaccurate book, *When the Daltons Rode*. In it he rather laments the end of the country-bred outlaw:

> One of the inducements to crime in the West was the presumed ease of escape into untrammelled lands. This supposed easy refuge was a fallacy, for in a sparsely settled land every stranger was a bid for curiosity. The colour of his horse was noted, the cut of his beard was marked, the directions he asked were remembered. A thousand-mile ride for the Western outlaw might harbour more pitfalls than a city block for the modern gangster.[4]

[4] Emmett Dalton, *When The Daltons Rode*.

Carl Sifakis gives an example of how out of touch with modern life the Daltons had been. Asked by a New York reporter in 1910 how the city should be kept crime-free, Emmett replied, 'Guard the entrances to the town.'[5]

The year before the First World War saw the end of the long-time stagecoach – graduated to train – robber and prison escaper Bill Miner, who is credited with the command beloved of the 'B' picture Western: 'Hands Up'.

He was born in Kentucky in 1847, becoming a cowboy at the age of 13 and going on to the Californian goldfields where, rather than panning himself, he stole from sleeping miners. From then it was into the Army as a dispatch rider and from there to his own mail delivery business and on to stagecoach robbery. His first arrest is given as 1869 near Sonora. Chased, he was captured when his horse died beneath him. Giving his age as 16 and so avoiding a hanging, he was sentenced to 15 years in San Quentin. As with many a prisoner before and after him, he now 'saw the Light' and was released for good behaviour in 1879. By now train robbery was becoming the crime of choice and Miner went to Colorado where there was light at the end of the tunnel, teaming up with a Bill Leroy. The pair had a relatively successful period of operations until Leroy was captured and hanged by a posse and Miner escaped to San Francisco and then, following the fashion of wanted American criminals, came to Europe. From there it was to Turkey, where he joined slave traders for a time, and then South America for a spot of gun-running.

The lure of the stagecoach and train was too great, however, and he went back to Sonora where he held up the stage, relieving it of $3,000. From there it was up to Colorado again with a new partner,

---

[5] Carl Sifakis, *The Encyclopedia of American Crime*. Bill Dalton, released from prison, had been killed in Oklahoma Territory in 1895. Afterwards Bill Doolin (b. 1863), very much more professional than his former colleagues, led his own gang until he married a minister's daughter in 1894 when he retired and the gang dissolved. He went to New Mexico, staying on the ranch of the author Eugene Manlove Brooks. There are a number of differing accounts of his death in 1896, the most attractive (if sentimental) of which is that he died of consumption. There was still a price on his head, so Marshal Heck Thomas shot the body to claim the $5,000 reward which he paid to Doolin's widow.

Jimmy Crum. San Quentin was the next stop after the pair had been caught, and this time the sentence was 25 years. Again 'the Light' shone and he emerged blinking in 1901, once more a reformed man. Two years later he was working trains in Oregon and Washington State. From there (after a failure in Oregon) it was a short hop across the border into Canada where for a time he settled in Aspen Grove in British Columbia – assuming, as George A. Edwards, the role of the Southern gentleman and, once again, taking up religion.

Then on 10 September 1904 he attacked the Canadian Pacific Railway Company's train, the *Imperial Limited*, on its way west from Toronto. About an hour out of Vancouver when it slowed to take on water, Miner and his team climbed over the coal tender into the engine cab and ordered the driver to stop a few miles down the track. The passenger cars were disconnected and gold dust and cash in the region of $7,000 were stolen. Some reports said that Australian and American bonds totalling $300,000 were also taken, but it is by no means clear that this was the case. Now the Pinkertons were called in. A trail was followed back into Washington, but it petered out and six months later Miner was still loose. In fact he was back in Aspen Grove.

On 30 April 1906 he and his men attacked the same *Imperial Limited*, but taking only $15 and missing $40,000 in banknotes. This time they were followed successfully and were captured at Douglas Lake. Miner was recognised by one of the mail clerks as the man who had robbed the train 18 months earlier. On 2 June he and his two colleagues were convicted and sentenced in Kamloops, in Miner's case to life imprisonment.

Once more he was a model prisoner with yet another dose of religion. He was allowed to keep his hair long – a clever ruse so that when he escaped he did not have the shaven head of the convict – and within a year, on 8 August 1907, he was out after tunnelling under the fence. Within weeks, white-haired and with a pronounced stoop, leading a small team, he carried out another series of train robberies. The Pinkertons were again enlisted, but this time they and others singularly failed to find the man as he worked his way across the continent. In 1910 he was thought to be living on the Flathead Indian reservation in Montana and a Pinkerton agent was sent to track him down, once more without success.

Then on 9 February 1911 he was caught in a swamp in Georgia after he had robbed the Southern Railroad Express in White Sulphur. He received his second life sentence but, game as ever, escaped three times from the prison at Milledgeville. On the last occasion he was found in another swamp by bloodhounds. One of his fellow-escapers had drowned and Miner became seriously ill from drinking the water, but he lived another nine months before he died on 2 September 1913. Local people paid for his funeral and a headstone for his grave.

There is no doubt that he was enormously popular, but why? Certainly, in his later years he may have threatened violence but there is no evidence that he used it. Most prison escapers grow a patina of daredevilry and there is always something amusing about seeing vast organisations such as the railroad companies and detective agencies thwarted. One attraction was the continuing rumours that he still held several hundred thousand dollars' worth of bonds from the 1904 robbery, and that he was negotiating their surrender in return for his release. Miner also displayed a good deal of old-world charm and courtesy. It was easy to forget – and forgive – that throughout his life he was a robber. A film *The Grey Fox*, with Richard Farnsworth, created a nostalgic view of his later life.[6]

Some prison escapers were more fortunate. In 1909 Frank Grigware received life imprisonment for a crime he did not commit. Shortly after being sent to the first United States Federal Penitentiary he and a number of other inmates escaped by hi-jacking a supply train and ramming it through the prison gates. He remained at liberty for 25 years until he was run to ground by the Mounties in Alberta, by which time he was a family man and ex-mayor of a small town in the province. When the American authorities asked

---

[6] See Pinkerton Archives Binder 130; Mark Dugan and John Boessenecker, *The Grey Fox*; Frank W. Anderson, *Bill Miner, Train Robber*; Martin Robin, *The Bad and the Lonely*; *Vancouver Sun*, 27 November 1940.

for him to be extradited the Canadians declined, saying he was 'the sort of man we want settling our frontier'.[7]

Some robbers never gave up. When on 3 January 1910 Arthur Heywood was shot by policeman Henry Decker as he was robbing a saloon on West 16th Street, Chicago, he was identified as the notorious Marion Columbus Hedgepeth, bank robber and safe-blower. Once known as 'The Derby Kid', he had served a number of sentences in both Missouri and California.[8] More interestingly he was the person who had given the Chief of Detectives Desmond information which led to the arrest of the Chicago serial killer, H. H. Holmes, whom he had met in prison. For this help he had been pardoned in Missouri.[9]

In his time he had led the well known Sly–Wilson gang of robbers and safe-blowers.[10] Having come to St Louis at the invitation of a local cracksman, Jim French, within two months they had blown over 50 safes. Hedgepeth's part in their activities culminated in the robbery of the Glendale train, for which on 28 September 1893 he received 25 years. Before then he had served 7 years for robbery in Missouri and had taken part in an escape in which a guard was badly injured.

Hedgepeth was arrested in San Francisco on 10 February and was taken back to St Louis in what was called the Oregon Boot, a leg-iron designed to break a man's ankle if he attempted to escape. He served 13 years before being pardoned in 1906, saying he had learned the trade of shoemaker while in prison and was now going straight; he thought he might go to Chicago. Aged 41 and said to look 55, he had almost lost contact with his wife who had been charged with the robbery and had twice tried to commit suicide in prison before being acquitted. She had remained in California. So

[7] Joe Jackson, *Leavenworth Train: A Fugitive's Search for Justice in the Vanishing West.*
[8] *Inter Ocean*, 4 January 1910; *Chicago Daily Journal*, 3 January 1910. See also 'Have Derby – Will Kill' in *True Western Adventures*, Number 8. Curiously, also shot in a separate incident on 1 January was Harry B. Featherstone, said by his sister Emma to be the rightful Lord Featherstonehaugh. He, along with two others, had robbed the Hunter saloon at 21st and Michigan and been shot by a patrolman as he tried to climb into a taxi to escape. His grandfather was the nephew and heir to the last Lord Featherstonehaugh, but had been disinherited when he married an Irish girl.
[9] Other reports say it was because he informed on potential prison mutineers.
[10] It was also known as the Hedgepeth Four. *Railroad Man's Magazine*, June 1907.

much for his good intentions: the next year he was sentenced in Omaha for robbery and served a year at Ford Madison, Iowa. From his release until a fortnight before his death he had been working in a shoe factory in Minneapolis.

Adelbert D. Sly, whose ambition was said to be a second Jesse James, was arrested in Los Angeles by Robert Pinkerton in January 1892, possibly on information given by Florence Waterman who claimed to be Hedgepeth's wife. He had been running a saloon in the name of Delabert Eyls, hardly a great cover, and was found in possession of a gold watch stolen from Messenger Mulrennan who had been injured when the safe on the train was dynamited. He had made rather a habit of being arrested by the Pinkertons who in 1882 had him for stealing from the American Express Company when he was employed as a driver. He served 7 years on that occasion, and while in the penitentiary in Jefferson City had teamed up with the Wilsons.

He was released along with Hedgepeth, 'old men, decrepit and broken before their time'. Sly is said to have gone into business in St Joseph but Hedgepeth . . .

> White haired, toothless, and stricken with fatal illness was thrown upon the world penniless, willing to take up 'odd jobs' to make a living.[11]

As for the Wilson brothers, their careers came to an end in Syracuse, New Jersey, on 31 July 1893 when Detective James Harvey was killed after he had arrested Lucius (known as Dink) and Charles and was taking them to the police station. They broke from him and shot him. Chased by a crowd, Lucius was captured and was electrocuted at Auburn on 14 May 1894. Charles was tracked down a month later and also sentenced to death, but this was commuted on 11 June 1895.

The last bandit of either sex to try to rob a stagecoach appears to have been Pearl Hart, born Pearl Taylor in Canada in 1878, who along with Joe Boot – variously described as her husband, boyfriend

---

[11] *Railroad Man's Magazine*, June 1907.

or more likely pimp – held up the stage between Globe and Riverside near Ajo in Arizona. It was a distinctly low-grade affair. The pair made the passengers dismount and took their valuables. Since they could not afford horses they then made off on foot and were easily caught. She was sentenced to 5 years in the penitentiary in Yuma and Boot to 7. Released in 1902, she had a short-lived career on the Orpheum circuit as 'Pearl Hart – The Bandit Queen' in which she re-enacted the hold-up. Two years later she was arrested for receiving – she had been working with a gang of pickpockets – but the charges were dropped. She is also thought to have robbed a train the following year. Pearl is believed to have died in 1925.

18

Lockett the Lionheart and the Great Receivers

'Lockett – the lion-hearted – the man who never knew fear', said ex-Detective Superintendent Charles Leach admiringly of James Lockett, from time to time during his long and illustrious career known as Preston, Harry Graham, Lockhart and Jim or James Howard. Lockett, who was born in Wild Street, Drury Lane, in 1862, is a genuine British claimant for the title of a 'Prince of Thieves'.

On 7 October 1898 he was sentenced to 4 years imprisonment in the name of Harry Graham for attempting, along with Hughie Burns and Yankee Jack, to steal a bag of silver in New York State. On his release he returned to England and was an original member of the Forty Thieves, owing allegiance to a woman known as The Swan-Necked Beauty or the Queen of the Forties.[1] He was married to Becky Cohen, who had previously been married to Yankee Jack. For her part

---

[1] Given the arrest rate it is not surprising that there were a number of Queens of the Forty Thieves. One, Helen Sheen, was arrested at Kensal Green Cemetery for a previous theft of jewellery worth around £100. On the arrival of the officers she sank to the ground and when challenged replied, 'How dare you come and arrest me when I am praying over my dear father's grave.' It was pointed out that the grave was that of a woman. The court adjourned sentence to give her the opportunity to disclose where the jewels had gone, but she declined. Sentenced to 18 months, she said to the judge, 'That won't break my heart, old tallow face. Good-bye, dearie.' *Morning Leader*, 19 May 1906.

Marm Mandelbaum, New York's
greatest receiver – *Private Collection*

Joseph Grizzard, London's greatest receiver
Private Collection

reconstruction of one of the Bonnot gang's robberies – *Private Collection*

1—George Carson, alias "Little George."   2—Harry Russell, alias Murphy.   3—"Sid" Yennie.
4—Joe Killoran   5—Charles Allen.

Five Aces – *Library of Congress*

unka Phillips did not want his
photograph taken – *Private Collection*

Nor did Micky Gleason – *Library of Congress*

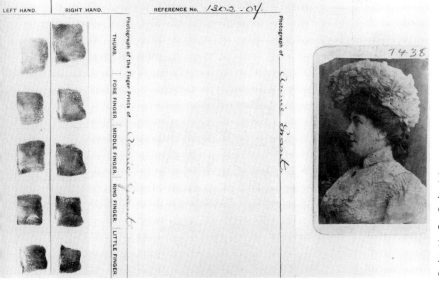

His wife
Annie
Gleason
didn't
mind –
*Library of
Congress*

'Doc' Pat Sheedy, sporting man about town and friend of the infamous – *Private Collection*

Jim Lockett 'the lion-hearted' – *Private Collection*

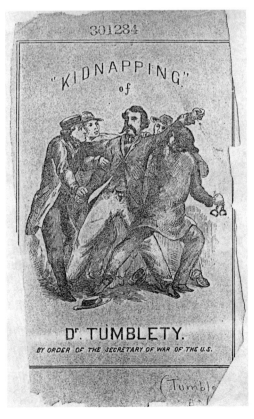

Tumblety is 'kidnapped' – *Private Collection*

dam Worth aka Harry Raymond –
rivate Collection

Kitty Flynn - his lost love –
Private Collection

Queen of more or less every scam –
Sophie Lyons – *Private Collection*

Casque d'Or – *Private Collection*

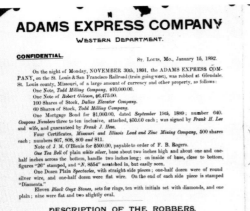

ADAMS EXPRESS COMPANY

WESTERN DEPARTMENT.

CONFIDENTIAL.

St. Louis, Mo., January 15, 1892.

On the night of Monday, NOVEMBER 30th, 1891, the ADAMS EXPRESS COMPANY, on the St. Louis & San Francisco Railroad (train going west), was robbed at Glendale, St. Louis county, Missouri, of a large amount of currency and other property, as follows:

One Note, Todd Milling Company, $10,000.00.
One Note of Robert Gileson, $6,475.00.
100 Shares of Stock, Dallas Elevator Company.
60 Shares of Stock, Todd Milling Company.
One Mortgage Bond for $1,000.00, dated September 19th, 1889; number 640.
Coupons Numbers three to ten inclusive, attached, $50.0 each; was signed by *Frank H. Lee* and wife, and guaranteed by *Frank J. Hess.*
Four Certificates, Missouri and Illinois Lead and Zinc Mining Company, 500 shares each; numbers 807, 808, 809 and 811.
Note of J. M. O'Blenis for $500.00, payable to order of F. B. Rogers.
One Tea Bell of plain *white silver*, base about two inches high and about one and one-half inches across the bottom, handle two inches long; on inside of base, close to bottom, figures "26" stamped, and "N. 8554" scratched in, but easily seen.
One Dozen Plain *Spectacles*, with straight side pieces; one-half dozen were of round silver wire, and one-half dozen were flat wire. On the end of each side piece was stamped "Diamenta."
Eleven *Black Onyx Stones*, sets for rings, ten with initials set with diamonds, and one plain; nine were flat and two slightly oval.

DESCRIPTION OF THE ROBBERS.

Marion C. Hedspeth, alias *Louis Marion Williams*, alias *George Scott*, alias *Marion Davis*, alias *Sam Woods*, alias *J. J. Morgan*, etc.
Age 28; 5 ft. 10 or 11; weight 170 to 180; dark mustache, which may be cut off, or may have full black or dark beard; dark complexion, black hair, brown eyes; lisps slightly; has false teeth in upper and lower front of mouth; has long scar across back of right thumb, usually wears glove to conceal; scar near right knee-cap; foot 11 inches long; rather affable in manner; disposition cool, but at times impulsive and reckless; dresses well, but not flashily; has

gold watch and chain, and may wear a large diamond stud in shirt bosom. Has served seven years in the Missouri penitentiary for larceny and jail breaking from Cooper county; committed November 19, 1883, discharged February 16th, 1889. Was married February 13, 1891, at Atchison, Kansas, to Maggie Graham, of St. Joseph, Missouri; the latter is a sister to "Burt" Sly's wife. Hedspeth was born in Missouri; mother, brother and sisters reside near Pisgah, Cooper county, Missouri.

Hedspeth is alleged to be a desperate thief, and has been engaged in numerous burglaries and train robberies in and about Omaha, Kansas City, Kansas, Kansas City, Missouri, St. Joseph, Missouri, and California. Was last heard from at San Francisco, California, December 30, 1891. The photograph hereto attached is a good one, and was taken in July, 1891.

L. R. Wilson, alias "Dink" Wilson.
Age 26 to 30; about 5 ft. 10, or more; weight 170 to 180; dark complexion, brown eyes; smooth face when last seen; face not full, broad chin; broad shoulders; stands erect; neatly built; lather by occupation.
The photograph of Wilson is said to be a good one. Wilson's home is at Omaha, Nebraska, where his parents and sisters reside. Wilson has relations in Salt Lake City, Utah.

Adelbert D. Sly, alias "Burt" Sly, alias A. S. Denton, alias Albert Silva, another of the robbers, is now in custody at St. Louis, having been arrested in Los Angeles, California, December 27th, 1891.

Mrs. Maggie Hedspeth, alias Florence A. Waterman (wife of Marion Hedspeth), is also under arrest at San Francisco, California, having been apprehended at Oakland, California, December 29th, 1891.

There are others in the Glendale robbery who are at present unknown; one of them is about 5 feet 5 or 6 inches; about 135 to 145 lbs.; complexion light; small, light, sandy mustache, thin face; age twenty-eight to thirty, or may be older.
Another, height 6 feet; weight 160 to 165 lbs.; eyes gray; face thin and peaked, like rest of his body. Had on, at time of robbery, light brown overcoat, brown or black derby hat; voice slow, deliberate, strong and full.
Hedspeth and Wilson, when last known of, were together. In case of arrest of either of above-named parties, look carefully for any associates that may be with them.
No official reward has been offered for the arrest of these men, but the Adams Express Company will deal fairly by any one who will give information leading to the identification and arrest of either one of the above described parties.
Communicate by mail, or telegraph, if necessary.

W. H. DAMSEL,
Manager Adams Express Company,
St. Louis, Missouri.

LAWRENCE HARRIGAN,
Chief of Police,
St. Louis, Missouri.

Or to PINKERTON'S NATIONAL DETECTIVE AGENCY,

Chicago, Ill., 193 Fifth Avenue.	St. Paul, Minn., Germania Bank Building.
Kansas City, Mo., 105 West 6th Street.	New York, 66 Exchange Place.
Denver, Col., 5 Opera House Block.	Boston, Mass., 42 Court Place.
Portland, Ore., 306 Marquam Block.	Philadelphia, 441 Chestnut Street.

Wanted: Marion Hedgepeth – *Library of Congress*

The arrest of the Carlisle police killers – *Illustrated Police News*

'Count' Lustig is arrested – *Library of Congress*

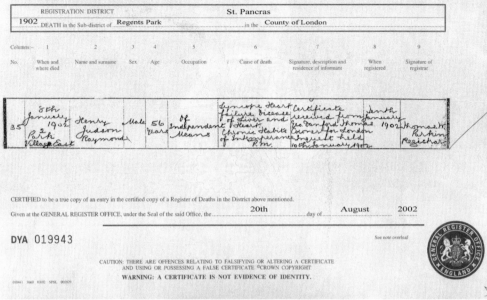

The End of Adam North – *Private Collection*

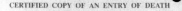

The bigamous marriage of 'Piano' Charley Wells – *Private Collection*

she organised a £30,000 jewel snatch in Brighton and, over the years, went to prison from courts in Brighton, Birmingham and Liverpool. On 13 February 1903, using the name of James Edward, Lockett was imprisoned in Italy for the theft of 8,500 lire in Milan.

Then in 1905 he took part in a skilled robbery in Birmingham. He and another man had targeted a Paris jewel dealer, Glattauer, who had been staying at the Grand Hotel. In a simple but well-worked trick, Lockett and his partner overtook Glattauer and his interpreter, Vyse, as they went into a chemist's shop-cum-post office in Colmore Row. There they played a small charade. One had bought liquorice and the other some pills; each complained and had their orders changed. Glattauer, tiring of holding his bag, sat down and put it next to him. The men then asked the way to New End Station and left the shop.

Glattauer picked up his bag to go to the counter and felt it to be much lighter. When he opened it there was nothing but paper. At first he thought his bag had been picked up accidentally and he and Vyse set out for New Street Station. It was only then that he realised what had happened. A reward of £400 was offered for the return of the jewels, said to be worth at least £10,000, but there was no sign of them. The men involved were said to be of middle height, clean-shaven and well-spoken. The preliminary work for the theft had almost certainly been carried out with the help of 'Blonde' Alice Smith who, immediately before the robbery, had been reconnoitring suitable targets for the snatch. Almost immediately afterwards she left for America and within a fortnight some of the jewels were found in the possession of a New York pawnbroker. As for Lockett, he was put on an identification parade but was not picked out. Released, he smartly followed her abroad.[2]

Jewellers, on the face of it, could be highly careless with their wares. In March 1906 a M. Edinow of Hatton Garden lost his wallet in Victoria Street Post Office, also curiously a chemist's shop, again in Birmingham. He had gone to post a parcel to his brother in Amsterdam, put his wallet containing £5,000 worth of diamonds on a ledge and walked out without picking it up. Then he met two

[2] *Birmingham Post*, 15, 18 March 1905.

men, had a drink with them and when he reached for his wallet to pay the bill remembered where he had left it. Unsurprisingly it had gone. He told the police he thought he had been followed by three men for some weeks.[3]

The month before, on 14 February 1906, under the name of William Preston, Lockett received 5 years at Liverpool Assizes for the attempted robbery of a man called Hutchinson, a travelling jewellery salesman. His partner, Arthur Norton, received 10 years. Along with two others picturesquely known as 'Red Bob' and 'Shirty Bob', they had trailed Hutchinson for some weeks and by scraping an acquaintance with him discovered he was going to Liverpool. They watched him leave his hotel and went to his room to search for the jewels, but unfortunately for them he returned to find Lockett standing holding the stones. Lockett was released on licence on 15 November 1909.[4]

Arthur Norton, also known as Arthur Anderson, was regarded as one of the – if not *the* – finest safe-crackers of the period. Always impeccably dressed and a resident in the best hotels, he would cultivate the bank clerks who frequented the hotels' bars and billiard rooms with a view to obtaining an impression of the keys they carried. On one occasion he persuaded a clerk to accompany him to a Turkish bath and after the man had taken off his clothes Anderson (as was his name on that occasion) went through his pockets for the keys. It was only a moment's work to make a wax impression.

Just before the Liverpool fiasco Anderson (this time known as Armstrong) had been released from another 10-year sentence after a raid on a branch of the North East Bank in Sunderland. On this occasion one of the team had ingratiated himself with the clerks at the bank and been allowed to warm his hands by their fire, which

---

[3] *The Umpire*, 18 March 1906.
[4] 'Shirty Bob or 'Bobs' is mentioned in the memoirs of Chicago May Sharpe. Apparently at one time he owned a fashionable club but when she knew him around the turn of the century he was an hotel thief working, among other places, the Langham Hotel. Although she often names criminals such as Dan McCarthy, who worked with Grizzard, and the receiver Ruby Michaels, she does not identify 'Shirty Bob'. *Morning Leader*, 15 February 1906; *The Umpire*, 18 February 1906.

put him in a position to see the set-up and location of the safes. It was something of a surprise that Anderson had actually gone to the Liverpool hotel, and there was speculation that he had unwisely regarded it as 'a soft job'.

The North East Bank produced a haul of £5,869 of which £3,554 was in gold. The robbery took place between 10 and 11 at night on 1 March 1897 and three respectably dressed men carrying Gladstone bags were seen outside the bank. A witness said he thought he could identify one of them. So far as they were concerned, the police were convinced it was a London job.

After the Sunderland bank robbery, the Durham police put a notice in the *Police Gazette* offering a £250 reward. Then came a most curious development. The Mayor of Sunderland revealed that two days before the robbery the manager of a grocery establishment owned by him had received a letter from a regular customer imploring him to advise the mayor that an attack was going to be made on a bank. It was thought that the writer of the letter was a relative by marriage of a well-known London burglar.

Armstrong was arrested for the Sunderland bank job in Soho after a brawl between the police and the local milieu.[5] Chief Inspector Jarvis had been looking for him for some time and found him as he and another man left a public house in Bateman Street. Armstrong and his companion were bundled into a four-wheeler cab by Jarvis and his officers, but then the crowd, said to be a hundred strong, tried to rescue them. With shouts of 'Chivvy them' they attacked the cab and after smashing the doors and windows managed to get Armstrong back onto the pavement. Then came extra police assistance in the form of the old Jack the Ripper hunter, the long-retired Abberline, who happened to be in the area. Armstrong's companion escaped – leaving behind, said the reports, 'his hat, a portion of his coat and waistcoat and a piece of his shirt and trousers'. As for the police, Abberline was said to be severely

---

[5] *The Times*, 4, 9 March, 9, 30 June 1897; *Sunderland Daily Echo*, 7 June 1897. John Hawkins, who helped Smith escape, was prosecuted for assaulting the police during the fracas. Despite calling an alibi he was convicted and sentenced to 3 months imprisonment. An appeal was dismissed and he was ordered to pay the costs. *Morning Leader*, 8 January 1898.

mauled and the other officers were reported to have been kicked and were bruised. The other man escaped into Oxford Street where he caught a bus. Police confidence that a second arrest was imminent was misplaced. The names of Armstrong's suspected companions at the bank and also photographs were released. The older man, originally described as being in his fifties, was the 61-year-old William Richardson, alias Richards. The younger was the very talented 'Long Almond', Frederick Smith, known confusingly also as Williams and Thompson, and previously heard of with 'Dutch' Alonzo in a Paris bank raid.[6] They were never caught. It was thought that Smith was the one who had escaped in the fight in Bateman Street.[7]

Armstrong appeared at the Assizes on 14 July, defended by Mr John Strachan Q.C. in a 'densely crowded court gay with the brilliant costumes of the ladies'. Objections were made to jurors from Sunderland and they were excluded. On the second day of the trial he was found guilty and sentenced to 10 years penal servitude. He had admitted a previous conviction at York in 1895.[8]

In her series in the *Empire News* 'Blonde' Alice Smith claims she was born at 108th St, Manhattan, on 19 February 1880. Her father John Smith was a native of Chicago who had married an Elsie Summers. She also claims that she was strictly brought up and went to elementary school at 102nd St. An early boyfriend was an artist whom she met at a magic lantern lecture. They eloped to England together on the SS *Minerva*, docking in Liverpool and then coming to London where they took rooms in Berners Street. It seems that her father sent a friend over to London to bring his daughter back, threatening charges of kidnapping, and she returned to New York, later followed by her boyfriend. They subsequently eloped again and this time married in the Anglo-Catholic Church in the Marylebone Road. Her daughter Bertha was born in 1900 and her son Roy in 1902. Her father died of grief shortly afterwards and

[6] 'Long' was a nickname applied to a number of criminals and may have derived from the fact that they had served a lengthy term of imprisonment.
[7] *Police Gazette*, 19 March, 25 June 1897.
[8] *Sunderland Daily Echo*, 15, 16 July 1897.

'besides being dreadfully short of money I found at the end of three years that my romance had faded'. Her husband had apparently begun a string of affairs, and she went to stay with the widow of a former steward on one of the American liners who lived in Kent. There she left her children while she tried to get a job as a shop assistant in London.

Alice is suitably vague as to how she actually came to meet Alice Jackson (with whom she says she was often confused) and her husband Cuban Jackson, a notorious confidence trickster who, under the name of Charles Bruce, hanged himself in the cells at Bow Street Police Court in 1925 or early 1926. She maintains she was penniless when they met her in Regent Street, took her home and after a week revealed how they made their money, inviting her to join them.

Jackson dressed her in his wife's finery and then took her to a jewellers at Marble Arch and showed her how the 'hoist' was worked. First he asked to look at some rings and then, diverting the shop-keeper's attention by asking for a cigarette case in the window, substituted some of his own in the ring tray. He then purchased the cigarette case and said he would be back for the rings another day. The same trick was worked over the next few hours in a number of shops before he suggested she try her hand in Briggs in the Holloway Road. But she panicked and dropped the fake rings, whereupon Jackson fled from the shop and she was taken to Dalston Lane police station. While in the cells she received a visit from a solicitor's clerk who told her that she could expect 6 months' impris-onment even as a first offender, and that she would be looked after during her stay inside. He was right on both counts. The first thing she did on her release was not to see her children but to go looking for Cuban Jackson. Unfortunately he had been arrested in Paris along with Ed Rice and sent to the Santé. However, there were others to advise her and she took up shoplifting and collected a further 12 months, but after that she was up and running in the big leagues.[9]

---

[9] For every gang of thieves from the Continent and America working in England, so there was an English one working abroad. In March 1903 Adair Johns, described as

In September 1909 Charles Gurron, then aged 44, along with Charles Knight, John and George Taylor (who were not related) and William Russell, appeared at the Old Bailey charged with entering Mappin & Webb, the jewellers in Poultry and Queen Victoria Street, and stealing £43,583. They had obtained keys and gone in when the watchman went for his dinner; on his return he was coshed. Once they were found guilty a string of police officers from across the country came to give evidence about their previous behaviour. Gurron, who had convictions dating back to 1900, was said to be the leader of this very dangerous gang of thieves based in the Elephant and Castle. Russell was on licence from Liverpool at the time and George Taylor had already racked up three sentences of 7 years penal servitude and one of 10 years from which he had been released on licence in the June. John Taylor was said to be a talented and notorious pickpocket.

Earlier that year a gang of American thieves had visited London and linked up with Gurron in a successful attempt to steal a motor trophy in the West End. Gurron and Russell were two of the men actually on the job, but they had escaped. William Henry and Albert Martin were arrested. A police officer saw three men go into the Shaftesbury Avenue entrance of the Rover Company and watched as the box containing the £30 cup was taken.[10]

Now, for the Mappin & Webb robbery, on 12 September the

---

an old man with a flowing white beard, a string of convictions in England and France and a member of a party of English thieves and swindlers, picked up 8 years. His speciality was thefts from railway carriages, and this time he was caught on the Marseilles-to-Nice Express.

In the following May 1903 Egan Patrick (in his absence) and James Robinson each netted 5 years following a theft in the Avenue de la Gare in Nice. It was a standard scam. Robinson went into a jewellers and asked to see a tiepin in the window. While he was pointing out the piece, Patrick cleared 1,600 francs from the till. *Illustrated Police News*, 18 March, 27 May 1903.

[10] *The Times, Morning Leader* 19, 26 May; 10 June 1909; *Illustrated Police News*, 14 May 1909. Martin, also known as 'Kid' Miller, was a gentleman thief and cracksman who stole £4 million from the Pacific Express Co. in New Orleans under the name of George Evans. He received a long sentence and bargained his release by agreeing to disclose where he had buried the money. His last trick was when he tapped a man on the shoulder as he was paying money into a bank in Newington Butts. When the man turned, he stole the money. Caught while watching the Boat Race in 1918, he received 5 years and prophetically said on hearing his sentence, 'This will kill me.' He died in 1922.

Taylors received 10 years each, as did Russell. Gurron went down for 8, while Knight was acquitted. Naturally, the Recorder of London had a few words to say: 'I am quite aware that in this age punishments are generally less than they used to be but not in the case of persons of your class.'

A regular face who was missing from the dock that day was 'Blonde' Alice Smith. Recruited as a message-taker and passer-in of tools, she was to stroll past the jewellers and when a piece of paper was pushed under the gate she would know the men were ready to come out with the jewellery. The idea was that she should then walk away with it. In fact her son was seriously ill and perhaps she was not concentrating as hard as the job required. When she saw a young man by a motor-cycle she became convinced that he was a police officer and she fled. In fact, the person who gave the alert was a cabman and after the trial everyone, except the Taylors and friends, was pleased to hear it announced that he was to be presented with a new horse and cab.[11]

A month after Gurron was sentenced, Aitchison Brothers, jewellers on Ludgate Hill, were relieved of £3,000 when on 11 October their premises were burgled. This was clearly a well-thought-out job because the owner discovered that his pocket had been picked and a key taken; he always kept it in the right-hand pocket of his overcoat. It had been the second key to disappear that year, and the locks had been changed in case the first was to have been put to bad use.

Although there was often no evidence against him, once the indomitable Lockett had been released on licence from his Liverpool sentence he was suspected of organising and sometimes executing a series of daring and successful burglaries throughout London and the rest of the country. The Glasgow Post Office had been robbed, as had the one in Goswell Road on 9 December 1909. There had been a dummy run the fortnight before when a hand-cart left behind the post office was taken away by the police. Then on 8 December a second hand-cart was left at the back door, and this time postal workers

[11] *Morning Leader*, 13 September 1909; *Thomson's Weekly News*, 10 April 1926.

propped it up against the wall. The safe was loaded on to it and taken to Rosebery Avenue, where seven men were arrested by the police as they took turns to try and break it open. The police had identified the house by freshly chipped stone at the doorway where the safe had been manhandled into the premises. Seven men were arrested.

Rather more successful was a major jewel robbery at Davidson's in Southampton Row on 25 February the previous year, when the thieves broke in through the next-door basement and cleared £4,000 worth of chains, rings and watches.

Another robbery came on 21 May 1913 when two night porters at the Berkeley Hotel in Piccadilly were attacked and the safe raided. Yet another little escapade in which Lockett's name was in the frame was when a man named Hopton was attacked by two men in broad daylight outside his home in Colvestone Crescent, Kingsland Road, and robbed of £3,000 worth of jewellery. A substantial but unspecified reward was offered. He was told to go to a spot near Soho Square where the jewels would be left, but either this was a hoax or someone else got there first because the police found nothing. Not every robbery in Britain can be laid at Lockett's door, but the police files suggest he had a hand in more than his fair share.

Thomas Morrell, regarded as one of the most expert and dangerous burglars in London, received 4 years on 19 February 1908. He always carried a firearm and boasted of being prepared to use it. 'Dead men tell no tales' was a favourite maxim.[12]

Given that Lockett was in custody over the Liverpool matter at the time, one which was certainly not his was the daring robbery from the newly opened London and County Bank at the corner of St James's and Jermyn Street on 20 May 1906. Using the tried and loved technique of George Leonidas Leslie, the thieves had tunnelled into the bank over the weekend and taken £1,000 from the tills.[13]

---

[12] *Morning Leader*, 20 February 1908. Another less dangerous but highly talented jewel thief of the period was George Baldwin, known as American Frank. In January 1897 he was arrested as he got off the Glasgow train and was charged with possessing housebreaking implements. Since this was not at night the charge was dismissed. He finally went to prison in February 1905 when he and George Stevenson were found trying to break into a jewellers in the Finchley Road. He received 15 months with hard labour. *Illustrated Police News*, 4 March 1905.

[13] *Morning Leader*, 21 May 1906; *The Times*, 28 August 1911.

After his release Lockett was under constant observation by the police and in 1910 he was reported to have an interest in the EIT Motor Works motor-car business in Finchley and what was rather charmingly called a 'Cinematograph Palace' in Golders Green, purchased with the proceeds from the robberies.

Where did all the jewellery go? The answer is that most of it went to Joseph 'Cammi' Grizzard who from the turn of the century and throughout the first decade of the 1900s was the great receiver of stolen goods and 'putter-up' of burglaries throughout London. More or less every major jewel theft could be laid at his door or that of his subordinates, who would bring the jewellery to him in Hatton Garden or to his home in the East End to fence for them.[14]

Born in 1867, by the early 1900s he was described as being of middle height and somewhat portly build, favouring a blond moustache and diamond rings on his fingers. Sir Richard Muir K.C., who would later prosecute him, thought . . .

> [he] possessed rather a fine face with nothing in it to tell the world of the evil, intriguing brain that had been responsible for some of the most amazing coups in the whole history of crime.[15]

Christmas Humphreys had a rather different view:

> . . . his impudence and swaggering self-assurance served to create a personality which dominated the smaller fry who hung about the 'Garden' and turned them when required into willing if not able tools.
>
> Like so many criminals he was a great man with a twist in his character which made him prefer to go crooked where he might go straight.[16]

Grizzard, who had a brother Abe working less exaltedly as a pimp,

---

[14] There were, of course, other receivers. George Powell who ran The Old Curiosity Shop in Holborn had been under police observation for 10 years before James Titlow, a burglar serving 18 months, gave him up. The proceeds of 12 recent burglaries were found in the shop and Powell, then aged 62, received 3 years penal servitude. *Illustrated Police News*, 30 July 1909.

[15] S.T. Felstead and Lady Muir, *Sir Richard Muir*, p. 130.

[16] Christmas Humphreys, *The Great Pearl Robbery of 1913*, p. 8.

was first convicted at Thames Police Court on 1 May 1880 and received 14 days for larceny. He did not then appear before the courts for some twenty years until he was charged with a heavy burglary including 78 gold watches, 24 gold chains and 70 diamond, pearl and sapphire rings at a jewellers in Richmond, Surrey, in which he was said to have been involved with David Jacobs, a cutter known as 'Sticks'. Despite an eyewitness who claimed to have seen him outside the shop at 5 a.m. on the night of 19 November 1902, backed up by a woman who said she had been sold a bracelet from the stolen jewellery by Grizzard, and a remark that he thought a piece of iron exhibited in court must have been his jemmy, he was acquitted.[17]

His greatest coup came six years later when he masterminded the jewel robbery at the Café Monico in Regent Street which led to the appearance of John Higgins and the former lightweight jockey Harry Grimshaw at London Sessions.

It is not clear where 'Blonde' Alice Smith met Lockett and through him Grizzard, on whose behalf she took part in the Café Monico robbery. On 20 June 1909 a French dealer, Frederick Goldschmidt, left Paris and travelled to London bringing jewellery with him and staying at De Keyser's Hotel. Grizzard, who maintained connections in Paris who had informed him of the vulnerability of certain dealers, had Goldschmidt watched by a number of people including Smith. Indeed Goldschmidt seems to have been doubly unfortunate because another gang which included the American Eddie Guerin, then still almost at the top of his form, was also seen at the hotel watching him. It was really only a question of who got to him first, and past the post was Grimshaw.

It became clear that the only time Goldschmidt ever put his case down in public was when he washed his hands, and on 9 July he was followed to the Café Monico. When he went to the lavatory he put his bag beside him and as he reached out for the soap, he was pushed off balance and the bag was snatched by Grimshaw. As Goldschmidt chased after it his passage was blocked by Higgins as the stallman. The jewels, worth some £60,000, were never found.

[17] *The Times*, 20 January 1903.

Had the pair struck the previous day, the haul would have been nearer £160,000.

Even more than today, it was apparent that only a handful of people had the ability to organise such a theft and dispose of the goods. Within a matter of hours the police obtained a search warrant for Grizzard's home at 73 Parkholme Road, Dalston, and found him at dinner with his guests, three potential buyers. Grizzard and his company sat at the dinner table while the police searched the house, but nothing was found. After they had gone Grizzard drank his now cold pea-soup and at the bottom of the bowl was a diamond necklace which was then cleaned and sold.

Alice Smith had been approached by Grizzard with instructions to watch the target. Harry Grimshaw maintained that when it was being decided who would do the snatch and who would do the stall Smith, whom he referred to as Diamond Dolly, shuffled the cards. The lowest card holder was to be the snatcher and he, Grimshaw, had drawn the two of spades. This just seems like a good story because given his size he would be the ideal person to do the snatch and one of the least likely to be an effective stall.

For the getaway she had a car waiting outside and Grizzard paid £21,000 for the pearls. After the robbery Grimshaw went down to Falmouth with Smith to keep out of the way. The effort was unsuccessful and while he was out walking she put a towel outside the bedroom window to try to signal to him that the police were in the hotel. It did him little good.

Higgins, defended by the talented and fashionable but dishonest solicitor Arthur Newton, ran an alibi defence that he had been with a police officer in the Old Bell public house in Holborn.[18] The officer accepted he had been with Higgins, but not at the crucial time. It was then announced that he was also going to call a character witness, a Mr Goldsmith. The cross-examination by Sir Richard Muir soon put a stop to this idea:

---

[18] Arthur Newton was one of the most sought-after London solicitors in the period 1890 to 1912, acting in the Oscar Wilde trial as well as in the Crippen and McDougal murder cases. He was given 6 months for conspiracy to pervert the course of justice in the Cleveland Brothel scandal and received 3 years in 1913 for a land fraud. After his release he established a dubious marriage agency and died in 1930. For a full account of his career see James Morton, *Gangland, The Lawyers.*

Q: What other names do you know him by?
A: Cammy, a nickname.
Q: Did you know that he has been tried at the Old Bailey for receiving as recently as 1903?
(Silence.)
Q: And that he has been arrested for the Monico robbery?

Higgins received 15 months and Grimshaw 3 years penal servitude to be followed by 5 years preventive detention. It was thought that altogether six men were involved in the snatch.[19]

Harry Grimshaw, alias Herbert White, Hartnell, Cracknall and Robert Jones, was born in Bolton in 1880. His father was a well-known jockey and his uncle Frederick won the Derby on the French horse, Gladiateur, who won the triple crown of the 2,000 Guineas, the Derby and the St Leger. Grimshaw's father, who was riding within Germany, took his son with him at an early age. In the 1890s Harry Grimshaw had himself been a successful jockey who could go to the scales at a pound or two over six stone, and in 1895 he won the valuable Manchester November and Liverpool Cup handicaps. Later he rode in Austria and Germany before returning to England, relinquishing his licence in 1904 and working as a tic-tac man. He would admit to nearly forty appearances before the stewards for pulling horses and rough riding.

In his own series of articles, he maintains it was he who set up the Monico robbery but Cammi Grizzard gave him £2,000 expenses. It is possible to put two and two together. He says Diamond Dolly, an American, had a car waiting for him, and from her account of the affair Diamond Dolly is clearly Alice Smith. Over the years Grimshaw reckoned he had made approximately £30,000 in the saddle and £50,000 from Grizzard.[20]

He first appeared in court two years after his retirement from

---

[19] Harry Grimshaw, 'A Famous Jockey's Downfall' in *Thomson's Weekly News*, 12 September 1925.
[20] Frederick Grimshaw was so shortsighted that he would lag behind the field by up to several hundred yards, relying on spectators to tell him what was happening in front of him. When Gladiateur won the Ascot Gold Cup by 40 lengths in 1866, he was at one time 300 yards behind the pacemaker. There is a statue of the horse, which became known as the Avenger of Waterloo, in the paddock at Longchamps.

the saddle when he was bound over at Clerkenwell on 20 October 1906 over the theft of £200 from a hairdressers, but the same year he received 3 months for a theft in Shaftesbury Avenue. From then it was a step up in class and soon he was the known associate of jewel thieves working on the Continent. October 1907 saw him collect 21 months at North London Quarter Sessions for the theft of a ring, and he followed this up with 3 years for a handbag snatch.

He was almost certainly the man who stole the Ascot Gold Cup in 1908, another escapade in which he worked with 'Blonde' Alice Smith. After his release from prison following the Monico sentence, Grimshaw received a total of 8 years following a conviction for theft at Marlborough Street Police Court. He was working as late as 1922 when, under the name Robert Jones, he was convicted of a theft from a hotel in Middlesbrough and received 21 months with hard labour.

It was after the Monico robbery that Grizzard's own fortunes began to decline. On 29 December 1909 he appeared at Greenwich Police Court along with his wife Sarah. They were both charged with receiving stolen jewellery from a burglary in Brighton and harbouring Samuel Barnett who had failed to appear at North London Sessions some 14 months previously. This time, unusually, the police did find a criminal to give evidence against him. Arthur Denville Sassoon Collinson, then doing 5 years on the Moor, said that during the six months prior to his current unhappy experience he had worked as a burglar for both men.

Barnett, wanted for burglaries around the South of England, had been given bail but fled abroad in 1907 after Grizzard stood surety for him in the sum of £100. On his return he was found living at Grizzard's house. He had, said Grizzard, only been there two days, and the generous man could not bring himself to evict the fugitive. On 8 March 1910 at the Old Bailey Grizzard received 5 months in the second division for feloniously harbouring him. Sarah Grizzard was discharged.

Grizzard was also behind the theft of jewellery from Vaughan Morgan, son of Sir Walter Vaughan Morgan, the City Alderman. Frank Ellis was his butler from 1904 until 1911, when he left to set up as a bookmaker. Before leaving he was asked to find another footman and he obtained a man called Robinson through an agency. In the three weeks before Ellis handed over, Robinson began betting with him. Ellis also knew William Bangham, one of Grizzard's men and a known jewel thief. By November 1911 Ellis's business was not going well and he was raided and heavily fined as an illegal bookmaker. He then persuaded Robinson to let him into his former master's house. After a successful trial run when nothing was taken, the second raid was successful, but the police dismissed the idea that there had been a break-in. So far as they were concerned it was an inside job. Robinson was arrested and discharged after naming Ellis. In turn he remained silent on the details of the raid but began crying in the witness box. 'Pluck up, Ellis, don't give way,' said his barrister. He received 21 months penal servitude. No amount of persuasion would make Ellis give up Grizzard.[21]

One reason for the loyalty was that Grizzard would help friends who came to grief with the police, and also their wives and children while they were away. He also had an unswerving loyalty to those with whom he worked. Unlike many a receiver, his word was thought to be his bond. He paid what he promised.[22]

Then in 1913 came Grizzard's greatest attempted coup and most abject failure – the theft of a string of 61 pearls, one of the finest collections then assembled, with an insurance value of £130,000. The parcel of pearls was sent from Paris to London, but the jewels had disappeared by the time it arrived. After a long investigation down went Grizzard and the faithful Lockett who seems to have been recruited only to deal with collecting the reward but remained stoic to the end. Two others, Leisir Gutwirth and Simon Silverman, were convicted with them.

Prosecuted by Sir Richard Muir, Lockett and Grizzard received 7 years penal servitude and Silverman 5 years at their trial in November 1913. Silverman was to be deported after his sentence. Gutwirth was sentenced to 18 months with hard labour. Despite

[21] *Empire News*, 21 January 1912.
[22] Henry Thomas, 'Harry the Valet', maintains Grizzard cheated him as a result of which he stole the receiver's jewels. See Chapter 14.

the fact that he had been in England for 25 years and was a married man, he too was recommended for deportation.

> *Mr Justice Lawrence:* That may be, but he is an alien and we do not want such aliens here.

Their appeals were dismissed in December. Throughout Lockett had contested the case only on the technical point that the theft had occurred in France and therefore the British courts could not try the case. After the arrests of the four principals the police had gone looking for 82-year-old Daniel McCarthy, a long-time fully paid-up member of continental teams specialising in jewel thefts. He was charged with them after admitting that he had changed some of the francs provided as part of the reward, but the technicalities of proving anything more against him were too great and he was discharged.[23]

A police report prepared after Grizzard's arrest establishes his high place in the pantheon of criminals of the time:

> He is a diamond merchant by trade, but has no established business premises. He does undoubtedly do a little business, but the greater portion of his time is taken up by organising crimes, and buying and disposing of stolen property. Much has been heard of him during the past fifteen years as having been connected with many serious crimes. A large number of statements made by prisoners are in our possession showing that they have disposed of property to him, but unfortunately we have been unable to prosecute him for a lack of corroborative evidence.

---

[23] Although McCarthy's name appears in the memoirs of a number of criminals of the time, little is known of him. However, while he was in custody awaiting trial over the Pearl Robbery, Scotland Yard received a letter from a Mrs A. Smith asking whether he was the father of a Michael McCarthy. The writer was Michael McCarthy's daughter who thought this might be the Daniel who had, at one time, emigrated to Australia. Scotland Yard could not assist. PRO MEPO 2 236B.

THE ENEMIES

19

The Forces of Good – Mostly

Arrayed against the train and bank robbers, the bank sneak-thieves, the forgers and confidence tricksters and often each other were the police and the private detective agencies.

First the police. The Metropolitan Police was founded by Sir Robert Peel in 1829, a mixture of jacks of all trades including many ex-soldiers but, resolutely, it had been decided that none should be from the commissioned ranks. The New York Police Department followed some 15 years later.[1] There had been an abortive effort to establish a police force in the city – as opposed to the system of night watchmen – in 1836, but it was thought that while there might be need for a police force in the future the present system was quite adequate. It was not, and the catalyst for change was the death of 21-year-old Mary Rogers in 1841, a stick held enthusiastically by the press and used to beat the authorities.

Mary Rogers was found dead floating in the Hudson River off the shores of Hoboken, New Jersey, in 1841. She had been missing for three days after leaving her mother's boarding house to visit an aunt in Greenwich Village. It appeared she had been raped. Like

[1] For a view of the foundation and early years of the NYPD see James Larner and Thomas Reppetto, *NYPD*.

the prostitute Helen Jewett who had been murdered a few years earlier, she was an exceptionally good-looking girl and had been employed by John Anderson to work behind the counter of his fashionable tobacco shop on Nassau Street.

Tobacco shops in New York were by no means the corner tobacconists of the England of 50 years ago. Particularly in the second half of the nineteenth century, they doubled as private male social clubs and effectively brothels. In his entertaining account of prostitution in New York, Timothy J. Gilfoyle recounts two anecdotes. The first is of the German immigrant who wanted simply to buy a cigar on the Lower East Side and was routinely asked by the proprietor if he wanted 'to be alone with a nice girl, it would cost only one dollar'. The second is of a West Third Street cigar store, 'the front portion of the store was divided from the back by a curtain from behind which emerge[d] half naked women whenever a customer enter[ed]'.[2]

James Gordon Bennett, who founded the *New York Herald*, 'the greatest organ of social life', in 1835, had already made a great deal of capital out of the Jewett case and now he played the Rogers case as one of official incompetence and apathy. At the time inquiries into mysterious deaths were undertaken by police court justices, a very rough approximation of the French examining magistrates. The Rogers case was in the hands of Robert Taylor and he was convinced that the answer lay in her sex life. The lace round her neck seemed to have been tied in a knot, which suggested a seaman, and one man William Kiekuck was held for several days before he was able to produce an alibi. His place was taken by Joseph Morse who, Bennett's reporters had discovered, was a frequenter of the cigar shop. He had left his home on the day Rogers disappeared and was found in Boylston, Massachusetts, living under an assumed name. He also was fortunate. The *Herald* had already produced a banner headline ARREST OF THE SUSPECTED MURDERER, and Morse admitted he had spent the night with a girl named Mary whom he believed to be Mary Rogers. That was why he had run off. Then

---

[2] Timothy J. Gilfoyle, *City of Eros*. His quotations are from Mayors' Papers, New York City Municipal Archives and Records Center, 22 August 1888, 9 March 1889.

his saviour appeared in the form of Mary Haviland, who said she was in fact the girl he had been with.

After that the *Herald* came up with all sorts of stories – she had been killed by a group of black men, by butchers' boys, she had been abducted in a boat – but there were no further arrests. Bennett was up in arms. New York City would be:

> disgraced in the eyes of the Christian and civilized world (which, even then were not apparently synonymous) unless one great big, one strong moral movement be made to reform and rein-vigorate the administration of criminal justice . . . Who will make the first move in this truly great moral reform?

There are no prizes for a correct answer.

The most likely explanation of Rogers' death is that she died as a result of what was euphemistically called 'a premature delivery'. Certainly that was the statement of a Mrs Loss, the keeper of Nick Moore's house in Hoboken, when she was dying in the autumn of 1842. It would account for the apparent violation.[3]

The *status quo* was not helped in November 1842 with the escape of John Colt from the death cell of the Tombs and the subsequent lacklustre investigation. Now the arrival of a more regular police force was only a matter of time and in 1844 the night watch and marshals were abolished and a full-time day and night police force of 800 men was created. Bennett was ecstatic.

His ecstasy did not last long, however. The Municipal Police were formed in 1853 and four years later during the second term of Mayor Fernando Wood they were regarded as so corrupt that a new force, the Metropolitans, was created. Unsurprisingly the Municipals

---

[3] Rogers lives on in 'The Mystery of Marie Roget' by Edgar Allan Poe who knew her socially if not biblically. The feisty Helen Jewett was regarded as the most desirable prostitute in New York in the 1830s. One of her admirers was the man-about-town Richard P. Robinson who, on 10 April 1836, axed her to death in Mrs Rosina Townsend's brothel where she was working. He was seen by a number of the workers and indeed made no effort to hide his identity. There was a wave of public feeling in his favour. Men wore caps and cloaks in his style and a popular chant was that 'No man should hang for the murder of a whore.' At the trial witnesses retracted their evidence and he provided a lame alibi. Robinson was acquitted in short order and disappeared from the city immediately afterwards. It was thought he became an outlaw on the Mississippi River.

were upset; some remained loyal to their uniform and in 1857 it was a question of 'criminals stood and watched' as a pitched battle between Metropolitans and Municipals was fought outside City Hall, in which 52 officers were injured. One Metropolitan was so badly injured that he was invalided for life. The National Guard was called in and surrounded Mayor Wood in his office.

Fighting between the forces continued throughout the summer, with an arrest by the Metropolitans countermanded by the Municipals and vice versa. Now gangs of thieves were robbing shops and stage-coaches with impunity. The final straw seems to have been a two-day pitched battle between the Dead Rabbits and the Bowery Boys which went unchecked. Following a decision by the Supreme Court, the Municipals were abolished by the Mayor. Several officers from both corps filed suits against Wood and each received an award of $250. It was left to the City to pay them.

It was Thomas Byrnes who changed policing in New York, not always for the better. At the age of six he had arrived with his parents from Ireland and leaving school early had been apprenticed as a gas-fitter before joining a volunteer fire company. In the Civil War he fought for the Unionists at the losing First Battle of Bull Run. He was demobilised in 1863, after which he joined the Metropolitan Police.

His first duty was at Mercer Street and for 5 years he was a patrolman in the Fifteenth Precinct around Greenwich Village. He progressed to roundsman, sergeant and, on 1 July 1870, Captain. He was promoted after he solved the Manhattan Savings robbery in September 1878.[4] He had already broken the Van Tine silk burglary case and captured Paul Law, the son of an ex-Governor of Maryland, who had shot four people in New York City. Now his star was high in the sky.

Police forces generally had been having a bad time, with the first kidnapping for ransom in America of the 4-year-old Charles Brewster ('Little Charley') Ross, snatched on 1 July 1874 from his

---

[4] See Ch. 19.

Philadelphia home. His father received a ransom note demanding $20,000 and warning him not to contact the police, but he immediately did so.

Over the next few months there were protracted negotiations, with three separate meetings set up, all of which were ignored by the kidnappers who, probably and correctly, suspected they were traps.

The kidnappers were almost certainly William Mosher and Joey Douglass, both clients of Marm Mandelbaum and of the law firm of Howe & Hummel, along with a former policeman William Westervelt. The police identified the handwriting of Mosher on the ransom notes, but on the night of 13 December 1874 both he and Douglass were killed in a burglary at the home of Judge Van Brunt in Bay Ridge, Brooklyn. Before dying Douglass admitted that both of them had taken part in the kidnapping, but he did not reveal the whereabouts of the child. With a fine command of grammar he is alleged to have said, 'It's no use lying now. Mosher and I stole Charley Ross from Germantown.'[5]

Westervelt – who had been seen loitering near the child's home and asking questions about the financial status of the boy's father – received 7 years after being found guilty of charges relating to the abduction. Over the years Mrs Mosher was besieged by what were described as amateur detectives, one of whom took her to the theatre in the hope that she would let something slip. Finally she gave an interview:

> Why shouldn't he be alive? I said that if the boy was alive and well – as I have every reason to believe – six weeks after the abduction, with all the hue and cry after him, the person who had him then could just as well keep him out of sight for six years.[6]

Charley Ross's father never gave up the hunt for his son. Now Mrs Mosher's brother was arrested, and she appealed to Ross to

[5] Herbert Asbury, *Gangs of New York*.
[6] *National Police Gazette*, 19 April 1879.

allow him to be released. Ross's parents spent the next twenty years tracking down leads, but were never able to discover to their satisfaction what exactly had happened to their son. It was the generally held Underworld opinion that Westervelt, left in charge of the child, had panicked and drowned the boy in the East River.[7]

The Detective Bureau in New York was then described as a force of broken-down policemen. It also had been going through a bad period with the kidnapping of a body, that of Alexander T. Stewart, which also remained a mystery. The body of Stewart, who had made his money from department stores, had been snatched from its grave in the churchyard of St Mark's on the Bowery in November 1878. The police agreed that an intermediary in the form of another shady lawyer, General Patrick H. Jones, should assist. Initially he tried to persuade the widow to pay the exorbitant sum of $250,000 for the remains of her husband. Matters dragged on for two years before he extracted $20,000. The body was re-buried in an alarmed vault in Garden City, Long Island.[8]

---

[7] One of the most curious of suspected kidnapping cases in England was handled rather better by the police. On 24 October 1907 Barbara Lapouline, the daughter of the head of the Russian Secret Service, went with her sister Marie and their governess to see *The Gay Gordons* at the Aldwych Theatre. As they left she vanished and, it seems, was held in Guildford Street almost around the corner from her home in Woburn Place. During the week a note was received at her lodgings. She clearly wrote excellent English:

> When you receive this letter, I shall be dead. I was seized and kidnapped outside the theatre. I do not know by whom, or why. I am now in a cellar, suffering and wounded. I am giving my brooch to a little girl so that she may post this letter to you. 'I am going to poison myself or I shall go mad. I shall be dead soon. B.L.

On 31 October her father arrived in London and 'remained with Chief Superintendent Froest for some time'. At 3 p.m. he telephoned Froest to say his daughter had returned home. It was never made clear whether the matter was political or Barbara had been covering a frolic of her own. *Illustrated Police News*, 23 January 1907. Two years later her father was arrested and charged in Russia with high treason.

[8] For an account of the Stewart case see George W. Walling, *Recollections of a New York Chief of Police*. Over the next 30 years there were relatively few commercial kidnappings in America. On 18 December 1900 Edward A. Cudahy jnr of Omaha, Nebraska, was kidnapped by two men one of whom, Pat Crow, fought in the Boer War before returning to America and handing over his share of the $25,000 ransom. He was triumphantly acquitted. In March 1909 a thoroughly botched effort was made by Helen and James Bogle who kidnapped Willie Whitlaw in Sharon, Ohio. The ransom of $10,000 was paid and the lawyer's 8-year-old son released. The pair was found in a Cleveland bar drinking the profits.

Almost immediately after his promotion to headquarters Byrnes transferred 21 out of the 28 detectives back to uniform and brought in replacements. By the time Byrnes was writing *Professional Criminals* in 1884 the Bureau had its own headquarters at 300 Mulberry Street and comprised two regular sergeants, 40 detective-sergeants and 14 patrolmen who were on assignment. The Detective Division had been transformed, with the press calling the members, each of whom earned $1,600 a year, 'the immortals' and their chief 'the great detective'. There was also the opportunity to earn extra money acting as guides to visiting English aristocracy and others who wished to tour the dives in safety.

To the delight of the bankers, on the day of his appointment Byrnes opened an office at 17 Wall Street. Offices were then provided in the Exchange and a telephone line was established from there to the finance houses in the district. Now detectives could be on the spot within five minutes.

It was Byrnes who created a notional line at Fulton Street, enforced by Detectives George Radford and John J. Dunn, 'Wall Street Johnny', promising immediate arrest of any known crook found below it without specific permission. As a result the robberies ceased and grateful businessmen such as Jay Gould, whose stolen wallet Byrnes had once restored, would pass on tips for the stock markets which, Byrnes said, made his fortune. He was particularly adroit in retrieving watches and pocketbooks stolen from the famous or influential and making the most of the resulting favourable publicity. When in the 1890s his salary was $5,000 a year and he had been appointed Chief Inspector his wealth was estimated to be some $350,000, the equivalent of $6–8 million in today's money.

Perhaps his greatest claims are that he forced detectives to keep notebooks of their movements and of where and in what circumstances they had seen a criminal. The benefit was never more clearly shown than when a prominent resident of Tarrytown had a storekeeper arrested as a burglar after his wife saw him in her room. Byrnes found that a criminal, Red Jack, had been seen by a detective looking exceptionally seedy when going north on a New York City train, and had returned a week later to the Bowery looking a swell. Brought in, he confessed. He was the almost exact double of the shopkeeper.

Byrnes also initiated the practice of photographing suspects as a means of identification. Before the Civil War busts of the top criminals had been the means of identification, but Byrnes' photographic record numbered 7,000. Fifty copies were made of each photograph and, with the history of the person on the back, were circulated.[9] Byrnes is described as:

> a robust broad-shouldered man, just under six feet, with a great jaw, a powerful neck and piercing eyes. He was erect in bearing, immaculate in appearance, meditative in manner; he puffed constantly on a cigar.[10]

The novelist Julian Hawthorne described him as '. . . a handsome man, large and powerful in every sense of the word'.

Not everyone was quite so uncritical. As a young journalist Lincoln Steffens was sent to police headquarters where Byrnes' favourite sergeant was called Mangin. Also present at the interview was the tall, handsome officer Alexander 'Clubber' Williams. Steffens recalls that Byrnes told him:

> I am going to put you on the same basis here as the old reporters who have been with us for years, most of them, and in return I ask you in all fairness, not to print the stuff you get from enemies of the police without submitting it to me for correction – or at any rate, comment.

Steffens was not overly impressed:

> I could see through this doughty chief of police; he was not the awe-inspiring figure I had imagined. For Tom Byrnes was a famous police chief; few people ever saw him; he was only a

[9] The police had no authority to take a picture of a man and place it in the Rogues' Gallery before his conviction. To this end the courts were strict and when Capt. Kuhne defied Justice Burr and 'mugged' Banker Jenkins who was still on remand, he received 30 days in Raymond Street jail and was fined $500.
[10] Arthur M. Schlesinger jnr, 'The Business of Crime' introductory article in Byrnes, T., *Criminals of America*.

name, but there were stories told about him, of his cunning as a detective, as a master of men, as a manhandler of criminals, and as a retriever of stolen properties. Stories that filled the upper world with respect and the lower with terror. He struck me as simple – no complications at all – a man who would buy you or beat you, as you might choose but get you he would.[11]

Byrnes, very sensibly, also ordered that damaged prisoners should be brought in from the rear of the building.

It was the police who suffered the backlash from the Reverend Charles Parkhurst's 1892 revelations. Prostitution was under their almost total control. It was a few weeks after Parkhurst began his campaign to reform New York's flourishing vice trade that Byrnes was appointed Superintendent, and he seems to have made some effort to have his officers close the saloons but he was unsuccessful.

> Gentlemen, did I not command you last Monday on this very spot in this same office to enforce to the letter of the last regulation the saloons in this city. Well, and what I want to know now is did youse (sic) do it?'[12]

Although his appointment was initially welcomed by the reformers, they soon turned against him as he fought back on behalf of the force. It was a classic example of a beleaguered police force regrouping against its perceived tormentors. Parkhurst took the view that if Byrnes did *not* know what was going on, then he should have done. If he *did* know, then some of his tactics were indefensible. Two years later in 1894 the State legislature appointed a committee under Senator Clarence Lexow to investigate the police department. He was assisted by John W. Goff – who gained the reputation of being the cruellest and most sadistic judge in New York – and the highly talented lawyer William Travers Jerome.[13]

---

[11] Lincoln Steffens, *Autobiography*, pp. 200–201.
[12] Lincoln Steffens quoted in Arthur M. Schlesinger jnr, 'The Business of Crime' in *Professional Criminals of America*, p. XXIII.
[13] Jerome's cousin was the wife of Lord Randolph Churchill and the mother of Winston.

And with it came a string of horror stories of institutionalised graft between police who took regular payments from both prostitutes and pickpockets and police commissioners who promoted officers for payment. One madam explained that she had paid the sum of $30,000 to the police.

Appearing before the Committee William S. Devery, a police captain, produced a masterly display of disinformation, turning questions aside with the ingenuous comment, 'touchin' on and appertainin' to that matter, I disremember'. Known as 'Big Bill', he was born in New York City in about 1855 and at first worked as a bartender before paying a bribe to Tammany Hall to become a policeman. He was promoted to sergeant in 1884 and to captain in 1891 when he obtained one of the most lucrative jobs running the Eldridge Police Station in a red light district. On one occasion, after he had recovered his temper – lost by actually being hailed by prostitutes from a brothel – he sent his wardman to tell the owner that in addition to a fee of $500 the monthly protection payment would be increased by $10 to $60.

Totally corrupt, Devery fined his men not for a breach of duty but for being caught. He would blackmail saloon keepers before elections, promising them protection if the ticket backed by Tammany Hall was elected. He was relentlessly exposed by Lincoln Steffens and others but to no effect. However, he lost his position when Seth Low defeated Mayor Robert A. Van Wyk in 1901. He then retired and divided his time between his mansion on West End Avenue and a real-estate business in Rockaway.

Other witnesses included 'Clubber' Williams who said he had made no attempt to close the brothels in the Tenderloin because, 'well, they're fashionable'. He had half a dozen large bank accounts, a yacht, an estate in Cos Cob, Connecticut, acquired, he said, through successful speculation in building lots in Japan.

The first weak link, however, was the German-born Captain Max Schmittberger, the collector for the Tenderloin which was between 5th and 9th Avenues and 28th and 48th Streets, roughly the Broadway and Hell's Kitchen districts. It was he who gave the game away. Even as a precinct commander he had been under instructions not to interfere with one of the premier brothels kept by Georgeanna Hastings. When first approached by the Committee he had complained of brain fever; but when one officer received 45 months for accepting a basket of fruit worth $6, Schmittberger realised that a $500 New Year gift left him in a much more vulnerable position and he rolled over. He named 'Clubber' Williams and exonerated Byrnes, something which did not please the Reverend Parkhurst. It is said that he sat there in his medals and confessed, giving away the whole system. Next in line was a former Civil War hero Timothy Creedon. In front of the Committee, at first he brazened things out, but he thought through his position overnight – particularly the $15,000 paid for his captaincy – and the next morning made a completely clean breast of his doings. His lies the previous day had, he said, been because of the terrible connotations for the Irish in the word informer.

The hearings, always political in nature, were shut down once they threatened to engulf the Republicans as well as the Democrats whom they were designed to embarrass. The Board of Police Commissioners was dissolved and a new Board appointed under the presidency of Theodore Roosevelt. Byrnes survived prosecution, but only just. Roosevelt wanted his dismissal and obtained his resignation along with that of 'Clubber' Williams. The journalist Jacob Riis, who later became part of the Roosevelt think tank, commented, 'Twice I held Dr Parkhurst from his throat, but in the end I had to admit that the Doctor was right.' Later he wrote of Byrnes:

> There was not one of us who had known him long who did not regret it, though I for one, had to own the necessity of it, for Byrnes stood for the old days that were bad. But, chained as he was in the meanness and smallness of it all, he was yet cast in a different mold . . . I believed that, untrammelled, Byrnes might have been a mighty engine for good, and it was with sorrow I saw him go. He left no one behind to wear his shoes.

On the day he left there were stories of both the high and low weeping for him. One was an old pickpocket to whom Byrnes had acted kindly who sat with his head in his hands on the steps of the police station. The other was a merchant banker who questioned who would protect him and his colleagues now.

In a lament for the policies of Byrnes and Williams the *New York Times* wrote:

> The use of the nightstick has become rare nowadays. In the old days a few raps over the head with a nightstick would stop the trouble but now it is different.[14]

On Byrnes' death, the *New York Times* mused whether he had been too big for the job or not big enough:

> He had been regarded as autocratic in his ruling of both the Bureau and the police. This had brought him into conflict with the civilians who were his superiors and there had been a good deal of 'pulling and hauling' between him and the Police Board. The Lexow Commission had left only him in the force unscathed. Although his enemies had not been able to find a peg on which to hang a direct accusation, the Lexow Commission had been the effective end of him.[15]

Byrnes retired on a pension of $3,000 a year and became the general manager of the burglary-insurance department of the United States Casualty Company. He passed his time sailing, acting as an unofficial private detective and fixer for the wealthy who had found themselves in trouble, and railing against the inefficiency of his former force. He died from cancer of the stomach on 7 May 1910 at his home at 318 W 77th – a building which the papers noted with some interest was valued at $550,000. He left some $8,000 to his wife Ophelia, but he had deeded the house at W 77th to her earlier in 1910 and had taken the trouble to divest himself of much of his property to members of the family over the years. There were no speeches or eulogies at his funeral, which was handsomely attended, and his body was buried at

[14] *New York Times*, 11 May 1910.
[15] Ibid., 8 May 1910.

Calvary cemetery. It was estimated that over the length of his career, sentences totalling 10,000 years had been passed on criminals he arrested.

It is ironic that the death of the man who had imposed a no-go limit for criminals below Fulton Street should occur at a time when the Car Barn Gang had imposed a similar no-go area for the police at 97th and 2nd Avenue. On 9 May Patrolman Lawrence J. Cummins tried to arrest Cornelius Lynch and was shot for his pains. This was the third attack on the police within the week.[16]

After the Lexow fiasco Schmittberger was exiled to an outlying district around which he rode on a white horse, but with suggestions that he was a mere dupe and anyway was an imposing figure. He was later reinstated. A small test was devised for him. He was offered the chance to go along with a wire-tapping swindle but, declining, badly beat the proposers and so was deemed to have been rehabilitated. Given a position on the Upper West Side he made a good job of things.[17]

Things were not easy for Theodore Roosevelt, however. Efforts were made to smear and compromise him, and the new Police Chief Peter Conlin wanted the informant system set up by Byrnes to be substantially reduced. The Wall Street line, which protected the bankers, was denied to have existed. In any event it was abolished. Roosevelt quarrelled with the members of the board and Steffens was never sure how he reached his decisions, sometimes apparently allowing himself to be swayed by politicians and sometimes not. He could easily be spun a story, as when he was deciding the case of an officer in dismissal proceedings. The man introduced eleven children into the hearing, telling Roosevelt of their mother's recent and tragic death; on retaining his position on the force, the man returned the children to their rightful parents. Roosevelt also deliberately tried to undermine the political rally at Madison Square Garden held by the Democrat William Jennings Bryan, a dangerous

[16] *New York Times*, 10 May 1910.
[17] In 1896 a police parade was held at which the crowd booed Schmittberger and cheered Devery who was marching. In turn, in 1898 Devery, now Chief of Police, banned Schmittberger from marching.

opponent of William McKinley, the Republican Governor of Ohio. Now the Chief was determined to leave Mulberry Street as soon and with as much dignity as possible, although the latter was not as important as the former. In April 1897 he was appointed Assistant Secretary to the Navy.

With his departure things did not change much for the New York police. Frank Moss, a Parkhurst man, replaced Roosevelt and the new Chief of Police was John McCullagh. He did not last long. He fell foul of the state senator 'Big Tim' Sullivan over the dismissal of Patrolman Matthew McConnell, who had raided a protected gambling joint. Sullivan demanded the dismissal of McConnell and when the chief refused it was his head which rolled.

The Detective Bureau now passed into the hands of Captain George 'Chesty George' McClusky and gambling into the hands of Sullivan, Frank Farrell and Devery. In 1900 gambling was thought to be bringing in around $3 million for the police and politicians. In today's terms this would be around $60 million. It was not simply gaming houses which paid for protection; the increasingly popular and expanding numbers rackets contributed substantially.

The greatest of the early numbers kings was Albert Adams, who had worked as a brakeman on the New Haven railroad. He then worked for Zacharias Simmons who after the Civil War took over from Reuben Parsons and John Frink as policy racketeers. Simmons made enough to be able to run the Kentucky state lottery. The saloon keeper Shang Draper was allowed as a partner of one of the banks and Devery was also a partner. Regarded as one of the great cheapskates of his era, Adams paid his employees slave wages and never made a contribution to charity. He did, however, educate his sons at Harvard and Heidelberg. He received little in the way of thanks for this because one son attacked him and Adams had him arrested; the boy received 12 months.

In turn Adams was exposed by the Reverend Charles Parkhurst. Now the *New York World* noted that he owned two breweries, hundreds of gambling houses and brothels, and controlled almost all the policy rackets in Manhattan. Adams went on trial in June 1902 and was sentenced on 27 April 1903 to a fine of a paltry $1,000, but more importantly to 18 months in Sing Sing. Pending his trial he had lived in the Waldorf, as did Boss Tweed when awaiting his. On his release Adams' wife and family shunned him and he moved into the Ansonia Hotel where he killed himself on 1 October 1906.[18]

There had also been the passing of the Raines Hotel Laws – introduced by Senator John Raines in 1896 – the results of which were a further source of income for the police. Since a liquor establishment which provided hotel facilities was now exempt from early and Sunday closing, it was a simple matter for the owners to put a bed almost literally in the broom cupboard.

In 1900 the Mazet Committee was set up to examine city government, and again there was the parade of witnesses telling of police-protected vice. The same year Roosevelt, by now Governor, pushed through a bill creating a single police commissioner. The sub-text was the removal of Devery; the bill was passed but Devery survived it. Mike Murphy, a National Guard colonel, became the Commissioner and Devery was appointed first deputy so maintaining his control. Disciplinary hearings degenerated into vaudeville. A patrolman found kissing a girl was found guilty, not for the offence but for being caught. Another who had fired his gun in the street was fined 30 days' pay 'for not hitting nobody'. More importantly, when George McClusky's officers arrested a confidence team McClusky was removed from office. He was said to have 'gotten too chesty'.

Devery's reign ended with the elections of 1894 won by Travers Jerome. Devery resigned and failed to acquire his hoped-for position in Tammany Hall. He won an election as District leader, but Tammany Hall refused to recognise the result.

Meanwhile Scotland Yard had already had its crisis with the detective force, one third of which was put on trial at the Old Bailey in 1877. The background to the so-called Trial of the Detectives is that of two high-class fraudsmen, William Kurr and Harry Benson, who operated a series of racing scams. Benson, educated in France,

---

[18] Curiously, with his death, policy rackets went into a temporary decline. Bob Mott, the policy king of Chicago, tried to keep Adams' empire alive, but social reformers won the day and most policies had closed down by 1908 with only a handful running by 1914. They opened up again as black crime in Harlem in the early 1920s, and within a matter of a few years they were seized by the likes of Dutch Schultz.

had previously run a series of swindles including one which, in 1872, saw him in London as the Comte de Montague, Mayor of Châteaudun, supposedly raising money for refugees from the Franco-Prussian War. He extracted £1,000 from the Lord Mayor but was arrested almost immediately. Fearful of a long prison sentence he set fire to the bedding in his cell and, badly crippled, he had to be carried into court on the back of a warder to receive his 12-month sentence. On his release he teamed up with William Kurr, the son of a wealthy Scottish baker.

From at least the previous year Detective Sergeant (later promoted Inspector) John Meiklejohn had been taking bribes from Kurr, whom he had met by chance in a bar, for tipping him off as to the progress of police inquiries in connection with racing frauds. Chief Inspector George Clarke, a freemason then approaching 60 years, was roped in, possibly with the hint of blackmail by Kurr. Clarke was at the time communicating with a man named Walters who had absconded bail and was using him as an informant, and Benson let it be known that a letter sent by Clarke was in their possession. One of Scotland Yard's most able if corrupt detectives, the multi-lingual Nathaniel Druscovich, was recruited, the excuse being that he had backed a bill for his brother in the sum of £60, a quarter of a year's salary, and could not pay. Kurr kindly lent him the money and he too was hooked. In fact, in the terms of the trade he had been well at it for some time. The fourth officer involved, William Palmer, was also recruited through Meiklejohn. The monies they received were considerable. For informing Kurr that a fraud charge could be 'settled', Meiklejohn received £100. Later Druscovich declined £1,000 for not travelling to Scotland to continue inquiries, but on another occasion took £100 and a piece of jewellery for his wife. He was also given a cigar-box containing £200 in gold as a *douceur* for delaying inquiries. Clarke received £150 in gold. For assisting in the changing of certain banknotes, Meiklejohn asked for £2,000 from Benson.

The most audacious of their racing swindles was perpetrated on the Comtesse de Goncourt in Paris in another example of greed dulling brains. She was persuaded to place bets on horses through a commission agent in London and to be sent her winnings by cheques drawn on a non-existent bank. In a matter of weeks she had been swindled out of £10,000. It was this which led the police to Froggatt and the others into the dock.

Their companion in the dock was Edward Froggatt, a noted criminal solicitor – in both senses of the phrase – of the time. He had appeared at the inquest following the death of Lucy Chapman, a case which had been investigated by Druscovich.[19] In the middle 1870s he also acted for the high-grade fraudsman, absconder and police informer, Henry Walters, who was a longtime associate of Edwin Murray. In February 1875 Walters and Murray had been arrested for an assault on a man named Berkley, but were discharged. They were then arrested for running the fraudulent Society for Insurance against Losses on the Turf, a charge which Murray stoutly denied when he later came to give evidence against Froggatt. Murray and Walters were bailed and fled to America where they worked a land swindle.

Walters advertised as an English gentleman wishing to lend money on landed property. When people applied for a loan he would refer them to Murray, posing as a surveyor. In fact it was often, Murray maintained, a matter of Greek meeting Greek, because many of the applicants were out to swindle the so-called English gentleman. They would try to enlist Murray's assistance and he would pretend to help them, taking a bribe on the side. He would then make an unfavourable report and Walters would require insurance against the loan; the insurance agent was again Murray. He frankly admitted the scheme which although it did not run for very long netted them $400 a day. After that they were arrested and acquitted on a charge of smuggling and following that Murray set up a pocket-book swindle.[20] He returned to England in December 1875 where he lived in Leytonstone under the name of Munroe. For the time being Walters remained in America.

Froggatt's part in the exercise which put them all in the dock was initially as a receiver of forged notes which he tried to sell on.

[19] *The Times*, 14 August 1908.
[20] A pocket-book swindle was a form of lottery in which the winners received no payment.

When his colleagues wanted to pay too little, he bought one himself. He also acted as a negotiator and indeed he seems to have grown into his part. When Benson, under the name of George Washington Morton, was arrested in Rotterdam it was Froggatt who devised a telegram:

> Find Morton and the two men you have in custody are not those we want. Officer will not be sent over. Liberate them. Letter follows. Carter, Scotland Yard.

This, he said, would set the cat amongst the pigeons. However, he was hoist with his own cleverness, his mistake being to say a letter would follow. The Dutch police nearly did let them go, but decided to wait for the letter of confirmation which never came.

One curious coincidence in the case is that Froggatt made an arrangement with a man Sawyer who had something to do with Middlesex Sessions. Along with Sawyer, Froggatt seems to have planned to get hold of the notes himself. Kurr, however, did not trust Sawyer and would have nothing to do with the scheme.

Meanwhile outside solicitors pressed Superintendent Frederick Williamson into pushing along the inquiries and, despite the efforts of Meiklejohn and Druscovich to delay matters, Kurr and Benson were arrested.

When Kurr sent for Froggatt and suggested he should take steps to prevent a witness named Flintoff from making an identification of him, Froggatt offered the man £50. Flintoff turned him down and Froggatt ingeniously tried to have him prosecuted for perjury. It did not help anyone, and Froggatt ended in the dock listening to the tale of his misdeeds told by Benson, Kurr and Murray.

Kurr received 10 years and Benson 15 years penal servitude. Setting a precedent they now began co-operating with the authorities in return, they hoped, for an early release. On their evidence Meiklejohn, Palmer, Druscovich, Clarke and Froggatt were charged. Clarke was acquitted, the others received two years apiece.

Sentencing the men Baron Pollock had a special, if misplaced, word for Froggatt:

There are no persons who know the duties and vicissitudes of the profession to which you belong but must feel for you in your present position, especially when, as you have yourself said, the necessary consequences of the crime go beyond any sentence the law can pass upon you.[21]

His Lordship clearly did not know of Froggatt's earlier misdemeanours, for the former (and certainly unfortunate) solicitor suffered what is known in the trade as a gate arrest. He had served most of his time in Newgate prison but then on 28 October 1879, just as he was leaving the House of Correction in Coldbath Fields, Clerkenwell, having completed his sentence, he was arrested. This time it was for embezzlement. In 1870 he had managed to induce the then Lord Euston into marrying Kate Walsh, a widow of doubtful provenance, and as part of the prize he had become one of the trustees of the marriage settlement. Over the years a great deal of the £10,000 settlement had disappeared. Froggatt at first blamed his previous imprisonment for not being able to produce the trust deeds and then, in time-honoured tradition, claimed that in his absence the responsibility lay with his managing clerk:

If I had not been in confinement this would not have happened but my clerk has taken away all my papers from my office and I don't know where they are.

This time Froggatt was sentenced to penal servitude for 7 years. He died in the Lambeth workhouse shortly after his release.

The case which followed the embezzlement was unique. Lord Euston petitioned for an annulment of the marriage on the grounds that his wife was already married and her husband was still alive.

---

[21] Meiklejohn was partly rehabilitated and was employed in obtaining evidence for the Parnell Commission. In 1903 he brought a libel action against the prison governor and author Major Arthur Griffiths over his book *Mysteries of Police and Crime*. His claim was that Griffiths had said he was guilty of a felony when he had only been convicted of a misdemeanour, and that the case was an old one. Meiklejohn did not give evidence and the jury did not leave the box before rejecting his claim. However, he must have had some money from somewhere because in the three-day case he was represented by Crispe K.C. The publishers immediately announced a further serialisation of the book. Meiklejohn died in 1912. See *Morning Leader*, 11, 12, 13 November 1903.

Kate Walsh had had what was then described as a 'gay' life. She seems to have lived with a circus performer for a number of years and was 28 at the time of her marriage; Euston was 21. They separated in 1875. The one piece of evidence which was accepted was that she had married a George Manly Smith on 6 July 1863; she could not therefore have contracted a valid marriage to His Lordship. The evidence came to light out of an action which she had brought against Froggatt for the recovery of her money, when she had told the court that Manly Smith died at sea when the *London* foundered. Not so, said His Lordship's lawyers. That was a George Maslin Smith. They had traced Manly Smith, alive and well, to New Zealand.

Game and set to His Lordship. But not match. In fact when he married Kate Walsh, Manly Smith already had a wife who died of cancer on 9 June 1867. His marriage to Ms Walsh being bigamous, she had therefore been free to marry Lord Euston. Petition dismissed.[22]

Harry Benson, who gave evidence against Froggatt and the detectives, did indeed obtain an early release and in 1886 he went first to Brussels where he was arrested for falsely representing himself to be a journalist and for dissemination of false information. Given bail, he promptly skipped across the Atlantic to Mexico where he ingratiated himself in the entourage of the singer Dame Adeline Patti who was on one of her farewell tours. First, posing as Charles Bourton, a journalist representing *Gil Blas* and the London *Referee*, he closely questioned her business manager Marcus Meyer as to how tickets were sold and then, as the brother of Marcus Meyer, he sold nearly $30,000 worth of those tickets in Mexico City. He left behind a trunk full of silver dollars and made for Switzerland where he ran a bogus bond swindle.

By the time Inspector Byrnes arrested him in New York on 12 January 1888 he was also wanted in St Louis. Benson was represented by Peter Mitchell who put up a long if ultimately hopeless fight, first for bail:

---

[22] His Lordship went to Australia to take up a government post. She returned to the stage and, described as 'the heroine of the suit', died in Fulham on 24 November 1903. *Morning Leader*, 25 November 1903.

For nearly two hours the lawyers argued in front of Commissioner Lyman who chewed a big red apple.

Then Mitchell fought against Benson's extradition, finally losing the battle when the Secretary of State signed the papers returning him to face trial. He was lodged in Ludlow Street jail, on the Lower East Side parallel with Orchard Street and, following an effort to bribe keeper McCane with $10,000, he was placed in a ground-floor cell under close watch. Now he said he was suffering from diarrhoea. There appear to have been no lavatories on his wing and throughout the day he was taken to the first floor. On 16 May on his 6.30 p.m. visit, on the way back to his cell he threw himself over the balcony, fracturing his spine. He died at 10 o'clock that night.[23]

The Met still had further troubles on its hands. From the turn of the twentieth century there were repeated allegations of brutality by its officers. The East End criminal Arthur Harding was very much more than a villain, he was a great baiter of the police – playing a considerable part in the Royal Commission into the Metropolitan Police 1908, and assisting in the prosecution of a number of officers for assault.

The catalyst which sparked the Commission was one of those cases which should never have happened. Once it was in the public domain, however, a great deal of capital was made of it to the general discomfort of all concerned.

On 1 May 1905 a French woman, Eva D'Angeley, was arrested in Regent Street for 'riotous and indecent behaviour', or, in plain language, prostitution. The charge was dismissed after a Mr

---

[23] *New York Times*, 13, 14, 15, 21 January; 5, 14, 16, 19 February; 17 March; 10 April; 17 May 1888. Another swindler by the name of Harry Benson, but who was no relation, operated around the same time. He had absconded in 1883 after being charged with fraud and had served a 5–9-year sentence in America under the name of Harry Phillips. In 1909 he received 4 years imprisonment for a fraud on the Feltham Bank which was wound up following a £25,000 loss. Fortunately not everyone had suffered. Mrs Benson had been wise enough to withdraw her investment of £7,000 immediately before its closure. Benson was another who complained of his physical condition. Appealing to be released on bail he told Lord Coleridge, 'I am suffering from diabetes, heart disease and [after a pause he added] Bright's disease'. This time no one was inclined to give him bail again and he received 5 years. Benson's name was originally Bebro. See *Morning Leader*, 22 September, 7 October 1909.

D'Angeley told the magistrate that he was married to the lady and that she was merely waiting for him, something she had done on a regular basis. Better still, the Sub-Divisional Inspector McKay told the court he believed the D'Angeleys to be a respectable couple. The experienced Marlborough Street magistrate, Denman, warning Mrs A. of the dangers of loitering in the wrong place, dismissed the charges. So another desert storm quickly blew up, with allegations of harassment, bribery and corruption. Within a fortnight a Royal Commission was set up to inquire into methods and discipline in the force.

Given that the D'Angeleys were the catalyst, it was wholly misconceived. Three officers, for whose heads the press and politicians were calling, had said that she had been waiting for her husband on most nights for the previous three months. Now McKay conducted further inquiries and came to the conclusion that he had been mistaken in his assessment of the pair. How could he have been deceived in the first place? Did not he or his colleagues know the French girls who worked his area? Could he not tell D'Angeley was a pimp? Why did he not ask for a short adjournment to make proper inquiries? Meanwhile the pair had retreated to Paris and sensibly stayed there, despite the requests of the police who offered to pay the lady's return fare so she could give evidence to the Commission. Sadly from the point of view of Anglo-French relations, their return to France had been hasty. When they caught the Dover packet they had not had time to pay for their lodgings, and had left behind a few empty trunks.[24]

They were now living in rented accommodation at 20 rue Berlin. Their landlady, a Marie Louise Hardy, who opened the door to an investigating journalist, was described as 'a buxom Frenchwoman of about 40 years of age part of whose costume was a white blouse with a black skirt and a large picture hat'. She was in no doubt of Madame D'Angeley's profession.[25]

There had been other problems in the force which came at the wrong time. A Detective Sergeant Rose was dismissed for prefer-

[24] *Morning Leader*, 3, 5, 14 May 1905.
[25] *Thomson's Weekly News*, 4 August 1906.

ring unfounded charges, and was also alleged to have fitted up two men who received lengthy terms of imprisonment.[26] Another case was that of a PC Rolls who, it was alleged, had planted a hammer on a cabinet-maker sleeping on a bench at London Fields and had then arrested him. The case was dismissed at the North London Police Court by the eccentric magistrate Edward Snow Fordham, who was continually at loggerheads with the police and who was not invited to give evidence to the Royal Commission. Rolls was later prosecuted at the Central Criminal Court and received 5 years penal servitude. Another officer was allowed to resign.

This led to the formation of the Public Vigilance Society; such success as the public had in establishing any misconduct by the police was largely due to this organisation and to Earl Russell, who appeared for the Society and who later wrote modestly:

> I was instructed by a curious body called the Police and Public Vigilance Society run by a fanatic called Timewell. He was prepared always to believe anything he was told against the police and to resent with some indignation the demand for proof which a lawyer always makes. However, we selected about twelve of the likeliest cases, and in spite of the extreme poverty on our side and the whole force of the Treasury and the police against us on the other we succeeded in getting home seven of them, largely on my cross-examination of the police.[27]

One of the cases which they 'succeeded in getting home' was that of PC Ashford, who is described by Arthur Harding as having a nice wife, '. . . but always after the women. He wasn't intelligent enough to catch a thief, but he was good at perjury and he could do a man an injury by strength.'[28]

In August 1906, Ashford came across a young man named Gamble out walking with a prostitute named Ethel Griffiths. It appears that he wanted the girl for himself and told Gamble to clear off. In turn Mrs Griffiths told Ashford she did not want him and

---

[26] *Morning Leader*, 5, 14 May 1905.
[27] Earl Russell, *My Life and Adventures*, pp. 304–5.
[28] Raphael Samuel, *East End Underworld*, p. 191.

the officer then knocked Gamble down and kicked him. A police sergeant, Sheedy, came up and told Gamble to get up and fight like a man, but when he saw how badly the man was injured he ordered Ashford to go away as he had done enough. Gamble was in hospital for four months and was operated on four times; he later spent nearly a month in a convalescent home. One member of the Commission compared his injuries with those which would have been sustained by falling on a railing.

This was one of the cases in which the Public Vigilance Society was aided and abetted by Harding. He discovered two witnesses and arranged for the Commission's investigator to take statements from them. Later another witness was found. The Commission found that PC Ashford was guilty of the misconduct alleged – that is, kicking Gamble – but that he did not intend to do him the serious injury which resulted. In Sergeant Sheedy's case, it was found he had not stopped the assault and that he had failed to make a report to his superiors. So far as the ineffective investigation of the incident by an Inspector Hewison was concerned, this had aborted when he found no trace of Gamble's name at the London Hospital – he had been wrongly listed under the name Pearce. The Commission found that Hewison had done 'all that could be reasonably expected'.

The aftermath was the prosecution of Ashford. Proceedings were commenced immediately after the Royal Commission published its findings and, at the Old Bailey in September 1908, the jury was instructed to disregard the evidence of Ethel Griffiths because she was a prostitute. The defence also claimed that there had been no proper identification of Ashford as the kicking officer. Nevertheless after a retirement of two hours by the jury, he was found guilty and sentenced to 9 months' hard labour. Leave to appeal was refused by the fledgling Court of Criminal Appeal.

Within days of the appointment of the Commission its members had been inundated with letters and postcards alleging corruption, perjury and bribery, often in language 'foul and intemperate'. In fact, apart from the assaults, there had been 548 complaints against the police for having improper relations with bookmakers, of which 208 had been made against particular officers. There had also been 105 allegations of improper relations with brothel-keepers. From these, 19 cases – including that of Madame D'Angeley – were closely scrutinised and a variety of witnesses came before the Commissioners who sat on 64 occasions over a period of 11 months.

Unsurprisingly, the Commission, increasingly bored with the East End evidence, exonerated the police and declared that, far from harassing street offenders, they were kind and conciliatory to them. True in some nine cases there had been reprehensible conduct but, by and large, the Commission found, 'The Metropolitan Police is entitled to the confidence of all classes of the community.'

The Times for one was enchanted:

> We have no hesitation in saying that the Metropolitan Police as a whole discharge their duties with honesty, discretion and efficiency.[29]

---

[29] *The Times*, 14 August 1908.

20

The Private Eyes

The first private detectives worthy of the name in modern times were probably the late eighteenth-century and early nineteenth-century Bow Street Runners, a semi-autonomous organisation under the nominal control of the chief magistrate at Bow Street whose members could be hired out privately for investigations and security work throughout the country.

The first recognised detective agency is the one set up by Eugène-François Vidocq, former criminal, former head of the Sûreté in Paris, who ran a bureau after his final resignation from the police force in 1832. However, it was probably not very much more than a credit-checking and debt-collecting agency. Because of the machinations of its owner and the hostility towards it of both the police and the government, Vidocq was imprisoned – although eventually acquitted – and his bureau largely destroyed in 1837. In any event his was such a personal operation that there was no question of anyone taking over the reins as the great man grew old. The agency died with his retirement.

So the credit for the most famous and enduring of detective agencies goes to Allan Pinkerton, who was born in Scotland in 1819 and fled to America after a warrant for his arrest was issued following his part in agitating for labour reforms in 1832. He settled in Kane County, Illinois, where, working as a cooper, he was heavily involved in the Underground Railroad which smuggled runaway slaves to freedom.[1] He became the first detective in the Chicago police and following the smashing of a large counterfeiting ring in 1850, opened the Agency which still bears his name.

In 1856 in one of his first notable cases he was hired to investigate the killing of a bank teller. He assigned one of his employees who bore a close physical resemblance to the dead man to shadow the chief suspect. The man, Drysdale, tormented by the sight of the man he had seemingly killed, confessed and committed suicide.

Pinkerton first met Abraham Lincoln when he obtained a contract to provide guards for the Illinois Central Railroad for whom the future president was working as a lawyer. In 1860 he uncovered a plot to assassinate Lincoln. The aim was to start a street riot in Baltimore and, with this as a diversion, kill Lincoln when he arrived by train at the Calvert Street Station. Pinkerton thwarted this by putting Lincoln, disguised as a woman, on another train. From then on the future of his Agency was assured.[2]

The Pinkertons were also employed to hunt down the Jesse James –Cole Younger gang who killed an agent trying to infiltrate them. In 1874 a senior Pinkerton agent Louis J. Lull and Sheriff Ed Daniel of Osceola, Mo., were killed by the gang. In return Pinkerton agents opened fire on a cabin, killing James's mother and his eight-year-old retarded brother.

Allan Pinkerton died in 1884 and his sons William and the more ascetic Robert took over the Agency. William was a great one for taking part in the forays into James country and also for associating with criminals. He was regularly warned in correspondence from his brother of the dangers of getting too close to the natural enemy.[3] Robert was pleased to say, if not wholly accurately, that for over half a century not one of 40,000 Pinkerton employees had been convicted of a crime. Paid informers did not count, but he

---

[1] In 1859 John Brown and 11 runaways hid out in the Pinkerton house.
[2] Allan Pinkerton, *The Spy of the Rebellion*.
[3] See e.g. RAP to WAP, 3 July 1901.

conveniently overlooked Tom Horn who was hanged for murder in 1903. Perhaps the omission was because he was an ex-employee at the time of the killing.

Much of the Pinkerton work in the 1890s came about as a result of an economic depression. In 1893 Jacob S. Coxey had led a tramps' army in a march on Washington. Now, in the smaller towns of mid-West states such as Nebraska, Iowa and Indiana smaller bands of tramps – far removed from the Worths, Leslies and Shinburns of the world – tormented local banks, blowing safes and moving on with their few-hundred-dollar takings to the next town. From rather less than one a year in the late 1890s the raids on American Banker's Association banks, protected by the Pinkertons, rose to 15 a year in the first decade of the twentieth century. To combat the growth of what was known as the Yeggman, the Pinkertons opened a series of new offices in the mid-West.[4] In their 1895 report to the American Bankers' Association they pointed to the convictions of 24 forgers, sentenced to a total of 121 years; five burglars whose sentences totalled 25 years and four sneak-thieves (17 years), making a total of 33 convictions and an aggregate of 163 years and 11 months or nearly 5 years apiece. In addition two professional forgers Charles Becker and James Cregan had each received life. Becker, the 'Wizard of Crime', was the prize of the collection. They were rightly pleased with themselves.

The Pinkertons were great ones for using infiltrators and under-cover agents and, well in advance of any police force of the time or for the next fifty years, employed women operatives. The first and perhaps the most notable was Kate Warne, with whom it was suggested Pinkerton, a noted womaniser, had a long-standing rela-tionship. It was she who convinced him of the need for women

---

[4] The Yeggman brought a whole new criminal vocabulary with him. Nitroglycerine was soup, a safe was a box, and a boxman was in charge of blowing the safe or shooting a drum. There is considerable discussion on the origin of the term Yegg. It is possible that a John Yegg was the first safe-blower to use nitroglycerine. It may derive from the German *Jaeger* or hunter. A third suggestion is that it is a corruption of beggar. In 1904 William Pinkerton, who believed an understanding of criminal slang to be invaluable, gave a lecture, 'Yeggman', to a body of police chiefs.

operatives.[5] From an early stage he also used black operatives such as John Scobell who posed as a groom to Southern lady Carrie Lawton, another Pinkerton, reporting on troop movements in Virginia.

One of the most remarkable of their undercover operators was James McParland who infiltrated the Molly Maguires, the terrorist branch of the Ancient Order of Hibernians, agitating for better pay and conditions in the Pennsylvania coalfields. His work can take its place alongside any others as an outstanding example of under-cover activity. After the break-up of the Maguires McParland then travelled west to Colorado where he became head of the Denver branch of the Pinkerton Agency. His work in infiltrating the Mollies was acclaimed throughout America and later formed the basis of the first Sherlock Holmes novel, *The Valley of Fear*, which led to a split between the Agency and Conan Doyle – something the rival Burns Agency was pleased to exploit. William Pinkerton believed that Conan Doyle, along with the dime novels, was distorting the detective industry, and Burns was only too happy to have his photo-graph taken with the celebrated author.[6]

Over the years, however, McParland's role has been substantially reassessed. It began in 1906 with the trial in Boise, Idaho, of Harry Orchard, 'Big' Bill Hayward, George Pettibone and Charles Moyer, the last three of whom were leading members of the Western Federation of Miners. Hayward went on to become a leading light in the Industrial Workers of the World, the Wobblies.

On 30 December 1905 Frank Steunenberg, a former Governor of Idaho, was killed by a bomb attached to his front gate. McParland found two informers, Steve Adams and Harry Orchard, whose

---

[5] Kate Warne joined the Agency in 1857 and was described as 'not remarkable for beauty, but persuasive, graceful and self assured'. After his death his sons discouraged the use of female detectives. See Allan Pinkerton to Robert Pinkerton, 26 May 1875; Frank Morn, *The Eye That Never Sleeps*; Richard Wilmer Rowan, *The Pinkertons*.
[6] There are numerous books on the breaking of the Mollie Maguires who, of course, feature in books on the Pinkertons. See e.g. Frank Morn, *The Eye That Never Sleeps*; Arthur H. Lewis, *Lament for the Mollie Maguires* and, for a particularly hostile account so far as the Agency is concerned, Patrick Campbell, *A Molly Maguire Story*. See also James Morton, *Supergrasses and Informers*. For an account of the trial of 'Big' Bill Hayward, see Irving Stone, *Clarence Darrow for the Defense*.

confessions led to the arrests of Hayward, Pettibone and Moyer. Adams later withdrew his confession, insisting that his statement was false and had been Pinkerton-inspired.

Orchard, whose real name was Albert F. Horsley, maintained that he had received the bombing instructions from Hayward. Leaving aside the Steunenberg case, Orchard was a self-confessed killer who had carried out a number of bombings for the Western Federation of Miners, including one in which 14 non-union members died in an explosion in June 1904. He had probably been involved in other attempts on the Governor's life.

The great lawyer Clarence Darrow, appearing for the defence, created massive inroads into Orchard's written confession in which corrections were probably in McParland's handwriting. There were good reasons for Orchard's killing of Steunenberg. In 1899 the then Governor had driven him out of Coeur d'Alêne in Idaho, so depriving him of a $^1/_{16}$th share of a mine which would have made him a millionaire.

As for the implication of Hayward and the others, it is thought that this was either part and parcel of a power struggle amongst the leadership of the Western Federation or, more likely, was inspired by the mine owners. The three Wobblies were acquitted, with Orchard's death sentence being commuted to life imprisonment. Later he petitioned William Pinkerton, then head of the Agency, to help him obtain parole. Pinkerton, rather contrary to the Agency's usual practice of helping their informers whether a conviction had been obtained or not, refused, writing in a memorandum:

> I know that McParland always thought Orchard should have been released for testifying, but I still regard Orchard as a cold-blooded murderer who killed many innocent persons and who testified only to save his own skin.[7]

---

[7] Orchard was never released, dying in prison on 13 April 1954 at the age of 86. By all accounts he was treated as something over and above the ordinary prisoner. Early in his imprisonment he had a room fitted with electricity. Private individuals gave him the money with which to buy machinery; the state permitted him to use convict labour

In fact, the incident gets scant mention in Rowan's adulatory account of the Pinkerton Agency. It suggests that Hayward and company were imprisoned – and indeed they were, although not quite in the way suggested by Rowan. Pinkerton agents had captured the men in Denver and put them on a special train to Boise, Idaho, where they were kept on death row until their trial. Nor is there any substantial reassessment in the rather more scholarly *The Eye That Never Sleeps* in which Frank Morn drily comments:

> Third degree methods on Orchard soon produced enough evidence for McParlan [sic] to arrest the three labour leaders and spirit them away to Idaho.

The fallout from the Orchard case was considerable. One Pinkerton man, the stenographer Morris Friedman, was so disenchanted with the affair that he left the Agency and wrote his own memoirs, *The Pinkerton Labour Spy*, in which he saw the Pinkerton management as a public menace masquerading as a public necessity and something not far from the Russian Secret Police.

His memoirs did not please the heads of the Pinkerton Agency, and operatives who subsequently tried their hands at unauthorised and therefore unadulatory reminiscences found themselves in considerable difficulties. When Charles Siringo wrote *Pinkerton's Cowboy Detective*, he was forced to change the name to *The Cowboy Detective*. Pinkerton becomes Dickenson and Tom Horn, the range rider/killer and another operative, appears as Tom Corn. There was worse to come. In 1914 Siringo wrote *Two Evil Isms* and sent the manuscript to the Agency for approval. Unsurprisingly, since one of the 'evil isms' was Pinkertonism, the management disapproved of the whole concept, took Siringo to court and the printing plates were confiscated.

Rather more serious for the Pinkerton Agency was the

---

for his own private enterprise, in which he manufactured shoes for prominent people in Idaho. By 1943 he was keeping a chicken farm, although he would tell visitors that he 'just can't bring himself to kill a chicken'. He was described as 'still fat and sleek, oily eyed and unctuous'. He complained if anyone discussed the 1905 case, 'The trouble with you writers is that you never come here to write about me. You always want to use me to write about somebody else.' See Irving Stone, *Clarence Darrow*.

unfavourable publicity, coupled with growing adulation for William
Burns who seemingly could do no wrong – and whose business
was the second of the great agencies of the time. Burns, born in
Baltimore in 1858, had been brought up in Zanesville, Ohio, and
then moved to Colombus where his father combined tailoring with
police work, later becoming the police commissioner in much the
same way as Allan Pinkerton had for a time been both a barrel-
maker and a detective.

In 1888 Burns began working freelance for the Furlong Detective
Agency of St Louis before entering the US Secret Police in 1891 –
where he was mainly used to break up the great counterfeiting
gangs – cracking the Bredall–Taylor counterfeiting ring. In 1905 he
was put in charge of investigating the huge Western land fraud in
which tens of thousands of acres of public lands were illegally fenced
or bought under false representations. Through Burns' efforts
Oregon Senator John H. Mitchell and Oregon Representative John
N. Williamson were convicted.

In 1906 Burns left the government service to investigate corruption in San Francisco and would eventually send Boss Abe Ruef to
prison.

His detective agency was now flourishing, and in 1909 when the
business was only three years old he took over the valuable contract
of the American Bankers' Association (with 11,000 member banks)
from the larger and stronger Pinkertons, whom he regarded as taking
on only safe cases and never going against public opinion. Now
the Pinkertons set up the rival Pinkerton Bank and Bankers'
Protection.

Then came Burns' next success, and with it a return by Clarence
Darrow to a defence of labour leaders. In 1911 the great lawyer
undertook the defence of the McNamara brothers, James and John.
Both were heavily involved in the labour union movement and both
had been charged with the bombing on 30 September 1910 of the
Times Building in Ink Alley, Los Angeles. In the subsequent explosion twenty people died, four as they missed a safety-net into which
they tried to jump from the burning building.

Burns, who was hired by the Mayor of Los Angeles to investigate the bombing, was convinced there was a connection between

the McNamaras and a previous outrage he had investigated in Illinois. After a six-month investigation he arrested the brothers, so earning fulsome praise. 'The only detective of genius, this country has produced', said the *New York Times*.[8]

Darrow did not really wish to appear in the McNamara trial; at the time he was a sick man and was tiring of the rigours of court work. However, partly because of his fee and partly through a suggestion that if he declined the brief he would be regarded as a traitor to the labour movement, he was pressed into service. The money put at his disposal by the unions was the equivalent of $3 million today, his fee being the equivalent of $500,000. He was also to be allowed to select his co-counsel and to set the trial strategy. However, it soon became clear to Darrow that the evidence against the brothers was overwhelming and the case hopeless.

One major difference between American and British trials is that in the United States there is pre-trial examination of the jury as to their beliefs, so that the jurors potentially most antagonistic to prosecution or defence may be eliminated. Some prefer to phrase it the other way and say it is so that the jurors potentially most favourable to the prosecution or defence may be selected. To this end, if the money is available in an important trial, inquiry agents are used to research the background of potential jurors.

On 6 October 1911 Darrow's principal investigator, Bert Franklin, approached a juror named Bain and, finding he was in financial straits, offered him $4,000 to acquit the McNamaras. The next month, it was increasingly apparent to Darrow that there was no defence likely to succeed and now it was a question of trying to save James McNamara, who had actually planted the bomb, from the gallows. Darrow was about to try striking a plea bargain when Franklin approached a second man – a big mistake, since this time he picked quite the wrong person. Lockwood, himself a former deputy sheriff and a friend of the District Attorney, reported matters and it was arranged that he should receive his bribe at 9 a.m. on

[8] *New York Times*, 4 December 1911; 'Dynamiters: A great case of Detective Burns' in *McClure's*, issue 37, August 1911.

28 November at the corner of Los Angeles Street and Third. Unfortunately, not only were the police watching but Darrow was in the area. Franklin was arrested.

As for the trial of the McNamaras, Darrow encountered difficulties, since James was by no means unhappy to face the gallows and so become a martyr to the union cause. Eventually on 1 December 1911 Darrow persuaded the brothers of their parlous situation and, to what was described as pandemonium in court, he announced that they would be changing their pleas to guilty. Four days later James received life imprisonment and John was sentenced to 15 years.

Darrow's actions are a good example of a lawyer doing what he can for the client rather than for the cause. However, now he was no longer a hero to the working class but their betrayer. On 29 January 1912 Franklin, who by this time had pleaded guilty to attempted bribery, gave evidence to a Grand Jury implicating Darrow. That afternoon the lawyer was arrested on a charge of jury tampering.

In the Lockwood case Darrow defended himself, also instructing the great (if corrupt) Californian lawyer Earl Rogers to appear as co-counsel. The two men did not get on and there were stories that Rogers was never paid. Nevertheless he made a stunning closing speech for his client. Darrow's own speech, which lasted a day and a half, was even greater. To the horror of the prosecution he not only moved the jury to tears, the judge cried as well. On the verdict of 'not guilty' Judge Hutton commented:

> Now the case is ended, I consider it entirely proper for me to congratulate Mr Darrow on his acquittal. I know that millions of hallelujahs will go up through the length and breadth of the land.

That left the Bain case, and now Darrow was in more difficulties. Both Rogers and his principal assistant, Horace Appel, withdrew from the trial leaving the up-and-coming Jerry Giesler to assist Darrow who now effectively defended himself. He could not argue that there was no point in bribing Bain because there was every point. At the time when Franklin handed over the money, the McNamara brothers were still intent on contesting everything. In March 1913 the jury was deadlocked, with 8 out of the 12 jurors wanting to convict Darrow. A plea bargain was struck and the District Attorney agreed not to re-try the case. Darrow, for his part, promised never to practise law in California again. It was not the great man's finest hour.[9]

Burns was triumphant, but then things started to go wrong for him. Within a year he was sued for making a false arrest, and the American Bankers' Association issued a statement disclaiming any responsibility for the mistakes of the detectives.

He was also involved in trying to secure the conviction of Alderman Thomas E. Glinnan for taking a bribe of $750. On 26 July 1912 Burns, under the name of James W. Brennan, had given him this money to vote one way in connection with the Wabash Railway, and later he gave evidence that Glinnan had told him this was the first time he had taken dirty money. Glinnan had stated that he thought he had tissue paper in his pocket. The judge directed the jury to acquit if they thought this was true and that, in effect, Burns had planted the money. Glinnan was indeed acquitted.

Then in the case of the Oregon Land Fraud Burns was accused by the then Attorney General George Wickersham of deliberately packing the box with prejudiced jurors. There were public rows with the International Association of Police Chiefs over the registration of hand-guns and Burns was dropped. However, he had a great success in the case of Leo Frank whom he proved was not guilty of the murder of Mary Phagan in Atlanta on 26 April 1913. The 14-year-old girl had gone to the pencil factory to collect her wages before she watched a Confederate Memorial Day parade, and had been raped and murdered. Sadly his efforts did his client no good, however. In a wave of anti-Semitic feeling – and in the first case in the Deep South when the word of an African-American, the janitor James Conley, was preferred to that of a white person – Frank was taken from the jail, driven 175 miles to the girl's home

[9] See Irving Stone, *Clarence Darrow for the Defense*, Chapter IX.

town and lynched. Burns was quite outrageously accused of professional misconduct.[10]

Unfortunately for Burns, one of his greater blunders took place very publicly and it was dealt with by the Pinkertons. From 1912 onwards there had been a man dubbed the 'Holiday Crook' and 'Christmas Keogh' who between then and 1918 tricked bankers and shopkeepers over the Christmas period with a series of forged cheques on the Dominion Bank of Toronto. The cheques would be passed on the Saturday before Christmas, so giving him two to three days headway. He seems to have been a very controlled and methodical thief because he did not work outside that period. The American Bankers' Association now retained Burns while the Jewellers' Security Alliance, in retaining the Pinkertons, brought his rivals into the case.

In fact in the early years, apart from posting seasonal warnings, neither agency seems to have devoted much time to the problem and 'Christmas Keogh' went on his way unmolested until in New York on 23 December 1916 he passed half-a-dozen cheques in clothing and jewellery shops. The day before, similar cheques had been passed in St Louis. In January 1917 Burns detectives arrested Alexander McCauley, a Canadian, in that city; he had been staying in a hotel with his family at the Christmas period. The local police were satisfied McCauley was not Keogh but eyewitnesses, handwriting experts and, embarrassingly, the Pinkerton agents in St Louis all agreed the Burns Agency had the right man. McCauley was extradited to New York.

Then in April 1917 the pattern changed and cheques were passed by a J.H. Paget in Chicago. The Chicago shopkeepers were agreed it was not McCauley, and witnesses brought to New York said that he and McCauley were not the same man. At the end of the year as the holiday season approached the 'Holiday Crook' struck again. Now McCauley was allowed to try on suits at Brooks Brothers where cheques had been passed the previous Christmas, and he was found

[10] *New York Times*, 11 December 1915. The local newspaper had already published an editorial, 'Our little girl – ours by the eternal God! Has been pursued to a hideous death by this filthy perverted Jew from New York.' There are many accounts of the case including James Morton, *Who's Who of Unsolved Murders*.

to have been far too small. He was released and to the Agency's great delight instructed the Pinkertons to investigate Burns. He spent some $50,000 proving his innocence, but his health cracked and later he suffered a stroke. McCauley then sued the American Bankers' Association, the National Retail Dry Goods Association and Burns for $100,000. He also began a series of actions against newspapers including the St Louis *Republican*, the *Post Dispatch* and the St Louis *Star*.[11]

'Christmas Keogh' – who was in fact Lawrence Farrell, and was also known both as Lawrence and Billy Keogh, as well as by at least eight other pseudonyms – was born in Wisconsin, and had been a prizefighter. He started his criminal career on 27 April 1895 when he appeared in Denver and was sentenced to 2 years for robbery and assault. This conviction was overturned and he was released, but in 1908 he started his long run as a fraudsman back in his home town of Lancaster, Wisconsin, and began his 'Christmas Keogh' swindles in 1912.

Farrell was released on parole in November 1926, but was almost immediately posted as a parole violator for failing to report and notify any change of address. He next reappeared in New York as Dr T. H. Lamar of Dover Street, London, trying to persuade the Canadian Bank of Commerce to cash some 1913 travellers' cheques. Because of their age the bank declined until these had been cleared by the head office. He returned a few days later and told the bank, who now reissued the cheques, that he had bought them from a man named Sousan, a patron of the famous Kit Kat nightclub. Later he demanded the return of the cheques themselves and foolishly left his address as 424 W 57th. He received 5 years, but was again released on parole after 30 months. Once more he violated the parole and completed his full sentence on 22 March 1930. Shortly after Farrell was arrested the Pinkertons opened a file on Burns' 'startling methods'.[12]

If ever there was anything to dispel the belief that there was

[11] See *Mail and Empire*, Toronto, 10 October 1917; *New York Times*, 17 January 1921.
[12] *New York Times*, 10 October 1917, 21 June 1918, 17 January 1921; *New York Herald*, 23 December 1918; Binder 27, vol. 1, *Lawrence M. Farrell, Check Swindler*; Binder 27, vol. 2, *Startling Evidences of Methods employed by W.J. Burns and His Detective Agency*.

honour amongst thieves it was the Pinkerton code-book of past and present informers. The 1904 edition is a roll-call of dishonour of those who had been recruited and who reported on their friends' and colleagues' as well as their enemies' moves. The average weekly salary to the paid informant was $12 but one with really valuable information – C.D. Long, who had been a member of the Dalton Brothers – was such a mine of knowledge on the thieves and police in Nebraska and Iowa that he was paid $75 a month.[13]

The paid informers had the suffix Stone added to their names. Unpaid informants were Wood.[14] Names were allotted with some whimsical humour, so 'Doc' Patrick F. Sheedy, man-about-town, gambler, one-time manager of the prizefighter John L. Sullivan and general fixer, the man who suggested Worth go to the Agency, was Prieststone. Worth himself was Jewstone. The Pinkertons had always considered him to be Jewish but, after he had appeared in William's office and had made disparaging remarks about Jews, they then thought he might not be.

Other notables included James Hope, working as Solidstone, and Johnny Hope who became Singstone. Little Horace Hovan, who had been with the Agency since 11 May 1898, was Duckstone.

Later editions show that 'Dutch' Alonzo Henne was Joystone and went on the books on 30 October 1906. Charles Becker was Gardenstone, while Paddy Guerin was Blackstone. His more famous brother, Eddie, was Rinstone; he had been with the Agency since 26 March 1900. Mickey Gleason, the husband of Annie, was on the books as Cimstone. It does not appear that she ever succumbed to the brothers' siren call. The famous Gondorff brothers, Charles, Fred and George, celebrated wire tappers and Big Store merchants, had signed up on the same day, 11 March 1907, as Yilstone, Jutstone and Nixstone. Collectively they were Vixstone. Max Shinburn was there as Plowstone.

John Considine from Detroit, defended by Bill Howe in one of his last successes, was Minkstone. Sadly, Mrs Mandelbaum's

---

[13] W.B. Laughlin to Asheter Rossetter, 30 January 1909.
[14] The agencies were also Woods, so New York was Plumwood, Chicago was Pinewood and Denver became Sailwood. Robert Pinkerton himself was Lowood.

surviving daughter Sarah, now Mrs S. Kohler, was on the books as Limestone, while her son Gus was Smallstone. In Sarah's case it was, perhaps, not surprising; she had married a detective.

To his credit the great Howe does not appear amongst the Woods, but in a later version of the code-book there is the name of A.H. Hummel, lawyer, as Mulwood. He was apparently used from 5 March 1906 when he was heavily involved in the Dodge–Morse case, and was probably looking for whatever help he could get from anyone on any side of the fence.

21

Forensics

At the beginning of the second half of the nineteenth century, detective methods were rudimentary. There was no fingerprinting, no science of ballistics. There was infiltration, there was questioning and there was torture. As for identifying criminals, the police went into the prisons to see if they recognised anybody. Photography was in its infancy.

At the end of a case when the defendant was found guilty, if previous convictions were not admitted – and there was no great incentive for a defendant to do so – police officers in the old case had to give evidence. The jury was often reluctant to heap more woe on the defendant. After Frederick Wilkinson was convicted at the Central Criminal Court in April 1885 of safe-breaking and the theft of silk, he denied that he had a conviction in the name of Henry Hillyer on 15 September 1856 and the jury gave him the benefit of the doubt. It was a small victory. He still received 10 years penal servitude.

Often criminals did the best they could for the authorities by having elaborate tattoos. Billy Forrester, wrongly suspected of the Nathan murder in New York, had a Goddess of Liberty on his right arm, an eagle, flag and anchor on his left leg, a full-rigged ship billowed on his left breast, the United States coat of arms on his left arm and red and blue bracelets on each wrist. To complete the picture both ears were pierced. Not to be outdone, Billy Porter sported a sailor with American flag and star on right arm; star and cross on outside of same arm; crucifixion of Christ, woman kneeling, man standing up on left arm. The police duly recorded the artwork, but it was a haphazard method at best.

However, in the last decades of the nineteenth century and the early years of the twentieth great strides were made in the development of forensic science in both fingerprinting and ballistics. In fact fingerprinting as a means of identification was nothing new. It had been used for centuries in India as a prevention against fraud in claiming pay twice over, as well as in Japan and China. Chinese orphanages took the fingerprints of abandoned babies and a handprint was usual on a Chinese divorce contract. The problem really lay in categorising fingerprints and introducing a system so that the collected data could be easily searched.

In Europe two early observations on fingerprints had come to nothing. The first was in 1686 when Marcello Malpighi, Professor of Anatomy at the University of Bologna, put down his thoughts, which were promptly ignored – as were those of John Purkinje at the University of Breslau who did the same in 1823.[1]

By the end of the century there were several rivals for the claim to be the Father of Identification and it was the Frenchman, Alphonse Bertillon, who bears the unquestioned title of being the first to establish a modern means of identification.

He started with the undeniable asset that he was grandson of Achille Guillard, a noted naturalist and mathematician, and the son of Louis Adolphe Bertillon – a distinguished physician, statistician and, even better from his son's point of view, the Vice President of the Anthropological Society of Paris. The Belgian scientist and statistician Adolphe Quetelet had for some years been trying to demonstrate an even distribution of human nature – there were as many dwarfs as giants, but the majority of men fell within a certain physical range. Quetelet's theory had already attracted some attention and in the 1850s the director of the Louvain prison suggested that

[1] For a detailed account of the development of forensic science see James Morton, *Manhunt*; D. Owen, *Hidden Evidence*. For a really excellent and highly readable account of its early development see Jurgen Thorwald, *The Marks of Cain*.

rudimentary measurements be taken of the head, length of ears, feet, height and the chest circumference of adult prisoners – the system would not, of course, work with juveniles. He argued that this would defeat disguises, false names and mutilations, but his suggestion was largely ignored.

Bertillon had a poor academic record and worse communication skills. It was more or less in despair that his father obtained a position for him as a clerk at the police headquarters at the Sûreté in Paris.[2] Nor initially was he any great success in this position. Ignored by his colleagues, he was set to work compiling cards in a corner, which was boiling hot in the summer and so cold in the winter that he was forced to wear gloves. His job was transferring arrest data to these cards. Each card had general remarks on the physical features of the prisoners such as 'tall', 'small', 'average' and so on. Additionally, there was a photograph, often badly taken, of the man to whom the card referred.

By this time in its career the archive section of the Sûreté had effectively outgrown itself. Criminals were categorised in sections of burglars, pickpockets, forgers and so on, with no thought that a robber might also be a coiner and so could fall into two or more categories. Then there was the problem of the collection of 80,000 photographs. Even if the photographs were a likeness – and the arrested man had usually grimaced at the camera in an effort to make himself unrecognisable – it was physically impossible to compare the library with newly arrested criminals.

Bertillon began comparing the photographs, studying the ears and noses side by side. He then obtained permission to measure suspects brought in. From these studies he decided that while people might have similar measurements of their ears or noses they never had four or five characteristics the same. By August 1879 he was convinced that he had devised a system for the easy and correct identification of criminals and accordingly he wrote a report to Louis Andrieux who, since the previous March, had been the Prefect of Police in Paris. It was ignored.

[2] There are a number of accounts of the career of Bertillon. See for example S. Bertillon, *Vie d'Alphonse Bertillon*.

Undaunted, Bertillon went on amassing data and obtained permission to take measurements at La Sante prison before he commenced work in the morning.

On 1 October 1879 he was promoted from assistant clerk to clerk, and it was then that he sent in a second and much more detailed report. Now he could say that the chances of two people being exactly the same height were 4-to-1. If a second measurement was added, then the chance of the two being the same decreased to 16-to-1. If eleven measurements were taken, then the mathematical probability of finding another criminal with exactly the same measurements was 4,191,304-to-1. He had also developed a system of arranging the cards on which the measurements were recorded so that there would be only twenty-three in each sub-section of a file.

Unfortunately Bertillon's second report was longwinded, repetitive and thoroughly obscure. Andrieux made no sense of it and passed it to Gustave Mace, the head of the Sûreté.

Mace was regarded as a brilliant detective who in 1869 had solved the Voirbo murder case which shocked and entertained *le tout Paris*. Part of a corpse, sewn in calico, had been found in a well, and Mace had traced it back to a tailor Voirbo. He was convinced that the killing and dismemberment must have produced a great deal of blood and although the shop floor had been well cleaned, the wood was uneven. Mace poured water through the cracks and then had the floorboards torn up. Underneath was a quantity of coagulated blood. Voirbo confessed that he had killed a friend, Bodasse.[3]

Sending the report to Mace was Bertillon's second misfortune. Mace had no time for theories and theorists, believing in the detective's 'nose' and practical experience. He reported back to Andrieux that the police should not be troubled with theorists' experiments, and consequently the report was ignored.

Despite the efforts of his father on his behalf, Bertillon had to wait until Andrieux's retirement seven years later when one of his father's friends, the lawyer Edgar Demange, persuaded the new

---

[3] For a detailed account of the case see Colin Wilson, *Written in Blood*.

incumbent, Camecasse, to give Bertillon the opportunity to prove his system. It seems this was simply a sop to Bertillon *père*, because he was given the assistance of two clerks and a three-month trial period for his system to root out one recidivist criminal.

Three months was an incredibly short time for a man to be charged, sentenced, released and rearrested, but it was all that was available for Bertillon. He took his data to a young Austrian woman, Amélie Notar – whom he had met crossing the street and who, possibly because of her short-sightedness, was almost as anti-social as he was – for her to complete the registration cards. Half-way through February 1883, with only two weeks of the trial period remaining, his index had grown to 1,800 cards. It was then that his luck changed. While he was taking the measurements of a man who gave his name as Dupont, a regular alias amongst the French criminal classes of the time, he correctly challenged the man, who had been arrested on 15 December for stealing bottles, as being called Martin. The newspapers reported the case and the politically astute Camecasse extended the trial indefinitely. Bertillon was given more assistants and an office of his own. In March he made another identification, and by the end of the year he had identified 49 recidivists.

Bertillon then began a rudimentary identikit, taking photographs of, say, noses, and cutting and pasting dozens side by side, eventually deciding that a photograph of the face in profile was the most satisfactory.

In 1884 he identified another 300 criminals, and now the previously unwanted Bertillon and his methods became fashionable. The Home Office sent Edmund Spearman to talk with him and Camecasse paraded him before politicians as well as Hebert, Director of the French Prison Administration, who announced to the press that he was going to introduce Bertillon's system – which he now called anthropometry – into French prisons. From then on the ugly duckling indeed became a swan with newspaper headlines championing him: 'Young French Scientist Revolutionises the Identification of Criminals'. On 1 November 1888 Bertillon moved into offices of his own. Now he was called Director of the Police Identification Service, and journalists coined the word *bertillonage*.

Thanks to a French genius, errors of identification will soon cease to exist not only in France, but also in the entire world. Hence judicial errors based upon false identification will likewise disappear. Long live *bertillonage*! Long live Alphonse Bertillon![4]

Next came improvements to the photographing of criminals, with Bertillon devising a chair in which the suspect was seated and which ensured regularity in the composition of the portraits. And after that came his pride and joy, the *portrait parlé*. He devised a series of words and phrases to describe visible characteristics; each was given a letter, and so a group of the letters explained and identified the man's features.

His major triumph was to come in 1892 after a violent explosion blew up the house of Judge Bénoit who the previous year had presided over the trial of a group of anarchists. Although the solution of the case was Bertillon's, the initial breakthrough came when one of the Sûreté's informers known as X2SI reported in. X2SI was female and had learned from the wife of Professor Chaumartin of the Technical School at Saint-Denis that her husband, a known sympathiser, had planned the outrage. The motive was, as surmised, revenge for the previous year's conviction. Chaumartin was arrested and implicated Leger, whom he knew under a number of aliases including Ravachol, as the man who had planted the bomb.

Ravachol's abandoned room on the Quai de la Marne was searched and bomb-making equipment was found. He was already wanted by the police for the theft of dynamite from a quarry in Soiry-sous-Etoiles. Chaumartin described him as being 5' 4" in height, with a sallow complexion and a dark beard.

The 43-year-old Ravachol, a known smuggler and burglar with a reputation for violence, had been arrested under the name of Koenigstein in 1889 but released through lack of evidence. However, his measurements and characteristics had been taken and these included a scar on his left hand near the thumb. From then on he had indulged himself in a one-man crime-wave across France. On

---

[4] Pierre Brullard quoted in Jurgen Thorwald, *The Marks of Cain*, p. 43.

15 May 1891 he broke into the funeral vault of the Baroness de Rocher-Taillier in St Etienne and stole a cross and medallion from the coffin. Just over a month later he strangled a recluse, who lived in the Forez mountains, and stole 35,000 francs; he was arrested but escaped. Then six weeks later, on 27 July, he killed two women who ran a hardware store in St Etienne; this time his take was a mere 48 francs.

On 27 March 1892 another bomb exploded in Paris, this time at 39 rue de Clichy, seriously injuring five people. On 30 March the owner of the Restaurant Very on Boulevard Magenta sent a message to the police to the effect that a man with a scar on his left hand was breakfasting there. He had been there before and, rather carelessly, had been spouting anarchism to the waiter. The man was arrested after a violent struggle during which he was said to have called out, 'Long live anarchy! Long live dynamite!' The day after his arrest he posed willingly for Bertillon and the measurements proved him to be Claudius François Koenigstein. In time he would admit that his anarchism was merely a cover for his professional activities, and that he had robbed the grave in St Etienne and killed the recluse. Ravachol sang on the way to the guillotine, 'If you want to be happy, hang your masters and cut the priests to pieces.' His last words were recorded as, 'You pigs, long live the Revolution!'

This was a coup of the highest order for *bertillonage*. Now its deviser could hope it would become standard police practice worldwide. It was not such a coup for the proprietor of the Restaurant Very for on 25 April, two days before Ravachol was due to stand trial in Paris, a bomb exploded on the premises killing him and a customer.

One of the great problems of the Bertillon system, and it was recognised by Mace from the start, was that it required some skill and commitment to record the measurements accurately. Since much of the measuring in prisons was left to marginally supervised prisoners who had no possible incentive in assisting the authorities, it is hardly surprising that there were considerable variations. For example, the celebrated American confidence trickster and jewel thief Annie Gleason had her measurements given variously as 5' ½", 5' 2" and 5' 3" on arrest records in the Pinkerton files.[5]

Almost from the time of his arrival in India in the late 1850s as a junior secretary assigned to the highland district of Hooghly, William Herschel began taking fingerprints. In a country where agreements and timescales were at best overlooked and more often forgotten, initially he had done so as a *procès d'impressement*, reasoning that this might instil some sense of commitment.

As early as 1858 Herschel had made a supplier of road-building materials, Rajadar Konai, seal a contract with a palm print. At first Herschel had only been interested in the contractual side of things, but as the years passed he became fascinated by the differences in the prints themselves and began to accumulate a collection of impressions of the first two fingers of the right hand. He found it no more difficult than making a fair stamp of an office seal, and by the middle of the 1860s he was using his system to ensure that pensioned Indian soldiers did not make multiple applications for money. Over the period he had taken thousands of impressions, and no one had refused to give one. He noted that not only was everyone's impression different but that, while the face, hair and stature might change over the years, fingerprints did not. In the prisons he had made each inmate place a fingerprint after his name in the register, thus almost instantly eliminating a wide variety of common practices such as having a substitute serve one's sentence.

On 15 August 1877 he wrote to the Inspector General of the prison in Bengal saying that by using his method he was able to identify every person in what he called his sign-manual. But just as Bertillon had fought against unbelievers to establish his measurement system, so Herschel went unrewarded. The letter in reply led him to think the Inspector General knew he was an ill man and believed his suggestions were simply delirious ramblings. Two years later he sailed for England and home.

---

[5] Library of Congress, Washington; Pinkerton Archives, Case Binder 33, Crimes and Associates of Sophie Lyons. For a time there was an erroneous belief that Bertillon had, in fact, discovered fingerprints. Ironically, in 1902 he identified Henri-Léon Scheffer as the murderer of Joseph Reibel on 17 October at 157 rue du Faubourg through them. This may have contributed to the myth.

Meanwhile in Tokyo, a Scottish doctor named Henry Faulds, who seems to have shared some of Bertillon's less admirable qualities, noticed fingermarks in some 'pre-historic' Japanese pottery and remarked on 'skin-furrows'. In 1880 he wrote to the English publication *Nature* pointing out his discovery.[6]

It is curious that Herschel, convalescing in Littlemore from the amoebic dysentery which had ruined his health, read the issue of *Nature* which printed Faulds' letter. He wrote to the editor saying that he had studied the subject for the last 20 years and only the recalcitrance of his superiors and his illness had prevented him from making his findings public. Faulds took up what he saw as a challenge to his discovery with enthusiasm. Off went letters to the Home Secretary, Charles Darwin, the Police Commissioner in London and to Andrieux, the Prefect of Paris Police, defending his claim of discovery. His contract ended in Japan and now he too set sail for England.

The man who undoubtedly made the greatest contribution to fingerprinting in Britain was Sir Francis Galton, born in 1822, the son of a wealthy Birmingham manufacturer who dabbled in science. Throughout his life he had an interest in anthropometry, and for the London International Exhibition in 1884 he had devised a highly popular show which for the admission price of 3d gave the visitor the chance to have his physical and mental characteristics measured.[7]

Once Galton had seen Herschel's papers, he recognised the deficiencies in *bertillonage* which he had been prepared to adopt wholeheartedly. At a lecture to the Royal Institution he gave an early indication that fingerprinting was a superior method of identification. Immediately after the lecture he began work, and within three years he had a greater print collection than Herschel. He also devised a workable system of classification based on four definitive types of print.

---

[6] *Nature*, 28 October 1880.

[7] A genuine scientific dilettante, Galton also tried to discover the source of the Nile and then took up ballooning before setting sail for South Africa where he studied and measured the native tribes. After the booth at the International Fair he established a permanent measurement laboratory in South Kensington where it was fashionable to have one's measurements taken by his assistant. Despite frequent breakdowns in his health he lived until the age of 90. See Sir Francis Galton, *Fingerprints*.

In 1891 he also wrote an article for *Nature* acknowledging his debt to Herschel. It elicited no great interest except for an angry response from Faulds, but Galton was undeterred. In 1892 he published his book *Fingerprints*, and this time there was a positive response. The Troup Committee was set up to make a report.

However, there was still one remaining major participant in the development of fingerprinting in Europe. Edward Henry, the son of a London doctor, had entered the Indian Civil Service and from 1891 he held the position of Inspector General of Police for Nepal. The story goes that having no paper with him he set down a comprehensive system for classifying fingerprints on his starched cuffs while on a train journey to Calcutta in 1896.

In 1894 the Troup Committee reported to the Home Office. It had been established to report on the merits of adopting either fingerprinting or *bertillonage* and the members – Charles Edward Troup, Major Arthur Griffith, Inspector of Prisons, and Melville Macnaghten, then Assistant Chief Constable of Scotland Yard – went to see Galton's laboratory at the South Kensington Museum where he was still trying to work out an improved system of sub-classifications. He felt he was progressing well, but when pressed admitted that it would probably be another two or three years before he had the problem solved.

Here was the nub of the problem. The Committee admired Galton's system, but classification was a serious problem. Should they therefore go for *bertillonage*, only to find that in a relatively short period the more accurate system had overtaken it?

When the Committee delivered its report on 19 February 1894, it was part Bertillon and part Galton. Anthropometry should be introduced but with only 5 instead of Bertillon's 11 measurements, and the cumbersome *portrait parlé* was out. Instead all ten fingerprints of convicts should be preserved on cards and, for the present, classification would be *à la* Bertillon. The then Home Secretary's acceptance of the Troup Committee's recommendations did not meet with favour amongst the officers at Scotland Yard. Particularly sceptical was Detective Inspector Stedman who himself travelled to Paris only to find Bertillon in a major sulk over the refusal by the English to adopt his system wholeheartedly, but also overjoyed to find police

forces from Russia, Belgium and Berlin queuing to sign up allegiance. *Bertillonage* also became the classification of choice in
Portugal, Holland and Denmark as well as Austria. Britain was
becoming isolated.

Edward Henry had met Galton at his home in Rutland Gate and
been given a free run of his laboratory and files. Now on the train
he devised a system which needed nothing more complicated than
a magnifying glass and a needle for counting ridges. It was the
beginning of the system we know today of plain and tented arches,
radial and ulnar loops and whorls. There was also a division into
the sub-patterns based on Galton's work.

In 1896, Henry ordered his officers to take not only Bertillon
measuring cards but also all ten fingerprints of convicts, and a year
later he suggested to the Governor General of India that an independent commission be appointed to consider the merits of the
respective systems. On 12 July 1897 the Governor General ordered
the abandonment of anthropometry in favour of fingerprinting.
What India did today Britain did three years later. In November
1900 a committee under Lord Belper recommended that *bertillonage*
be dropped. In March 1901 Henry was appointed Acting Police
Commissioner of London, and through his personal efforts he
converted doubting officers to the cause. In the first year over 1,700
convicts were identified.

One of the great days of the English social sporting and criminal calendars was the Derby meeting run at Epsom, a mecca for
thieves from around the country. It was usual for temporary magistrates' courts, with the power to impose 6 months imprisonment,
to be set up behind the stands to deal with the stream of pickpockets and it was here that the usefulness of the fingerprinting
system proved itself; in 1901, 54 men were arrested on Derby
Day and fingerprint officers found that 29 of them had previous
convictions.

However, it was one thing to convince tame magistrates that a
prisoner's record was correct but a completely different matter
convincing a jury that fingerprints correctly identified a defendant.

The opportunity occurred in the summer of 1902 when a

burglary took place in Dulwich, South East London, where Stedman, the Scotland Yard detective – once a committed opponent of finger-printing – found a print on a newly painted board. It was identified as that of a Henry Jackson who had previously served a sentence for burglary. He was arrested and taken to Brixton prison where he was once again fingerprinted. It was essential that fingerprinting could be explained to a jury in simple terms, and the barrister chosen to do so was Richard Muir.[8]

Muir was known as an extremely hard worker and one of the rising men who prosecuted. He was said to allow himself no more than five hours sleep a night, and he would appear in court with a number of cards with notes in different colours to assist his cross-examination. He distrusted eyewitness evidence. To Edward Henry he seemed ideal. Contrary to the usual practice of the Bar of the day, when barristers never left their chambers except for court or to go on circuit, Muir spent four days at Scotland Yard being briefed on how the system worked. His preparation paid off. Jackson appeared at the Old Bailey in front of the Common Serjeant, where the odds were stacked against him because he was unrepresented. *The Times* reported that Muir told the court that fingerprint evidence was commonly used to identify criminals in India, and a demonstration with the use of photographs as to how finger-prints were identified had been received 'with much interest by the jury'. Jackson was convicted in short order and received 7 years penal servitude.[9]

Gradually, despite cries from the dock, juries began to accept fingerprint evidence more readily. Thomas Wilson who, along with his friends Joseph Taylor and John Jones, was arrested for a large burglary despite the fact that they were all over sixty, voiced the general criminal opinion that the idea of fingerprints was:

[8] It was certainly not yet an exact science. At the same time as the Jackson case, finger-prints taken at Guildhall showed a man with convictions to be in Birmingham, but in fact he was actually in jail in London. *Morning Leader*, 16 September 1902.

Muir began his working life as a bank clerk and then an agent for a sugar company before reading for the Bar. His many notable cases included the defence of Eddie Guerin and the prosecution of Harvey Hawley Crippen. See S.T. Felstead, *Sir Richard Muir*.

[9] *The Times*, 15 September 1902.

A fallacious one imported from our French neighbours to whom
it has done as much mischief as it is doing here.[10]

The jury found against them, but they had picked a lenient judge
at Berkshire Assizes who noted that all three had served long periods
of penal servitude in the past for offences which he did not think
merited them. In the circumstances, coupled with their ages, he
would sentence them to 6 months hard labour apiece.[11]

The same month there was great acclaim both in England and
America when the so-called International Gang were caught by their
fingerprints following a major raid on the galleries of the auctioneers Knight, Frank and Rutley.

As for the French friends, Bertillon was still claiming his system
was the one and to gain the confidence of the public held annual
anthropometrical tests outside the Palais de Justice. In 1903, out
of 125 tests there was an accurate recognition in 101 cases and
only one mistake. It seems to have been a good-humoured public
relations exercise. The son of the Paris police chief Lepine was
spotted in the crowd and was promptly 'arrested' and tested.[12]

Although the Jackson and other cases were dramatic steps
towards the general acceptance of fingerprinting, it would be a
quantum leap to convince a jury that they should convict a man
of murder, and so sentence him to death, on fingerprint evidence.
This came three years later on 27 March 1905 with the murder of
the Farrows at their shop at 34 High Street, Deptford, a depressing
South East London suburb. A cash-box was examined for fingerprints and there was indeed a smudge on the varnished inner tray.
The box was sent for fingerprinting and, for the first time in London,
fingerprints were taken from a corpse. The next morning the reports
came through. The fingerprint did not belong to the victims. The
bad news was that it did not correspond with any of the 80,000
prints currently on record. However, it was a good print which,
when it had been enlarged, was particularly clear.

The investigation proceeded on the usual lines with inquiries

[10] *Morning Leader*, 31 October, 11 November 1903.
[11] Ibid., 17 November 1903; *New York Times*, 18 November 1903.
[12] Ibid., 4 December 1903.

being made in the neighbourhood, and in a public house one evening a detective overheard a conversation to the effect that the Stratton brothers were 'capable of it'. The police found Alfred Stratton's mistress, Helen Cromarty, living in squalor in Brookmill Road. She had been given a recent beating by him and now was prepared to say that he had wanted her to give him an alibi for the night of the murder. He had also dyed his brown shoes black, and since that night she had not seen him wearing the overcoat he had on when he left her.

The brothers, Alfred and Albert, had no previous convictions but locally they were regarded as small-time ponces with no regular work. From the prosecution's point of view it was a good murder in which to try introducing fingerprint evidence. Defendants such as the brothers, alleged to have battered two old people to death for a few pounds, were not likely to garner much public sympathy.

There was little evidence against them – a vengeful girlfriend and a woman, Ethel Stanton, who had seen two men running up the High Street. The first problem, therefore, was persuading the magistrate to remand the pair in custody and to allow the police to take their fingerprints. Eventually the magistrate agreed and, when it came to it, the brothers were rather amused. The process tickled, they said.

They were not tickled to know that the mark on the cash-box tray was that of Alfred Stratton. The magistrate committed the brothers for trial at the Old Bailey and now Muir, who once again had been briefed for the Crown, was faced with the very serious problem of getting a jury to understand fingerprinting in a capital case. Meanwhile the Strattons' lawyer indicated that he would be calling two experts to challenge the prints.

One of the experts turned out to be a Dr Garson who had long argued in favour of *bertillonage* and had then developed his own, inadequate, system of fingerprinting. The other was the unfortunate Dr Henry Faulds who was still smarting because Herschel rather than he had been given the credit for the discovery of fingerprinting.

As for the fingerprint evidence, after further lessons from Scotland Yard Muir had arranged for a large blackboard so that an Inspector

Collins could clarify his evidence with examples. He displayed a substantially enlarged photograph of the thumbprint on the cash-box tray, alongside the print of Alfred Stratton and pointed out no fewer than eleven similarities.

Unfortunately for the Strattons, neither Curtis-Bennett nor Harold Morris who appeared for them had any great understanding of dactyloscopy and had to rely heavily on their experts. Nor did they know much, if anything, of the in-fighting which had gone on in the scientific journals to establish supremacy. Now Curtis-Bennett argued that Collins' photographs showed discrepancies which were clear to anyone examining the prints carefully – another example of careless behaviour at the Yard.

Muir and Collins met this challenge by having the latter finger-print every member of the jury several times. They were then given their prints to examine so that they could see for themselves that the discrepancies were simply the result of different pressure being applied to the fingers during the printing process and nothing at all to do with the basic characteristic patterns. Faulds lapsed into silence. At least he maintained his integrity.

The defence, after some lengthy deliberation, decided to call Dr Garson, who did not last long under cross-examination. Had he written to the Director of Public Prosecutions offering himself as a witness for the prosecution? How could he explain this behaviour? 'I am an independent witness,' he told the court, and Mr Justice Channell added as he ordered him to leave the witness box, 'I would say a completely untrustworthy witness . . .' The judge regarded the mark made through perspiration as less satisfactory than if the murderer had made a definite impression in ink, but he instructed the jury that fingerprint evidence could, to an extent, be regarded as corroborative. The jurors retired for two hours before returning the verdict of guilty.[13]

Even before that trial the star of Alphonse Bertillon had begun

---

[13] The brothers were hanged together by John Billington at Wandsworth prison on 23 May 1905. Collins retired as a Superintendent in 1925, dying in 1932. His superior, C.H. Stedman, had retired to Gorleston-on-Sea in 1908 when given only a few years to live by his doctor. In fact he survived to write a congratulatory letter to the Fingerprint Bureau when it held its 50th anniversary dinner in 1951. See Fred Cherrill, *Cherrill of the Yard*.

to fade. In 1902 Hungary began fingerprinting, as did Austria, along with Denmark and Spain, followed by Switzerland. In the next year Saxony introduced fingerprinting, followed by Hamburg and Berlin. A Belgian anarchist was traced by his fingerprints on anonymous letters. A man broke into a morgue where his wife's body lay; through fingerprinting he was identified as her murderer. That convinced the Belgian authorities. Italy followed suit and Russia adopted fingerprinting in all major prisons in 1906. Six years later a Russian jury convicted a man of murder on fingerprint evidence. Now it was only a matter of time before *bertillonage* was completely outmoded. Really only Romania, Luxembourg and Monaco were left amongst European adherents.

Part of the trouble was that Bertillon was unwilling to shift his stance. His colleagues Dr Lacassagne and Dr Locard in Lyons had been urging him to do so, but he would not listen. Locard, for example, had been burning his own fingers with oil and hot irons to prove that fingerprints never changed.

In a more practical demonstration of the immutability of fingerprints in the early 1900s, an old lag who had not been recognised in court but who had been remanded in custody for a week, 'excoriated (with a pluck and perseverance worthy of a better cause) the papillary ridges of his thumbs and fingers by means of a metal tag attached to his bootlace'. On his arrival at Brixton prison his hands were in such a state that it was feared that if the ink for fingerprinting were applied it might result in blood poisoning. As a result he was remanded from week to week until his fingertips had healed and the impressions revealed his identity.[14]

Perhaps Bertillon's downfall came about with the theft on 22 August 1911 of Leonardo da Vinci's *Mona Lisa* from the Salon Carré in the Louvre. The theft caused an international political scandal, with suggestions that the painting had been stolen on the orders of Kaiser Wilhelm II. In fact the answer was much more mundane; it had been taken by an Italian house-painter, Vicenzo Perrugia, who simply removed it from the wall, hid it under his painter's smock and walked out with it. In circumstances reminiscent of

[14] Melville Macnaghten, *Days of My Years*, p. 106.

Adam Worth and the Duchess of Devonshire (see Chapter 7), the painting remained under his bed in a room on the rue de l'Hôpital Saint-Louis for over two years until he offered it to a Florentine art dealer, Alfredo Geri. The suggestion then was that he wanted to return the painting to Italy because it had been stolen by Napoleon. In fact it hadn't.

The difficulty for Bertillon was that Perrugia's fingerprints were on the files. His prints had been taken in 1909 when he tried to steal a prostitute's purse, but unfortunately the files had become far too cumbersome to search. The matter was hushed up by the resourceful Lepine, who did not want to cause damage to a national treasure such as Bertillon even if he had, by now, become a liability. The good news for Lepine was that Bertillon was dying of pernicious anaemia and progress could soon be made. He died, now blind, on 13 February 1914.

In the spring of that year an International Police Conference was held in Monaco, one of the last strongholds of *bertillonage*. There his successor M. David proposed that the standard method of identification be fingerprinting.

Meanwhile, for the past 30 years the police forces in the United States had been experimenting with both *bertillonage* and fingerprinting. As far back as 1882 Gilbert Thompson, a railroad engineer, had been taking a thumbprint from each of the workers on their wage slips to safeguard himself against forgeries. In 1885 it was suggested that thumbprints should be stamped on railroad tickets, and the same year there was another proposal, this time that the ever-increasing number of Chinese immigrants be registered by their thumbprints.

It was not, however, until 1903 that the great value of fingerprinting over *bertillonage* was recognised. Quite by chance McCloughty, the Warden of Fort Leavenworth, had been sent a copy of the Henry book on fingerprints together with a rudimentary test kit. Apparently the Warden experimented and was not impressed. Then some months later a black prisoner, Will West, was being measured and photographed under Card No. 3246 when one of the guards discovered his exact Bertillon measurements (within the tolerated discrepancies) on Card 2626. West protested that he was not the same man, who was found in fact to be in one of the work-shops. The discovery spelled the slow death of *bertillonage* in the States.

Fingerprinting came to New York through Police Commissioner William McAdoo who heard of the identification of West. Since the process had been a great attraction at the Louisiana Purchase Exposition in St Louis, he sent a Detective Sergeant Joseph A. Faurot to London to learn the techniques. However, by the time he returned, full of enthusiasm, McAdoo had been replaced and Faurot was told to forget the system. However, like so many other pioneers he continued with his own experiments, assembling a private collection of fingerprints.

On 16 April 1906 Faurot, on patrol for hotel creepers, saw a shoeless man, otherwise in full evening dress, leaving a suite in the Waldorf-Astoria. The man explained that he was British, that his name was James Jones and that he had just been leaving after an assignation. He demanded to see the British Consul and nearly bluffed his way out of the situation, but Faurot insisted on having 'Jones' give his fingerprints which he wired to Scotland Yard. Back came the reply that he was in fact Daniel Nolan, otherwise known as Henry Johnson, who had 12 previous convictions for burglary.

The first American murder case officially solved with the use of fingerprinting was the strangling of a nurse, Nellie Quinn, in 1908. As in the Stratton case, the crime scene had become contaminated with beat policemen and others on the premises who had touched a number of objects in the room. However, they had not touched a whisky bottle on the table and Faurot was able to obtain prints, some of which were the nurse's and some those of a neighbour. Faurot was able to establish that the girl had only purchased the bottle earlier in the evening and the neighbour confessed.[15]

Another early American case in which fingerprinting was used to convict and hang a suspect was that of Thomas Jennings in

---

[15] Faurot was regarded as very much the father of American fingerprinting. After his success in 1911 he went on to establish the police department's fingerprint bureau. He retired in 1930 with the rank of deputy commissioner and three years later set up a company to provide 'clean fingerprinting' instead of messy inkprinting. It did not catch on. He died in 1942. See *Time*, 23 April 1933.

Chicago. On 19 September 1910 Clarence Hiller awoke at his home on W 104th Street and, going out onto the landing, found a burglar. The men fought and Hiller was shot dead. The evidence was strong: Jennings was arrested within a mile of the shooting and he was carrying a loaded revolver; three bullets were found by Hiller's body; Jennings was wearing bloodstained clothing – caused, he said, when he fell from a street-car.

More important, however, were the fingerprints found in paint in the kitchen. With echoes of the early discovery by Herschel, Hiller had been painting the kitchen railings and the paint was still wet. Four perfect prints had been left by Jennings.

So far these had been cases where there was either a confession or a good deal of corroborative evidence. It was an entirely different matter to persuade a jury to accept fingerprint evidence on its own, particularly when ranged against a defence which called five alibi witnesses. In May 1911 Caesar Cella, a well-known New York burglar, raised $3,000 for his defence to a charge that he had broken into a millinery shop. His alibi was that on the night of the burglary he had been to the Hippodrome and then home with his wife.

Faurot had found and photographed the prints of several dirty fingers on the shop window and identified them as those of Cella. Just as Collins had done in the Stratton case 15 years earlier, Faurot enlarged the prints so that the jury could see the points of identification more clearly. During Faurot's evidence the judge stopped the proceedings, ordering him from the room and again, as in the Stratton case, an experiment began. In Faurot's absence various lawyers and court personnel pressed their fingers on panes of glass in the windows of the court, noting carefully whose print was where. Additionally, one man placed his fingerprint on a glass desktop. When Faurot returned and, after examining the prints, made the correct identifications, Cella changed his plea to one of guilty.

Before he was sentenced Judge Rosalsky promised that there would be no indictments against his alibi witnesses if Cella told the court whether he had really committed the crime and how:

It is most important in the cause of justice and science that you tell the whole truth. It is invaluable to us to know whether the expert testimony given during this trial was correct.

Cella said that his alibi had in part been correct; he had been to the theatre and returned home with his wife, but while she was asleep he had gone out and committed the burglary. He received 6 months imprisonment.

It was reported that before the plea of guilty the jury was split 7:5 – seven for a conviction, because of Cella's previous record, while five, in view of the strong alibi, would not have convicted on fingerprints alone. 'That is beautifully characteristic of the jurybox – conservatism,' commented the editorial.[16]

Almost everyone concerned with the early days of fingerprints had some scientific background and was acting, if sometimes mistakenly, in good faith. The same could not be said for the early gun experts. For a good twenty years charlatans in America moved through rudimentary police laboratories and the courts selling their 'expert' evidence to whichever side paid the better. And, of course, they produced some terrible and tragic results.

Probably the first fully recorded case of an identification through ballistics came when on 9 December 1860 a labourer, Thomas Richardson, stood trial at Lincoln charged with the murder of Constable Alexander McBrian on 25 October that year. At about 4 a.m. McBrian had been on duty patrolling near the churchyard at Wyberton when he saw Richardson wearing a billycock hat pulled over his eyes and with something in his pocket. When McBrian went to question Richardson he shot the officer and fled. Badly

---

[16] *New York Times*, 11, 12, 13 and 20 May 1911. In February 1922 the highly talented Russian-born Lucas Panchenro, along with Englishman Harold Jones, was found burgling the offices of the Catering Trades Approved Society in Piccadilly, London. Jones received 5 years penal servitude to be followed by 5 years preventive detention for his pains. The Russian, said to be an absolute expert with safes, received 6 years penal servitude followed by his deportation. The pair were betrayed to the police because the safe had been emptied in readiness for their attack. Panchenro was said to have been another who would leave his sleeping wife in bed, do the job and be back before she woke up. Jones was not regarded in Panchenro's class with a safe. He was also either careless or unlucky; this was his 36th conviction for some sort of theft. *Thomson's Weekly News*, 18 February 1922.

wounded, McBrian managed to arouse the vicar, but he died later that morning after giving a description of his attacker.

This time the murder was solved not by matching the bullet but with the paper plugs used to stuff powder and bullets into the barrels of muzzle-loaders. Superintendent Manton found the singed remains of a tampion made from a page of *The Times*. When Richardson's home was searched he was found to have a double-barrelled pistol, one barrel of which had been fired while the second contained a matching piece of *The Times* from 27 March 1854. At his trial the jury was invited to return accident, manslaughter or wilful murder, with the judge seeming to favour a manslaughter verdict. They returned a verdict of wilful murder and Richardson was sentenced to death, but the sentence was respited on 20 December.[17]

Nearly 30 years earlier there had been an identification of a suspect through a bullet. In 1835 Henry Goddard, one of the Bow Street Runners, that semi-private band of detectives, had taken a bullet with a curious ridge from the body of a householder. In those days bullets were often homemade, and at the home of the suspect Goddard found a bullet mould with a slight gouge and a ridge on the bullet which matched the mould.

Ballistics were used in England in 1882 to trace the killer of PC George Coles, who was shot while trying to arrest a young man he had seen acting suspiciously outside the Baptist chapel opposite the Reeves paint factory in the Dalston Road, London. The man drew a pistol and fired two shots, one of which killed the policeman. A set of housebreaking tools was found behind a low wall of the chapel, but for nearly two years there was no sign of the murderer.

The bag of tools did provide one clue. A chisel had a crude 'ROCK' marked in the handle, and it was believed that a tool repairer had scratched the name Orrock into the wood when the owner left the tool for sharpening.

Inquiries led the police to believe that a young man, Thomas Henry Orrock, had acquired a pistol from *Exchange & Mart*. Initially he was placed on an identification parade, but he was not picked

---

[17] *The Times*, 10, 21 December 1860.

out and so was released. Later Sergeant Cobb was told that Orrock had used a tree on Tottenham Marshes for firing practice and the detective went there, found the tree and took out the bullets, matching them with the one which had killed Coles.

The police were also able to find youths who had been drinking with Orrock on the night of the murder, and they confirmed that they had all planned to burgle the church under cover of the prevailing fog. Orrock was traced to the jail at Coldbath Fields, Clerkenwell, where he was serving a short sentence, and was convicted at the Old Bailey. He was not as fortunate as Richardson and was hanged by James Berry on 6 October 1884 at Newgate prison.[18]

In the United States there was an early use of ballistics when in Oregon in 1852 a local sheriff was asked to examine a hole in a victim's shirt and give an opinion. With the firearm likely to have been used in the incident, the sheriff fired a shot into a shirt and produced a similar hole.

Another case in 1879 in Georgia involved a man named Moughon, charged with murder, who maintained he had not fired his gun for over a year. The trial judge sent for a gunsmith who found both barrels mildewed, which exculpated him. Three years later in Minnesota another gunsmith gave evidence about rifling which tended to show that a particular gun had been used.

The first murder case in England in which the new science of ballistics really came into play was that of Samuel Dougal, the Moat Farm murderer. Camille Holland, a wealthy spinster who lived at the farm at Audley End, disappeared in 1899. She had been living with Dougal whose two previous wives had died of oyster poisoning. Dougal having been found in the room of one of the servant girls, Miss Holland had decided he must go. The result was rather the reverse; he shot her and buried her in a trench. Well-wishers were told she was away on a yachting trip. It was only in 1903 – after Dougal had been seen trying to teach a naked girl to ride a bicycle and one of Miss Holland's cheques was found to have been forged – that a full inquiry began. Dougal claimed the shooting had been

---

[18] For a full account of the case see Belton Cobb, *Murdered on Duty*.

accidental, but the gunsmith E.J. Churchill carried out a series of tests using a .32 revolver on a number of sheep skulls. He then gave evidence that the shots had been fired from a distance between 6" and 1'.[19]

From then on the use of ballistics was generally accepted in the English courts. The Americans had a much harder struggle, with charlatans such as the *soi-disant* 'Dr' Albert Hamilton (who had begun his life as a patent medicine salesman) giving evidence to the highest bidder.[20] The science only became established there after the Chicago St Valentine's Day Massacre when Calvin Goddard was able to prove that the bullets fired had come from the same guns found at the home of the Detroit killer, Fred Burke, after his arrest a year later in Missouri.

There were also early attempts at criminal profiling, which uses the analysis of crime scenes and a vast amount of crime data to try and predict as accurately as possible what kind of person the criminal may be. This in itself is nothing new; it is the application which has produced a troubled history, particularly in recent years.

The traditional approach to detective work has been that the only clues of value are fingerprints, discarded equipment, bloodstains and the like, whereas profiling relates to the 'invisible' clues which help to define the perpetrator, such as the location and choice of victim, whether the victim is allowed to live and the type of assault. These factors are applied to create a profile and also to eliminate suspects. Many might say that this is only good police work based on experience. A burglar will usually operate within a limited range of his own home; unless the killer is a transient he also is likely to operate in a known area in which he feels comfortable. Even if he is a transient,

---

[19] For an account of the case see Gordon Honeycombe, *The Murders of the Black Museum*. Churchill's nephew, Robert, became perhaps the most famous of all ballistics experts giving evidence in countless trials, usually on behalf of the Crown. His biography is Macdonald Hastings' *The Other Mr Churchill*.

[20] Hamilton advertised himself as 'Micro-Chemical Investigator' and claimed to be an expert in chemistry, microscopy, handwriting analysis, toxicology, identification of bloodstains, causes of death, embalming and anatomy as well as gunshot wounds, guns, identification of bullets, gunpowder and high-explosives. Particularly adroit with a camera, realising how much blown-up photographs appealed to juries, he worked for $50 a day and expenses. One of his more ignominious appearances was in the celebrated trial of the anarchists Sacco and Vanzetti in 1921.

he is still likely to operate in an area which is 'safe' to him – a railway or bus station, a fast food complex and so on.

Offender profiling is the art – profilers will say science – of making correct deductions based on both physical and psychological clues such as the background of a likely offender. It is also a combination of appraisal and statistics. Another factor will be the type of similar offences committed by similar offenders. So if, for example, rapists statistically are shown to have previous convictions for indecent exposure, a profile of a rapist is likely to include a man who has at least one previous conviction for that offence.

The father of the criminal profile, as indeed of criminology itself, was undoubtedly Caesare Lombroso, an Italian army doctor. In the 1860s he began seeking the answer to whether criminals were physically different from ordinary people, and to this end he conducted studies of criminals imprisoned in Turin and Pavia.

In 1871 he made what he considered to be a breakthrough when he studied the skull of an Italian thief, Vilela:

> I found in the occipital part, exactly on the post where the spine is found in a normal skull, a distinct depression as in inferior animals, in particular rodents. I suddenly saw, lit up as a vast plane under the flaming sky, the nature of the criminal. An atavistic being who reproduced the ferocious instincts of primitive humanity and of the inferior animal.

Lombroso believed he had found evidence that a criminal's brain was different from that of a non-criminal, and he claimed that this was clearly displayed in the shape of the criminal's face:

> A criminal's ears are often of a large size. The nose is frequently upturned or of a flattened character in thieves. In murderers, on the contrary, it is often aquiline like the beak of a bird of prey.

As for the rapist:

> The lips of violators of women are fleshly, swollen and protruding. Swindlers have thin and straight lips.

Lombroso's controversial criminal typology does not stand up to modern scientific scrutiny, but at the time when it was fashionable it was hugely influential. Nowadays the studies he conducted can be ridiculed in their simplicity, but it was a beginning. He laid the foundations on which later generations would build houses if not skyscrapers.

It is the corrupt but highly successful New York police inspector Thomas Byrnes who is credited with the invention of the Third Degree, but he surely only refined and improved previous methods. One of the techniques credited to him is the sweatbox in which a cell was heated until the prisoner, unable to endure it, would promise to give the required answers. Another method of police interrogation in America at the time was dragging a cat's claws across a suspect's bare back.

In the case of Mike McGloin, the murderer from the Whyos street gang, Byrnes decided that he should not be allowed to sleep for more than 15 minutes at a time, and that his meals should always be late. He was put in a place where he could see the bloodstained clothes of his victim carried by, and he was allowed to see all the people who could have connected him with the murder coming and going around the prison. Another murderer gave up when he was made to sleep in the bed of his victim, and yet another when he was forced into the coffin in which the murdered man was to be buried.[21]

James Munro, the lay missionary who wrote *The New York Tombs*, was in no doubt as to how confession should be obtained:

> You know crooks are the worst kind of liar; unless the police gave them a moderate cuffing they would tell them a fake story which it would be a waste of time to listen to.

---

[21] A very similar situation occurred in the first case in Argentina to be solved by finger-printing. Ramon Velazquez, the suspect in the 1892 murder of the two young children of Francisca Rojas, apart from being beaten was bound and laid by the corpses overnight. But he did not confess, and the case was solved when a bloodstained fingerprint in the children's room turned out to be that of Rojas herself. This was regarded as the first time a murder had been solved in Argentina by the use of fingerprints and was, of course, some 15 years before that of the Strattons. The credit for the introduction of fingerprinting into the Argentine goes to Juan Vucetich.

The good pastor thought he was not in a position to state whether the police were actually justified, but he seems to have had a secret admiration for the German police who put a rat into a woman's cell so that it 'may exhaust her nervous system and her inner strength till she is unable to stick to her story'.[22]

'It was generally a case of the strain being too much for the human brain to stand,' said Lieutenant Edward F. Rayens when visiting London from the New York District Attorney's office shortly before the First World War. He took the opportunity to give an interview to the press explaining the Third Degree:

> The old Third Degree consisted chiefly of brutality. The suspects were not allowed to sleep. Whenever their cell door was opened a policeman or two would give them a couple of wallops with their fists or a blow or two with their clubs. Food was some-times denied them.
>
> You can take it from me that the stories that float across the 'pond' regarding the brutality and unfairness of our methods are exaggerations, and frequently pure inventions, but it is true that a prisoner is treated differently in America from the way in which he is treated in this country.
>
> If we have good grounds for suspecting anyone of a crime we try to make him confess. We tell him we 'have the goods' – to put it in English, we make him believe that we can prove his guilt and that it will be easier for him to confess. If we know that a man is guilty but cannot prove it, what possible objection can be taken to persuading him to confess?

But Lieut. Rayens maintained that things had indeed changed from Byrnes' day, and it was to be emphasised that kindness was the way to confession. As an example he enthusiastically quoted the New York detective, George Dougherty, as plying the suspect with Havana cigars until he confessed.[23]

---

[22] James Munro, *The New York Tombs Inside and Out*, p. 183.
[23] 'Truth about famous "Third Degree"' in *Thomson's Weekly News*, 12 July 1913. The previous year in the notorious Conway case in Chicago a woman had confessed to the murder of her husband after 48 hours' continuous questioning. She had not been struck or beaten by the officers, merely questioned until, after several fainting spells and an attack of hysteria, she confessed.

Perhaps the gesture was not wholly altruistic and it was simply to make the suspect sick. In fact this kindly treatment had been adopted by the Paris Sûreté since the days of the thief turned detective, Eugène-François Vidocq. It was certainly a technique of the great French detectives Gustave Mace and Marie-François Goron. They found that a good meal and a bottle of burgundy helped loosen the criminal throat no end. If that didn't work, there was always the reward of a visit by a prostitute for a really good confession.[24]

---

[24] Goron was the Chef de la Sûreté from 1887 until well into the 1890s. He had been appointed assistant to the then Chief, Taylor, in 1886 and succeeded him the following year.

22

Prisons and Escapers

The Tombs, situated on New York's West Side at White and Leonard and which covered Lafayette and Mulberry, opened its doors for business in 1838. It had been built on marshland to provide work for the poor. Officially it was named the Hall of Justice, but took its name because its design was copied from an ancient mausoleum. Like Dartmoor, it was cold and damp and the conditions provoked something of a scandal.[1]

In the 1880s the lay missionary James Munro wrote of the Tombs:

> No prison on the American continent has had such an unsavoury reputation as a corrupt grafting institution as the New York Tombs. For many years the Tombs prison has been the happy hunting ground for graft and rake-offs of various kinds given in return for all kinds of privileges.[2]

However, it was an immediate success in the neighbourhood mainly because locals could charge between one and five dollars,

---

[1] Another prison which survives, Riker's Island, south-east of the Bronx and named after the family which owned it, was bought from them in 1884 as a prison farm. It was converted into a prison in 1932. In 1902 the Tombs began to sink.

[2] He found there were some 80 boys a week in the Tombs, around half of whom had venereal disease. 'Here they learned to become expert pickpockets'. James Munro, *The Tombs of New York Inside and Out*, p. 13.

depending on the notoriety of the condemned man, to watch hangings there. Hangmen were encouraged to prolong the proceedings so that more money could be spent in local shops.

Generally, New York prisons of the nineteenth century were by no means secure. There is no doubt the jailers were susceptible to bribery and, even when they weren't, the walls do not seem to have been all that thick.

It was only three years after its opening that the 22-year-old socialite John C. Colt, brother of the more famous gunsmith Sam, who had killed the printer Samuel Adams, escaped from the Tombs. Colt had quarrelled with Adams over the production of a book. The playboy's friends included Washington Irving and James Fenimore Cooper and he received, as was his due, considerably better treatment than the run-of-the-mill inmates. His luncheon was sent in and afterwards he was allowed a cigar; he wore his own cherry-coloured dressing-gown; his cell was filled with flowers and in a cage on the wall was a canary; on his exercise walks he carried a gold-headed switch.[3]

His fiancée, Caroline Henshaw, was a constant visitor to the Tombs, and the greatest concession was that she was allowed to marry him four hours before his execution on 18 November 1842. The witnesses were Colt's brother and John Howard Payne, the composer of 'Home Sweet Home', with the Reverend Anton performing the ceremony. The bride arrived at about 11.30 by carriage and, because of the crowds, was obliged to enter the prison through a side entrance. As a courtesy, during the actual ceremony the carpenters erecting the gallows stopped their hammering. The bride and groom were allowed one hour alone during which champagne was served, the curtains to the cell were drawn and the hammering recommenced. All this was faithfully relayed to the crowd which cheered and groaned accordingly. The hour up, Mrs Colt departed and Colt then asked to be left alone, no doubt for a little quiet reflection and perhaps even prayer.

Just before the warden was to collect Colt for the hanging the

---

[3] Charles A. Dana in the *Tribune*.

fire alarm was raised and the cupola of the prison was found to be ablaze. Panic broke out and prisoners demanded to be let out of their cells. When the sheriff returned, Colt was lying dead with a knife in his heart. At 7 p.m. that night a coroner's jury returned a verdict of suicide. The body was taken from the prison and buried in a grave at St Mark's Church. The best interpretation of events is that a substitute corpse had been found, the coroner was aware of the deception and the jurors were selected for their ignorance of Colt's appearance. Mrs Colt disappeared and Colt escaped to Texas where the pair lived in style on a hacienda in the Santa Clara Valley.[4]

In fact the Tombs did not have too bad a record for escapes. In the first 35 years of its existence there were only 28, including six youths who got out through a window on the Franklin Street side on 11 April 1859 and were never recaptured. One of the more celebrated escapes was that of Conrad Smith, also known as Schrader, who on 19 September 1863 with the help of some other prisoners removed an iron lintel, so creating a small gap. He then soaped himself from head to toe and slid through it. He hid out for a month before the lure of the Bowery proved too much and he was recaptured in a bar.

Another of the more daring escapes from the Tombs was that organised by Maggie Jourdan, the girlfriend of William J. Sharkey who, on Sunday 1 September 1872, shot dead Robert Dunn, a one-time faro banker, over a debt. Sharkey and some others had been at the funeral of James Reilly that afternoon. Dunn was also there. The killing took place at the liquor saloon of Charles Harvey, known appropriately enough as The Place, at 288 Hudson Street.

Sharkey and Jourdan seem to have come from relatively respectable backgrounds. Said to have been the son of a prominent

---

[4] Some discount the story of the substituted corpse, but the coincidences seem too great. For example, why did Mrs Colt disappear that night? In 1850 Edgar Allen Poe and Lewis Clark, the editor of the *Knickerbocker* magazine, each received a manuscript which they identified as being written by Colt. Two years later Samuel Everett, a close friend of Colt, reported that he had visited him and his wife at the ranch. It is encouraging to note that a number of the prisoners released from their cells also escaped during the fire.

clergyman, he slipped from the paths of righteousness to become a talented pickpocket and then a stolen bond businessman, as well as managing cracksmen's jobs at which he was regarded as a star. He then took up with the disreputable Louisa Jourdan, later known as Mrs Derrigan, and organised the Sharkey Guard who ruled the corner of Wooster and Houston. It was then that his talents came to be noticed by the Ring. And once he was under their tutelage and patronage, 'there was no better-dressed man in the city, after a certain style, and his diamonds were of a true Tammany Hall brilliancy'.[5]

He had been nominated as Assistant Alderman, but lost the contest through internal juggling. Disgusted with politics, he turned back to gambling and loaned Dunn $600 to start a faro bank in Buffalo, something which Dunn promptly lost.

If it is correct that Maggie Jourdan came from a good family she did not merely slip, she fell. She was at one time the companion of Thomas Murphy, the well-known pickpocket, a profession in which her sister Josephine was similarly involved. It was about the time when their brother was charged in Connecticut with bond robbery that Maggie fell in love with Sharkey.

Now Sharkey wanted the $600 repaid. When Dunn said he did not have it, Sharkey produced a single-barrelled hair-trigger Derringer. Dunn said, 'Don't shoot, Billy.' But Sharkey shot him dead. As Dunn lay on the floor Sharkey said, 'Bov, I did not mean to shoot you' and made his escape. He was traced to a house in Washington Street and arrested where again he repeated that it was an accident.

In June the following year he was found guilty of murder in the first degree and was sentenced to be hanged. It was while he was running through a series of appeals that he escaped, disguised in women's clothing and using the pass of Mrs Wes Allen whose

[5] Born in England in 1844, Louisa Jourdan was described by Thomas Byrnes as 'lady-like in appearance and matters'. She was first married to Tom McCormack, the bank burglar who killed Jim Casey in New York. As the companion of a Brazilian lady, she stole her mistress's jewels and received 40 lashes and had part of her right ear cut off. As a result she wore her hair long to cover the deformity.

husband was then doing 6 years in Sing Sing.[6] An odd-looking woman who kept her veil close to her face was suspected and followed but, wearing a pair of new gaiters and French high heels, she nimbly leaped on a tram for Bleeker Street and was away. When the tram conductor was later questioned, he said that far from the character being a woman it was a man who had descended at Walker Street.

Maggie Jourdan, described as 'rather pretty', was charged with helping Sharkey to escape. She was defended by Bill Howe and ex-Judge Beach who, given Howe's known talents, somewhat surprisingly appears to have had the closing speech. The jury could not agree and she was discharged.

Sharkey stayed in New York for some three weeks before taking a small schooner to Baraca and then travelling to Havana where he was joined by Maggie. It would be good to record that they lived happily ever afterwards, but it would not be correct. In short order he began to mistreat her and she returned to New York.

Sometimes it appears that the function of some of the other American prisons of the period was simply to facilitate escapes; one of the more successful from Sing Sing at Ossining up the Hudson River was from the death house when, in the early hours of 20 April 1893, Thomas Pallister and Frederick Roche got clean away. Just how much co-operation they received is another matter.

In theory, however, it was simply enterprise. In the death house there was a stove on which food could be warmed throughout the night, and prisoners were allowed out of their cells to brew tea and coffee. Roche asked to be allowed out and, since he had done this many times before, Keeper Hulse agreed. Roche threw pepper in his eyes, took away his keys and locked him in his cell. He then unlocked Pallister and together they climbed through a skylight, dropped into the prison yard and made off in a waiting boat. It was nine hours before the authorities knew of the break. The pair were never recaptured and it was thought they had either drowned or reached the safety of South America. It was suggested but never proved that bribes of $5,000 had been paid.

[6] See *New York Herald*, 20 November 1873.

There is one slightly sad note to the story. They offered to take another man, Carlyle Harris, along with them, but he claimed he was innocent and would wait for the court's verdict. It was a poor decision, since he was found guilty and electrocuted.[7]

The arrest of the shoplifter 'Long Mary' Moon led to an explanation as to why there were so many escapes from Sing Sing. When the police searched her room they found a wax impression of a key to Gallery 19 of the prison.

There was certainly no doubt as to how the handsome Edward Biddle and his brother Jack, the leaders of a gang of burglars, escaped from Butler's jail in Pennsylvania on 30 January 1902. The brothers claimed they had been wrongly convicted of the killing of a storekeeper and a private detective. The jailer's wife, 26-year-old Katherine Scoffel, had fallen in love with Edward, having met the brothers in the first instance because it was her practice to attempt to bring the solace of religion to condemned men. Now she supplied them with files, hacksaws, guns and ammunition. The brothers threw a warder from a landing and escaped with Mrs Scoffel in tow. The alarm was raised but they made it to open ground and, chased by the police, took a sleigh. A gun battle resulted in all three being shot. The Biddle brothers died of their injuries in short order, with Katherine Scoffel begging Ed to kill her. Scoffel, the jailer, resigned, leaving the prison and taking his children with him. He said that he suspected – probably quite correctly – that he had been chloroformed by his wife.

Katherine Scoffel survived and was sentenced to 2 years in the prison where her husband had worked. Asked how she could have fallen in love with a vicious killer like Biddle, she was reported as saying she could forgive him anything except not killing her so that they could have been together in death.[8]

Even in the early days, stays on Death Row could be lengthy. In

---

[7] The situation was repeated when Dennis Stockton, wrongly believing he would eventually be proved innocent, declined to join an escape from Death Row at the Mecklenburg Correctional Center, Virginia, on 31 May 1984.

[8] She was released after 18 months and lived, ostracised, until 1926. The story was turned into a melodrama, *The Biddle Brothers*, which played throughout America for some years. *New York Times*, 31 January 1902; *Illustrated Police News*, 8 February 1902.

1909 Raefello Casonea was finally acquitted after spending 31 months and 23 days in the death house. He had the No. 1 cell and during his tenure had been permitted to shake hands with the 12 men who were electrocuted in that time. After being released he was shot by the 17-year-old brother of his victim, and he died on 10 August that year.

They ordered things very differently in England where the majority of the prisons were built throughout Queen Victoria's reign. Pentonville, designed as a model prison, was opened in 1842; Parkhurst, for juvenile male offenders, came six years later and Wandsworth in 1849. Brixton, designed originally as a female prison, was first opened in 1853 and Holloway, then the City of London jail, the same year. But Wormwood Scrubs did not open until 1874 and was not completed – by convict labour – until 1891.[9]

Until the report of the committee under Sir Henry Gladstone in 1895 prisoners were treated as unworthy, hopeless wretches set to perform meaningless tasks such as the treadmill, or cockchafer as it was also known. Frank Fraser, now nearly 80, recalls one man whom he met in 1943 in Wandsworth who had been on the treadmill:

> He must have been well over eighty. Johnny Ryan or Grey he called himself. He went in the nick first in the 1880s. He used to say that men would cry when they were forced onto it to climb the required 8,700 feet a day. If you didn't climb high enough then there was a cut in your rations, which weren't much, or a whipping or both. When you went to church of a Sunday you was all hooded and you had to have your hand on the shoulder of the man in front. He was a sort of trusty and didn't have a hood. You could only take it off when you was in your pew which was high sided so you could only see in front.[10]

---

[9] The great prisons around the country opened in the same period: Birmingham in 1845, Liverpool in 1854 and Manchester in 1869.
[10] Conversation with author, 21 August 2002.

The crank was doubly useful because this task could be performed by the prisoner in his cell. The prisoner turned the equivalent of 12 lbs per revolution and was required to do 20 revolutions a minute. The 1,200 revolutions an hour were recorded on a dial and 10,000 were required daily from the prisoner, a total of 8 hours 20 minutes' work, if it can be called that. When it was discovered that some men could do their 10,000 stint in under the time allowed, a screw in the wheel was tightened to make it more difficult. The legacy of the crank is the name give to prison officers. Another (this time outdoor) activity was moving what looked like stone cannonballs from one end of the prison yard to the other and back again all day. It was not until the Prison Act 1896 incorporating Gladstone's report that prisoners were given useful work.

There were also efforts to reform the young criminal. A new prison at Borstal in Kent which was opened for young people seems to have been a highly risky enterprise by today's standards. Boys could earn marks for industry and when they reached a total of 300 their conditions improved dramatically. Not only could they receive and send letters and have visits every month instead of six weeks; they could have cells with iron bedsteads, a strip of carpet and – the most prized possession of all – a looking-glass, which seems rather dangerous. The boys worked an 8-hour day, reproducing conditions in the outside world.

In New York a court for children was opened on 3rd Avenue, where there were two waiting-rooms with toys and books. The first case, that of a girl charged with stealing a loaf of bread for her invalid father, was said to have reduced Magistrate Olosted to tears, while he glared severely at two boys charged with tossing pennies in the street.[11]

Dartmoor prison with its inscription *Parcere Subjectis* – Spare the Humbled – over the gates was built in 1806 to hold French prisoners from the Napoleonic Wars. When transportation to Australia was under attack in the 1830s, largely by the Australian government which rightly complained that the structure of its

[11] *Morning Leader*, 5 November 1902.

society was being undermined by wave upon wave of prison ships, prisoners had to be housed somewhere. The cold, inhospitable and – because of difficulties in getting off the Moor – supposedly escape-proof Dartmoor was the answer. In 1836 there had been a plan for the prison to house 700 juveniles, but the estimated cost of conversion was £72,000 and the project was dropped in favour of Albany Barracks on the equally escape-proof Isle of Wight. By 1842 Millbank prison was full, and Pentonville was over-subscribed even before it was completed. It was not until 1850 that a small number of artisan convicts from Millbank were sent to Dartmoor.

The first Governor as such, Sir Joshua Jebb – after whom Brixton prison's approach road, Jebb Avenue, is named – was one of the more enlightened. Prisoners were given the luxury of white bread, and senior prisoners had a glass of beer on a Sunday. Children from the Moor were sent to collect the leavings, and in turn their leavings were fed to the local pigs. It would be pleasant to report that this carrot approach promoted good conduct amongst the inmates, but it did not. There was slack discipline, a good deal of profanity amongst the prisoners, and warders in charge of working parties were repeatedly pelted with stones. For their part the warders were poorly paid and poorly educated. Unlike the police, of which there was no lingering officer class, the warders were subject to discipline by ex-Naval and Army officers, mainly those who had failed to gain promotion. Infringements of regulations were punished severely and warders were encouraged to spy and report on their colleagues.

But escapes could and did take place. In 1850 prisoners John Brodrick, John Thompson and Charles Webster managed to have themselves sent to the infirmary by faking mental illness – putting on the barmy stick, as it was known. Once there they took up the floor of the ward and managed to get into the basement where tools were stored. They forced a door and, using a scaffolding plank as a ladder, were over the wall and away. For the first time descriptions of the convicts were circulated in the locality and four days into the escape Thompson was arrested in the village of Ashburton. They had clearly been travelling as a party because a short time later Brodrick and Webster were caught a mile away. Brodrick was held, but Webster wriggled free and escaped; he was never seen again.

A few months later Gordon Taylor tried his luck and reached Plymouth before he was caught. For his pains he was transported to Bermuda. It cannot be said that after that the escapes came thick and fast, but there was a fairly steady stream of attempts. To counter them locals were paid £5 a head for each prisoner recaptured; but in April 1851 John Cotton and John Jones escaped, robbed a man and were never caught. Thomas Clutch managed, with amazing agility, to get through the bars and climbed the wall by digging his hands and toes into spaces between the stones.

The prison was now becoming something of a place to go for an outing. In August 1851 there were so many sightseers that the military guard could not get through and two prisoners Baker and Griffiths took advantage of the situation to break through the wall. They survived only a few hours on the outside.[12]

With the death of Jebb in 1862 so prison discipline changed, from the prisoners' point of view not for the better. The last few years of his office had been marred by a series of incidents. Attacks on warders had increased. In September 1861 four convicts had captured, tried and flogged a man named Kean whom they suspected of being an informer. The previous year two prisoners on their way to Chatham had managed to leap out of a train between Reading and Maidenhead. When it was discovered that their chain had been cut, Assistant Warder White was discharged and Principal Warder Brown was reduced in rank. Part of the discontent was caused by the new rule that re-convicted ticket-of-leave men could not earn remission.

The new Governor Colonel Henderson cut the rations, ordered that the men march properly to work and tightened discipline generally. Now a man worked in his cell for the first nine months of his

---

[12] Merely because prisoners were not recaptured does not mean the escape had been successful. There were bogs and mires all over the Moor and some men simply died of exposure. On 5 January 1959 the house-breaker William Day escaped along with Dennis Stafford. Day fell into a reservoir and, although Stafford threw him a lifebelt, he drowned.

sentence. Unsuccessful escapes were rewarded by a public flogging naked before the rest of the men. Twenty-four to 36 lashes were considered the norm, but there could be more. The men were tied to a triangle with a leather pad protecting the lower part of their backs. A doctor was present and could stop the flogging if he thought the man could stand no more. However, this was not the end of the matter, since the flogging was resumed when he was deemed fit again.

In 1878, by which time Captain Harris was Governor, a Commission of Enquiry on Penal Servitude was established to examine conditions in the prison. One of the men who gave evidence was the one-armed Michael Davitt who had been sentenced to 15 years for felony treason in 1870.

Davitt's first job had been breaking stones, which ended when his hand blistered from using the hammer. He was then sent out to work in an eight-man party pulling a cart loaded with stones, rubbish or manure around the prison. To do this he had to wear a kind of halter which covered his chest. When the halter caught the end of the amputated arm and almost pushed the bone through the skin, he was excused and sent back to breaking stones. After that he had to carry tubs of water to men mixing mortar, and then was put to winding an iron crank used to shift blocks of stone. The next job was breaking putrid bones into powder, and finally back to stone-breaking. These were considered light duties.

The Governor now denied that men were searched naked in front of others, but he was unable to say when the practice had ceased. The men had one bath a fortnight and a footbath once a week. They could be made to have their hair cut on a daily basis. Punishments less than a flogging could include withdrawal of letters for a month. By the turn of the century there were still some 1,700 men in the prison, with a third punished annually: bread and water, cell confinement, and restraint which meant wearing a broad leather body-belt fastened at the back with an iron handcuff at each wrist. Despite assurances by the Governor Captain Frank Johnson to the subsequent Gladstone Committee that convicts were healthier both mentally and physically on their release, Dartmoor had a far higher death rate than any other prison.[13] Two years later Visitors to the prison were appointed with the intention of providing a rudimentary check on excesses by the staff.

One man actually broke back into Dartmoor. Towards the end of the nineteenth century there were a few black convicts, none of whom was regarded as a model prisoner. On 17 August 1890 Joe Denny was trapped when he activated a rudimentary alarm inside the prison. He had walked from London, apparently with the express intention of killing the Chief Warder and firing the prison. He had been living rough and was later charged with killing a ewe from which he had cut a handful of raw meat.

Nor, when convicts complained, did anyone take very much notice of them. When Richard Wooley (serving 18 months) and George Harris pleaded guilty at London Sessions on 4 September 1909 to smashing tiles and glass worth £27 at Wormwood Scrubs prison, Wooley took the opportunity to tell the court about the conditions in the jail. Until the time of this minor mutiny it was accepted that he had been a model prisoner. Now he told the court he had been suffering from malaria but despite this had been required to perform hard labour. He had received tyrannical treatment and been taunted and bullied by the warders, but could not complain without being himself put on a charge and also put on bread and water. He had been reduced to the First Stage, which meant he could neither write nor receive letters, nor have visitors, and had lost library privileges. Added to that, he was in strict solitary confinement. Punishments were imposed for such things as not paying attention at Divine Service, making communicatory gestures to other prisoners and looking out of the cell window. He and Harris had staged their demonstration to 'open the eyes of the Governor'. After the demonstration he had been kicked and beaten and thrown off a roof into the flower-beds of the prison exercise yard.

His outburst did him no good whatsoever. A senior warder was called to say that conditions in the jail were little less than perfect, and the judge said that discipline in prison must be maintained.

---

[13] For an account of Dartmoor's early years, see Tom Tullet, *Inside Dartmoor*.

Wooley received another 6 months and Harris 9 months.

Their cases could be contrasted with the experience of a short-term prisoner who found that communication between experienced prisoners was relatively easy. During Divine Service while the Old Hundredth hymn was being sung, one convict sang:

> How long are you in for?
> I'm doing 60 days
> I nearly broke a copper's jaw
> Sing low or else they'll maybe hear.

The second replied:

> You are a lucky pie-can
> I've got twelve months to serve
> Tried to break into a house.
> Someb'dy must have gi'en me away.[14]

A very few people did manage to get clean away from a prison. By 1898 the only man to escape from Portland, the prison on a Dorset peninsula, had been William Beckett in 1870 while serving 10 years for burglary. Somehow he obtained a rough tool with which he removed stones from his cell. He then managed to enter the ventilation shaft, having previously saved some of his bread ration which lasted him six days while he waited for a favourable tide to swim to the mainland avoiding the guards. There he broke into the house of a clergyman, fed himself and made off with the man's clothing. He was stopped by a policeman who saw Beckett, dressed as the vicar, gorging himself on blackberries. It seems he bluffed his way out of trouble until the constable noticed he was wearing prison socks. In 1871 he received another 8 years for the escape and theft of the clothing. In December 1898 he was back in court for failing to report as a ticket-of-leave man; this time he received a further 9 months.[15]

---

[14] *Illustrated Police News*, 4 September and 16 January 1909.
[15] Ibid., 10 December 1898.

There was no other successful escape from the prison for over 30 years. In 1902 James Westcliffe, who also went under the names of Wantage and Winter, escaped while serving 10 years. Westcliffe's stock-in-trade was a version of the pigeon drop. He would go to a jewellers and then take the man out to luncheon, at the end of which he would seemingly drop a nugget. Casually he would ask the value and on being told £75 would ask for £50 as he was temporarily embarrassed. The jeweller would end up with a heavily plated nugget.

One day Westcliffe simply did not answer at the roll-call. About three weeks later a young girl sighted a nearly naked man in a nearby village; but when she alerted other men, of Westcliffe there was no further sign. He was believed to have escaped dressed as a stewardess on a liner to Montreal, because when the boat docked two suits of men's clothing were found to be missing from a passenger's cabin. The company also reported the loss of a stewardess. It was thought that he was back working in England in the early 1920s because jewellers up and down the country were reporting identical frauds.[16]

Even when a prison escape was temporarily successful, the convict could not expect any sympathy from the authorities if he received a rough handling from the public.

When on 24 April 1909, Johannes Witer, a Belgian waiter convicted of three burglaries carried out in one night in Belgravia, escaped from Winchester he was treated rather as a fox, with the local gentry out on horseback following the bloodhounds, Solferino and Waterloo.

Witer's initial capture had come about when he was sitting on a seat on Ramsgate promenade. His nerve was not what it should have been because when he thought a policeman was looking at him suspiciously he ran away. Chased, he turned and shot at the officer; missing, he turned the gun on himself, shooting himself in the eye. Subsequently he received 15 years at Maidstone Assizes.

Somehow Witer had managed to obtain a pair of scissors and taken off the lock of his cell. He survived on the outside for rather

---

[16] *Empire News*, 1922.

over a week, carrying out a series of burglaries to provide himself with food and clothing. At the end of one day during which they had followed a wrong trail, and with Witer nowhere to be seen, Solferino was described as tired and Waterloo dejected.[17] Things improved with the introduction of a third dog, Tsar, and Witer was spotted by a police officer who wittily called, 'Gone away.' Witer was caught by a sergeant who was given £5 on the spot by the Chief Constable who had been following the chase on a horse. There was much local rejoicing and cheering as the man was marched through a village and 'the village parson swung his straw hat in the air'.[18]

Witer at least fared rather better than another escapee, John Jones, also known as Coch Bach and Little Turpin, who died at the hands of the 19-year-old Old Etonian Reginald Bateman. Jones, a man with six sentences of penal servitude behind him and convictions for wounding with intent and office breaking, escaped from Ruthin Gaol on 6 September 1913 by digging through a 2' 6"-thick wall. Dressed in sacking and carrying a monkey wrench, on 3 October he encountered Elizabeth Jones and Bateman on land owned by the Naylor-Leyland family. Apparently Jones threatened to kill them, struck Bateman and then swung at him with the monkey wrench. In return Bateman shot him in the feet. Jones collapsed and was left to die where he fell as the others went for the police. A coroner's jury returned a verdict of manslaughter, but the authorities were having nothing of it. When Bateman appeared for committal to the Assizes the next week, the Attorney General indicated that he did not wish to intervene and the Chief Constable told the court:

> I may add that on the facts at present before me were I to undertake the prosecution of this case I should do so only for the purpose of suggesting that this was not a case in which the magistrates ought to commit the accused for trial.

---

[17] They must have come from the same family as the bloodhounds who were hired to find Jack the Ripper and who lost themselves and their master.
[18] *Illustrated Police News*, 1 and 8 May 1909.

The bench agreed with him and Bateman was discharged to cheers from the public gallery.[19]

[19] *The Times*, 6, 8, 14, 17 October 1913; *Thomson's Weekly News*, 18 October 1913. Prisoners could be shot with impunity while trying to escape. On 1 July 1909 James Henry, then serving 4 years, was brought down by a bullet in the thigh when trying to escape from a Dartmoor working party. There was some surprise expressed at his attempted escape, since it was a bright clear day with none of the fog for which convicts would normally try to wait. *Illustrated Police News*, 10 July 1909. Even so, this does not compare with the efforts by the German authorities to prevent escapes. After the notorious burglar Bertram broke his handcuffs and tried to escape for the nineteenth time while serving a sentence of hard labour in Aachen, his cell was filled with water to the level of his mouth. *Illustrated Police News*, 21 January 1905.

For sheer endurance, one of the great escapes must be that by Joseph Creswick, sentenced in Rhodesia for forgery. While being transferred in leg-irons between Bulawayo and Salisbury, he jumped from the train. Eight months later he was found exhausted about 200 miles from Leopoldville in the Congo by some explorers. They nursed him back to health and furnished him with cricket flannels and a football jersey. He managed to work his passage to Antwerp and then came to London where, sadly, recognised by Detective Inspector Belcher of Scotland Yard, he was arrested and deported. *Morning Leader*, 27 December 1909.

23

Death

Throughout the period there were also what might generously be described as improvements in the techniques used to execute criminals both in Britain and in the United States.

Until 1868 hangings in England and Wales were conducted in public, but now there was something approaching squeamishness in the air.[1] The novelist William Thackeray had printed his tract against public hanging, and it was decided that in future executions should be held within prison walls. This did not mean to say there could not be a fair number of privileged spectators invited to witness the event. The last public execution was that of the Fenian Michael Barrett, hanged on 26 May 1868 at the Old Bailey for his part in the Clerkenwell Explosion. Three months later, the first private execution was that of 18-year-old Thomas Wells who had been convicted of the murder of Edward Walshe, the stationmaster at Dover Priory station where Wells was employed. Wells was facing

[1] Between 1867 and 1874 there were seven unsuccessful attempts to pass bills in Parliament designed to establish degrees of murder. There was continual agitation by organisations such as the Howard Association to obtain reprieves, and on occasion they were successful. At the Winter Assizes at Gloucester in December 1871, six out of seven condemned were reprieved. The only failure was at Cheltenham when a number of clergymen intervened on behalf of 20-year-old Fred Jones who had cut the throat of his girlfriend Emily Gardner on 10 December.

dismissal for poor work and while Walshe was discussing the matter with his supervisor, Henry Cox, the boy shot him at the station and then made a futile attempt to hide in a railway carriage. Earlier on Wells had been nearly crushed to death by a train, and this was said to have affected him but a defence of insanity failed. Sixteen journalists watched the execution on 13 August 1868 and reported that Wells, who struggled for several minutes on the end of the rope, had died hard.

The method then in use was the so-called short drop, and the hangman in the Wells execution was the Londoner William Chalcraft who had held the position since 1829. Until the beginning of the nineteenth century hangings were of the most rudimentary variety. The condemned person was taken to a tree on the back of a horse or cart, pinioned, a noose put over his or her head, and when the cart was removed or the horse whipped away, fell into space. Sometimes a ladder was used, and earlier a stool was simply kicked from under the prisoner's feet.

Then in 1818 came the collapsing scaffold, first used in Northamptonshire and which proved so popular that within a year almost every prison had one. The gallows was a platform around 6–8' high and reached by a staircase usually of 13 steps. The size of the platforms varied but generally averaged 10 feet square and consisted of two upright beams, a crossbeam, trapdoor and lever. The beam was about 8 foot, with a chain on which a rope would be fixed. The trapdoors could be either single or double; later, double doors became standard. The gallows worked by pushing a lever which released a hinge on the trapdoor, which then fell open. The rope, usually Italian hemp, 13 feet long and around $5/8''$ thick, was supplied by the hangman who could cut it in pieces and sell it after the execution. The more notorious the criminal, the higher the price. The hangman was also entitled to the dead person's clothes and possessions which, again in famous cases, could be sold to waxwork museums.

Until the late 1870s a temporary scaffold was usually erected in the prison yard, but by the 1880s an execution chamber was becoming more common in prisons. It was also increasingly apparent that it was far easier to hang a man without having to get him up a series of steps. Pits were dug, or hangings took place over stairwells or ventilation shafts. Refinements now included the condemned cell being placed next to the execution chamber, thereby cutting down the time from the entry of the hangman to the actual execution.

Chalcraft was a silent, happily married man who disliked talking about his work and whose chief hobby was breeding rabbits. He also owned a pony which would follow him about like a dog. His first hanging was that of the child murderer Esther Hibner on 13 April, only nine days after his appointment. The woman had tortured one of her apprentices to death and the crowd was very much on Chalcraft's side, something which was not always the case later in his career. On New Year's Eve that year he also executed Thomas Maynard, the last man to be hanged for forgery. Apart from being the public hangman, he was also required to flog miscreants at a fee of half-a-crown a flagellation, with an allowance for birches and the cat-o'-nine tails. His retainer was either a guinea or 25 shillings a week, and he received an extra guinea a head for actual executions. Hangings outside London meant special fees of up to £10.

The problem with Chalcraft was that despite his long years of experience he was never a proficient hangman. Throughout his career he persisted in the short drop, which resulted in death by strangulation, rather than the long drop which broke the neck and was nearly perfected by his successor William Marwood.

Before his compulsory retirement Chalcraft had steadily been losing his nerve even after executions took place in private;[2] reportedly he was in a cold sweat when he went to Manchester to hang three Fenians for the murder of a police officer, as well as being in terror at the execution of Michael Barrett. Chalcraft's career ended on 25 May 1874 with another botched execution, that of the wife murderer James Goodwin. The fact that his nerve had gone is hardly surprising since he was 75 at the time. He died on 13 December 1879.

---

[2] 'Private' is a relative word. When on 21 December 1875 Chalcraft hanged Henry Wainwright for the murder of his mistress Harriet Lane, the local sheriffs had invited

Marwood, a cobbler by trade from Horncastle in Lincolnshire, did not become a hangman until middle age when he carried out experiments in his so-called long drop for the Governor of Lincoln prison and was then hired to hang – 'execute' was the word he preferred – William Horry on 1 April 1872.[3]

The long drop worked on the principle that instead of strangulation the prisoner's neck was broken by the fall and death was therefore instantaneous. The length of the rope to be used was based on the weight of the prisoner. With Chalcraft's contemporaries – George Smith, Thomas Askern and Anderson (whose real name may have been Robert Evans and who was possibly the son of a lawyer and a qualified but non-practising doctor) – still advocating the short drop, Marwood's star shone brightly. There is little doubt that he did improve on Chalcraft's work, something he was forever pointing out to visitors to his shop over the door of which he had a sign, 'Crown Office'.

Once Marwood had been appointed in 1875 the number of hangings increased fairly dramatically, which may have been because officials could now deceive themselves into thinking that executions were being humanely carried out and there was no necessity to grant reprieves. Marwood became something of a celebrity. He brought dignity to what he saw as a profession and was invited to lecture in Sheffield, but this was not a success. Unfortunately he wished to speak about the monarchy and the Fenian troubles, but the audience wanted to hear stories from the

---

some 100 people to watch the execution. It did not please Wainwright who turned on the spectators, calling them curs for having come to see a man die.

[3] Horry, a Staffordshire publican, was convicted of shooting his wife after she refused to return to him. He had taken to drink after becoming jealous of her habit of talking to customers at the bar.

In his excellent record of executions, Steve Fielding suggests that although he has the credit Marwood did not actually invent the long drop but that it had already been used successfully in Ireland. Again 'success' is a relative term. In the first recorded case of its use in Dublin in 1870 a 14-foot drop was used, which tore the condemned man's head from his shoulders. It was a problem which continued over the years and led to the end of the career of Marwood's successor James Berry, who retired after he hanged 62-year-old John Conway in Liverpool on 20 August 1891 for the murder of 9-year-old Nicholas Martin. Berry had his way after a dispute with the prison doctor over the length of the drop, which he insisted should be a long one. The result was that Conway was nearly decapitated. See Steve Fielding, *The Hangman's Record*, Volumes One and Two.

scaffold and the meeting broke up in some disorder. He died in 1883, having contracted jaundice on a visit to Ireland where he hanged the Phoenix Park murderers. For a time it was suggested in the national press that he had been murdered as a reprisal for the hangings, and an inquest was ordered, but an autopsy showed that he had died from pneumonia aggravated by a liver disease. He was remembered in a children's riddle: 'If Pa killed Ma who would kill Pa? Marwood.'

In 1885, following a number of botched hangings, politicians in New York were becoming squeamish. One reason for the failures was that they were generally carried out by Deputy Sheriffs who lacked both the technique and the temperament for the job and were still using the short drop. There was also a suggestion that the hangmen were prolonging the proceedings so that the crowds could spend more money with local shopkeepers.[4]

Now the new Governor David B. Hill suggested that 'The present mode of executing criminals by hanging has come down from the Dark Ages.' The following year a committee known as the Death Commission and chaired by Elbridge T. Gerry – who in happier circumstances had organised the Society for the Prevention of Cruelty to Children – undertook a study of 40 methods of execution. When it came to it the field was narrowed down to four – the garotte, a hypodermic injection of poison, the guillotine and electrocution. There were practical and political objections to three of the methods. The garotte, a screw slowly tightened until it broke the neck, was both a painful and a lengthy operation. In any event it was used in Spain, a country with which the United States was not then on the best of terms. The guillotine, although undoubtedly quick, was regarded as messy and un-American.[5] As for

---

[4] Craig Brandon, *The Electric Chair*, p. 27.
[5] The guillotine, perfected at the time of the French Revolution, was highly thought of in France. There had previously been a German version in the thirteenth century and both Halifax and Edinburgh had 'maidens', the latter being reserved for erring gentry. It was introduced by the Earl of Morton, who himself fell foul of it. Guillotine execution had fallen into disuse in the century before Joseph-Ignace Guillotin, a professor of anatomy in the medical faculty in Paris, reintroduced it. Earlier research had been carried out by Antoine Louis, while a harpsicord maker Tobias Schmidt set up the first models. For a short period the guillotine was known as a Louison or Louisette.

poisoning, there was a fear that, since a number of those to be executed would be drug addicts, they might have developed a resistance to the dose of morphine intended to kill them. That, rather by default, left electrocution.[6]

At the time there were rivals to provide electricity for the chamber: the direct current, propounded by Thomas J. Edison, and George Westinghouse jnr's alternate current. Trials were conducted, with Edison providing the members of the Death Commission with the use of his staff who executed four dogs, two calves and a horse to demonstrate the efficiency of his scheme. His provision was chosen.

However, as mentioned earlier in Chapter 5, there was something of a hiatus when the wily, highly talented and totally unscrupulous Broadway lawyer William J. Howe argued that his client, Harry Carleton (known to his friends as Handsome Harry), could not be hanged for the murder of a police officer because the state had passed a bill ruling that all future executions should be by electrocution. Since this was not yet in force, Howe argued, his client must go free.

Sentencing was postponed for a week and now Howe produced one of his great coups: Carleton could not be sentenced in any way. The Assembly, in passing the Electrical Death Penalty Law the previous spring – abolishing death by hanging and substituting electrocution – proposed to abolish hanging as from 4 June but prisoners convicted after that date were to be kept alive until 1 January 1889 when they could be electrocuted. At least that was the intention. According to Howe:

When the execution of its first victim, the burglar Nicolas-Jacques Pelletie, passed off successfully on 25 April 1792, a Paris newspaper commented that the device 'in no way stained any man's hand with the murder of his kind and the speed with which it struck is more in accordance with the spirit of the law, which may often be severe but which should never be cruel'. There were, however, complaints that there was not enough pageantry attached to the spectacle. Local residents also complained that at midnight after the execution dogs were still licking the blood. See Rayner Heppenstall, *French Crime in the Belle Epoque.*

[6] The gas chamber was first introduced in Nevada in 1922 when Gee Jon, a hatchetman for the Hop Sing Tong in San Francisco, was executed on 8 February that year for the murder of Tom Quong Kee in a tong war. The state was followed by Arizona and Colorado in 1934, North Carolina in 1936 and California a year later.

> He [Carleton] says that Your Honor cannot now pass any sentence
> of death upon him. He says that the Legislature by its enactment
> of Chapter 499 of the laws of 1888, a statute passed, approved,
> and signed by the Governor . . .

The judge agreed and, while the prosecution appealed, unsurprisingly panic followed. If Howe was right, then not only had all murderers to be released but also the logical extension was that until 1 January 1889 they could kill with impunity. Chief of Police Thomas Byrnes and the District Attorney released statements assuring the public that measures would be taken to ensure public safety over the Christmas period.

Howe, with Hummel supporting him, was adamant that Carleton could not be punished 'because of the slipshod drafting of the bill', but other lawyers were not convinced. Of course, in practice, Howe's reading of the law could not be allowed to stand and the appeal court held that while it was strictly correct, a mere slip of syntax should not allow the guilty to go free.

On 5 December 1888 Carleton became the last man to be hanged in the Tombs prison. By now the papers had become less hostile to him. One of his children had died during the year, and he was generally accepted to have behaved well throughout his time in the condemned cell. As he walked to the scaffold he was described as having:

> . . . a high retreating head; a long thin face scarred with smallpox,
> a curling brown mustache and blue eyes. His face looked intelligent and not unkindly.

As for the hanging itself:

> If it had been designed particularly to be an argument for the
> swiftness and painlessness of the old method of inflicting the
> death penalty it could not have been more effective. Electricity
> could not have been more humanely expeditious and certain.[7]

---

[7] *New York Herald*, 10 October, 3, 4, 6 December 1889.

Hanging continued in other states, and if more evidence was needed that changes were necessary it came with the execution of Mrs M. M. Rogers in Windsor, Vermont. At the age of 19 on 13 August 1902 she chloroformed her husband and, after writing a suicide note for him, with the help of two others she rolled him into the river where he drowned. The aim had been to enable her to marry Maurice Knapp, with whom she then set up home aided by $100 of Rogers' life insurance money. She was hanged on 8 December 1905, in the first execution in the state since 1892. It was not a success. She apparently looked fetching and composed in a low-cut dress and gave a crucifix to the priest to be passed to her sister. Unfortunately she weighed 11 stone 6 lbs and her weight stretched the four-strand manila rope so that she landed on her feet. Deputy Sheriffs then hauled her up where she swung for 14 minutes as she strangled to death. To their credit the spectators turned away from the scene.[8]

The man to actually hold the dubious distinction of being the first to die by electrocution was the otherwise unremarkable William Kemmler, who had killed his mistress in a drunken fit. He was convicted on 6 May 1889 but with a series of appeals conducted on his behalf it was over a year before, on 6 August 1890, he was electrocuted at Auburn prison in a scene of what was for the witnesses appalling horror. The arguments advanced on his behalf by lawyer W. Bourke Cockran had been that the punishment was cruel and inhumane.[9]

In the time between sentence and execution Kemmler had, as do so many, 'seen the Light' and had become philosophical about the whole unhappy procedure. According to a newspaper report:

> The first jolt lasting 17 seconds had failed to kill him and his chest began to heave and his heart restarted. The current was turned on for another 70 seconds whilst some of the witnesses

[8] *New York Times*, 9 December 1904; *Illustrated Police News*, 4 March 1905.
[9] Cockran was a well-known politician and expensive attorney. He was instructed for Kemmler, who was in no position to pay his fees, 'by Philanthropy', but there were many who thought that in this case philanthropy was spelled Westinghouse.

fainted and vomited. Some made for the door. Kemmler's back was badly burned and his muscles carbonized. At the autopsy it was described as resembling well-cooked beef.[10]

The public in general nevertheless liked the possibility that things would not go smoothly, and when four murderers were executed at Sing Sing in 1891 the roads from the town of Ossining to the prison were jammed with spectators. They were disappointed on that occasion, but would have been happier two years later when at Clinton prison Fred Van Wormer, one of three executed brothers, began to move in the autopsy room. The executioner was recalled to the prison and, although Van Wormer had by then ceased to move, he was returned to the chair and given an extra 1,700 volts as a precaution.[11]

Even if, which is arguable, execution methods had improved with Marwood's long drop in England and the introduction of the electric chair in America, they clearly had not done so in Western Australia. In January 1906 in Fremantle there was a thoroughly botched triple hanging following the convictions of a Norwegian, Charles Hagen, and two 'natives from Manila', Espada and Marquez, for the murder of Mark Leibglid, a jeweller. Leibglid, who was known to have carried a deal of money, had been lured onto a schooner under the pretext of buying a valuable pearl, then robbed and his body thrown overboard. Now at the execution, as befitted his superior status as a white man Hagen was hanged first, but not before he had given a 15-minute speech protesting his innocence. By the time Espada and Marquez were brought to the scaffold they were quarrelling, which thoroughly unnerved the hangman who failed to secure Espada properly. The

[10] For accounts of Kemmler's last days, execution and the public reaction see *New York Times*, 2–8 and 6–18 August 1890.
[11] There was certainly no squeamishness in America when crowds turned out in force on 5 January 1903 to watch the execution of the elephant Topsy, for 28 years a favourite on Coney Island but now sentenced to death as a rogue. She had killed two men who had been tormenting her and, it seems, had tried to rescue her keeper from a police station where he was being held for drunkenness. The execution was finally conducted semi-privately. The unfortunate beast was first given cyanide-drenched carrots, then given an electric shock of 6,600 volts and was finally hanged from a steam crane. *Morning Leader*, 6 January 1903.

man then tried to clutch the rope and haul himself up on it. Chief Warden Webster, who was assisting, had his foot on the trap-door and fell through, badly injuring himself when it opened on Espada. The unnamed hangman, so the report says, was 'terribly affected and cried like a child'.[12]

By the second half of the nineteenth century the French, or at least the authorities there, had also become somewhat squeamish about their use of the guillotine. When Marlini was executed on 23 July 1892 in Montpellier for the murder of the police officer Ambert, it was the first public execution in the town since 1854. Marlini had a glass of rum and a cigarette on the scaffold while the crowd hissed the executioner, Deibler; they were annoyed that Marlini was to be executed when his partner in the crime had been reprieved. Overall French juries would, if they could, find extenuating circumstances which saved the accused from the guillotine, sometimes to the dismay of the press which wondered if there would ever be another execution. One particularly gross case was that of Paul Martin, a young man who befriended an ageing demi-mondaine, Berthe de Brienne, and then murdered her and stole her jewels. He fled to Glasgow from where he was retrieved. The jury found extentuating circumstances which enabled him to be transported for life. The Paris correspondent of the *Morning Leader* thought that if there was no guillotine for Martin there never would be for anyone.[13]

Happily for the newspaper, there was. On 12 January 1909 the Pallet Gang – the brothers Abel and Auguste Pallet, Canut Vroman and Théophile Deroo – were guillotined before an excited crowd in Béthune. It was the first execution for three years and tickets for the inner circle around the guillotine were sold for the modern equivalent of between 50p and £2.[14] Permission to film the proceed-

---

[12] *Thomson's Weekly News*, 20 January 1906.
[13] *Morning Leader*, 31 January 1904.
[14] Capital punishment was much rarer in France than in Britain. The last execution in Marseilles had been that of Vitalis in 1877. There had been something of a resurgence of opinion in favour of capital punishment, particularly after the Prime Minister Fallières and President Clemenceau were shot at near Etoile on Christmas Day. There had also been particular anger over the reprieve of the child-murderer Soleilland. Fallières had reprieved six murderers the previous year, commuting their sentences to life in five

ings had been refused, but it was believed that the film company might stage and film a mock execution. If so, said the Prefect, he would ban the display. Abel Pallet, who was the last to be guillotined, was defiant to the last, calling out, 'You pack of do-nothings. Down with the priests! Lead the social revolution!'[15] It was thought that this might be the last public execution because of the perceived bad behaviour of the crowd, and *Le Temps* suggested that if there had to be a headsman he should at least be kept out of sight. Other newspapers had some sympathy with the people of Béthune. Over a period of years the Pallet Gang had perpetrated at least 25 murders or attempted murders and more than 100 robberies in the area, and it was understandable that the locals should be happy and relieved.

Their bodies were taken to the Academy of Medicine at Lille where four days later Deroo's brother, who worked nearby, managed to burst into the lecture room where the students were examining the corpses and tried to seize his brother's head. According to reports he roundly abused it, saying disgrace had been brought to the family. He then collapsed on the floor.[16]

The Pallet Gang was one of three gangs which terrorised rural France in the middle of the first decade of the century. The Pallets operated in the north, in the south-west a gang was led by Branchery (an inn-keeper from Langon) and in the Drôme, where the peasants barricaded themselves in at night, perhaps the most feared of them all were the Chauffeurs.[17] They were led by Berruyer, a failed priest, along with David, and Liottard who posed as an itinerant pedlar in order to reconnoitre houses for occupants worth robbing.

Liottard seems to have been particularly vicious and killed a retired railway worker at Livron on 5 November 1905, an old lady

---

cases and 20 years in the other. There was now a suggestion (based on the fact that he had been moved from Aix prison) that the murderer Camajore would soon be executed. See *The Times*, 11 January 1909.

[15] *The Times*, 12, 13 January 1909.

[16] *Morning Leader*, 16 January 1909.

[17] Roasting victims to persuade them to disclose their valuables was a long-standing sport of French criminal gangs. Before Vidocq, the poacher-turned-gamekeeper, was recruited into the Paris police in 1810, he had associated with a gang of feetwarmers who operated around Santerre in northern France.

at Alixon on 20 September 1906 and a gardener at Peyrons in April the next year. David, who had been orphaned at the age of 12 and had fought in Indo-China, joined the gang in 1907 when a pensioner had his feet roasted but survived. He had previously killed a Russian sailor in a knife attack in Sète. At Suresne, with the help of a prostitute he had lured a German gambler into a brothel and killed him for his winnings at the racecourse before dumping the body in the Seine.

The Pallets were certainly not the last to be publicly executed for at 9 p.m. on 22 September 1909 a crowd of some 2,000 people met the train at Valence and along with it Monsieur de Paris, Anatole Deibler, the executioner. The meeting got off to an inauspicious start because Deibler tried to hide himself in the station lavatory but was eventually forced to show his face. He then went to his hotel, La Tête d'Or. At 2 a.m. the guillotine arrived and at 4.30 Deibler went to the prison. Reports of the execution record that every window opening on to the prison was let for 200 francs and a pitch on a rooftop went for 5 francs. Did David not have pity for his victims? 'No they suffered for five minutes. I have suffered for 35 years.'[18]

With his wife, Lucia, Branchery kept the Café de la Gare in Langon not far from Bordeaux. The speciality of his team was robbery of the locals, and until his arrest he maintained something of a reign of terror in the region. His downfall came when an insurance agent, a M. Monget, was killed in his café on 6 February 1907. One of the gang, Parrot, struck Monget from behind as he was sitting at a table and Branchery then half-strangled the man with a napkin before he was taken to the cellar and the job completed.

---

[18] Marcel Montarron, *L'Histoire du Milieu*. The last acknowledged public execution in France took place at dawn in Versailles on 18 May 1939 when Eugène Weidmann, a German-born multiple murderer who killed six people, was guillotined before a large and unruly crowd. He had been convicted of a series of robbery-murders along with Roger Million who was reprieved. This time the process was filmed. I am indebted to crime historian Matthew Singer for the information that public executions took place in the French penal colonies until the 1960s and that after the Second World War there were some public executions in northern France. For an account of Weidmann's career see Rayner Heppenstall, *Bluebeard and After*.

Lucia and the servant girl, Henriette Courrièges, then disposed of the man's valise while another member of the team, Garol, helped to throw the body into the Garonne.[19]

[19] *Morning Leader*, 27, 29 February 1908.

RECREATION

24

Sex

The late 1880s saw social reform movements springing up in both London and New York. Some were predominantly politically motivated; some were genuinely aimed at improving the social conditions of the underclasses. An example of the first came when, on St Valentine's Day 1892, the Reverend Charles Parkhurst began his campaign, 'Ye are the salt of the earth', from the pulpit of the Presbyterian Church, Madison Square, by castigating the democratic administration of Tammany Hall as the Devil and lacing into the front man, Mayor Hugh J. Grant and the real power, Richard Croker, who had taken over from Boss Tweed as the head of the Democratic Party. He then turned his attention to the New York police for doing nothing about the brothels and gambling houses which 'flourished almost as thick as roses in Sharon'.

It was not a sermon which appealed to the authorities and on 23 February he was hauled in front of the Grand Jury. When questioned he admitted he could not swear on his own knowledge that what he said was correct. Six days later, the jury rebuked him for 'instilling unwarranted feeling of distrust in officials'. Had they said nothing Parkhurst might just have let sleeping whores lie, but now he began to collect evidence. In the long term this evidence led to the Lexow Committee examining the New York police. Meanwhile, however, he recruited a reformed criminal turned private detective Charles W. Gardner at $6 a night and a parishioner John Langdon Erving, known as 'Sunbeam' – as in Jesus wants me for a – because of his virtue, for a tour of the red-light district. Decked out in turtle-neck sweaters and checked caps, they carried out personal research into the hell-holes in which, so that his disguise was not penetrated, he played leap-frog with naked prostitutes at midnight. The sermons continued until the District Attorney sent his detectives to raid the 27th Street brothel of Hattie Adams where, said the good pastor, most of the worst indecencies had occurred. It was there that a nude can-can had taken place.

Hattie Adams knew the rules of the game perfectly well: a plea of not guilty in the magistrates' court followed by one of guilty at the Court of General Sessions where she would be represented by Bill Howe or Abe Hummel. The fine was up to $50 and the whole thing was little more than an inconvenience before order was restored. This time Thomas Byrnes thought of a little ruse which would put paid to the Reverend Parkhurst. Hattie was to plead not guilty at the Sessions and then the tiresome clergyman would have to give evidence, an experience which should shut him up once and for all. Byrnes, under pressure, did however enforce the Sunday closing laws and after a raid on a 31st W brothel turned the girls out into the snow without letting them get their coats. They marched to Parkhurst's vicarage at Madison Square where he and his wife served them tea and cakes.

Unfortunately for the forces of evil, Parkhurst was not the fool that Comstock was. Nor was he a coward. Despite Howe at his most ornate, 'I cannot elevate him to the level of my contempt. Speak as you will of her, Hattie Adams is worth a thousand of his kind' – aided by a cute but giggling chorus of girls who at appropriate moments looked shocked when Parkhurst told some of the more outrageous stories of his investigation – the clergyman held firm.

Hattie Adams was convicted and went to prison for 6 months and, as the closing hymn inevitably follows the sermon, so the Lexow Committee followed the case. Byrnes, the originator of the scheme, survived, but only just. The hit music-hall song of the time had a new verse quickly added:

> Dr Parkhurst on the floor
> Playing leapfrog with a whore
> Tarara Boom-de-ay[1]

Parkhurst's campaign was certainly politically motivated but in both London and, rather later, in New Orleans, Chicago and San Francisco campaigns were developing to deal with what the middle classes saw as the accelerating menace of prostitution. These campaigns, which were intrinsically bound in with the growing women's rights' movements, were designed to expose the double standards of men as well as the political corruption which allowed vice, with a capital 'V', to flourish unchallenged.

In 1881 a senior police officer gave evidence to the Select Committee of the House of Lords on the Law relating to the Protection of Young Girls:

> . . . the state of affairs which exists in this capital is such that from four o'clock, or one may say, from three o'clock in the afternoon it is impossible for any respectable woman to walk from the top of the Haymarket to Wellington Street, Strand. From 3 or 4 o'clock in the afternoon Villiers Street and Charing Cross Station are crowded with prostitutes who are there openly soliciting prostitution in broad daylight. At half past twelve at night a calculation was made a short time ago that there were 500 prostitutes between Piccadilly Circus and the bottom of Waterloo Place.

By 1894 the Haymarket may have been cleared of prostitutes, but this was not apparently the case in Regent Street where during the

---

[1] Parkhurst continued his life as a reformer until his death in 1933 when he fell off a roof while sleepwalking; he was 93. In 1892 Gardner was framed by Tammany on a charge of living off the immoral earnings of his wife. He spent a year in the Tombs after the conviction was overturned by the State Supreme Court, but by then he was both a broken man and penniless. He wrote an account of the case, *The Doctor and the Devils*, and then went West. 'Sunbeam' Erving apparently suffered a breakdown. See Luc Sante, *Low Life*.

Empire scandal a man wrote to *The Times* saying that while he was free from solicitation in the Promenade there he could not walk down Regent Street unless it was in the company of his daughter without being accosted.[2]

The *cause célèbre* of that year was the closure of the Empire, Leicester Square. It had been opened with the best of intentions but as the years passed its productions of theatre, spectacle, drama and grand opera had not produced the profit expected by the shareholders (including the moneylender Lord Coleridge, who owned the Café Royal). The management had then resorted to acrobats, performing dogs and ballet girls, at which time it came to the attention of Ormiston Chant (née Laura Ormiston Dibbin in Chepstow), a woman concerned with temperance, suffrage and the less easily defined 'social purity'. It was she who wrote the verse:

> We are standing on the threshold, sisters
> Of the new and brighter day
> But the hideous night of savage customs
> Passes, with the dark, away.

What particularly worried Mrs Chant, a committed official of the National Vigilance Association, was what went on in the Promenade area at the back of the circle which, she believed, amounted to little more than open prostitution.[3] The Empire was warned that unless it cleaned up its act, particularly at the back of the Circle where 'rigidity of decorum is not, as a rule, insisted on by its patrons of either sex', there would be an objection at the next licensing hearing of the Middlesex County Council on the grounds that the Empire was 'a habitual resort of prostitutes in pursuit of their traffic'.

There are certainly some grounds for thinking that Mrs Chant might have been right. Young men were enjoined not to go to the Empire. The young Winston Churchill received a letter from Anne Everest, his former nanny:

---

[2] *The Times*, 15 October 1894. In 1921 the pattern had shifted slightly. Tottenham Court Road and King's Cross were now favoured as well as Charing Cross.
[3] There are also suggestions that the closing of the Empire was not because of heterosexual prostitution but rather of homosexual behaviour.

I hope you will be kept from all evil and bad companions & not go to the Empire & not stay out at night, its too awful to think of, it can only lead to wickedness & everything bad.

Churchill did not heed her words, visiting the music hall the following week; in its turn, nor did the music hall heed Mrs Chant who duly objected. She gave evidence that dressed in her 'prettiest evening frock . . . I myself was accosted by men'. She had also overheard one outraged Frenchman say to his companion (male) during the ballet in which the participants wore flesh-coloured tights, '*C'est trop fort*', and they had both upped and left. Apparently the *trop fort* had been an extra high kick.[4] Two Americans had been upset by the vulgar coster songs of Albert Chevalier and had also walked out. There had also been some pretty outrageous cross-talk, with a young woman saying to a comedian playing the part of a shop-walker, 'I want to see your underwear.' Later George Edwardes, the manager, told the Committee that while he excised such vulgar repartee sadly this line had been overlooked.

Perhaps Mrs Chant was fortunate that of the more prominent members of the Licensing Committee (which totalled eight), one was a promised abstainer and two others were members of the NVA. The Committee recommended that the licence be refused unless the Promenade was abolished or fitted up with seats.

As might be expected, battle lines were now drawn with some unexpected names announcing their support for the Empire. These included the Reverend Stewart Headlam, who perhaps was not such a surprise since he later stood bail for Oscar Wilde. The London Cab Drivers' Union and the Grand Order of Water Rats came out for the stage, while the Central Prayer Meeting Branch of the YMCA stood behind Mrs Chant, Lady Burton (who had burned her husband's memoirs) and Josephine Butler who, as might have been expected, supported her. Our friend Victoria Clafin, now Mrs Woodhull Martin, editress of *Humanitarian*, kept interest alive with a column: 'Should the same standard of morality be required from

---

[4] *Daily Telegraph and Morning Post*, 11 October 1894.

men as from women?'[5] Which after all was what it was all about. Not all the sisters, however, rallied.

Miss Helen Matthews, the novelist, wrote, 'Nature by establishing a considerable excess of women over men, seems to say that males are at a premium and have special privileges', which was not at all what was hoped for, and W.T. Stead rallied to the flag damning her words as 'a harlot's gospel'. The critic William Archer called the NVA 'a pudibund fraternity' and said of the debate, 'The whole thing is so new to me that I have not yet considered its moral bearing.' Pudibund, presumably a combination of purity and moribund, seems not to have become part of the dictionary.

Before the full Council met on 26 October 1894 Mr Edwardes had tried to pre-empt matters. In an announcement in *The Times* he told readers that if the licence was refused there would be financial ruin for the owners. There would than be no alternative but to close, putting 643 employees out of work and affecting another 3,000 who depended 'for their daily bread' on the house. Girls would now be out on the street. It was pointed out that the same had been said some thirty years earlier when the Argyll Rooms and the Haymarket establishments were closed. A protest meeting was organised and a Mrs Evans of the Strand Board of Governors proposed a motion objecting to the decision of the Licensing Committee.

Neither Mrs Evans' motion nor Mr Edwardes' threats carried any weight. By a majority of 43 (75–32) the Council refused to renew the licence. There was talk of writs of *certiorari* and *mandamus* but, when it came to it, with a chorus of 'Rule Britannia' and a tableau of weeping ballet-girls embracing each other the Empire closed its doors.

The *Methodist Times* called it a 'Great Defeat of Lust and Lucre and Lying'.[6] The *Sporting Times* termed it 'The Triumph of Cant'. That paper had already had the greatest of fun with Mrs Chant:

---

[5] For the adventures of the redoubtable Clafin sisters see James Morton, *Sex, Crimes and Misdemeanours*.
[6] *Methodist Times*, 8 November 1894.

The comic song is to be abolished and the experiment of the Chant is to be tried in the Empire.

A lot of meddling and nasty-minded busy-bodies have obtained sufficient power to be able to dictate to the sightseer what he shall and what he shall not look at.

Shrieking sisterhood.

A couple of women earnest and well-meaning, no doubt, go to the Empire. They see things that nobody else sees, hear things that nobody else hears. The ordinary man about town uses the lounge of the Empire as a club where he is sure to meet his friends. It will be shameful if one of the pleasantest clubs in London is interfered with without good cause. To anybody who knows the perfect organisation of the front of the house at the Empire the idea of women accosting men there is absurd.[7]

What is the result of the present Government being in office?

Why the interests of the Empire are in danger all over the world – from Afghanistan to Leicester Square.

What woman calling herself a lady would go to a night promenade without an escort? (Letter)

Prudes on the prowl.[8]

The *Daily Telegraph*'s correspondence columns were filled with letters from 'Britisher', 'Fallen Woman' and 'Lover of Truth'. It was pointed out that the girls were charged 5/- entrance or a levy of £70 a year. The management responded by saying that the levy was not always enforced. On 5 November Mrs Chant, cartooned by *Punch* as Pauline Pry, was burned in effigy. There were suggestions of a mass meeting in Hyde Park, and the ever-useful Stead secured the Queen's Hall for a rival gathering where the afternoon session entitled 'If Christ came to London what would he say?' found George Bernard Shaw leaving at the opening prayer, while the evening

---

[7] *Sporting Times*, 13 October 1894.
[8] Ibid., 20 October 1894.

session, 'If Christ came to London what would he do?', produced the unhelpful response from a Mr Anton, 'He would put a stop to the Temperance Movement.'

Mrs Chant was as well-received as she had been the night before when she attended at the Princes Hall. She was so moved by the proceedings as to disclose her age:

> I'm 47 (giggle) and I don't mind telling you (giggle) and I'm proud of it (giggle).[9]

When it came to it the quarrel over the Empire was really not necessary except as a piece in a scheme of greater things. Within a week the Empire re-opened and on the opening night the crowd tore down the screen which separated the bar from the Promenade. One of those in the throng was the young Winston Churchill who, in his autobiography, claimed that it was there that he made his maiden speech. He wrote to his brother, 'Did you see the papers about the riot at the Empire last Saturday? It was I who led the rioters – and made a speech to the crowd.'

His cry, he said, had been:

> Ladies of the Empire, I stand for Liberty!
> You have seen us tear down these barricades tonight. See that you pull down those who are responsible for them at the coming election.[10]

Some campaigns, such as those of Father Bernard Vaughan in Mayfair, never really left the pulpit. Perhaps this was because his approach was slightly muddled. His August 1906 sermon on the topic that 'if people heard what the smart set's servants had to say they would never visit the Chamber of Horrors', received some short-lived publicity, and the flame was held for a week or so by Father Ignatius in Wandsworth, but his shared thoughts on 'Are we becoming less religious?' met with scant attention.[11]

[9] *Sporting Times*, 10 November 1894.
[10] Martin Gilbert, *Churchill: A Life*, p. 47.
[11] *The Umpire*, 11, 25 August 1906.

As for New York venues, Greene Street W off Broadway in the 1850s and 1860s was an avenue of sin. Any house not a brothel was an exception. One madam, Josie Woods, expected clients to appear in white tie and tails – and they did. It was suggested that some of the girls married well out of the brothels. Some may have done, but far more of them ended down on Water Street.

The Haymarket was a three-storey brick and frame building painted a dull and sulphurous yellow on Sixth Avenue just south of 30th Street. Once evening came, it blazed with light. Women were admitted free but men paid an entrance of 25c. Working girls who showed their ankles were not admitted, but galleries and boxes extended around three sides of the main floor and contained small cubicles where the women frequenters danced the can-can and gave exhibitions 'rivalling the French peep shows'. It survived several closures and was in operation until late 1913.

The ex-pugilist Harry Hill's Concert Saloon in West Houston Street, east of Broadway, was a sprawling two-storey frame structure with two front entrances: a small door for ladies, who were again admitted free, and a large one for 'gents' who also paid 25c. The house rule was that all men must call for refreshments as soon as they arrived, and this was to be repeated after each dance. If a man did not dance he must leave. Hill was described as the complete pugilist, he was always present during business hours and did not hesitate to knock a man down if he infringed the house rules. The saloon was closed by order of Mayor Abram S. Hewitt in 1886. At the lower end of the scale John Allen had a brothel-cum-concert hall on Water Street. There the girls wore bells on their shoes which could be heard tinkling as they worked. Allen had studied for the ministry at the Union Theological Seminary and, in a form of each-way betting and certainly preceding the Gideons, put a bible in each of his rooms.[12]

In the late 1880s Norton's Point on Coney Island was the place for prize-fighting, gambling and prostitution. The Gut had dance halls, brothels and peepshows.

---

[12] For accounts of sex in the city see Timothy J. Gilfoyle, *City of Eros* and George Chauncey, *Gay New York*.

One of the earliest of the successful Chicago madams was Lizzie Allen, also known as Ella Williams. Born in Milwaukee, she originally worked for Mrs Hernicks in the brothel called the Prairie Queen and in 1865 moved to the Senate which had opened in Wells Street six years earlier and which was destroyed by the Great Fire in 1871. She then opened a two-storey brothel in the appropriately named Congress Street in competition with Carrie Watson. Later she took up with Christopher Columbus Crabb and, at a cost of $125,000, opened the three-storey, 50-room House of Mirrors at 2131 South Dearborn Street in 1890, leasing it to Effie Hawkins six years later. Williams was buried at Rosehill cemetery; on her headstone is the engraving 'Perpetual Rest'.

In 1900 Crabb, who was suspected of having a hand in Williams' death but was never charged, leased the brothel to the Everleigh sisters, Ada and Minna.[13] Originally working in a theatrical troupe, in 1898 they had begun what were illustrious careers in Omaha, Nebraska, which was hosting the Trans-Mississippi Exposition. Having acquired some $5,000 capital, they used it to purchase a whorehouse. New girls were acquired and wine was sold at $12 a bottle, $2 more than the temporary purchase of an inmate. After the exhibition ended the local citizens were unwilling to pay these inflated prices and the pair moved to Chicago – buying the lease to (and the girls from) Effie Hawkins' brothel at a reputed figure of $55,000 and opening on 2 February 1900. The parlours were soundproofed, there were three orchestras and a minimum of 15 cooks. There was a library, an art gallery, and each private room had a fountain which squirted perfume into the room. There were 25 gold spittoons, each costing $650. Butterflies fluttered throughout the premises.[14]

From the beginning they enraged their competitors, indicating that only 'the best people' – who included the celebrated newsman Ring Lardner, John Barrymore and the boxer 'Gentleman' Jim Corbett – would be admitted, and again putting what were seen as fancy prices on the wine list. The basic $10 fee was really only the

[13] It is said that their name was really Lester but they adopted Everleigh in memory of their grandmother who signed letters 'Everly Yours'.
[14] The house had originally been built in 1890.

admission charge, and a minimum expenditure of $50 was required to secure readmission. The girls who worked there were the cream of tarts. There was a waiting list of applicants and a girl could very often marry a patron. At one time they had employed Belle Schreiber, the woman later involved in the downfall of Jack Johnson under the Mann Act.

> I talk with each applicant myself. She must have worked somewhere else before coming here. We do not like amateurs . . . To get in a girl must have a good face and figure, be in perfect health, must understand what it is to act like a lady. If she is addicted to drugs or to drink, we do not want her.[15]

The unfortunate death of Nathaniel Ford Moore was seen by their competitors as an opportunity to bring down the house. Moore died of a drug overdose, probably a mixture of morphine and champagne, while staying in the rival establishment run by Vic Shaw and her husband, Roy Jones. The idea was to move the body to the Everleigh Club and then have the police called, but the plan was thwarted when a girl who had previously worked for the sisters told them of the plot.

It was the vice purge of 1910 which finally closed the club. The sisters went on an extended trip to Europe, and then to New York where they lived on W 71st near Central Park and off their former earnings. Mixing in polite society, they became patrons of the arts. Minna died on 16 September 1948 and Ada died in Charlottesville on 3 December 1960.[16]

Next door to the Everleigh Club was the Weiss Club which Ed Weiss and his wife, the former prostitute Aimée, opened in 1904. The girls were said to have been sufficiently good-looking to have had an opportunity of working for the sisters and the prices were, for residents anyway, half those of the Everleigh, but most of the work came from ripping off the Everleigh Club. Weiss had a lock on the cab-drivers in the area. When a fare seemed to be sufficiently drunk he was driven to the Weiss Club where he was charged full

[15] Minna Everleigh quoted in Carl Sifakis, *The Encyclopedia of American Crime.*
[16] Their premises became a hotel housing black transients until it closed in 1933.

rates and left in the belief that he had been to the more celebrated establishment. The Weiss Club was also closed in the 1910 purge, and for a time Ed Weiss himself worked as a manager for the Capone brothels.

Panel houses went hand in hand with prostitution. The panel house, to which men were taken for the purposes of prostitution and then robbed, seems to have originated with Moll Hodges who ran brothels in Philadelphia and New York. Sliding doors were installed in the walls and the men would have their clothing and possessions taken while occupied with the girl. An advantage was that the girl could not be charged with, or at least convicted of, the robbery. One of Hodges' girls, Lizzie Clifford, is credited with taking the concept to Chicago where there were thought to be 200 such houses by the early 1890s. They were all closed by 1900 following the efforts of the Chicago policeman, Clifton Wooldridge, who arrested the landlords of the premises.

Art, or what passed for it, could also benefit from vice. In 1913 came *The Lost Little Sister*, the first of the White Slave plays. By Edward E. Rose, it was based on the exposures by Virginia Brooks in the Chicago *American* and had been through a number of doctoring hands before it opened in Detroit. Based on the old-fashioned melodrama, in the first act the country girl is seduced and in the second is whipped into prostitution. In the third act, when the slavers try to seduce her little sister she rebels and the brothel goes up in flames. In the final act, redeemed, she is reunited with her original country-boy love. The play cost $3,000 to produce – most of it in advertising handbills – and grossed $6,800 in the first week. It was said to be still playing the riverboats in the 1930s.[17]

The Underworld does not seem to have controlled male prostitution with the same enthusiasm as it controlled the girls. The

---

[17] There had been trouble in finding the right title and it was originally called *The Little Sister* until, in a stroke of genius, the play's backer Frank A. P. 'Apple Pie' Gazzolo suggested that 'lost' be used as an additional adjective. Other popular but less successful White Slave plays included *The Lure* and *The Traffic*. Ironically, with the profits of *The Lost Little Sister* Gazzolo bought the Everleigh sisters' home at 5536 Washington Boulevard from them. They had encountered considerable difficulty in selling it.

reason is explicable, in that the main controllers of prostitution were the police who operated a licence system. Even though they took the money sent them, many claimed to be appalled by male prostitution. In New York the main gay hangout in the 1890s was the Columbia Hall, also known as Paresis Hall, on the Bowery at Fifth Avenue, but at the turn of the century there were certainly half a dozen others on or south of the Bowery alone. They included Little Bucks, Manilla Hall, the appropriately named Palm Club and the Black Rabbit which was at 183 Bleeker Street and where the French floorman was known as the Jarbean fairy. A woman engaged in sodomy with two men was part of the floorshow, along with a hermaphrodite whose contribution to the evening's entertainment was to display his or her genitalia.[18] There were a number of places immediately north including the Jumbo, and the Artistic Club on W 30th which was regularly raided.[19]

Abortion fell into legal disfavour on both sides of the Atlantic, not through moral but through economic reasons. It became a crime in England during the Napoleonic Wars when the Government was looking for more and more little soldiers and sailors to defend the country against Napoleon and his successors. After the American Civil War the factories and mills needed restocking. Depriving the country of long-term workers was simply not acceptable. However, there had been some earlier legislation.

The New York Criminal Code of 1828 made any attempt of an abortion on a pregnant woman by drugs or instrument – unless necessary to save her life and attested as such by two physicians – a crime punishable by a fine of $100 and/or a year in prison. The crime could be committed both before and after quickening. The previous year the unauthorised practice of medicine had been made a misdemeanour. However, the laws were rarely enforced. The New

[18] Society for the Suppression of Vice record books, vol. 4, 100–101, 5 October 1900. The papers are in the Library of Congress, Washington.
[19] For raids on the Paresis see The Report of the Special (Mazet) Committee of the Assembly appointed to investigate the Public Offices and Departments of the City of New York and of the Counties Therein Included (Albany, 1900); Jonathan Katz, *Gay American History*. For an account of another gay bar, the Slide, see *New York Herald*, 5 January 1892.

Yorkers considered they had a 'God-given right to purge, puke or even poison themselves as they saw fit'.[20]

There was of course a thriving trade. Pills were sold on the basis that the girl was suffering from an obstruction arising from a cold. 'I will not sell medicine for anything else but a cold, nor will I treat any lady for anything else. Your young friend has only taken cold and if she is not relieved by these pills she had better come and see me herself' – this was the abortionist's line of patter. And the leading woman who supplied the stuff to make them purge and puke was Ann Trow Lohman, or Madame Ann Restall as she was known. She administered 'Female Pills' mostly to high-class women and built a mansion for herself on Fifth Avenue at 52nd on the proceeds.

Born in 1812 in Painswick, Gloucestershire, the daughter of a labourer named Trow, she first married Henry Somers, a journeyman tailor, and came to America where she was widowed. Her second marriage was to Charles Lohman, a printer. They borrowed money and put an advertisement in the *Sun* most weeks from 1836 to 1840 billing her as a 'beautiful young female physician'. Ostensibly it was a rational appeal for limiting families. Her brother Joseph did the chemical work and at the age of 30 she was boasting she had done 30 years' work in European hospitals. Another story was that she had been the mistress of a New York physician from whom she learned her trade. Once she had done so she aborted the relationship.

She appeared in court on 22 July 1840 wearing:

> . . . a black satin walking dress, white satin bonnet of the cottage pattern and a very elegant white veil. In her hand she carried a parcel of printed papers which made some persons mistake her for the lady presidentess of the Tract Society.[21]

The real allegation against her was not that she performed abortions but that she provided advice on contraception, so promoting

[20] Clifford Browder, *The Wickedest Woman in New York*, p. 14.
[21] There is a pamphlet, *The Trial of Madame Restall, alias Ann Lohman for abortion and causing the death of Mrs Purdy* (1841).

immorality in general and infidelity in particular. The prosecution's opening speech to the jury was pitched in terms which – today anyway – would be called a bit high:

> Seamen, you are going on a three years' voyage and have this security for the good behaviour of your wife . . . Not at all, all this is at an end. Madame Restall shows your spouse how she may commit as many adulteries as there are in the hours of the year without the possibility of detection.

The quarrel with Mrs Purdy which brought Madame Restall to court was not over a botched abortion but the price. Mrs Purdy had deposited jewellery against the $20 fee and wanted some of it back. When told she was not having it, and that anyway she had received a cut-price bargain, she threatened to go to the police. Madame said that would mean state prison for both of them. Mrs Purdy did nothing at the time but when Dr Samuel Smith was treating her, he discovered 'foul play' and reported the matter to the Mayor. The jury retired a bare ten minutes before convicting. The writer in the *National Police Gazette* was quite clear where things lay:

> It affords us high gratitude to be able to state to our readers that the monster in human shape, who has so long flourished among us under the appellation of Restall, has, after an impartial trial by jury, been convicted of one of the most hellish acts ever perpetrated in a Christian land!

He went on to praise the prosecution '. . . for their zeal in bringing this woman to justice and thus wiping a foul stain from our city and country'.

Initially there were threats of arson and mob violence, but on her conviction for second-degree manslaughter Abe Hummel recorded 'the spasm of public morality with a soft sigh fell asleep'. In fact judgement was stayed while an appeal was made against the admissibility of Mary Purdy's evidence against Madame Restall. Her conviction was quashed and a retrial ordered. But without Mrs Purdy, now in her grave, there was no case and the charge was finally dropped on 12 February 1844, whereupon Madame returned in triumph to her home at 657 Fifth Avenue.

Once out and about again, she bought a new property on Chambers Street and then 10 lots on Fifth Avenue for a cost of $10,000. There was another outcry when it was learned that the stables cost $20,000 and two Italians had been employed for an entire two years producing frescoed ceilings. She declined offers to sell the property, which would have given her a $5,000 profit.

Throughout her career she ruthlessly fought off competitors such as Mrs Birds who kept a 'lying-in hospital' and who advertised a cure for 'all untoward afflictions incident to females', and Catherine Ames alias Madame Costello.

Madame Restall was hunted down again simply because she flaunted herself. Unlike many of her rivals, it seems she was a very competent operator and never lost a woman patient. In this she differed from the saloon keeper from Chatham Street, Jacob Rosenzweig, also known as Asher and given the courtesy title of Doctor, who took up a career as an abortionist as an easier way to make money. On 27 August 1871 a dreadful smell had come from a trunk checked through at the Hudson River railroad depot on 30th Street to Chicago. It was found to contain the dismembered body of one of his patients, a young woman, Alice Augusta Bowlsly. Defended by Howe, he was given 7 years in state prison, 'a sentence so obviously out of all proportion to the enormity of the crime that a howl of public indignation went up to the skies'. Rosenzweig went to Sing Sing to await representations by Howe and Hummel on the quashing of his conviction, which duly followed. He was later prosecuted in another case and acquitted.

In February 1878 Madame Restall was arrested by Anthony Comstock of the Society for the Suppression of Vice and eventually given bail in the sum of $10,000.[22] It transpired that he had

---

[22] Born on 7 March 1844 as one of ten children in New Caanan, Conn. (where his father owned a saw-mill) his mother, to whom he was devoted, had died when he was ten. Brought up a strict Congregationalist, he always had a reforming zeal. At the age of 18 he shot and killed a mad dog and then campaigned against its owner. Later he would refer to those he prosecuted as 'mad dogs endangering the community'.

In 1871, supported and financed by the YMCA, he formed the Committee for the

lured her into supplying the damning evidence of equipment by saying that his wife was yet again pregnant and it would be the ruination of the family if she had the child. In fact Comstock had married a woman 10 years older than himself who, it was said, replaced his mother; they had a daughter who died and had adopted another. Restall, now in her mid-sixties, like so many criminals could not face another term of imprisonment. After Comstock refused an offer of $40,000 to drop the case she committed suicide, cutting her throat in her bath on 1 April 1878.[23]

There were the usual suggestions that the body was not hers and that she had escaped, but it was wishful thinking. There were all sorts of rumours following her death and – as with Kennedy, Elvis, Robert Maxwell and Lord Lucan – numerous sightings. One suggestion was that she had poisoned her husband and then killed herself in remorse; another that she had gone to Europe, and a third that the body in the tub was that of a client. Comstock commented, 'A bloody ending to a bloody life', but there were many who were not happy with the way he had entrapped her and he was roundly criticised in the press over his behaviour.[24]

In the long term the trickery used by Comstock does not seem to have done him any harm at all. At the next meeting of the Society he was asked if that was what he had done and when he replied that he had, the matter seems to have rested. Later he would say that by her insolent and provocative attitude she had brought the prosecution on herself.

Suppression of Vice and two years later went to Washington where he forced through the passage of new postal legislation preventing the communication of obscene material through the mails. It was then that he was appointed a special agent of the Post Office Department in New York and Secretary of the Society for the Suppression of Vice. He held the former post without pay until the Government forced him to accept a salary of $1,500 in 1906. During his years in the position he campaigned tirelessly against 'quacks, abortionists, gamblers, managers of lotteries, dishonest advertisers, patent medicine vendors and artists in the nude'. He was regarded as a rather more sinister American Thomas Bowdler.

[23] Clifford Browder, *op cit.* See also William Howe and Abe Hummel, *In Danger*, pp. 164–6; *New York Sun*, 18 March 1839.

[24] *New York Sun*, 2 April 1878. For accounts of her arrest and death see *New York Times, Herald, Sun* and *World*, 12–16 February 1878 and throughout April 1878. Two years after her death the comic paper *Puck* published a cartoon showing Fifth Avenue thronged with nurse girls and baby carriages.

In his time he claimed to have seized 50 tons of indecent books, 28,425 lbs of plates for printing, 4 million obscene pictures and 16,900 pamphlets, as well as driving 15 people to suicide.

In the early part of the twentieth century the linked questions of prostitution and White Slavery were high on the agenda of any self-respecting puritan organisation. Both in Britain and particularly in America in the years before the First World War, prostitution had become an obsessive topic. It was thought that prostitutes, many driven out of their homes by disease, were entering from Europe in their thousands. It was originally suggested by the United States Senate's Immigration Commission in 1909 that the French and the Jews (strongly denied) were the principal controllers of prostitution, but then it was suggested that young Italians were taking up the business.[25]

The shift in emphasis of courting came from the overcrowded working-class tenements where there were no parlours in which a young girl could entertain her beau to a glass of lemonade. Now the man paid for the outing and expected a kiss or even sexual intercourse at the end. Girls who traded sex for the excitement of an outing, or shoes, clothing or other presents were known as charity girls. And, of course, the step from an unsupervised kiss to the pavement was seen by vigilant and watch societies as less than half a step away.

Over the next few years, even after the passing of the so-called Mann Act, there was almost hysteria over the plight of young women kept in the degrading conditions of the brothel. Figures varied, but in 1910 the Illinois Training School for Girls warned:

> . . . some 65,000 daughters of American homes and 15,000 alien girls are the prey each year of procurers in this traffic . . . They are hunted, trapped in a thousand ways . . . sold – sold for less than hogs! – and held in white slavery worse than death.[26]

---

[25] S. Doc. No. 196, 61st Cong., 2nd Sess. 23 (1909); George Kibbe Turner, 'The Daughters of the Poor' in *McClure's* 34 (November 1909). For protests see e.g. 'White Slave Story False, says Guide' in *New York Times*, 28 October 1909.

[26] Superintendent Ophelia Amigh quoted by Representative Russell of Texas, 45 Congressional Record 821 (1910).

Ice-cream parlours combined with fruit shops, naturally run by foreigners, were seen as one of the first steps to potential slavery. Books and films including the highly successful 1913 *Traffic in Souls* abounded.

Clearly, what was in the air was that curious cloud, Moral Panic, an intangible which blows around from time to time and place to place and is often accompanied by a highly successful symbolic crusade in which the apparent motives of the organisers are not always on all fours with the ulterior ones.

The promoters (in the wide sense) of the Act which would bear the name of Congressman James R. Mann included the United States Attorney in Chicago, Edwin W. Sims, who is thought to have at least partly drafted the Bill. The year before he had written:

> The legal evidence thus far collected establishes with complete moral certainty these awful facts: That the white slave trade is a system operated by a syndicate which has its ramifications from the Atlantic seaboard to the Pacific ocean, 'clearing houses' or 'distributing centres' in nearly all of the larger cities; that in this ghastly traffic the buying price of a young girl is from $15 up and that the selling price is from $200 to $600 . . . that this syndicate . . . is a definite organisation sending its hunters regularly to scour France, Germany, Hungary, Italy and Canada, for victims; that the man at the head of this unthinkable enterprise it [sic] known amongst his hunters as 'The Big Chief'.[27]

So far as young American girls who became 'white slaves' were concerned, they were 'enticed away from their homes in the country to large cities'.

The Bill was introduced on 6 December 1909 and, like so many bills such as the Criminal Law Amendment Act 1885 which do untold harm, went through Congress with only minor amendments and was signed into law by President Taft on 25 June 1910. It was now an offence to transport a woman across a state line for the purpose of having sex.

One of its by-products was that it expanded the power of the

---

[27] Quoted in Stanley W. Finch, 'The White Slave Traffic' in *Light* (12 July), p. 17.

Bureau of Investigation – later to be renamed the Federal Bureau of Investigation, and run by Stanley W. Finch – in whose interest it certainly was that the Act should come into force. By 1912 White Slave investigations constituted by far the largest part of the Bureau's work.

The first success of the Act came almost immediately when on 8 July 1910 a madam was arrested at Chicago's Union Station transporting five perfectly willing prostitutes to her brothel in Michigan. Throughout the operation of the Act most of the successful prosecutions have been of this nature.

The *New York Times*, which had been plumb against White Slavery, was overjoyed when on 30 April 1910 it was able to banner headline WHITE SLAVE TRAFFIC SHOWN TO BE REAL. It went on to recount the arrest of Belle Moore and another who had sold two girls to two female investigators. The girls were little more than children, giving their ages as 17 and 18, one of whom wept because she had to leave behind her teddy bear while the other clutched a tattered doll. This, the District Attorney claimed, had 'netted the leaders in the traffic in the city'.

Sadly, as is so often the case, the reality turned out to be quite different. The girls were in fact 25 and 23 respectively. Both admitted to being prostitutes of long standing and during the hearing one 'swung a patent-leather toe in the neighbourhood of the stenographer's left ear'. They had been given money for the trip to their new brothel in Seattle and had spent it on clothes for the train journey.

The *New York Times* was less than pleased, recording that the convictions were 'not a victory of which anybody connected with the prosecution can or should be very proud and there was not in it anything obviously relevant to the traffic in white slaves'. It turned its face away from the panic and by 1916 was writing that 'the myth of an international and interstate 'syndicate' trafficking in women was merely a figment of imaginative fly-gobblers'.[28]

From 1914 to 1916 inclusive there were over 300 convictions annually, with a one-in-three success rate. Punishments ranged from

[28] *New York Times*, 2–3 May, 19–21 May 1910, 20 September 1916.

a fine for a man who took his girlfriend across the state line to 5 years in bad commercial cases. One man who fell foul of the Act was the black heavyweight boxer Jack Johnson who had had the temerity to knock out Jim Jeffries, the white former champion who came out of retirement to 'remove that golden smile from Jack Johnson's face'. The new champion was now seen as a symbolic threat to white America. There was an attempt to prosecute Johnson over his involvement with the prostitute Lucille Cameron who had come to Chicago from Minneapolis, but she maintained that her move had occurred before she met him. Her lack of co-operation earned her a spell in Rockford prison.

The Bureau of Investigation now tried another tack. Johnson was known for his huge sexual appetite and his predilection for white women, and the Bureau mounted a targeting operation. Eventually they found Belle Schreiber, who had been sacked from the Everleigh Club for entertaining Johnson and then travelled with him to his training camps. In 1910 she was again working in a brothel, this time in Pittsburgh, and was sacked this time for rolling a customer. She telegraphed Johnson for help and he sent her train money, asking her to meet him in Chicago where he set her up with her own establishment.

When agents found her they put her in front of a Grand Jury and obtained an indictment charging that he had transported her from Pittsburgh to Chicago for personal sexual use and for the purposes of prostitution. Governor Cole Blease of South Carolina spoke for the white South, and indeed much of America, when he said '. . . the black brute who lays his hands upon a white woman ought not to have any trial'.[29]

The charge against him of the transportation of Lucille Cameron was dismissed. She was released and now, much to the fury of white America, he married her. Twice he tried to plea bargain a fine rather than be imprisoned, but eventually in May 1913 he was convicted of the Belle Schreiber offence and sentenced to a

---

[29] Proceedings of the Fifth Meeting of the Governors of the States of the Union, Richmond, Virginia, 3–7 December 1912, quoted in Al-Tony Gilmore, 'Jack Johnson and White Women: The National Impact', in *Journal of Negro History* 58 (January 1973), p. 20.

year's imprisonment. It had not exactly been a fair trial, with the prosecution playing the race card throughout. Afterwards the Federal Prosecutor announced:

> . . . this negro, in the eyes of many, has been persecuted. Perhaps as an individual he was. But it was his misfortune to be the foremost example of the evil in permitting the intermarriage of whites and blacks.[30]

Meanwhile, back in London, the Radcliffe Highway was known as the poor man's Regent Street because of the prostitution there. In 1887, at any time there would be 20–30 Jewish prostitutes at the East India Dock gates. Prostitutes' pubs included the Globe and Artichoke, the Gunboat, Malt Shovel and, the doyen of them all, the White Swan at the Shadwell end of the Highway, known as Paddy's Goose, the proprietor of which had, during the Crimean War, recruited for the Navy 'in a small steamer with a band of music and flags'.[31]

Flower and Dean Street was regarded as perhaps the roughest of streets in the East End and one notorious for prostitution. In the early 1870s the Reverend Samuel Barnett gave notice to the local Guardians to have the area demolished under the so-called Cross Act, the Artisans' and Labourers' Act passed 30 years earlier which was designed as an answer to the challenge presented by criminal slums. The notice followed a severe outbreak of cholera in the street. Although the improvement scheme was signed in 1877, nothing was done because the authorities fought shy of making 13,000 people homeless in a time of severe depression. It was not until 1883 that part of Flower and Dean Street was demolished and the Charlotte de Rothschild Buildings were constructed. This now created quite separate communities in the street.

In October 1885 efforts were being made to clear out brothels

---

[30] *Chicago Tribune*, 14 May 1914. Jackson fled to Europe where he appeared in France as a wrestler while the Supreme Court was considering his appeal. They allowed it in part, confirming it on 'other immoral purposes'. He lost his title in Cuba in 1915 and returned to serve his sentence in 1920. He died in a car accident in 1946.

[31] Quoted in Kellow Chesney, *The Victorian Underworld*, p. 381. Chesney remarks that despite this apparently wholly successful display of patriotism the proprietor soon fell out with the authorities.

from Lady Lake's Grove and Oxford Street leading into Bedford Street, when Messrs F. N. Charrington and E. H. Kerwin went round the houses with a black book. As parishioners, if they gave notice to the police of the keeping of a disorderly house, on conviction the overseers of the street would pay them £10. They were attacked with rotten fish and other filth and the next day they were stoned. One feature of the attack was the 'extreme scarcity' of the police. They had in fact watched a police officer visit the brothel of a Mrs Hart in Canal Street.

At the turn of the century, Sol Cohen ran the Jewish Association for the Protection of Girls and Women. His research into the White Slave trade showed that many of the girls had been prostitutes before going to South America, and equally that there had been no coercion in many cases. The Association was involved in 125 cases in 1900, 128 in 1901, and there was a massive leap in 1902 when there were 206 instances of girls who had disappeared and were thought to have been abducted or exported to South America.

His experiences were rather different from those described in a Metropolitan Police report of 1906 which recorded that cases of procuring innocent girls for immoral purposes were few and far between. There were perhaps half a dozen genuine instances, but these were mostly French and Belgian girls brought to work here before being sent to South America or South Africa.[32]

However, the Home Office was not wholly deaf to the worries of the vigilance groups and on 17 October 1912 a small White Slave Traffic Squad was launched. It consisted of one CID inspector, one CID constable, two uniformed constables in each of C, D and H divisions and one constable in E and L. The constables were to be given 7 shillings a week to enable them to perform their duties in plain clothes.

Thirteen months later, on 7 November 1913, John Curry, the Detective Inspector in charge of the Squad, reported:

At the time of the formation of the Branch the country was being aroused by a number of alarming statements made by religious,

[32] PRO MEPO 2 558; PRO MEPO 2 1006.

social and other workers who spread the belief that there was a highly organised gang of White Slave Traffickers with agents in every part of the civilised world, kidnapping and otherwise carrying off women and girls from their homes to lead them to their ruin in foreign lands, and were thereby reaping huge harvests of gold.

I have to state that there has been an utter absence of evidence to justify these alarming statements, the effect of which was to cause a large shoal of complaints and allegations [many contained in anonymous letters] to be received by police, against persons of all classes.

The year's work had produced a total of 51 arrests. Two were for procuring, and two for attempting to procure. Forty-four were for living on immoral earnings, and the three who were aliens and who were suspected slavers were deported.[33]

The Inspector thought that 'the Criminal Law Amendment Act 1912 has had a salutary effect on foreign ponces'. Happily, there was 'No case of unwilling or innocent girls being recruited into white slavery' and anyway 'Mostly [they are] Jewesses of Russian or Polish origin [who] go to Argentina and Brazil'.

The size of the Squad was accordingly reduced.[34]

He was probably correct when he said that most were Jewesses, but note the anti-Semitic tone. With the pogroms, poverty and the forcing of the Jewish community in Russia away from rural communities and into the cities, there was undoubtedly a trade in young Jewesses.[35]

One such case where the victims escaped was followed by the prosecution of Joseph Karmeler and Sam Scheffer who had prepared mock marriage certificates in Hebrew and who were trying to lure young girls on board a ship bound for South America. The girls

---

[33] There were, however, undoubtedly gangs with international connections. One such was headed in London by Aldo Antonious Celli (alias Carvelli, Shanks, Cortini, Ferrari and Leonora) who had convictions in Australia and was said to be of Swiss origin. Girls recruited in Belgium were told they would be taken to Wellington, New Zealand. On 30 November 1910 he and a Frenchman, Alexander Nicolini, pleaded to a general conspiracy to procure women within the King's Dominions and were sentenced to 6 months hard labour and deportation. The authorities had a hard time returning the girls home. PRO MEPO 3 197.

[34] PRO MEPO 3 184.

[35] Edward J. Bristow, *Prostitution and Prejudice: The Jewish Fight against White Slavery 1870–1939*.

very sensibly went to their parents, as a result of which – in an unsuccessful effort to save himself from the inevitability of prison – Karmeler, who was known to have a direct link to a brothel in Rio, was obliged to hand in a written statement:

> Dear Judges
> I am innocent of these charges . . . This is written not with ink but with the blood and tears of my eyes.

He received 15 months imprisonment and Scheffer three months more. Each received 12 strokes of the cat.[36]

In fact, possibly because there was no money around, prostitution was not that much of a problem in many parts of the East End and it was confined largely to the Pennyfields, Limehouse and Aldgate areas. Nor, of course, were all prostitutes Jewish:

> The brides were mostly down the other end of Brick Lane where the lodging houses were in Flower and Dean Street. The 'Seven Stars' next to Christ Church School was mostly used by the ladies of the town, and the 'Frying Pan' on the corner of Thrawl Street and Brick Lane was famous for being the centre of the red light district.[37]

Certainly, while prostitution down in the East End at the turn of the century was rife it could not necessarily be called a lucrative trade:

> There were two kinds of girl. Those who went up West and mixed with the toffs. They would get as much as ten shillings a time, or even £1, and they would ride home in hansom cabs . . . The girls who stayed at Spitalfields were very poor. That was what you called a 'fourpenny touch' or a 'knee trembler' – they wouldn't stay with you all night . . . Even if you stayed all night with the girls like that it was only a couple of shillings.[38]

[36] *East London Advertiser*, 11 August 1914.
[37] Raphael Samuel, *East End Underworld*, p. 109.
[38] Ibid.

Dock prostitutes were known as trippers-up. Three or four would band together when ships docked and it became a battle of wits to separate a sailor from his money. The sailors' defences included pads in which they kept their money which they wore in their shoes; pouches sewn in waistbands; and leather bags under shields attached to belts.[39]

It was a far cry from New Orleans, described by Herbert Asbury as 'the promised land of harlotry', where prostitution went almost unchecked until September 1897. There had been a successful closure of Smoky Row on Burgundy Street in September 1886 which had evicted prostitutes from the ground floors of all houses on Burgundy, Customhouse, Bienville, Dauphine, St Louis and Conti, but the parlour-houses remained unaffected. Mainly they were two- and three-dollar houses, with those on Basin Street charging a grand $5.

It is difficult to know exactly what freedom the girls had in their work and the degree of control exercised over them. Although in today's world this form of controlling prostitution was organised crime, it was not recognised then with the same opprobrium.

And, of course, New Orleans was not alone in this respect. There are reports of closed brothels in London with girls kidnapped, raped into submission and then kept under lock and key with old-time pugilists taking them for accompanied walks, but these are rare.[40] It is a generalisation that prostitutes tend to exaggerate the circumstances in which they became prostitutes, but it is not wholly an unfair one. They had a tendency to claim to be daughters of clergymen or, perhaps even better, to have been defiled by them.

Giving evidence before the House of Lords Committee of 1881–2 on the Protection of Young Girls, two senior officers who had been in the Metropolitan Police force for over twenty years said that neither of them knew of a girl detained against her will in a brothel.[41]

---

[39] For an account of some of the schemes and counterschemes see James Berrett, *When I was at Scotland Yard*, Chapter 3.

[40] Henry Mayhew, *London Labour and the London Poor*, Vol. IV with J. Binney, B. Hemyng and A. Halliday, quoted in Kellow Chesney, *The Victorian Underworld*.

[41] Kellow Chesney, *The Victorian Underworld*, pp. 405–6. The situation on the Continent, as Chesney points out, was police controlled and consequently very different. Once the woman had signed a statutory declaration and had been entered in police records as being attached to a particular brothel the chances of freedom, unless someone could be found to purchase her, were remote.

As for New Orleans:

From Bienville to the First World War commercialised vice was the most firmly entrenched phase of Underworld activity in New Orleans; it was not only big business on its own account, owning some of the best property in the city and giving employment to thousands, but was also the foundation upon which the keepers of the concert-saloons, cabarets, dance-halls and other low resorts reared their fantastic structures of prosperity.[42]

Clearly the top echelon of girls there could hope to make a marriage, at least move into the position of a mistress or open their own house, but for the great majority it was a downhill spiral of ever-increasing speed. Expulsion was a substantial risk. The courts could be used to protect the rights of the workers, however. In October 1894 Cecile Torrence was arrested after biting off the finger of Josie Vinton. One of the witnesses, Helen Frank, said that when one of the bouncers had tried to separate the fighting girls the owner of the brothel, Queen Gertie Livingstone, had told him to let them fight it out. This piece of evidence had not pleased Livingstone and she expelled Frank but retained the girl's trunk. Now the court ordered its release. The local newspaper *The Mascot* was delighted:

Among the things in the box are four dozen towels, which Helen does not think Gertie has any right to withhold, as they come under the act that provides that a workman's tools cannot be retained.[43]

Prostitutes generally provided good advertising and gossip copy for the papers:

Clara Henderson is now occupying the beautiful cottage 1554 Conti Street and has living with her Cleona Miller, a lovely blonde who is in the 20 karat class. Clara is well known by the rounders and is a thoroughly good fellow.

[42] Herbert Asbur, *The French Quarter*, p. 256.
[43] Ibid., p. 210.

Or less encouragingly:

> Tillie Thurman or Carlisle who keeps a joint on Basin Street near
> the corner of Conti next to Pelican Four's truck house, is certainly
> a Pelican of the first water. Boys, if you are out looking for a
> good time and wish to save a doctor's bill we severely advise you
> to give the above establishment all the room possible. When it
> comes down to the real thing in the way of low-down tarts, then
> this is the house you are looking for.[44]

One of the most popular girls in the early 1890s was Mary E. Hines,
known as Abbie Read. A striking strawberry blonde, she had saved
enough money from her time in the Basin Street brothels to open
up on her own account at 15 Burgundy Street. From there she
struck out socially and in January 1893 she married Jules Kuneman,
grandson of a wealthy planter. It was not a success; he beat her
and in the September attempted to kill her. The cause of the quarrel
was either, as *he* said, because she had told him she preferred life
in the *bagnio* and was returning to work with Queen Gertie
Livingstone to whom she had rented her Burgundy Street property,
or – *her* version – that he had wanted her to sell her properties in
order to to set him up in business. After she recovered from her
injuries she retired to Pensacola, Florida, where she lived for 10
years before returning in 1904 to work as Countess Kuneman in
Fanny Lambert's brothel on North Basin Street. The *Sunday Sun* was
pleased, commenting that her friends would be glad to hear that
she was getting along so nicely.[45]

By then, however, times had changed. In the early 1890s there
had been some ineffective efforts to recognise a brothel quarter or
even eradicate prostitution. The Rev. E.A. Clay had tried his best
and in true Parkhurst style he had denounced open prostitution:

> I am now going to speak to you, Beloved, of things which I
> wish could be told without words. I am going to speak of those
> houses of darkness and death and blackness and despair, of

[44] 'Scarlet World' in the *Sunday Sun*, 31 January 1904.
[45] Quoted in Herbert Asbury, *The French Quarter*, p. 309.

those human slaughterhouses, of the gravest things of all the pitfalls in the way of virtue in this great city . . . There are over five hundred of these dark places and they run the gamut of condition from the palatial palaces of velvet and gilt down to the veriest stinking and reeking pesthole of foul hags and noisomeness. Fifteen hundred angels of death and damnation inhabit these places. They affect and inhabit the virtue and honor of every girl in the city.[46]

Curiously, these regulatory efforts fell foul of New Orleans society who saw it as an insult to that delicate flower, 'Southern Womanhood'. It was not until 26 January 1897 that the ordinance was proposed by Alderman Sidney Story which provided two distinct areas in which prostitution was permitted. One was above Canal Street and the other in the French Quarter. In effect there was a 38-block red-light district. Fines of up to $25 with a maximum 30 days for non-payment backed up the measure. From then, although it never recaptured the glory of the *post-bellum* days of the carpetbaggers, it became an essential part of any evening tour of the city. Storyville, as it was known to the displeasure of the Alderman, was closed in November 1917.[47]

[46] Rev. E.A. Clay, 'Some City Pitfalls and Snares', a sermon delivered to the Dryades German Methodist Church. Clay knew what he was talking about. Unlike Parkhurst, who had undertaken a quick if exciting tour in New York, he was the President of the Society for the Prevention of Cruelty to Children and had actively worked for some years retrieving young girls from the brothels.

[47] Story is one of the few who have given their name to a district. It was also sometimes known as Anderson County after Tom Anderson, political boss of the Fourth Ward, saloon keeper, owner of a restaurant and cabaret on Rampart, two other saloons and at least one brothel on North Basin, with an interest in several others. In 1928 after a serious illness he married Gertrude Dix who had run his brothel at 209 North Basin. He was by then a wealthy man with interests in the oil industry.

25

This Unsporting Life

Throughout the nineteenth century there were allegations that horse-racing was crooked and despite the efforts of the members of the Jockey Club, notably Admiral H. J. Rous, it was true. One of the most notorious examples was the 1844 Derby, the premier classic for three-year-olds, when the winner Running Rein was in fact a four-year-old named Maccabeus. At level weights a top three-year-old cannot be expected to be a top-class older horse. Maccabeus had been switched as a yearling for the foal, Running Rein. There were doubts of his age as a two-year-old and one writer put it succinctly enough after the colt had won at Newmarket, 'to speak plainly, the colt is as well furnished as many of our *bona fide* three-year-olds.'

The running of the Derby itself was a disgrace. The favourite Ugly Buck was the victim of deliberately foul riding. The second favourite was not only got at the night before but his jockey Sam Rogers was warned off as a result of his riding. Leander, who was leading at the time, was so badly struck into by Maccabeus/ Running Rein that he broke a leg and had to be destroyed. A subsequent examination of his jaws showed he also was a four-year-old; his owners were warned off and in a fit of temper one of them disclosed that far from being a mere four he was in fact a six-year-old. What was perhaps most extraordinary was that there had been an objection to Running Rein before the race on the grounds of his age, but it was decided he should be allowed to run subject to the withholding of the stakes and an inquiry if he won.

Another dubious Derby result was that of 1880 won by Bend Or, ridden by the great Fred Archer. That year Prince Soltykoff's Mask ran third. There were suggestions that Bend Or was in fact Tadcaster, and in truth the matter was never really cleared up. Whatever the case, Bend Or proved to be a success at stud and in his first season was the sire of the great Ormonde.

Things took a turn for the worse towards the end of the century. In 1892 the Duke of Westminster's Orme was suspected of being poisoned to prevent his running, but if an effort had been made it was not successful. The horse won £33,000 for his owner. There were all kinds of scares of doping and allegations of foul riding. A number of American horses had come over along with American jockeys, the leading rider being Tod Sloan of whom – because of the regularity with which he finished in front – the expression 'On Your Tod' was coined.[1] Unfortunately Sloan, a man of immense talent and a brilliant shot who won international events at Monte Carlo, was in the hands of the bookmakers. He won thousands, and then lost even more and so was easy prey. The jockey Jack Leach wrote of him:

> . . . flagrant dishonesty ended the fabulous career of Tod Sloan. Tod had the ball at his feet, but kicked it the wrong way so often that he had to be got rid of. Here was a man who had every-thing needed by a top jockey, but a kink in his brain unbalanced him.[2]

He was not the only jockey thought to be tilting the odds in his favour:

> A stroll round Newmarket would show the bulk of the palatial establishments are in the hands of jockeys who never ride winners,

[1] Tod Sloan = alone.
[2] Jack Leach, *Sods I Have Cut on The Turf*.

and trainers whose favourites always get beaten; and yet with it all these two classes contrive to wax fat. 'How is it done?' is a frequent question and rumour supplied many ominous answers.[3]

However, Sloan was undoubtedly a brilliant and winning jockey. The Hon. George Lambton, the master trainer, described him as 'wonderful'. He arrived at the back end of the 1897 season and rode 20 winners out of 58 mounts. The next full season he managed 43 out of 95. In 1899 it was 108 out of 364, and in 1900 83 out of 311, an amazing percentage.

Recently a defence of Sloan has been published, in which it is claimed that all he did wrong – apart from being what was regarded as an upstart American – was accept a present from an owner in the event of his horse winning the Cambridgeshire, and also that he (Sloan) had placed bets on the race.

Having been asked to ride Codoman in the *Prix du Conseil Municipal* for a fee of £200, according to the story he took the ride and insisted that the horse be shod with American plates before the race. If so his advice was good; an outsider, the horse won handily. Sloan had bet heavily on the race and had marked the cards of his friends. The owner gave him a present of £700.

The horse was then entered for the Cambridgeshire at Newmarket and Sloan, although he had said he wanted to ride Berrill, agreed to ride Codoman on condition that he could supervise the final days of training. Sloan had accepted a present from the Australian gambler Frank Gardner with whom he wished to go into a form of partnership if Gardner could obtain a trainer's licence. There was a very substantial sum of money on Codoman, on which Sloan himself stood to win nearly £100,000. In the event he was beaten into second place by four lengths. Probably he was beaten by the better horse, but it was noted that he had been finishing second on highly fancied mounts all too frequently and that there had been a good deal of place betting on Codoman. He might have survived had it not become public knowledge that he was likely to be offered a retainer to ride for the Prince of Wales the following season. This

---

[3] *Spirit of the Times*, 13 October 1900.

really could not be allowed. Bertie might have survived the Tranby Croft Baccarat Scandal of 1890, but for the future King to be linked publicly with a crooked jockey could not be permitted.[4] An inquiry was held and Gardner, who claimed he was unaware that he could not give presents to jockeys unless he was the owner, was fined £25. Sloan was told he need not apply for a licence for the following season.

Sloan then turned his mind if not talents to investing in motor cars and setting up a factory in America. It was a disaster. He had intended to import five cars as prototypes for his factory, but discovered that a 45 per cent duty was payable. His partner was fined for underestimating the value of the cars to the Customs, and to make matters worse Sloan lost $30,000 in one day at the racetrack and more at cards. His career as automobile magnate lasted a bare month.

He had always been a brilliant shot and entered some of the big contests in France. He was now so hard up that when he entered the *Grand Prix du Casino* at Monte Carlo in 1903 a friend had to lend him the entrance fee and enough money to back himself at 50 to 1. He killed all his birds and won the first prize of 10,000 francs. The way Sloan played the game, however, pigeon shooting was not necessarily that great a financial support. His gun had been bought in Bond Street. The 50 francs for the man who picked up his birds was the least of his expenses, for two ladies claimed the wings of the last pigeon and these had to be suitably mounted as jewellery on a hat for each of them. He gave a champagne dinner with a bill of 1,400 francs; he was also betting and losing heavily in the casinos, particularly at baccarat. Then there was the best suite in the hotel and a valet and a chauffeur to be paid for, as well as a string of *demi-mondaines*.

---

[4] The Great Baccarat Scandal involved allegations of cheating by the Baronet Gordon Cummings at a house party attended by the Prince of Wales at the Doncaster meeting on 8 September 1890. Cummings, supposedly to prevent embarrassment to the Prince, accepted he had cheated by increasing his stake. The *quid pro quo* was that details of his behaviour would not be made public. Of course they were, and he sued. The Prince of Wales was called as a witness in the case and Cummings lost, but the verdict was an unpopular one and the better view is that he was innocent. There are many accounts of the case and certainly one of the best is John Welcome, *Cheating at Cards*.

He continued to slide. The next allegation against him was over the filly Rose de Mai in the spring of 1903. He had some sort of financial interest in her and she was due to run in the *Prix de Diane* (the French Oaks) on 20 May, but after exercising her on the morning of the race he put it about that she was coughing and unlikely to run. Her odds drifted to 12 to 1. But he backed her heavily and she won readily. The trainer was fined and Sloan was warned off for spreading rumours. He sued the French Jockey Club and won on the technicality that, as he had been merely galloping the filly, he was outside the remit of the Club. But there were no damages and he was required to pay his own and the Jockey Club's costs. His action came against a background of expulsion of American jockeys from France and dopings in small races where the horses had no stud value.

From then on Sloan appeared in Vaudeville and the impresario George Cohan wrote the musical *Little Johnny Jones* which was based on Sloan's English riding career. Those were the ups. The downs were many.

In September 1907 he married the 'Queen of American Musical Comedy', Julia Sanderson, but it was not a success. In 1915 he was declared an undesirable alien and deported from England following a conviction for running an illegal gaming house in the West End with a young French woman Mlle D'Herlys, who never became one of the several Mrs Sloans. She travelled back to France first class with her mother; he went steerage to New York. There was a minor outcry, with questions being asked in the House of Commons as to why he had been deported and whether in fact he was the fall man for someone rather more important. No, said Sir John Simon. The deportation was necessary. There may well have been someone behind him. Given his financial state, it is difficult to think that Sloan was his own backer. The reason for the deportation was that his establishment was attracting young Army officers who were losing their pay and so making themselves possible prey to foreign agents who would lend them money in return for information.[5]

---

[5] *Illustrated Police News*, 24 November 1915; *The Times*, 24 November, 15 December 1915.

There followed a short spell of riding in New Orleans, then the equivalent of an unlicensed track, a failed business as a racing tipster, a lavish and ultimately failed billiard hall on Broadway and in 1920 another, ultimately failed, marriage. This time he had met Betty Saxon Maloney, described as even smaller than the diminutive jockey, on 15 June and married her in early July. Towards the end of his life he worked on the gate of the racecourse at Tijuana, Mexico, where the writer Damon Runyon noted that he was, 'A bit heavier but still able to smile with a nonchalant toss of the head.'[6]

Sloan died of cirrhosis of the liver on 21 December 1933 in Los Angeles. There had been rumours of his ill health the previous month, but he had denied them and to prove his well-being sent out for a box of cigars. The story is told that his coffin was put in a room at the funeral parlour next to that of a celebrated gangster. Sloan did not have too many floral tributes, but when the boxers Jim Jeffries and 'Gentleman' Jim Corbett went to pay their respects Corbett removed most of the gangster's flowers and put them on Sloan's coffin. 'Tod always travelled first class,' he said to Jeffries.[7]

It was at the turn of the century that allegations of doping were rife, when it was suggested that this was done with a mixture of cocaine and a weak solution of nitroglycerine under the mane. It would be applied on the way to the start and the effect would last 5–10 minutes. However, this could cause a problem. If the start was delayed the effect might have worn off and the horse, reacting to the stimulant, would come home half asleep. In one French case, where the fashionable dope of that time was strychnine and ether, the horse lay down and slept at the starting post. The other method was in the form of a pill, made of ginger or cayenne and cocaine, which took much longer to act. Generally the horses doped were of little or no stud value and raced at the minor tracks.[8] There were also suggestions that mechanical aids were being employed,

[6] Charles Parmer, *For Gold and Glory: The Story of Thoroughbred Racing in America*.
[7] Jack Leach, *Sods I Have Cut on The Turf*, p. 40.
[8] *Pearson's Magazine*, 8 August 1914.

including a mechanical saddle which stimulated the horse by its vibrations and an electric spur. In the forefront of these allegations was Sloan.

In 1906 a libel action was begun by de Wend Fenton, who had been warned off by the Jockey Club following a match between his Pitchbattle and Lord Gerard's Piari at Sandown Park on 5 November the previous year.

'Blonde' Alice Smith maintains she was involved in the nobbling of The Panther. It started a hot favourite at 6–5 for the Derby in 1919, with the runner-up Buchan and the third horse, Paper Money, next best price at 7–1. The Panther broke the tapes and then refused to line up. Finally, at the 'off' it threw up its head and initially refused to race. It was hopelessly beaten by the time the field reached Tattenham Corner. Again badly beaten in both the Irish Derby and the Champion Stakes, the horse was sent to stud in Argentina. Brought back to England, The Panther died suddenly of heart disease.

Of the many racing swindles, and there have indeed been many, one of the greatest ever must be that of the Trodmore Races never run in August 1898. This was a coup which was thought to have netted something in the region of £250,000, though it would have been considerably more had it not been for a printer's error. In those days many small jumping and flat meetings were held on August Bank Holiday and the editor of The *Sportsman* received a press release announcing the first running of the Trodmore Races in Cornwall on the Bank Holiday; no doubt the paper would wish to cover the meeting and report on the betting? No doubt it would, but there was the problem of staff.

The difficulty was solved when an English sporting gent arrived unannounced in the editor's offices and offered to report on the meeting. Runners and riders were provided with possible betting odds and there was heavy betting. At the end of the day the correspondent, 'G. Martin', wired in the results and starting prices with one animal, Reaper, having won at 5-2. The *Sporting Life*, not wishing to be outdone, then reprinted the results and this time the odds of Reaper were given as 5-1. A bookmaker wishing to know the correct odds made inquiries, but of G. Martin there was no trace. There was no registered horse named Reaper and, worst of all, there was no place named Trodmore. The perpetrators, suspected to be a group of journalists, were never caught. In an article commemorating the centenary of the coup, the *Racing Post* speculated on just how many previous Trodmores there had been.[9]

In December 1902 it was proved that there is no fool like an old fool when 24-year-old Thomas Victor Parker and Edith Julia Ashley, a year older, were charged with conspiracy. They had told Walter Charles Douse that, because Parker worked for the owner, they were in a position to obtain valuable inside information regarding racehorses owned by a Mr Lindermere. They persuaded him to give them £100 and half his house, to resign from his job with the London and North West Railway (which he had held for 19 years) and to draw out his share from the superannuation fund. Douse said he believed that his, Lindermere's and Parker's share of the profits would come to £250,000.[10]

In America the Pinkertons, who had provided a policing service at the Coney Island track since the 1880s, waged a war with the New York poolroom syndicate over the transmission of the race results. The trouble broke out at the spring 1891 meeting. This was the beginning of the wire service, and the Brooklyn Jockey Club which owned the Gravesend track indicated that the fee for receiving the results from the track via Western Union would in future be $4,000. The syndicate replied that they would not pay in excess of $2,500, whereupon the owners said that there would be no more results. The syndicate was not impressed, replying that they would transmit the results themselves. The Pinkertons were consulted.

The syndicate posted men outside the gates so that legmen would leave the track and give them the results. In turn the Pinkertons locked the gates 20 minutes before the first race and only unlocked them after the last. The next move on behalf of the syndicate was to provide men inside the track with a number of tennis balls,

[9] *Racing Post*, 2 August 1998.
[10] *Morning Leader*, 10 December 1902.

pencils and paper; the results were to be put in the slit balls which were then thrown over the track wall. The Pinkertons evicted the ball-throwers. The syndicate offered $25 to the thrower of the first ball with the results. Now the Pinkertons threw their own balls containing the wrong results. The syndicate then erected a tower outside the track so that they could read the results as they were posted. The Pinkertons built the fence higher so that they could not. The syndicate built a further storey on the stand. The fence went higher, so that eventually the tower was so high it swayed dangerously in a breeze.

And so it went on, with one female pickpocket smuggling a cage of pigeons under her dress with the idea of releasing a pair after each race. One man was found to have a bulb, battery and telegraph key under his large hat. However, by the end of the season the Pinkertons had driven out the syndicate. Now they turned their attention to the problem of ringers, the then king of whom was Benjamin A. Chilson.

More than any other sport, boxing has always had its share of dubious characters. Curiously enough, in the old days of the prize ring there seem to have been few confirmed examples of the boxers throwing a fight by lying down and refusing to come up to scratch. This may have been due to the fact that the Underworld of the time did not have control of the sport, which was in the hands first of the aristocracy and then later the middle classes. The more usual way of throwing a fight was simply not to turn up for the contest, in which case bets were forfeit.[11]

The great days of the always illegal prize ring with its bouts lasting 100 rounds and three hours really came to an end in Britain with the Heenan–Sayers contest.[12] Now it largely went underground. The Railway Act 1868 prohibited the railway companies from

---

[11] One possible example of nobbling a boxer was before the Tom Maley–Sam Merryman contest in June 1840. Maley, who had been training at a regular boxing headquarters, the Five Bells at Finchley, was suddenly taken ill with vomiting and diarrhoea. He was moved from the public house and his backers successfully applied for a three-week adjournment. The younger man, he recovered and after losing the first ten rounds won the 11th with a cross-buttock and afterwards dominated the Nottingham veteran. Examples such as this were, however, rare. Tony Gee, *Up to Scratch*.

[12] The contest in 1860, near Farnborough, lasted over 2 hours before the crowd broke the ring, leaving the bout drawn.

carrying spectators to prize fights, but it was still possible to purchase tickets for special trains known as 'There and Backs' where the fancy could watch bouts over 50 to 100 rounds.

In London the home of the prize fight was the celebrated Pelican Club which opened in Wardour Street in 1887 before moving to Gerrard Street.[13] Generally, the wealth and rank of its members kept the fights safe from the prying eyes of the police. One intruding officer was told by Sir Robert Peel, 'My father did not invent you to interfere with me.' Wagering was heavy and one of their protégés was Jem Smith, the all-England Heavyweight Champion who fought a 106-round draw with Jake Kilrann. Shortly after that, in a glove match with a black American, Peter Jackson, on the Club premises, Smith was badly beaten when he was disqualified for trying to push Jackson out of the ring.

The Club members lost heavily and had to recoup. Smith's next match was promoted by 'Squire' George Alexander on the tennis court of Atkinson Grimshaw, a retired major in the Cameron Highlanders, in Bruges on 21 December 1889. This time he was matched with the Australian Frank Slavin, known as the Sydney Cornstalk. The Club members had backed Smith cleverly, 'not to lose', and they were determined their man should have the best possible support.

Smith's party turned up accompanied by 30–40 of the roughest villains that ever disgraced creation. They swarmed round the ropes forming the ring and with bludgeons, knuckledusters and even knives, attacked Slavin whenever he came within reach.

Nevertheless Slavin punished Smith so badly that he was insensible at the end of the 15th round and it was thought he would not come up for the 16th. It was then that 'Squire' Baird, Smith's backer, led the charge into the ring. Slavin was defended by Lord Mandeville with a Bowie knife, and to the delight of the members the contest was declared a draw.

It was reminiscent of the days of Bendigo, whose Nottingham Lambs behaved in a similar fashion towards his opponents and

[13] The club took its name from a stuffed bird which was kept proudly on display along with a stuffed flamingo. See Douglas Sutherland, *The Mad Hatters*.

supporters. On this occasion, however, the police arrived and the Mayor of Bruges applied to the military for support. The principals were jailed.[14] Baird was brought before the Club committee under the chairmanship of Lord Lonsdale and was expelled. It was, however, the effective end of the Club.[15]

In America the reputation of prize-fighting disintegrated after the Civil War. There were allegations that fights were fixed, the contestants were paid to lose, and that referees were in the hands of gamblers. In San Francisco in 1863 the contest between Johnny Lazarus and Pat Dailey ended with the crowd breaking into the ring. Lazarus fell to the ground without a blow being struck and Dailey then refused to fight, whereupon the crowd rushed the ring and the referee declared him the winner. A proposed rematch never took place. Four years later the crowd forced the referee to decide in favour of the badly beaten Charlie Collins on Fisher's Island, New York. The same thing happened the next year in St Louis when Tom Allen lost the decision to Charles Gallagher. No fewer than three contests between Joe Wormald and Ned O'Baldwin came to nothing, and the belief was that these were out-and-out swindles designed to cheat the spectators and gamblers alike.

Even the 1870 contest between Tom Allen and Jem Mace, generally regarded as the best match of its time, was thought by some to have been a fix and believed that Allen had been bought out. Nor were Mace's two fights with Joe Coburn in 1871 much better. The first lasted over an hour without a blow being struck until the

---

[14] J.B. Booth, *'Master' and Men: Pink 'Un Yesterdays*. For an account of the prize ring in its heyday see J.P. Bean, *Brave as a Lion*. In 1846 the Irish prize-fighter Peter Rafferty was convicted of the murder of Brian Patrick Daley following a four-hour bout in Limerick. Sentenced to death, he was reprieved and transported to Australia. On the voyage he saved the captain's daughter from drowning and, on condition Rafferty never returned to Ireland and also changed his name, the man agreed to smuggle him back to England. Joe Robinson, *Claret and Cross-Buttock*.

[15] The heir to a shipbuilding fortune who squandered millions on the prize ring, racing and women, 'Squire' George Alexander Baird was a throwback to the Regency days. He died in New Orleans in 1893 at the age of 35. He had gone on the town after the defeat of Jem Hall, whom he seconded, by Bob Fitzsimmonds. His body was dressed in full evening clothes, placed in a coffin and returned to England. See J.B. Booth, *Old Pink 'Un Days*.

sheriff and militia of Port Dover stopped the proceedings. It could not be called a fight. In the second Coburn outfought Mace for 11 rounds until he decided he had done enough, and no further work was done by either man until the referee got into the ring and declared a draw. There were suggestions that he had done this on a sign from Mace's second, none other than Tom Allen.[16] It was also suggested that a small shot of strychnine applied between rounds could generate enough energy for a boxer being beaten on points to go for a knock-out.

The courts seem to have taken a fairly lenient view of the contests. When Nelson Stead was indicted along with his seconds for the manslaughter of Isaac Tetley in a fight on 5 September 1909 near Doncaster, he was advised by the judge to plead guilty. The judge, commenting that this was an illegal fair fight, sentenced them all to a week's imprisonment, backdated to the beginning of the Assize which meant their immediate release.[17]

Even when there were properly controlled gloved contests there were dangers for the participants. In 1898 Thomas Turner collapsed and died during a fight with Nat Smith at the National Sporting Club. A police inspector had been at the ringside and prior to the contest had warned the pair and the promoters that in the event of damage he would step in. The coroner's jury returned a verdict that the death was accidental but that all boxers should be examined by a medical man before being allowed in the ring. This did not prevent a prosecution against Smith and his seconds for manslaughter. The test was whether the contest had been for money, in which case it would be deemed to be a prize fight. In the seven years of the existence of the National Sporting Club there had been over 2,000 contests and only two fatalities.

The National Sporting Club's contests may have been well run, but the same could not be said for the Lennox Club in New York. There, during his contest with Tommy West, Jack Bonner's gloves were painted with oil of mustard. The effect was temporarily to blind both West, as well as the referee who was sprayed with the

---

[16] These were of course not the only examples. See Elliot J. Gorm, *The Manly Art*.
[17] *Morning Leader*, 10 December 1909.

mixture. Recovering, he disqualified Bonner and a series of fights broke out in the audience.

Dick Burge was one of the more louche characters of the British ring, at least at the start of his career. Born in December 1865, Burge won the British title by defeating Jim Carney on 25 May 1891 on a foul in a skin gloves match. He had long been associated with the highly talented but doubtful Birmingham heavyweight, Charlie Mitchell, in a series of crooked fights before he stepped up in class in 1906 and was used as the heavy in what became known as the Liverpool Bank Fraud.[18] A clerk, Goudie, was lured into betting first with his own money and then, when inevitably he lost, with the bank's. In a few weeks he lost £64,000 and began a series of forgeries which over a year produced a total of £160,000. Things then went from bad to worse. A bankrupt bookmaker and a swindler, Marks, saw that Goudie's previous tormentors were suddenly in the money and wanted to share in the profits. They brought in Dick Burge to do the heavy end of the business and in a few weeks poor Goudie lost another £90,000. Eventually the terrified Goudie simply left his hat in his room at the bank and disappeared. Immediately there was an inquiry and all but one of the conspirators, Manches, were arrested. He was thought – a precursor of Lord Lucan – to have committed suicide on a cross-Channel steamer, but as with His Lordship the body was never found – nor was a considerable part of the proceeds he took with him. Goudie died in Parkhurst half-way through his 10-year sentence.

Chartres Biron, who along with F.E. Smith defended Goudie, wrote in his memoirs that he considered Burge had taken part in the scheme as a way of 'finding some help towards furnishing the house and meeting the responsibilities of matrimony'.[19] Burge received 10 years and, it is reported, burst out crying.

Burge is also said to have been shot while trying to escape from Dartmoor and to have received a flogging for his pains. In the

[18] *The Times*, 5, 6, 8, 11 October, 2, 6, 7 December 1892; *Illustrated Police News*, 15 October 1892, 1 January 1893.
[19] Chartres Biron, *Without Prejudice*, pp. 169–73.

end, however, he was released early for good behaviour and his is a story of total redemption. In 1901 he married Leah Belle Orchard, the adopted sister of the celebrated music-hall comedienne Marie Lloyd, and after his release he became one of the driving forces behind The Ring at Blackfriars, a venue which almost drove the East End boxing arena Premierland out of existence. He died, completely rehabilitated and much loved, in the flu epidemic of 1918.[20]

Not so Charles Mitchell, born in 1861, who was another pugilist of the era to visit prison. In his case it was only two months with hard labour for assault. The actual offence was assaulting an old man, George Salvage, just off the Strand in October 1892. Mitchell, walking home, had intervened in a quarrel between two prostitutes and a drunk. There was some suggestion that he also had been drinking. His version of events was that Salvage came to the front door of the premises where the girls were manhandling the drunk and Mitchell, thinking he was going to be attacked, hit the old man who struck his head on the pavement. Mitchell was stopped by a policeman when he was running away. Salvage's son had told the constable, 'He's killed my father.'

By the time the case came to Bow Street things had been patched up. There was Mitchell under the alias Charles Smith. There was the receipt for £10 compensation, and there was no Salvage. Bernard Abrahams for Smith/Mitchell told Vaughan the magistrate that the matter was at an end, but Vaughan would have nothing of it. He must have known who Smith really was because he asked if he was known to the police and was told by the court staff that there was nothing against the boxer, said now to be the manager of a music hall. Vaughan adjourned the case so that Salvage could be brought to court and full inquiries could be made. On 7 October it all became clear. Salvage, his head bandaged, said he did not want to prosecute and had been paid off, something which earned him a lecture. There was still other evidence against Mitchell and he was convicted; this time his record was produced. Six weeks on 17 October 1881 for prize-fighting at Reading; £5 for assault

---

[20] There is a full account of the case by Richard Whittington-Egan, *Liverpool Shadows*.

on 12 March 1889 at Marlborough Street, and a further £5 on 1 August 1891 for an assault at Brighton. That year Mitchell had been awarded the New York *Police Gazette* Medal made of gold and diamonds, something the court did not hear. There was also a discharge in March 1890 for an assault on another pugilist Goode. Now it was a question of keeping Vaughan from sending Mitchell to the Sessions for sentence.

'You used your great size and strength for dealing with weaklings,' said Vaughan. Mitchell was unhappy: 'There have been no witnesses called for me. Is this an English Court of Justice? As there are no witnesses I must speak for myself.' 'Remove that man,' said Vaughan. Mitchell appealed but, realising his sentence could be increased, surrendered in December to serve his time in Pentonville.

Unfortunately Mitchell did not behave all that well there. At the end of 1892, suspected of supplementing the prison diet, he scuffled with a warder while being transferred to another cell. He was found to have 1 lb of beef and bread and butter on him. A convict cleaner received 21 days solitary confinement and a warder on the landing was discharged.

Overall Mitchell was one of the more intelligent prize-fighters of his day. His father-in-law Pony 'George Washington' Moore kept the Washington Music Hall, Battersea, which Mitchell managed, and until the time when he met the reprobate 'Squire' George Alexander Baird, Mitchell had been a clean-living pugilist.[21] Under the Squire's doubtful tutelage he developed unsavoury and physically weakening habits.

Baird kept a stable of pugilists with whom he sparred and who egged him on. In the bare-fist bouts which he fought with them, a little charade was played. The pugs would take his blows while one would call out warnings such as, 'Careful, Think what you did to 'Arry.' This was a reference to an elderly pugilist whom Baird thought he had killed and to whose family he paid substantial compensation. After a length of time 'Arry reappeared, something which Baird took in good part.

---

[21] He promoted boxing and wrestling matches there, appearing himself both as boxer and wrestler. *Sporting Life*, 2, 16 November 1889, 16, 24 December 1890.

He took Mitchell to New York to fight Jim Corbett, but unfortunately he had not arranged a date and when they arrived they found the current world heavyweight champion appearing in the play *Gentleman Jack* and showing no signs of wishing to interrupt his appearances. Mitchell finally fought Corbett in 1894, but by then he was ageing and certainly not at his peak; he was also giving weight away and Corbett beat him readily. Mitchell died on 2 April 1918. His son had been killed in the First World War and he never really recovered from the blow.

Sometimes it seems as though boxers could not keep their hands off non-combatants. In May 1903 the heavyweight John L. Sullivan was arrested for attacking a one-armed lawyer, Lizotte, in a sleeping car at Boston. It seems that the lawyer, shaking hands with one of the great man's entourage, disturbed him and paid for it.[22]

Another of the great East End boxers was 'Pedlar' Palmer, whose family had long been associated with the Watney Streeters fighting gang and whose career was punctuated with appearances in court and finally in prison. His father had once fought on the marshes at Plaistow for the Barefist Championship of Essex, and Palmer and his brother Matt were at one time a music-hall act, 'Palmer's midgets'.

In 1900 he was living in Bow, a district which his cousin described as 'not a health resort'.[23] A good drinker and an inveterate smoker, two years later on 17 October he went to the Coborn Arms, Coborn Road, when drunk. The licensee, Alexander Stokes, refused to serve him, whereupon Palmer produced a gun and threatened to shoot him. Bystanders ran out in panic, but this time when the matter came to court things had been sorted out. Palmer had written a letter of apology and agreed to be bound

[22] *Illustrated Police News*, 27 May 1903. He died in Brighton in 1918. His ring record was a short one for the time; he boxed 27 times, winning 13 and with draws declared for one reason or another in 11 of the remaining 13.
[23] The unhealthiness of the area is borne out by the memoirs of the stipendiary magistrate H. Cancellor who wrote that when he was told he was being posted to Thames Police Court in Arbour Square he was warned he must take regular holidays. His predecessor had been appointed in the August, 'and told he could have a holiday in November. When that month came, poor P. was so worn out by the hard work and smells of Thames Police Court that he had no strength left to resist a fatal attack of pneumonia.' H.L. Cancellor, *The Life of a London Beak*.

over in the sum of 40 shillings for a year. All was forgiven and forgotten.[24]

He left his wife in June 1906 and was promptly summoned for desertion at Old Street Magistrates Court; he had earned, so she said, some £25,000 in the previous ten years. He told the court that he was not the great fighter he once was and was ordered to pay £1 a week. At his peak, Palmer's admirers had given him a belt studded with diamonds valued at £1,000. It was stolen and when returned the diamonds had been removed and substituted with paste.

On 24 April 1907 he killed Robert Choat, also a one-time boxer, on the 6.30 p.m. train back from Epsom Races. Choat had got in the carriage and asked, 'What will you have, a song or a dance?' Palmer said, 'Don't forget there are ladies.' 'I'm not afraid of little people,' was the reply and Palmer hit him. Choat died instantly. Charged with murder, Palmer had been the life and soul of the court at Maidstone Assizes but when in a matter of minutes the jury convicted him of manslaughter he almost collapsed. He had several previous convictions and received 4 years imprisonment on 20 July.

Money, as has always been the case, was to be made from gambling on horses, prize fights, the gaming tables and, for the working classes particularly, a variety of coin games. These included Nudgers in which one player acting as banker tossed five coins into the air one at a time, catching them in his free hand. After they were all collected he would take bets on how many had come up tails or heads. Another game was Nearest the Mottie, in which a small piece of crockery was placed against a wall. The person who pitched his penny closest to the piece won the money chucked by the other players. In Pitch and Toss, perhaps the most enduring, the person who threw nearest to the crockery then tossed all the coins in the air, keeping those which fell heads up. The coins were then thrown again by the runner-up who kept the heads and so on. To an extent this version of Pitch and Toss was regarded as a young person's game, and the version for real men was the equivalent of Australia's national pastime Two-Up.

Although the real Pitch and Toss was predominantly a working-class sport, tradesmen were equally happy to take their chance. At

[24] *East London Advertiser*, 6 December 1902.

some rings there were gold, silver and copper rings, just as today a casino will run different levels of minimum betting at different tables.[25] Some masters of the Tossing Ring included the well-regarded Two-Ton Titley of Cannock, loved and tenderly regarded by his wife, but generally the rings were not there for the benefit of the punters. Winning players without protection could expect to be robbed as they made their way home.

Another sport in which the upper-class gull could be plucked was appropriately enough the pigeon shooting at which Tod Sloan excelled. In 1903 Robert Sievier, gambler, man-about-town and owner of the wonderful filly Sceptre, was sued on a cheque for £4,000 which he had dropped on betting on a pigeon shoot in Monte Carlo in the spring of 1901. Sievier claimed he was not liable in law as it was a gambling debt, but was also keen to tell the court why he had stopped the cheque. He had been betting on a man named Baratz and claimed that when he called 'pull', a 'very tame pigeon came hovering out of the trap' and Baratz shot three yards below it. When the bird settled six yards from him on the mat and, under the rules, he was entitled to kill it, Baratz failed to do so. There was also a suggestion that he was firing blanks. Sievier claimed he had only issued the cheque because he was warned that when Sceptre was running in Paris she would be got at. She ran unharmed and he stopped the cheque forthwith. Judgement to Sievier.

Pedestrianism was another sport on which there was heavy betting. At one time it had been the preserve of the gambling aristocrat, but in the last two decades of the nineteenth century it became the sport of the professional. The first six-day walking event was promoted by Sir John Astley at the Agricultural Hall in Islington in March 1879, and the sport quickly gained in popularity. Sometimes the races were designated 'go as you please', which allowed contestants to lope or run as they wished. Wagers could be made on the result, the number of miles covered in an hour or half-hour, when rests were taken, and probably on the number of flies surrounding a walker.

One of the more demanding of wagers was that won by Madame

[25] Norman Smithson,' Those Bygone Days of Pitch and Toss' in *Yorkshire Life*, August 1975.

Anderson who at King's Lynn in August 1886 was the subject of a bet that she would walk a quarter of a mile every five minutes for six days. This was an incredible feat. Wagers such as hers had been getting more and more difficult and imaginative since Captain Robert Barclay won a bet that he would walk 1,000 miles in 1,000 hours, in theory a fairly simple requirement. The problem was that he had to complete a mile every hour, with the inevitable and draining loss of sleep. Part of his scheme was to complete his first mile in the first few minutes of an hour and his second mile at the end of the next, so that he could snatch an hour here and there, but he suffered dreadfully.

Shortly before Madame Anderson put on her walking boots, William Barnett of Leeds covered 3,000 half-miles in 3,000 consecutive periods of 20 minutes at St Helena Gardens, Rotherhithe. He had already completed 1,200 miles in 500 hours at the Wellington Street Baths, Leeds, in March 1878. Other targets achieved were 1,000 miles in 1,000 hours, as well as 2,000 quarter-miles in 2,000 quarter-hours. Imagine the sleep deprivation undergone by him and Madame Anderson. She was reported to have completed the course 'but little fatigued'.[26]

Given the gambling however, it was a sport at which nobbling and fixing were rife. Long-distances walkers often had to be protected so that they were able to come up to the start at the given time. Then, quite apart from simple threats or bribes, there were all sorts of little tricks which could be played such as putting stones in their boots.

Professional cycling was also becoming popular, with six-day events ridden indoors with all the problems of a pedestrian event. Outdoors, the Tour de France was originally a 1,510-mile race over six stages, with several periods of rest days between the stages. The first prize was 20,000 francs. The riders were soon victims of skul-

[26] *The Times*, 26 August 1886; *Lynn Journal*, 27 July 1878. The latter paper records Barnett's walk but not that of Madame Anderson. For a thoroughly entertaining account of Captain Barclay's walk and life and times, see Peter Radford, *The Celebrated Captain Barclay*. Matches for women pedestrians were becoming increasingly common on both sides of the Atlantic. In April 1879, 14 females competed in a six-day race at Gillmore Gardens, New York.

duggery. In 1904, 53 riders fell into an ambush on the already sufficiently difficult Col de la République to allow Bénoit-Faure to get to Marseilles first. There was also a similar incident at Nîmes in favour of the local hero Payan who had been disqualified. At the end of the race five riders were disqualified. One, Pothier, was suspended for life but was reinstated in 1910, and the four others received suspensions of 1–2 years. The next year roads were deliberately strewn with nails on the Paris to Nancy stage.

THE NEW KIDS

26

Street Gangs and Politicians

Just as today Belleville in Paris's 13th *arrondissement* has an unhappy reputation as a hangout for gangs, so it did towards the end of the nineteenth century. In March 1889 police officers stopped four men carrying heavy packages along the rue du Point du Jour at the corner of Boulevard Excelmans. They stopped them and for their pains were fired on – two bullets hitting the thick coat of police officer Laplanche. Three of the men escaped, leaving behind Antoine Ravel who claimed he was a turner at Belleville. He and his companions had been on a housebreaking expedition and the packages which the thieves had dropped included linen with the marking G.C., clocks and jewellery. A bloodstained knife was found in Ravel's pocket.

The same afternoon the body of a gardener-cum-caretaker Jules Bourdon was found lying on an iron bedstead at 10 rue Poussin, where he had been looking after the house for a family who were wintering in Nice. His throat had been cut from ear to ear and he had been stabbed in the heart and the stomach; there were bloodstained fingerprints on his cheek and his face was convulsed. The house itself had been ransacked. On the dining-room table a long candle was still flickering alongside four dirty glasses. The initials on the linen found that morning by the police matched linen in the house. Ravel, when questioned, denied that he was a murderer.

However, he was soon identified by another officer as Joseph Allorto, Joseph the Italian, a member of a gang of thieves known as the Pantin or Auteuil Gang because they had operated in that area. The remainder of the gang – about 15 in number – had been sent to the French penal colony in New Caledonia or to Cayenne, but Allorto had not been caught. He was identified by his Bertillon measurements and a photograph. The next day, following standard French police procedure, he was taken to the rue Poussin where Bourdon's body remained on the bed.

Allorto's initial defence was that he had been walking down the street when people whom he did not know had given him a package and the knife. In time he changed this to three men whose names he did not know having offered him a soft job at which he was merely to keep watch. It was his knife, but he had no idea to what use it had been put. The bloodstains were from a nosebleed. It was only a matter of time before he confessed and implicated his companions – Sellier known as Le Manchot, and Cathelin.[1]

This was one of the more celebrated cases of the Detective Chief of the Sûreté Marie-François Goron. His mother wished him to be a priest and he wanted to join the Army; instead he was apprenticed to a chemist. In 1867 he enlisted in the 99th regiment of the Line and served in Mexico and Martinique. He was then bought out of the Senegalese Tirailleurs which he had joined. After the Franco-Prussian War he married and went to Paraguay before returning to Paris in 1880. Five years later he was appointed police commissary at Pantin, and in 1887 succeeded Taylor as Chef de la Sûreté. On his retirement he worked as a journalist for *Le Matin* and then set up a detective agency. He also published a number of novels based on his cases with engaging titles such as *The Pariahs of Love* and *The Market of Women*. He was heavily criticised for having a notecase made out of the skin of the executed serial murderer Pranzini.

By the turn of the century Paris was littered with gangs such as

---

[1] For a full account of the case and others of Goron, see Philip A. Wilkins. *Behind the French CID.*

the Apaches and the Mohawks. Their girls, *gigolettes*, were expected to take part in crime; indeed the gangs probably would not have been able to function without their active participation. Like the girlfriends of Glasgow gang members 30 years later, they would cache weapons in dance halls for their lovers, and were used both as lookouts and as the lures for robberies.

The Apaches were not, however, the only teams in Paris at the end of the nineteenth century. The highly successful detective Gustave Rossignol was credited with bringing down the armed robbery gangs of Maillard and Regnault in 1876, followed by those of the robbers Raab and Siroux. The next year saw the end of the *bande* Moreau and the arrest of 18 thieves from the teams of Rutes and Lochenoz. He was equally successful some 6 years later when in 1883 he arrested 15 members of the *bande* Marquelel. Rossignol was another who fell into disgrace over the skin of Pranzini.[2]

Perhaps the most famous of the Apaches was known, because of her mop of blonde hair, as Casque d'Or, l'Algérienne. One version of her story is that she was born Julia Dalmazzo. Her father was said to have been a wrestler and her mother Anna Delmas had in her time been a music-hall star. Dalmazzo was the queen of a gang which ran the northern side of rue Lafayette and her exploits were legendary. She is said to have evaded capture for many months and, after the team had been broken up by the Lepine-led police, she (having been found in a brothel) so captivated the jury that she was given a nominal sentence. Afterwards, for a time, she appeared topping the bill in Paris music halls.

There have even been doubts expressed as to whether this Amazon actually existed, but Harry Greenwall wrote that he remembered her quite well.[3] The detective René Cassellari wrote in his 1930 memoirs of an expedition on which he embarked with

---

[2] *La France*, 25 July 1887.
[3] See René Cassellari, *Dramas of French Crime*. There is a picture of her in Cassellari's book. On the other hand many sources, including Marcel Montarron's *Histoire du Milieu*, give her name as Amélie Heye. There are pictures of her in that as well, but it is difficult to see if it is the same woman. The French film director Jacques Becker cast Simone Signoret in a romanticised version of her life, *Casque d'Or*.

Casque d'Or to retrieve some paintings stolen in Amiens which he suspected her former lover was fencing. Having left him in an hotel, she went out and picked a man's pocket. Then she told the arresting officer that Cassellari was her gigolo, as a result of which he was arrested and beaten.[4]

Another (and probably the correct) version of her story is that her real name was Amélie Helie and that she was the mistress of both of two Apache gang leaders: Marius Joseph Pleigneur known as Manda, head of a gang in Belleville, and his rival François Dominique Lecca who ran the Popincs, a gang in Popincourt at the turn of the century. The relationships seem to have been short-lived. One account has Lecca meeting her in a debit on the Boulevard Voltaire on 22 December 1901, and their setting up together in a hotel on the rue Godefroy-Cavaignac between Chaonne and Roquettes in the 11th.[5]

In January 1902 the men fought at the corner of Popincourt and Chemin Vert, not far from the Bastille, allegedly over her favours but, in reality, more prosaically the money she made for them, and Lecca was shot. Manda was arrested and Lecca fled from his hospital bed to Brussels where he was found playing cards and held in Saint Gilles prison awaiting extradition. According to legend, Lecca was visited in hospital by La Grande Louise and Amélie Helie and was asked which of his girlfriends he preferred – 'Le Casque d'Or' or 'Le Casque d'Ebène'. He chose Amélie. In fact descriptions of her show a dark rather than a blonde girl with a generous mouth and a tendency to weight.

At his trial Manda, described as having 'small yellow eyes like nuts and a boxer's nose', was dressed all in grey with an impeccably clean collar. He gave evidence, saying that Lecca had challenged him and, 'I replied, "Accepted – whenever you wish".' As for allegations of pimping, nothing could be further from the truth. He was a varnisher by trade and so could not possibly be a *souteneur*. If Mlle Helie gave him money it was merely tobacco money. He was sentenced to life imprisonment with hard labour and died in

[4] René Cassellari, *Dramas of French Crime*, p. 115.
[5] Claude Dubois, *Apaches, Voyous et Gozes Poilus*.

1936 in the penal colony of St Laurent. Six months after Manda's trial Lecca appeared before the court and received 8 years as did one of his men, Erbs.

Shortly after his trial, while awaiting transportation to New Caledonia, Lecca married Mlle Van Mael, known rather exotically as the Panther of the Throne district. If he served his time well she would be allowed to join him after 5 years. A French Salvation Army Captain then offered to look after Mme Lecca, as she had now become, pending her being able to join her husband. He also called on Lecca to repent, but was told that Lecca had 'seen no indication of divine clemency towards himself'.[6] He was killed by gold prospectors after an escape attempt during his imprisonment.

There were varying reports about Casque d'Or's life after the trials. In the early months of 1903 she seemed to be leading a rackety sort of life with suggestions that she was working in a brothel. There were also reports that she had been stabbed by Lecca's men, or stabbed herself while drunk, and that a potential suitor had shot at her in a police station, which seems a foolish place to choose.[7]

Amélie Helie wrote her life story, *Memoires de Mes Nuits*, and on 27 January 1917 married another varnisher André Nardin, 15 years younger than herself. She later opened hat stalls at the markets in Montreuil and Lilas, and died well loved in her neighbourhood at the age of 55 in 1929. She is buried in the cemetery at Bagnolet. When the film *Casque d'Or* starring Simone Signoret appeared, Nardin tried to have it banned on the grounds that it infringed privacy, but it was ruled that she was a public name and the distribution continued.

Meanwhile, undeterred by sentences to two of their leaders the Apaches fought on a regular basis. After Le Bicot de Montparnasse, 'The Billygoat', was shot and knifed in 1903 five men were arrested – one of whom, Leclere, rather sportingly accepted that he was the perpetrator. The other four were acquitted and Leclere went

---

[6] *The Umpire*, 4, 11 January 1903.
[7] Ibid., 11, 18 January 1903.

to penal servitude. Shortly into his sentence he called for the police to say that it was in fact a man named Dierez who had killed the Billygoat, that it had been one of those arrangements which all too often go wrong. Leclere had accepted responsibility on the basis that he would be paid 20 francs a week while he was in prison. Once the payments dried up he thought to rearrange things.

In a week in which 50 murders were reported Ernest Person, called Nenesse de la Rapée, stabbed a café proprietor. He was quickly arrested and when it was pointed out that this was his thirteenth offence he replied that he should have killed another before dawn to get off the unlucky number.[8]

Numbers clearly counted for something, as did being seen in the company of a recently released murderess. In 1890 Gabrielle Bompard – a streetwalker at the Madeleine end of Boulevard Malesherbes – and her pimp, Michel Eyraud, murdered Gouffe, a client, with the help of a pulley in an alcove. His body was found on the banks of the Rhône and the victim was traced, because of his luggage, to the Euston Road, London. Eyraud was arrested in Cuba, while Mlle Bompard turned up again in Paris with an American businessman she had found in New York. Meanwhile the murder room was on view for sightseers. She received 20 years hard labour. Eyraud was guillotined on 3 February 1891.

Now in 1903 Bompard had been released and could be found being wined and fêted at the Grand-Prix de Paris in the Bois de Boulogne by a variety of notables including the Brazilian aeronaut, Santos Dumont. That afternoon between races he flew in his balloon with the number 9 on its silks; this was taken as an omen and punters rushed to bet on the winning number in the next race. No one seemed at all perturbed to be in the company of a none too high-class prostitute.[9] Perhaps it is no surprise that Mlle Bompard went on to publish her memoirs.

Like so many she attracted hangers-on. At her trial there had

[8] *The Umpire*, 15, 22 March 1903.
[9] Ibid., 28 June 1903.

been an unsuccessful application to allow her to be hypnotised so that she could give the true account of what had happened. Now she was in the hands of a Dr Gaston Kardos who had the idea that they should tour America together giving demonstrations. But she was refused admission and returned to England where she was found to be destitute when she landed in Liverpool. There was a whip-round amongst the passengers to get her a ticket to Paris. There are no reports on the fate of Dr Kardos but doubtless, as these men do, he fared perfectly well.[10]

By 1907 the public had tired of the Apaches, and that year a campaign was started against them by the press calling for police action. The First World War seems to have been the marking point of their decline. Afterwards the Apaches had refined their craft to include simple but organised robbery and protection of bars and small shops. These and the long-standing trick of robbing prostitutes' clients seem to have been about the highest form of crime to which they aspired. Higher-class enterprises such as safe-breaking seem to have been quite beyond them.[11]

One of the more celebrated Apaches was one named Liabeuf, sometimes called Leboeuf or Lacombe[12], who wore a bullet-proof waistcoat and a suit, both fixed with spikes to prevent an arrest or attack. The day after the killing of the post-mistress's husband in Besons, the police raided a house in Passage de Clichy to arrest him. He escaped, but another man and two women were arrested in his place. Finally, either caught in a dawn raid or as he watched a wrestling match at a fairground, he attacked a policeman/warder bringing him food and made his way to the station/La Santé roof. Despite the entreaties of both his lawyer, Maître Boucheron, and Lepine, he remained on the roof until it became apparent that the fire brigade was being enlisted to retrieve him. Calling out 'To hell

---

[10] *Morning Leader*, 1 February 1904.
[11] There is a long account by Harry Greenwall of their dress and habits, and as with other criminal enterprises they had their own *patois*. The Black Maria was a salad basket. Prison was a violin. To take a drink of absinthe was to strangle a parrot, and to order the drink itself the purchaser would call for two vitriols. A policemen was either a cow or a *flic*.
[12] The name seems to have been coined by the French journalist Arthur Dupin.

with the police and long live anarchy!' he threw himself into the yard.[13]

It was the time for criminals to persuade themselves that they were anarchists. Although they would prefer to be remembered as the former, the first great criminal gang in Paris of this century was the one led by the ex-racing driver Jules Bonnot.[14] Functioning at a time when there was considerable violence on the streets, they were the first to exploit the use of the motor car as an essential element in a successful robbery.[15]

Bonnot was able to put together a team of younger men and off they went. At the start the gang numbered around 15 members and an early enterprise was a raid on a gunsmith's shop in Boulevard Haussman off the Grandes Boulevards. Now they had the necessary revolvers and ammunition. The next step was to obtain a motor car and change its appearance. Then came the robberies. At first

[13] Readers may take their pick of which version is the more entertaining. One comes from Jean Belin, *My Work at the Sûreté*, p. 42, the other from Harry Greenwall, *The Underworld of Paris*, pp. 118–19. More likely is the account by Georges Claretie in *Drames et Comédies Judiciares: Chroniques du Palais*. The radical journalist Gustave Herve received 4 years for praising Liabeuf's action as not lacking 'a certain beauty, a certain grandeur'. Another version of the story is that Liabeuf, sentenced previously for 'exploiting women', was killed in a struggle in rue Aubrey-le-Boucher with the police officer Debray who died from his wounds ten months after a gold police medal had been pinned on him by Lepine. *Thomson's Weekly News*, 15 January 1910
[14] Greenwall suggests that Raymond Callemin, known as both Raymond le Science and Raymond L' Auxerrois, was the true leader of the gang. He may well have been more of an intellectual, but the name Bonnot is the one by which the gang remains known. It was Callemin who was suspected of murdering Garnier, the policeman. He was described as possessing 'the singular skill in disguising himself as a woman' and when witnesses had claimed a woman was seated in a car it was thought that this was Callemin.
[15] For example on 9 January 1910 a police officer was killed by Apaches when he interfered in a quarrel and was shot and stabbed. It followed hard on the murder of an elderly lady by soldiers in a first-class compartment in the Paris–Fontainebleau train. One of the reasons for the outrages was believed to be the new law which allowed offenders to enter the same Army battalions as boys of decent type instead of being sent to the African corps where they would be subject to more severe discipline. In 1911 there were estimated to be more than 11,000 criminals serving in French battalions.
They may have developed the robbery by motor car, but there were earlier instances. In August 1906 a series of motor-car robberies took place in New York in which a large red touring car was driven by a woman but thought possibly to be a man in disguise. Targets included the Meadowbank Hunt Club and the Westbury post office. *The Umpire*, 1 September 1906. In earlier years robberies had been by butcher's carts which were stolen and used because of the speed of a butcher's horse as a getaway.

things did not go well; they picked the wrong targets and the profits were negligible. Then Bonnot decided that they would rob the cashier of the Société Générale when he left the headquarters to go back to his own branch at 146 rue Ordener.

The man, Gaby (or Caby), invariably followed the same route and took only one assistant with him for protection. At 9 a.m. on 21 December 1911 Gaby was shot in the chest and back as he struggled to hold on to his bag. A second robber went through his pockets. The two men jumped into their Terrot car which took off at an estimated 40 m.p.h. with the occupants firing at anyone foolish enough to give chase. It was the world's first recorded hold-up and getaway by motor car. The haul was little short of sensational – a third of a million francs in gold, notes, small change and share certificates. The Société Générale offered a reward of 12,500 francs, increased to 50,000 and finally to 125,000.[16]

The Bonnot gang continued to plunder. On 3 January 1912 they murdered a 91-year-old man and Mme Arfunx, his house-keeper, at Thiais in the south of Paris. The following week a raid at a factory in northern France failed when the night-watchman knocked down a member, Callemin. A smash-and-grab raid on another gunsmith followed. On 26 January a smart Delaunay-Belleville car was stolen at St Mande near the Bois de Vincennes, and the next day a policeman was shot as he tried to stop the car near St Lazare station.

The first of the gang to be arrested was Eugène Dieudonne, a joiner by trade whom Gaby, who had miraculously survived his injuries, identified. He was also recognised by Inspector Jouin who was being helped by a woman informant. Almost certainly the gunman was Garnier, another member of the gang, and now he wrote a letter to the police claiming responsibility. In a postscript he added:

[16] Another account has the haul in mostly worthless paper and the bandits nearly caught at a customs post on the outskirts of the city. This version has the car abandoned near Dieppe and the penniless bandits getting third-class tickets back to Paris. It may have been Raymond Callemin's idea to abandon the car in the hope that the police would think the gang either were English or had fled across the Channel.

I know that you will get the better of me in the long run, for all the strength is on your side, but I will make you pay for it dearly.

Two months later at about 8.30 a.m. on 25 March a blue and yellow Dion-Bouton belonging to the Colonel Comte (some reports say Marquis) de Rouge, a Paris society sportsman, was stolen on the Montgeron road in the forest of Senart. Céleste Mattine, the 32-year-old driver from the Dion-Bouton company, was shot dead and 18-year-old Louis Cerisol (who was on the box seat) was hit four times by bullets. They had been on their way to Nice to deliver the car to its new owner.[17] After the theft, the injured Cerisol managed to struggle into Montgeron and raise the alarm. Bonnot put on the goggles and coat of the dead driver and used the car the same day for a getaway following a bank raid on a small branch of the Société Générale in Chantilly. A considerable sum of money was stolen but, worse, two employees were killed and a third was shot in the shoulder but survived.

The tubercular André Soudy was next to be arrested. He was captured on 30 March at Berck-sur-Mer when he was leaving for Amiens. 'I may die, but plenty of others will die with me,' he told the police. He had with him a Browning automatic, cartridges and a phial of potassium cyanide. He had been living in an isolated cottage belonging to a railway worker, Barnaille, who was also arrested. When questioned by the examining magistrate Soudy said that his adherence to anarchism was the real reason for his arrest. Then Carouy and Raymond Callemin, both printers and both Belgian by birth, were traced and captured. On 3 April 1912 Carouy tried to commit suicide by using what he believed was potassium cyanide. It was not a successful attempt; all he had done was swallow an emetic. Soudy was now positively identified as the man with the carbine outside the bank at Chantilly sweeping the square with rifle fire.[18] There was

---

[17] Coincidentally this was the same place at which the Lyons Mail was robbed in 1796. All the robbers escaped, only to be captured after a number of innocent men had been executed for that crime.

[18] *The Times*, 5 April 1912. The English press took a great deal of interest in the exploits and capture of the Bonnot gang and there are numerous references to the case in *The Times* for the years 1911–1913.

now a suggestion that Carouy was not involved in the Chantilly robbery or the Montgeron murder and, tempted by the reward offered by the Société Générale, might turn informer. He was, and he did not.

On 23 April Bonnot was reported to be at Ivry, then a derelict area outside the fortifications of the old city, trying to put together another gang. Jouin, now the deputy head of the Sûreté, led a police raid on a second-hand clothes store with rooms above owned by a dealer named Gauzy. Bonnot was hiding in a back bedroom and in the ensuing gunfire Jouin was killed and his colleague, Colmar, badly wounded. Bonnot, hit in the wrist, leaped from a window and escaped.

On 28 April Bonnot, betrayed by an informant, was caught in Choisy-le-Roi and on this occasion he did not escape. The raid was led by Lepine himself, who this time had taken the precaution of calling in the Army. Watched by a large crowd, Bonnot held both the military and the police – commanded by the head of the Sûreté, Xavier Guichard – at bay for six hours before the police, under cover of a hayrick and behind a screen of mattresses and pillows, stormed the building. Bonnot had been badly wounded and shot himself. As he lay dying he had written a note:

> I am famous now, My fame has spread throughout the world. For my part I could have done without this kind of glory. I have tried to live my own kind of life and I have a right to live.

In his blood he had added a postscript: My mistress is innocent and so are Gauzy and Dieudonne. I am dying now. Bonnot.[19]

Despite the efforts of the crowd to lynch him, the police managed to put the semi-conscious Bonnot in a taxi-cab and drove to the Hôtel Dieu, the hospital near the Préfecture of Police, where he died shortly after 1 p.m., twenty minutes after his arrival there. Another man, Dubois, suspected of being involved in the Montgeron

---

[19] *The Times*, 30 April 1912. There are other versions of the note's contents.

murder and theft and the Chantilly murders and bank robbery, had been found dead on the premises.[20]

On 14 May two other members of the gang – Garnier, said to be the most violent, and Vallet – were traced to the Villa Moulin Rouge, Nogent-sur-Marne, where they had been trying to negotiate stolen bonds. Once again Lepine took command and at about 5 p.m. the villa was surrounded. Lepine narrowly escaped being shot as he led his troops from the front, and with the siege beginning the local townsfolk turned up to watch the spectacle. By the end of the evening Paris taxi-drivers were taking spectators out to Nogent. The siege continued into the night until Lepine decided that the building should be blown up. At 2 a.m., with the crowd shouting 'A mort; à mort' the sappers launched a mine, but this appeared to do little damage and the attack was called off until dawn. By then there was no answering fire from the house and, when it was charged by the police, the bodies of Garnier and Vallet were found propped against the window frames.

It was a comparatively simple matter to round up the less active members and hangers-on. Defended by the Corsican lawyer, Maître More de Giafferi, they were charged on 12 September 1912 with 8 murders or attempted murders and 18 thefts, and stood trial with Dieudonne and the others arrested earlier. The three-week trial began on 3 February 1913 when one of the key witnesses was the messenger, Gaby, who would not shift from his belief that Dieudonne was his assailant.

On the last evening the trial was attended by *le tout Paris* in evening dress and ball gowns. The jury acquitted four, 12 received sentences of 5 years and more, including Metge who was sentenced to penal servitude for life. Dieudonne and three others were sentenced to death.

After his conviction Callemin said that Dieudonne had not been involved in the first raid in rue Ordener. Carouy committed suicide in his cell by taking poison. Soudy bequeathed his burglary tools

---

[20] An examination of the body of Dubois, born in Odessa, the son of a French father and Russian mother, showed he had been shot three times probably at an early stage in the siege. He had served in the French Foreign Legion and genuinely was a car repairer.

to the Minister of War. Mounier gave his revolver to his lawyer in the hope that he would in turn donate it to a museum; he wanted 'Thou shalt not kill' to be engraved on the barrel. He also left his books to the Paris municipal library, and to society a wish that 'one day life will be ordered so as to give the individual more time for the study of beauty of knowledge'. The three were executed on 21 April 1913. It was reported that during his last hours Callemin had read *Revue des Deux Mondes* while Soudy had tried to complete his autobiography.[21] The first to die was Soudy whose words on the scaffold have gone down in criminal literature: 'It's all very cold. Goodbye, all.' Callemin shouted abuse at the crowd, calling out that it was not nice of them to come to witness a man's agony. The last, Mounier, was still arguing with Monsieur de Paris, the executioner Deibler, when the guillotine fell.

Perhaps as a result of the efforts of his colleagues to exculpate him, Dieudonne was reprieved and sentenced to penal servitude for life. He survived his years in Guiana, from which he once escaped to Brazil before being recaptured in July 1927. Later his conviction was re-examined and was overturned. He returned to Paris where he worked as before as a carpenter, making bookshelves for the crime writer Marcel Montarron and indeed for the detective Jean Belin.

After the siege of his Villa Moulin Rouge the landlord, who had chosen his tenants badly, charged a fee for the large number of visitors who wished to see where the anarchists died. He argued that he had to do so to pay for the repairs to his property.

There is some evidence that Bonnot operated for a time in England. In his memoirs Detective Inspector Charles Leach recalls how he received information that a gang of counterfeiters was at work in Netley Street, Hampstead. The workshop was kept under observation and when finally the raid was carried out there was a complete mint on the premises, with two dozen moulds for making French and Belgian currency along with 194 counterfeit examples. Following that raid Leach made a raid on another house in the area and:

---

[21] *The Times*, 22 April 1913.

When I entered with my colleagues, someone got away very hurriedly through the back entrance and over the wall. Though we pursued him, the unknown fugitive made his escape.

I was afterwards informed that he was none other than the notorious Bonnot. Had I arrived at the house a little earlier and surprised him before he could effect an escape I might not now be writing this tale – or possibly Paris might have been spared a series of the most brutal and callous murders of modern times.

The raid resulted in the arrest of two coiners, Alexander Estegny aged 39 and Jules Barault who was ten years his junior. Described as a dangerous anarchist, Estegny had previously received 2 years for embezzlement and had been found in possession of six motor-cycles in Lyons, from where Bonnot originated. Now he was sentenced to 5 years imprisonment and Barault to 4.[22]

Back at street level, in 1881 a war broke out between gangs of schoolboys which ran for nearly 25 years. The Irishers and the Bohemians were not racially named, rather from the districts where they lived. Their final battle took place in December 1905 when the Irishers led by Mike and George McGinnis fought Joe Fischer, now leading the Bohemians. Although numerous shots were fired in the fight which raged for hours, no one was hurt. It seems to have been rather like the battle between the gangs of Paul Kelly and Monk Eastman in New York some years later when the only casualty was a passer-by.

In the last 15 years of the nineteenth century the Johnson Street gang, led by Buff Higgins, Edward 'Red' Geary and Johnny Murell – who received life for killing a patrolman in 1880 but was paroled within two years – was regarded as one of the most dangerous. Higgins, born in Ireland in 1871 and who came to Chicago at the

---

[22] *The Umpire*, 17 December 1911; Charles Leach, *On Top of the Underworld*, pp. 44–5. There followed a little homily about how Bonnot never went unarmed. Leach had his share of troubles. In 1918, along with Alexander Duncan Lawrence, he was accused of accepting bribes. He was defended by Sir Patrick Hastings at the Old Bailey and was acquitted on 8 February 1918 after the judge told the jury that the accusers were men of appalling character and that corroboration in a material particular was required. Leach later became a private detective.

age of two, was regarded as a murderous coward. He was believed to have murdered two men and from 1891 had served two years in Joliet for assault with intent to kill. Certainly at the time of his arrest he had only been out a few months and was already wanted for the shooting of a barman at 16th and Morgan the previous July. Then on 3 September 1893 he, along with Harry Feinberg, broke into the home of Peter McCooey at 153 Johnson. McCooey (who lived near Higgins) was said to have drawn out his life savings, and Higgins came to hear of this potential booty. At 3.30 a.m they broke into the house where Higgins while jemmying a trunk accidentally dropped the lid, which woke McCooey who came to investigate. Higgins shot him at point-blank range. They escaped with less than $2 and on the way home robbed a milkman of his $10 takings.

The police set up a dragnet and at 5 a.m. Higgins was found hiding under the sidewalk on Halstead which was being repaired. He threatened the officers with his gun but, seeing he was outnumbered, surrendered. In true Third-Degree style he was taken into a room with the body and a young man was sprung on him saying, quite falsely, that he had seen Higgins climb out through the window. At that, according to the police officers, one of whom was conveniently a notary public and so took down the statement, Higgins confessed. His trial was a confused affair. He withdrew his confession and witnesses were produced, and discredited, to say that they had seen the murderer running away and it was not Higgins.

Showing that an unhealthy interest in a criminal's memoirs is nothing new; the *Chicago Daily News* published a long, self-exculpatory life story in which Higgins blamed the police for all his misfortunes.[23]

He was hanged at Cook County jail at noon on 23 March 1894 and the paper brought out a special late-night extra detailing his last hours:

[23] *Chicago Daily News*, 4 September 1893, 23 March 1894.

The thought that the rope would strangle the life out of his body apparently weighed no more heavily on the mind of Thomas Higgins than did lighting and smoking a cigarette.

There was an account of how he had seen two priests, asking them to wait until he had dined, and some of his own words:

Yes, this is my day, sure I reckon everybody in Chicago is saying, 'I'd hate to be in Higgins' boots today.'

One thing which pleased him was that another man, due to hang with him for a separate offence, had been granted a stay of execution. Higgins did not consider him a worthy gallows mate.

Another gang was the Henry Street Gang led by Chris Merry, describing himself as a pedlar, who eventually was hanged for kicking his invalid wife to death. The Bill Mortell–Jack McGraw team were highly regarded, as were the McGanns whose leader Jimmy had only one leg but still retained a high degree of mobility. For some years he led his five sons but, as the *Chicago Journal* reported, by 1903 one of them had been killed by him and three of the remainder were in prison.

The Weiss or White Gang really only flourished from the time when the six sons and two daughters of the widow Margaret Weiss (who lived on Maxwell) married into the Renich family of 10 daughters and two sons. They operated for a period of years from an isolated house in Cooper Street, Lake View. The gang may have been named Weiss but the brains was certainly Eva Gussler, known as Eva the Cow, who amongst other things ran a pickpocketing and shoplifting school. Like many others at the time, she specialised in silk, which was really a generic name for anything which could be found in a tailor's shop – buttons, bolts of cloth, irons and even sewing machines.

The Daly Gang, from 42nd and Taylor Street, which specialised in stripping cars, was relatively short-lived, but the Valley Gang lasted for something like 40 years, eventually breaking down in the Prohibition era.[24] Early Valley members included Big Henry Muller

---

[24] James Morton, *Gangland International*.

and Jimmy Farley, along with Billy Hughes and Cooney the Fox. Later came Red Bolton who received life imprisonment and then Paddy Ryan, Paddy the Bear, who was killed in 1920 by Walter Quinlan, known as The Runt, and who in turn was killed by Paddy the Bear's son, Paddy the Fox.

Another of the gangs was the Formby Gang led by Jimmy Formby who had with him David Kelly and Bill Dulfer. Formby killed a street-car conductor in a robbery and when arrested only for the robbery is reputed to have said, 'Charge me with murder. I'm a killer not a robber.'

In the first six months of 1906 in Chicago there was a burglary every three hours and a hold-up every six hours. Murders ran at one a day. The *Chicago American* complained that Mayor Carter Harrison jnr had pardoned 110 criminals between 1 October and 15 November 1903.

The Rev. W.H. Burns, who headed the Law Enforcement League and was one of the many clerics throughout social history with a liberal disposition, commented, 'Chicago is worse than it has been since 1879. In those days I saw two men hanged to lamp-posts and it did some good, too!' This comment followed the rape and murder of Mrs Frank C. Hollister who on 12 January 1906 had left her home to go to sing at a funeral. Her naked body bound with copper wire was found the next day on a disused site. She had been beaten mercilessly.

The 39th precinct, south of Division Street and north of the Chicago River, and 22nd precinct on the Westside were regarded as the worst areas with 400 saloons, one for every 80 of the population, and a further 200 blind pigs (illegal drinking joints). Little Hell was a network of brothels and low hotels between LaSalle and the River, with a number catering for specific types of behaviour: this one for male degenerates, that for cocaine addicts and so forth.

The sweep following the death of Mrs Hollister may not have produced her killer but it certainly produced a clean-up. In the first five months of 1906 there were 900 arrests of which 100 were for murder, rape and robbery. The feeling was that had the police been better staffed and organised there could have been twice that number.

By the end of the nineteenth century there were signs that gangs in London and elsewhere in Britain were becoming a little more structured. They were no longer only fighting gangs; now they were preying on women. The Green Gate Gang in the East End was rather more correctly suspected of the killing of a woman who from time to time is suggested as a victim of Jack the Ripper.

Emma Elizabeth Smith was killed on the night of 2–3 April 1888. She lived after she was attacked and said she could identify one of the four men involved. Having been seen talking to a man with a white scarf shortly after midnight in Fairance Street, Limehouse, she then reappeared at George Street lodging house, telling the deputy that she had been assaulted and robbed in Osborn Street. She was taken to the London Hospital where she was found to have had an instrument, not a knife, inserted in her vagina. As she staggered back to the lodgings, she must have been in great pain but had made no complaint to any police constable she must have passed in the street and was indeed reluctant to be taken to hospital. Two days later she died of peritonitis. Unfortunately it was not until 6 April that the police were informed. Members of the Green Gate Gang or the old Nichol Gang who operated in the area at the time as ponces, extortionists and as street robbers generally were regarded as her killers.

Also in the East End was the Silver Hatchet Gang and south of the river, as a forerunner of the Elephant Boys, were the Manchester Boys, a collection of youths from Scotland Road, Liverpool, Manchester, Leeds and Bradford. There was also the South Tottenham Gang, otherwise known as the Mardell Hooligans. In Peckham there was a gang of street robbers, The League of Rattlesnakes.[25]

More or less any town of size had its own fighting gangs which would do a bit of what they saw as tapping of local shopkeepers.[26] Synonyms for tapping might include blackmail and demanding with

[25] *Illustrated Police News*, 14 January 1899; *Thomson's Weekly News*, 8 September 1906.
[26] In Sunderland for example there was a gang which called itself The Nuts, two of whose members, James Boyd and Stanley Coates, appeared at the Assizes charged with the manslaughter of a bookie's runner.

menaces. In July 1906 the Italian Joseph Ventura, a shopkeeper, was charged with the murder of John McAndrew, head of the Village Boys. McAndrew had already served a three-month sentence earlier in the year for breaking into Ventura's shop. The Italian, who displayed the 'characteristics of the sons of the Sunny South', had to be rescued by the police after he had shot McAndrew. Neighbours spoke of the activities of the Village Boys and their persecution of the man.[27]

The end of Hull's Silver Hatchet Gang came on 30 July 1913 when John C. Hutchinson was kicked and beaten with pit-props after he had intervened in a fight at Hull Alexandra Docks. Various members of the gang had set on a labourer, Curley Howlett, and Hutchinson had said that 4–1 was not an English way of settling things. 'And it was not,' said Mr Justice Scrutton. The fight had been over a girl who at one time had lived with Howlett but then transferred her affections to Herbert Yeaman. Howlett was said to have been following her and trying to persuade her to return to him. On Hutchinson's intervention the gang had simply turned on him.

The Hatchet Gang were said to have repeatedly been in breach of 'public morals' and violence over the previous two years. Now Yeaman along with Walter Davis, John William Petch and the 19-year-old Harold Cummings were charged with Hutchinson's murder. Some 15,000 watched his funeral at which the Wilson Band played the 'Dead March' from *Saul*.

There was little evidence against Cummings and, surprisingly, although the magistrate committed him for trial he allowed him bail. Things must have been poorly with the gang by this time because although he turned up at York Assizes at the end of the first day, he asked to be taken back into custody since he did not have the money for the night's lodgings. On the second day the other three pleaded guilty to manslaughter and Yeaman received 7 years. The previous year he had been convicted of four assaults. Davis now received 5 years and Petch 3. Cummings was found not guilty, but was made by the judge to stay and watch the sentencing

[27] *Thomson's Weekly News*, 21 July 1906.

of the others and hear him have some harsh words to say about violence in Hull.[28]

Of course these rough and ready gangs bore no resemblance to those of New York with their relatively sophisticated political affiliations. Politicians in England had used mobs to control voting, but this was much earlier in the nineteenth century. Now, as a general proposition, there was no way that gangs in England were going to be associated with politicians, whereas in America politics and gangs have continued to be inextricably linked since that time.

In the second half of the nineteenth century the first pre-eminent political gang in New York was the Tweed Ring run by the eponymous William Marcy 'Boss' Tweed and including the lawyer 'The Elegant' Abraham Oakey Hall along with Peter Barr Sweeney (known as 'Brains' or 'Bismark') and Richard 'Slippery Dick' Connolly. Together they built and masterminded a political organisation which dominated both city and state politics.[29]

Hall was born in Albany, New York, on 26 July 1826. He was the District Attorney for New York City in the 1850s and in 1862 joined the Democratic Party. Described as a 'nervous witty little man who delighted New York with his rhetoric of inanities and his absurd pince-nez', Oakey Hall was mayor from 1868 to 1872. He wrote and acted in some of his own plays including *Let Me Kiss Him for His Mother*. In his early years he had prosecuted in a number of cases though not always with outstanding success. In 1855 he appeared for the prosecution of Lew Baker, accused of the killing of William Pool – something which he certainly did and in which the evidence was almost overwhelming. Nevertheless he was acquitted.

---

[28] It may not have been completely the end of the gang because on 24 May 1919 four men were convicted of being drunk and disorderly and of assault on the police at the Duke of York Inn at Sutton when Edgar Featherstone said, 'We belong to the Silver Hatchet Gang' before throwing a bottle at the police officer. This may have been an attempt to trade on an old name because if the gang still did exist it cannot have been very active; or else its members were adroit because none of the four appears to have had previous convictions. *Hull Daily Mail*, 23 May 1919.

[29] An Australian version of Tammany Hall was that run in Sydney by John Norton, William Willis and Paddy Crick in the late 1880s. For an account of their careers see Cyril Pearl, *Wild Men of Sydney*.

The lawyers Howe and Hummel were never directly related to the Ring. Nonetheless they provided invaluable assistance because, if at an election a repeat voter such as the experienced and much valued Reddy the Blacksmith and often provided by the Whyos gang was caught, Howe and Hummel were there to have him released to vote again before the day was out.[30] On one occasion Tweed naturalised 60,000 immigrants in a three-week period. Few knew sufficient English to understand the nature of the oath of allegiance, but they soon understood how they were to vote on election day.

Running at full strength from approximately 1860 to 1875, it is estimated that the Ring took one dollar out of every two paid out by the city. Huge bribes had to be paid to the Ring, which in turn awarded contracts and waived tax payments. Some of their operations were staggering. Pencils worth $75 cost $10,000; chairs and tables worth $4,000 went through the books at $171,000 and a building contract worth $50,000 went for $1.8 million. The Ring also paid out huge sums to non-existent charities and hospitals. Since it controlled the police and District Attorney's office as well as having the physical power of the Whyos at its disposal, it was almost exempt from criticism let alone attack.

But all good things come to an end. By the mid-1870s the Ring had almost bankrupted the city and an anti-corruption reform movement headed by Samuel J. Tilden overturned their power.

It is believed that the Ring-owned Judge Albert Cardozo was bribed a staggering 200 times by Howe and Hummel to release their clients. When the Tweed Ring was dismantled Cardozo resigned but was never prosecuted. Judges Barnard and McCunn were impeached, but neither was prosecuted.

Tweed stood trial in 1874 and his first trial ended with a bribed

---

[30] Little is known about Reddy except that he was a prominent member of the Bowery Boys and was a brother of Mary Varley, a notorious fence and confidence trickster, who kept a house in James Street. He killed the Philadelphian, Jimmy Hegarty, uncle of Johnny Pope, in Eagan's Saloon, Houston Street at the corner of Broadway, known as Murderers Row. Hegarty had tried to make Reddy stand on his head.

and hung jury. The second had every juror watched by a plainclothes officer, himself watched by another detective who, in turn,
was watched by a private detective. Tweed received 12 years,
reduced on appeal. He was released in 1875 and now faced a civil
action. Held in the less than secure Ludlow Street jail, he broke
out in December of that year, travelling to Cuba and then to Spain
where he was recognised from a political cartoon and returned to
the United States. He made a partial confession and offered to tell
all and name names, but this was rejected. He died in prison in
1878.

When the Ring collapsed Oakey Hall was the only other who
stayed to fight. In all he faced one Grand Jury and three trials,
and in essence he was charged with misfeasance in public office.
He had signed some $6 million of fraudulent vouchers. His
defence was that he had only been acting in his ministerial
capacity and the real villains were Tweed and Connolly. His law
partner, who appeared as his counsel, did what he could to help
him by saying he never considered Hall had the talents of a
businessman.

Hall's final trial began on 22 December 1873 and concluded on
Christmas Eve with the judge in poor humour. He had been asked
something of a technical question by the jury and, in retaliation,
said that if they did not reach a verdict soon he would lock them
in their chambers all night. They responded promptly by acquit-
ting Hall.

Immediately after his release Hall wrote another play, *The Crucible*,
described as an artfully contrived drama with a simple plot, the
gist of which was that he had never conspired with the Tweed Ring.
It was not a success; opening on 5 December 1875, it ran for only
22 performances. Hall went to England for a time before returning
to New York where he resumed his career as a lawyer and journalist. On 25 March 1898, this one-time mocker of organised religion was baptised into the Roman Catholic Church. He died seven
months later.

After the fall of the Ring things did not improve that much.
Tweed's position was then taken by Richard 'Boss' Croker, a one-
time member of the Fourth Avenue Tunnel Gang. Born in Ireland

in 1843, he came to America at the age of three and lived in what was described as a shantytown in the vicinity of what is now Central Park. In turn he was a machinist and a prize-fighter. He was twice elected an Alderman in the 1860s and in 1873, surviving the fall of the Ring, he was appointed Coroner. The next year, however, he was involved in a quarrel in the Gas House district in which a bystander, John McKenna, was shot and killed during election day shenanigans. The disagreement by the jury is thought to have been due to Howe's behind-the-scenes efforts. Croker was never retried; he was then re-elected Coroner and after that Fire Commissioner, and held control of Tammany Hall from 1886 to 1902.

He was more or less compulsorily retired that year and, visited in Ireland by Abe Hummel, he sent back a message saying that he had no intention of returning to politics. 'Depend on it Richard Croker has burned his political bridges behind him. He is without political ambition,' reported Hummel, who could always be relied on for a quote or two on return from his travels.[31]

Throughout the nineteenth century there had been a series of New York street gangs including the Plug Uglys – from the hats they wore – and the Dead Rabbits because one was carried into battle on a stick.[32] The last of the period and one of the longest-lived in New York was the Five Points Gang which ruled a territory bounded roughly by Broadway, Canal Street, the Bowery and Park Row. The writer Herbert Asbury is, of course, right in saying that many of the gangs of that time were basically fighting gangs. The 1,500-strong Five Pointers were direct descendants of the Whyos who flourished, in succession to the Chichesters and the Dead Rabbits, from about 1874. In their early days the Whyos were an almost entirely Irish gang who specialised in contracted beatings and murders, preferably of Englishmen. When in 1883 one of their top men, Piker Ryan, was arrested he had in his possesion a tariff for services to be rendered. A punching came relatively cheap at $2; a broken nose or jaw cost $10; a broken arm or leg an

---

[31] *New York Times*, 11 August 1903.
[32] For an account of the early fighting gangs see Herbert Asbury, *Gangs of New York*.

additional $9. A stabbing or shooting in the leg was $35, and 'the Big One' was priced to start at $100.

So powerful were the Whyos that they were able to extract a street tax permitting traders to operate. As they grew more sophisticated, and when their predilection for alcohol did not disable them, they moved into protecting stuss parlours, extracting a high proportion of the profits from the owners.[33] About that time membership was reserved to those who could show they had killed a man. One of the leaders was Dandy Johnny Morgan who, apparently not content with basic street robbery, had devised a patent eye gouger to be worn on the thumb. He was keen to display both the proceeds of his crime and the eyes of his victims in the Whyos' club house, a bar known as the Morgue in the Bowery. They faded from sight before the turn of the century because they were unable to harness their undoubted talents to new political interests and, lacking protection in high places, became increasingly vulnerable to arrest and imprisonment.

However, the Whyos were sufficiently sophisticated, or intelligent enough, to retain Howe and Hummel on a long-term basis. Howe defended Mike McGloin, one of their early leaders who was hanged in the Tombs on 8 March 1883 for the murder of Louis Hanier, a saloon keeper of 26th St W. Hanier had tried to prevent McGloin making off with the till takings and was killed with a sling-shot. The day after the murder McGloin is said to have remarked, 'A guy ain't tough until he's knocked his man out.' It was McGloin who was a victim of Thomas Byrnes' Third-Degree technique of having him in a cell with the corpse of the murdered man.

In 1887 Howe defended Danny Driscoll, charged with the murder of a girl called Beezy Garrity. She had been keeping company with both Driscoll, then the leader of the Whyos, and a John McCarthy. In a gunfight between the men, Driscoll accidentally killed her.

---

[33] Stuss, a variation on faro, was particularly popular amongst the Jewish community. In theory it was a game in which the players had an almost even chance of winning. In practice a good deal of sleight of hand could be exercised so that heavily favoured numbers were matched by the first card dealt.

Howe had battled long and hard to save him, but when he failed he seemed to display none of the angst the modern lawyer shares with his unfortunate client. By now he had turned his attention to his feud with the Tombs' warden with whom he had a long-standing quarrel over the smuggling of a knife to Driscoll. Now he accused the warden of bribery and favouritism. Not a word about the unfortunate Driscoll. Instead:

> Lawyer Howe ate walnuts and sipped sherry yesterday while he said that there was proof enough in existence to warrant the instant removal of Warden Walsh from his office.[34]

Six months later he defended Driscoll's successor-in-title, Danny Lyons, who on 5 July 1887 shot Joseph Quinn, the lover of 'Pretty' Kitty McGown, a prostitute in Lyons' stable. With a string of appeals, Howe managed to keep the Whyo alive for the better part of a year before the inevitable happened.

The *New York Times* wrote a short tribute to Howe's client, 'Simple story of Commonplace Life':

> He knew better than to steal, but he stole and was sent to the reformatory. He stole again and was sent to the penitentiary. He stole again and was sent to State Prison. He murdered and he was hanged.[35]

Another relatively unfêted gang were the Buckhoos, men (principally from the Fourth Ward) who took one short trip to sea and picked up enough of the talk and practice to be able to strike up with sailors on leave and rob them.

The leader of the Five Points Gang was the ex-boxer Paul Kelly. Born Paolo Antonini Vaccarelli, he spoke fluent English, French, Italian and Spanish. When he retired from the ring he invested his winnings in a string of brothels in the Italian quarter and also east of the Bowery. He held court in the New Brighton Dance Hall in Great Jones Street, and it was there that the middle classes found

[34] *New York Herald*, 24 January 1888.
[35] *New York Times*, 22 August 1888.

it entertaining to go slumming. Kelly, unlike the Whyos, was astute enough to link himself to politics and the corrupt Tammany Hall machine.

Perhaps the zenith of his career came in the 1901 campaign for political control of the Second Assembly district, in which he threw his army behind the Irish politician Big Tim Sullivan who, in turn, was supporting Tom Foley against the sitting member, saloon keeper Paddy Driver. Driver at least was trying to keep the neighbourhood reasonably respectable.[36] His campaign slogan was 'Don't let the Red Lights into the old Fourth Ward.' It was not a slogan which appealed to Kelly. During the primary, Driver's voters were attacked and kept away from the polls at gunpoint. Kelly's men went in to vote unhindered, one apparently recording his choice over 50 times. Foley won by a 3–1 majority, and in came the Red Lights. Prostitution in the Assembly was now controlled by Kelly who provided an army of streetwalkers, mostly young Italian girls charging 50c a time, half of which went to him.

One difficulty in being a leader was that Kelly obliged himself to lead by example. From time to time he performed a street robbery, and it was in the act of one of these that he was caught by the police. His political contacts now served him well. Robbery then carried a sentence of 10–20 years but to the fury of the judge, Recorder John W. Goff, the charges were reduced to simple assault.

Kelly served 9 months, and it was then that he established his Athletic Associations, in theory to provide recreational activities for youngsters in deprived neighbourhoods but in reality well-controlled youth gangs. One of his younger members was a man himself destined to become a legend, Johnny Torrio. Under Kelly's patronage he formed a youth gang which over the years included Lucky Luciano, Frankie Yale and Al Capone. All in turn graduated

---

[36] In his younger days Sullivan had been a prominent member of the Whyos. He aligned himself with the notorious Richard 'Boss' Croker and became the sachem of the Assembly District in 1892.

to the Five Points Gang whose operations included strike-breaking, contract beatings and murder. Now began the inexorable march to organised crime as we know it.

27

The Immigrants

By the end of the nineteenth century the Irish gangs were facing new challenges. In the 1860s the great Jewish migration to the East End of London and then on to America began, gathering pace after the assassination of Tsar Alexander II in 1881.

The Lower East Side of New York was the breeding ground for Jewish crime. Quite apart from controlling prostitution and the usual protection work, some was relatively sophisticated. Back in 1879 Joseph Levy, Charles Bernstein, Isaac Perlstein and Abraham Freeman conspired to defraud insurance companies by over-insuring buildings and then setting them on fire. Sixteen years later in 1895 Vernon Davis, the District Attorney, indicted the largest gang of incendiaries ever at work in New York. The head was Isaac Zuker who received 36 years hard labour.[1]

It was hoped that the Hawthorne School in Westchester which opened in May 1907 would be the reformatory which would eliminate Jewish crime. The hope was a pious one. The next year 250 Jewish delinquents had to go to non-Jewish reformatories because of overcrowding at Hawthorne.

By 1910 it was estimated that rather more than half a million

[1] *New York Times*, 13 February 1879; *Jewish Messenger*, 1 January 1879. See also 'The Epic of Incendiarism' in *Leslie Illustrated Weekly*, Vol. 82, 18 February 1897.

Jews lived in a 1.5 square-mile area. It was then that Joseph 'Yoski Nigger' Toblinsky led a gang of horse poisoners. Styling themselves on the Italian Black Hand and calling themselves the Yiddish Black Hand, they were protection racketeers preying on new immigrants. Letters were written to stablemen and businessmen demanding money to insure their horses against unforeseen accidents. Toblinsky boasted that he himself had poisoned over 200 horses and styled himself 'King of the Horse Poisoners'. The East Side Horse Owners Protection Association was formed in 1912 and within a year the poisoning of horses had ceased altogether.

Although the original Black Hand gangs had been operating in Italy as early as the 1750s, it was in the first two decades of the century that this became a favourite Italian sport in America. To make the threats more sinister and terrifying, the threatening letter was signed with the outline of a black hand. The first major outbreak seems to have come in New York in about 1901, and by 1908 there were over fifty separate references in the *New York Times Index* to different Black Hand incidents that year. They included the note which the Reverend J.A. Gray, pastor of the Congregational Church in Orient, Long Island, received in the collection plate on 20 February. He ignored it at his peril. The church was burned two days later. The same month, Dr C. Volini, President of the White Handers – dedicated to the defeat of the Black Handers – received a death threat note. In June 1909 the Black Hand leader Sam Lima was arrested in Marion, Ohio, but things did not slow down. In 1911 in Chicago it was estimated that there were 18 Black Hand murders, 100 bombings, and that blackmail collections totalled $500,000. It seems that in Chicago there were some 60–80 Black Hand gangs functioning in the city until 1920. All were independent gangs; no two were ever linked together. Now there was no city in America with an Italian community which did not have at least one Black Hand gang and probably many more.[2]

---

[2] There was an outbreak in the Hamburg area in 1902 and another in 1910. The letters contained no threats, simply a drawing of a black hand. One woman told the police she had paid over the equivalent of £30,000 over a period of years. There was a late rash of letters sent to farmers near Prestatyn, Wales, in January 1925. *Thomson's Weekly News*, 16 April 1910, 25 January 1925.

Nor were the targets always the *paisans*. The celebrated opera
singer Enrico Caruso was a victim, paying, so it was said, $1,000
out of every $10,000 he earned. The notes he received warned that
if he did not pay, lye would be slipped into his wine or tea.[3] An
early warning was often the removal and return of a finger of one
of the victim's children. One example is the letter in 1905 sent to
Gaetano Costa, a Brooklyn butcher:

> You have more money than we have. We know of your wealth
> and that you are alone in this country. We want $1,000 which
> you are to put in a loaf of bread and hand to a man who comes
> in to buy meat and pulls out a red handkerchief.

Costa refused to pay and was shot dead in his shop. His killers
were never arrested but they were thought to be working for the
almost tautologous Lupo the Wolf (also known as Ignazio Saietta
or Ignazio Lupo), a Black Hand chief in Italian Harlem who had
arrived in New York in 1899. Saietta owned what became known
as the Murder Stable at 323 East 10th St.[4]

On 14 April 1903 a woman named Carmelina Zillo, emptying
trash into the street, saw a barrel which she thought might be of
use. Unfortunately, on closer inspection it was found to be full
of sawdust and a man's head with his genitalia poking out of his
mouth. By the end of the day Joseph Petrosino, the only Italian-
speaking detective then on the New York force, had been sent
for. A squat man who wore a derby hat, he was known amongst
his colleagues as 'The Dago'. Petrosino was highly regarded
amongst the Italian community for not taking bribes, and by the
criminal fraternity for the ferocity with which he beat them to

---

[3] History tends to repeat itself. In May 1997 Luciano Pavarotti's home near Modena
racecourse was the target of an arson attack. It was thought that this was a warning
to the tenor to pay protection money to the Mafia. His girlfriend, Nicoletta Mantovani,
was at pains to point out that there was no Mafia in Modena. Others such as the Rome
daily newspapers, *Il Messaggero* and *La Repubblica*, were not so sure. John Phillips,
'Mafia and the Maestro' in *Daily Express*, 19 May 1997.
[4] Some reports have it that eventually the bodies of over 60 victims were found. Many
of the victims were thought to be those who had disobeyed Black Hand letters, but
there is little doubt he was also operating an early contract killing agency.

obtain confessions or, if he was unable to extract one, simply to teach them who was the master.[5]

Petrosino was relatively successful in concluding the case of the man in the barrel. He seems to have been able to identify a *toscano*, a cheap Italian cigar, a religious medallion with INRJ[6] and the testicle stuffing as marking the victim as Italian, probably Sicilian. Initials W.T. on the barrel showed it had been made for Wallace & Towney who supplied cafés with pastries. One of them was a German establishment on Prince Street which could be eliminated from the inquiry and the other, a much more likely candidate, the Star of Italy bar run by a Pietro Inzerillo at 260 Elizabeth Street. From reports in the newspapers it seems that dozens of Italians were brought in to see if they could identify the body and indeed, as is often the case, there were a number of false hopes and leads as when Michele Bongiorno identified the victim as Antonio Quattrocchi. For a time there was some excitement over this because Quattrocchi came from a family of smugglers of illegal immigrants, but that line proved to be useless when the supposed victim reported to police headquarters.

However, at the time there was a completely independent inquiry going on into a counterfeiting operation run by Italians in New Orleans and Pittsburgh as well as in New York. The Star of Italy was the meeting place of the New York end of the operation and Petrosino became convinced that the victim was in some way connected to the counterfeiters. Guiseppe Di Primo, a Pittsburgh counterfeiter, had been arrested and was in Sing Sing. It was from there that he identified a photograph of his brother-in-law, Benedetto Madonnia, from Buffalo, as being the dead man.

---

[5] Petrosino, born in Italy, had joined the New York police department in 1883 and was promoted detective in 1895. In 1899 he was instrumental in smashing a large insurance fraud in the Italian community. The more gullible were persuaded to take out policies with life insurance companies. The 'agent' would lend them the money for the premium and the policy-holder in return made him the beneficiary while the debt was outstanding. It was unusual for the policy-holders to survive a year. After his death Petrosino's body was brought back to New York and buried at Calvary cemetery. His widow, Angelina, received a pension of $1,000 from the City of New York and $10,000 collected by the Italian community. She died in Brooklyn in 1957 at the age of eighty.

[6] The Latin initials of Jesus of Nazareth, King of the Jews, said to have been the mocking inscription on the Cross.

Petrosino believed that Madonnia had been to see a Guiseppe Morello, generally believed to be the leader of the counterfeiting ring, had demanded money and been killed for his pains. It is also possible that he was trying to use some of Morello's outlets to dispose of his own counterfeit money. Either that, or it was feared that he was an informant. A sweep of the patrons of the Star of Italy was arranged and Morello, Lupo, Guiseppe Fontana – who in Italy had been accused of the murder of the Marquis Emanuele de Notarbartolo – were arrested on counterfeiting charges. With them in the raid came Tommaso Petto, a bodybuilder and male beauty contest winner known as 'The Bull', and Vito Cascio Ferro, a known man of respect, who had only recently arrived from Sicily with his family.[7] Petto, living up to his nickname, required four officers to arrest him. In his pocket was a pawn ticket for a watch.

Bail was set at what was, for seemingly penniless Italian immigrants, a high sum. It was raised within 24 hours as their lawyer, the noted Le Barbier, told the court, 'by a collection throughout the Italian community' – whatever that may have meant.

Petrosino had the watch (now redeemed from the pawnshop) identified by the family as belonging to Madonnia. From his inquiries he was able to reconstruct the circumstances of the man's death. After Di Primo's arrest in Pittsburgh, Madonnia had been sent to Morello to collect the imprisoned man's share of the counterfeit money. He had been turned away and had threatened to go to the police, hence the castration. Petto was identified as the killer. With the exception of Vito Cascio Ferro, who had prudently absented himself to New Orleans, the gang were rearrested in the Star, this time for murder. Now Petto gave no trouble; indeed, although he had identification papers in his pocket he took some pains to deny that was his name.

On 29 April 1903 the murder trial began – and effectively ended immediately, with the man once more denying he was Petto. He had good reason, since he was in fact a ringer, Giovanni Pecoraro. He was discharged. In the end only Morello and Lupo were

---

[7] Ferro was probably the Don of Manhattan, the underboss of the shadowy Don Balsamo who controlled Brooklyn.

convicted. Di Primo was released in 1905 and in the summer of that year the real Tommaso Petto, who had changed his name to Tom Carrillo, was killed by an unknown assailant on his doorstep in Wilkes-Barre, Pennsylvania. On his release the police had put a tail on Di Primo, but he easily eluded them.

For a time Petrosino prospered. He persuaded the Police Commissioner, William McAdoo, that it was hopeless trying to police the growing Italian community with only 13 officers who could speak the language. In 1905 he arrested the Camorra Black Hander Enrico Alfano, discovered he was wanted for a double murder in Naples, and arranged for his deportation. He now became convinced that many other Black Handers actually had criminal convictions in Italy and so were liable for deportation. He persuaded the New York police to send him to Sicily to make inquiries, where he was assured of co-operation from the local authorities. It was with some reluctance that the then commissioner, Theodore Bingham, allowed him to go, since there were fears that the Mafia had infiltrated the police department and Petrosino's safety could not be guaranteed.

At 8.45 on the night of 12 March 1909 Petrosino was shot dead in the Piazza Marino in Palermo, having been lured there in the belief that an informant would disclose the names of the local *mafiosi* leaders. Unsurprisingly, there were no identifying witnesses of his killers. His old enemy Vito Cascio Ferro, now Don Vito and one of the *mafiosi* chiefs, was charged with the murder, but the allegation was swiftly dropped. He maintained that he was dining with a member of the Italian parliament. Later, however, he would claim that he fired the final bullet into Petrosino.[8]

Ignazio Lupo Saietta continued his criminal career. He was again convicted, this time of a plot to smuggle forged dollars into the United States, and in 1920 was sentenced to 30 years imprisonment. Paroled, he was allowed to go back to Italy. Unfortunately he did not stay there, returning to New York two years later. By now, however, he found that the world he had once controlled had changed beyond recognition and he took less of an active part in

[8] For a fuller account of Vito Cascio Ferro's life see James Morton, *Gangland International*.

matters, although in 1936 he was sent to prison on racketeering charges – he had been running a lottery for Charles 'Lucky' Luciano as well as a small-time protection racket on local bakers. By this time the leaders of the old brigade, or Mustachio Petes as they were ironically known, were Guiseppe Masseria, Salvatore Mauro and Umberto Valenti. Their rivalry would ultimately lead to the infamous Castellammarese War which Saietta, now a nonentity, survived. He died in Brooklyn in 1944, probably in his early seventies.

However, he was not the only extortionist of the early years. According to one account a leading exponent and moneylender was a mannish, red-haired woman named Pasquarella who ran stables between East 108 and 109 Streets. She operated them as a school for murderers and thieves, and also had ten stable grooms trained to be horse thieves. Horses 'found' were returned for reward.

It was Don Nicholas Morello who, decades before 'Lucky' Luciano thought of a national crime syndicate, had that same idea. His family had arrived in New York at the end of the nineteenth century after emigrating from Corleone. The founder of the clan was Antonio, believed to have personally committed between 30 and 40 murders, and succession passed to his brother Joe, the brother-in-law of Saietta, and then to Nicholas.

Unfortunately Nicholas Morello did not have the muscle to impose his wishes. While his Sicilian gang controlled the rackets in East Harlem and Greenwich Village he was unable to explain the wisdom of his vision to Don Pellegrino Morano, the leader of the Camorristas, who ran Brooklyn. Instead of co-operating to make one happy family, Morano continually cut into the interests of Morello until in 1916 he sued for peace. A meeting was arranged at the Navy Café and as Morello stepped from his car he and his bodyguards were ambushed and killed. Morano was sentenced to life imprisonment. The succession then passed to the artichoke king, Ciro Terranova.[9]

As for London, in his autobiography published in 1931, Frederick Wensley wrote:

---

[9] G. Selvaggi, *Rise of the Mafia in New York*, pp. 22–42.

Any reader of the daily papers these days might come to the conclusion that Chicago is the only place in which organised bands of desperate criminals ever existed. The public have a short memory. It is not so very long ago that we, in the East End and some other districts of London, were engaged in stamping out groups of criminals, many of whom carried arms, and who waged a sort of warfare among themselves and against the public.

He continued:

In the early part of the century there was one gang of this class who had established a real reign of terror among certain people in the East End.

The victims were those same people who are always the victims:

In the main, however, the victims were persons who for some reason or another were a little shy of bringing their troubles to the notice of the police. Keepers of shady restaurants, runners of gambling dens, landlords of houses of resort, street book-makers and other people on the fringe of the Underworld were among those peculiarly open to trouble.

And of the others:

Sometimes small tradesmen were offered 'protection' against other gangs at a price. If they did not take kindly to this blackmail all sorts of unpleasant things were liable to happen to them . . . Persons who had resisted their extortions had been brutally assaulted, their premises wrecked – in one case an attempt to burn down a building had been made – and any portable property stolen.[10]

By the late 1890s there was a considerable amount of anti-Semitic feeling which continued into the twentieth century:

[10] F. Wensley, *Detective Days*.

Foreign Jews of no nationality whatever are becoming a pest and a menace to the poor native born East-Ender – [they have] greater responsibility for the distress which prevails there probably than all other cases put together.[11]

The West London magistrate for one was not at all pleased with the number of immigrants who appeared in his court:

These foreigners come here as into a foreign country, parcel out the public streets like territory and fight amongst themselves like savages. Their trade is a lucrative one and they are a well organised trade union so that if money can prevent it one of their number rarely goes to prison.[12]

The principal East End immigrant gang which operated around the turn of the century was the 40-strong pack, the Whitechapel-based Bessarabians, sometimes known as the Bessarabian Tigers or the Bessarabian Fighters:

The Russian Jews with their ingrained terror of the police would, in practically every case, rather put up with the gangs than risk the consequences of complaining to the police . . . we were continually having to let cases drop through lack of evidence.

They levied a protection toll on timid alien shop-keepers, proprietors of coffee-stalls and so on. The faintest shadow of protest on their part at this blackmail and the gang descended on them in force armed with guns, knives and such weapons as broken bottles.[13]

In *Lost London* the former Detective Sergeant B. Leeson gave another example of their methods:

---

[11] 'Judenhetze Brewing in East London' in the *Pall Mall Gazette*, 18 February 1886. See also Simeon Singer's reply in the edition of 23 February.
[12] *Illustrated Police News*, 7 March 1903. The previous year it was announced that eight powerful associations for criminals had been formed in New York. They included a Lady Shoplifters Association, one for racecourse swindlers, one for con-men etc. The Association had paid a leading lawyer a large fee to go to Paris to instruct counsel for two members. *Illustrated Police News*, 3 January 1903.
[13] George W. Cornish, *Cornish of the 'Yard'*, p. 4.

Lists of people to be blackmailed were drawn up by the gang-sters, and amongst these prospective brides provided the happiest and most productive results. A few days before the wedding cere-mony a gangster would approach the bride's parents and threaten to expose all sorts of imaginary indiscretions of which their daughter had been guilty if their silence was not bought. The victims, fearful of the scandal that might ensue, invariably paid up.[14]

The Bessarabians ruled for almost an entire decade with their chief rivals the Odessians, so named because a man named Weinstein – also known as Kikal, the proprietor of the Odessa Café – took on the Bessarabians. He refused to pay protection money and according to Leeson fought them off with an iron bar when they came to demand their wages. The rival gang, which did not include Weinstein, took the name as a tribute to his courage.[15]

For the first couple of years of the twentieth century there were the usual gang skirmishes. The effective end of the Bessarabians came in October 1902 following an attack by them on a Yiddish music hall held in the York Minster, a public house in Philpot Street off the Commercial Road where a number of Odessians were thought to be. There had been trouble the previous Saturday and witnesses spoke of Bessarabians going up and down the Commercial Road asking the whereabouts of their rivals.

One man, sometimes called Henry Brodovich but also known as Kaufmann, was stabbed to death. In the ensuing confusion the public was either less discreet or more likely less frightened than usual and names were named. As a result the boxer Kid McCoy (whose real name was Max Moses), Samuel Oreman and Barnet Badeczosky were arrested. 'If that man had not died £15 would have squared it,' said McCoy, who claimed it was he who had been attacked.

It was clear that witnesses were at risk and the stipendiary magis-trate Mead issued a warning that those convicted of threats would

[14] G. Leeson, *Lost London*, p. 147.
[15] Weinstein was not always the complete hero. The *Police Gazette* had a wanted notice for him, 'Said to be a Russian Jew of around 50 he has absconded his bail and might be found at seaside towns.' 6 February 1903.

face imprisonment. This intelligence seemingly failed to percolate to Woolf Selvitzky – a restaurant keeper and said to be the leader of the Bessarabians – and Marks Lipman because the following week they were promptly convicted of an assault on Marks Mieland. Selvitzky had punched him saying, 'My pal is in trouble through you.' Two months hard labour each.[16]

The week after that Woolf Kigesky and Joe Zelkowitz each received a month's hard labour. They had been trying to raise funds for their friends' defence, and Morris Goldberg had refused to pay up until threats were made.[17]

Meanwhile the committal proceedings on the murder charge continued and, somewhat against the perceived wisdom, E. S. Abinger called witnesses to show that McCoy was indeed the victim of a planned attack. Evidence was called that certain people, including the dead man who was said to have been armed with an iron bar, had been out looking for and threatening to harm McCoy that night. For the present it did neither him nor the others any good, since they were all committed for trial.

Alleged heads of the Bessarabians kept popping up. After the imprisonment of Selvitzsky, presumably Woolf Schaberman had taken over, for he was described as the head of the gang when he appeared charged with being concerned in the robbery of Max Goldman, a butcher, and stealing the watch of Harris Harman. This seems to have been a curious affair. Schaberman is said to have knocked Goldman down and then bitten him before stealing £8 in gold and his chain. Harman's watch was found in Schaberman's possession. It is difficult now to say exactly what happened or, indeed, who was batting for whom, because the police officer in the case said that Goldman had been very drunk, and despite the finding of the watch Schaberman was discharged.

With their leaders in prison the Bessarabians faded from power, although they were still hired to break up Anarchist and Social Democrat meetings. When not working they could be found playing cards in a Romanian restaurant at the corner of Setters Street and

---

[16] *East London Observer*, 1 November 1902.
[17] Ibid., 8 November 1902.

the Commercial Road. Meanwhile the police chipped away at the Odessians, many of whom went to America where they joined forces with the local crooks. One known as 'Tilly the Burglar' is said to have become a Chicago policeman.[18]

By no means all immigrant crime was the fairly amateur mugging and rolling of sailors or preying on their own communities. In 1901 a middle-aged German woman Bertha Weiner, from Shadwell, came to grief along with her 12-strong gang of housebreakers and thieves. Their targets were big suburban houses standing in their own grounds, and up to five of the gang would go on what were meticulously researched expeditions. The raids were carried out with seeming impunity.

Wensley claims that it was when he saw a number of men in the Shadwell area who appeared to have money and the leisure to spend it that he became suspicious. He began shadowing the area and discovered that many of the men lived in a house in Albert Street which was regularly visited by Bertha Weiner, who paid the rent. She herself lived with a sailor named Rebork in Ship Alley, about a mile away. She had a brother Ludwig who with his two sons lived in Tredegar Square, Bow, and were auctioneers.

According to Wensley, Bertha Weiner was the putter-up and financier. The men from Albert Street were the burglars and disposed of the articles to her, while the better pieces were auctioned by her brother and nephews.

A raid scheduled for 28 October was aborted when Wensley's father was taken seriously ill and the next night a housebreaking took place in Willesden with the windows and doors forced, the silver and wines removed from the cellar and much of the owner's clothing taken. The police raided on 31 October when eight men were arrested in Albert Street. One had put on a pair of stolen socks and another had a hat taken in the burglary. Wensley went to Ship Alley and broke in on the home of Rebork and Bertha Weiner at the same time as other officers raided her relations in Tredegar Square. One of the curious pieces of evidence against them was a

---

[18] According to Leeson, McCoy also went to America on his release and became a successful businessman.

small badge which had been presented to Sir Montague Sharpe, then deputy Chairman of Middlesex Sessions, by his fellow judges. A member of the gang named Wald, a professional wrestler, wore it with pride, claiming he had won it in a tournament in Germany.

Bertha Weiner received 7 years penal servitude at the Old Bailey in December 1901 and, with the exception of a nephew who received 12 months, the others were sentenced to 5 years. Bertha was released early on licence, but she was soon back in custody charged with theft at Clerkenwell. Her licence was revoked on 27 July 1907 and she was finally released from Aylesbury prison on 26 August 1909.[19]

It should not be thought that the indigenous London gangs of the period were shrinking violets. There were a considerable number of highly talented gangs of thieves such as The Titanics, a gang of pickpockets who lasted until well after the First World War.

There was also Arthur Harding who ran the Blind Beggar Gang (also known as the Vendetta Mob) from around 1906, which made a speciality of the armed robbery of Jewish gambling clubs. One of Harding's ventures, along with his friends Dido Gilbert, Tommy Taylor and Danny Isaacs, was to hold up card games in the Jewish spielers and take the proceeds, often as little as £3 or £4 a time. Harding justified the raids by claiming the victims were all crooked men who regarded the raids as little more than a minor inconvenience:

> Yiddisher people make a laugh of it. They said, 'Give them a few bob and get rid of them.'[20]

Eventually, however, the card-players became bored with these raids in which they were made to stand with their hands in the air, and they recruited some of their own to deal with Harding and the others. A meeting at Mother Woolf's public house in Whitechapel

[19] F. Wensley, *Detective Days*; PRO P Com 6 28.
[20] Raphael Samuel, *East End Underworld*, p. 120. Gilbert was killed in the First World War, Taylor became a ponce and, according to Harding, died of syphilis in 1915. Harding later fell out with Isaacs over a girl they both knew and whom, so Harding believed, he was beating.

saw the Vendettas badly beaten. Finally Ruby Michaels, fearing there would actually be fatalities if the raids escalated, explained the facts of life to Harding through his henchman Tommy Hoy:[21]

> Ruby Michaels was the most noted receiver of stolen property. He was the biggest buyer of stolen jewellery in East London. His headquarters was the Three Tuns in Aldgate. He had several front men – Leon Behren, the man who got killed in 1911, was one of them. They picked the stuff up from the daylight screwsmen at the spielers and took it to Ruby at the pub. Anyone who had any diamond rings to sell, they took it to him, and the buyers came from all over the world. In Portland I met a crook who had come all the way from America to buy something off Ruby.[22]

Michaels had a long and successful career. He was friendly with 'Chicago May' Sharpe and it was she who tipped him off that Tim Oates, who was regarded as the King of the Panel Workers and who owned an antique shop in the City Road, was unfortunately also a police informer.[23]

Shortly before Sharpe was arrested for shooting at her former lover Eddie Guerin, Michaels put up a jewel robbery for her in the Strand. A young Italian thief, Louis Lorenzano, who worked with Sharpe and her then partner Charles Smith, was to be the coachman and drive her in an open barouche – on which had been placed a temporary coat of arms – to the jewellers not far from Charing Cross. Usually the jeweller was left on his own during the lunch period. Lorenzano, fine in livery and with a birthmark painted on his cheek, was then to go into the shop and ask the jeweller to come to the carriage as his mistress was an invalid. Smith would then snatch a tray of diamonds which were on display. Unfortunately the jeweller noticed Smith working on the hasp and staple which secured the jewels and ran after him. To maintain her cover, Sharpe

---

[21] From reports in the local papers Hoy was clearly a man with whom to be reckoned. At least twice he was charged with shootings. He was friendly with Billy Chandler of the bookmaking family and was an expert dealer at faro. *East London Observer*, 9 January 1909, 28 January, 11 February 1911.

[22] Raphael Samuel, *East End Underworld*, p. 134.

[23] A panel was a brothel or low boarding house in which theft from the customers was rife.

found herself obliged to buy a solid gold collar-button. As she remarked, Michaels was 'out his expenses'.[24]

However Michaels generally kept a low profile, surfacing in court only in 1915 when he and Aaron Lechenstein – who, in his salad days, had been a police court interpreter – pleaded guilty at the Old Bailey to trying to bribe a police officer to allow them to conduct illegal gaming in East End clubs. The payment was to be £10 a week for each of three clubs, totalling £1,500 annually, and an amber cigarette holder was delivered to the officer as a mark of esteem. The proposal followed a raid in the previous June when a club owner had been fined £500, and Michaels thought that prevention was the best cure.

Under the direction of his superiors the officer played along with them and the pair were arrested at a meeting to which they had brought a document for him to sign. There was clearly money about because Michaels had Sir Edward Marshall Hall K.C. to defend him. The receiver was, said Hall, now paralysed and prison would be a death sentence. Chief Inspector Wensley put his oar in, saying he had known Michaels as a gambler and receiver for some 24 years, but Marshall Hall won through. Michaels was fined £100 and Lechenstein, said to be in a poor financial way, a mere £10.[25]

In New York it was Edward 'Monk' Eastman who controlled the Lower East Side and – one of the early great Jewish gangsters – became the Five Pointer, Paul Kelly's principal rival. 'Monk' Eastman was the antithesis of Kelly. The latter may have been a former prize-fighter but he was also a cultured man. Apart from his linguistic abilities, he dressed well, could and did read books and appreciated both art and classical music.

Eastman, a former bouncer, was a wild man with a following said at its height to have numbered over 2,000. He had no time for a man he considered effete.[26] Eastman was also unreasonable.

---

[24] May Churchill Sharpe, *Chicago May – Her Story*, p. 116–17.

[25] *East London Observer*, 18 September 1915. It was around this time that it was decided that, as a sufficient number of immigrants now spoke English, the services of a full-time Yiddish interpreter could be dispensed with at Thames Magistrates' Court.

[26] Eastman seems to have had one quality. He was devoted to animals. He could often be seen with a cat under each arm and a parrot on his shoulder. At one time he had

It was impossible for Kelly to negotiate with him and, with an overwhelming numerical superiority, Eastman made inroads into Kelly's territory. This culminated in a 50-a-side battle on Rivington Street near the Second Avenue El in 1903, by the end of which three were killed and seven wounded. Tammany Hall stepped in and drew demarcation lines between the gangs, which were now run on Italian-Jewish loyalties. The line held for a time and then an Eastman man was badly beaten by the Five Pointers. Again Tammany Hall stepped in and at a second peace conference Kelly and Eastman were told in no uncertain terms that all political support would be withdrawn if fighting continued. Now, according to legend, the two leaders agreed to battle and a two-hour bare-fist fight took place in the Bronx ending with the collapse of both men.

But, when it came to it, Eastman was unable to appreciate the need for care if political backing was to be forthcoming. He also liked joining his men on the raids too much and was caught after a robbery on 2 February 1904. Seeing a young man staggering drunk at the corner of 42nd and Sixth, it seemed that here was a pigeon ripe for the plucking. Unfortunately the pigeon had a guard with him in the shape of a Pinkerton detective. Unlike Kelly in his time, however, Eastman could not call on the aid of Tammany Hall and off he went up the Hudson river to Sing Sing for 10 years. In his absence Kelly regained his territory, but in turn he fell foul not of the politicians but his own men. After 'Eat-'Em-'Up' Jack McManus, the bouncer at the New Brighton establishment, had been killed, Biff Ellison was incensed not to be appointed in his place. Along with Razor Riley, Ellison walked into the dance hall where Riley shot Kelly's bodyguard, Bill Harrington. Kelly was hit three times himself, wounding Ellison who fled with Riley. As befitted a gang-leader, Kelly was repaired in a private hospital in Harlem before surrendering himself to the police. No charges were preferred. As befits renegades, Ellison and Riley were not so lucky. Ellison was arrested in 1911 and sent to prison for 8 to 20 years, and then to an asylum where he died. Riley hid out in Chinatown – some

---

a pet store in Broome Street in Lower Manhattan, but apparently could rarely be persuaded to sell any of his stock.

accounts say in Hell's Kitchen on the West Side – where he died of pneumonia in a basement before the police could find him.[27]

The shooting marked the end of Kelly's reign. Police Commissioner William McAdoo closed the New Brighton dance hall and Kelly moved his operations to the Italian community in Harlem from where, for a time, he ran strike-breaking operations. A sideline of this was destroying properties so that the owners were obliged to sell out at knock-down prices. He did return to the scene of his former glory, opening the New Englander Social and Dramatic Club, but it was not a great success. He was continually being raided by the police, although these raids were usually telegraphed in advance because they never found anything more than some elderly gentlemen playing dominoes. He retired shortly afterwards, living until 1927 when he was one of the few gangsters of this or any era to die in bed. Some accounts have it that Jack Sirocco took over the Five Pointers, but it is more likely his career took off through 'Monk' Eastman's outfit.[28]

'Monk' Eastman, born Edward Osterman, is described as having a bullet-shaped head, a broken nose and cauliflower ears. He had scarred cheeks which were heavily veined, sagging jowls and a short bull-neck. He usually wore a derby hat several sizes too small and carried a variety of weapons – brass knuckles, a blackjack and pistol, although it was his proud boast that he never used them on a woman. In his early career he worked as a bouncer in Silver Dollar Smith's, across from Essex Street courthouse, where the floor was inlaid with silver dollars. Immensely strong, he is credited as

[27] McManus was almost certainly killed on the orders of Chick Tricker who had been criticising the way ladies at the New Brighton threw their feet in the air while dancing, something he considered inappropriate. In a quarrel over the conduct of the dancers McManus shot Tricker in the leg. While the latter was in hospital, on his behalf Sardinia Frank bludgeoned his rival with an iron bar. In turn Frank became the bouncer at the Normandie Grill at Broadway and 38th. When asked what he was doing so far away from home he invariably replied, 'I'm here to keep out everybody I know.'

[28] The Five Points Gang had held sway in one form or another from the 1820s. The 500-strong Gophers ruled and spent much time raiding the railway sidings in the area of Hell's Kitchen. They were one of the few gangs of the time to have a women's section. The Lady Gophers, officially known as the Battle Row Ladies' Social and Athletic Club, could be hired in industrial disputes to play the parts of the wives of strikers or strike-breakers, or both. The Gophers were eventually destroyed by the predations of the railway police who first cleared them out of the yards and then drove a wedge in their activities in Hell's Kitchen.

having survived being wounded during a shoot-out with the Five Pointers. Hit twice in the stomach, he pushed his hand into the wound and staggered to Gouverneur Hospital. Although Eastman's men worked sporadically for Tammany Hall, he mainly worked with and for music and dance halls and protected the up-and-coming gambler Arnold Rothstein, as well as working for both sides in the labour strikes which were beginning to proliferate at the time. The sentence in Sing Sing proved to be the effective end of him as a force. He took to pickpocketing and peddling small quantities of dope, unfortunately too often testing his own supplies in quality control exercises. He returned to the Lower East Side, where he eked out an existence before being arrested in possession of narcotics in his apartment on E 13th Street in 1912 and sentenced to 8 months imprisonment. He was acquitted of burglary in Buffalo and then spent nearly 3 years in Dannemora for a robbery in 1915. In 1917 he was discharged by a court for fighting and the next day enlisted.

In France he served with considerable bravery and distinction. On 3 May 1919, following a petition by his commanding officer, his civil rights were restored to him; but back in America he soon went to the bad and was shot by a Prohibition agent, Jerry Bohan, while liquor-running on 26 December 1920. The police found his body outside the Blue Bird Café on E 14th near Fourth Avenue. He was buried with full military honours. Bohan, who said he had been quarrelling with Eastman over a tip for a waiter, pleaded guilty to manslaughter and was sentenced to 3 to 10 years. He was paroled after two years.

Eastman's time was the heyday of the early Jewish gangster. When he went to Sing Sing the leadership of his gang was assumed by Max 'Kid Twist' Zweibach who managed this only after a lengthy struggle with Richie Fitzpatrick – just as Italians of the time assumed Irish *noms-de-guerre*, so did many of their Jewish counterparts. The story goes that after skirmishing the men agreed to meet in a Chrystie Street bar. Fitzpatrick arrived first and almost immediately the lights went out; when they were switched back on, he was found dead on the floor. Twist, also known as Kid Sly Fox, lasted only some four years as the leader of the former Eastman gang, continuing to give support to Tammany Hall at elections and providing protection for the stuss parlours and brothels. His end came not really in battle but because of his love for Carroll Terry, sometimes described as a music-hall artiste but probably a dance-hall girl. Her affection was shared by the 19-year-old Louie 'The Lump' Pioggi, a Five Pointer. Or that at least is one version of the story. On 14 May 1908 Zweibach, together with his bodyguard, a former circus strongman Samuel 'Cyclone Lewis' Teitsch, was shot dead outside a Coney Island bar. In another version, Pioggi and Zweibach were in the dance hall and the latter was teasing him about the girl and threatening to make Pioggi jump out of a window. However, the killing may not have been that of *crime passionelle*. It was reported that Pioggi had telephoned for permission to kill Kid Twist and that a horse-drawn busload of Five Pointers arrived to watch the killing. By shooting at a policeman they were able to effect his escape. However, either the courts were convinced it was gang warfare or Tammany Hall was pleased to see Zweibach go. Pioggi pleaded guilty to manslaughter and received a term of 11 months rather than years. In true gangster tradition, he is said to have commented that he could do the term standing on his head.

After Zweibach's death, Big Jack Zelig, who had risen through the ranks, proposed a split in the former Eastman gang. Jack Sirocco and Chick Tricker were to be the other leaders and members could choose whom they followed.

Zelig, with the support of Jacob 'Whitey Lewis' Seidenschnier, Louis Rosenberg and particularly Harry 'Gyp The Blood' Horowitz, whose talents lay in a back-breaking wrestling hold which he was always pleased to demonstrate, took the cream of the talent. Within three years the four men were to feature in one of the great criminal trials and mysteries of the early part of the twentieth century.

Born in 1882, Zelig was a slightly different character from the usual run of gangleaders. His real name was William Alberts and he at least had a different upbringing in that he was born to middle-class parents on the Lower East Side. A talented pickpocket, robber and contract killer, apparently with huge eyes which served him well with social workers, he had graduated to being a hired gun with Eastman's gang by the time he was 20 years of age. He mainly avoided prison until shortly before that time by the use of his looks and the assistance of a girl waif who would come to court to plead on behalf of her 'young husband and our baby'. This would normally have been sufficient to avoid a custodial sentence, but Zelig ran up against the formidable judge John Goff. The girl gave her mitigation and, at the judge's order, was taken out of court. Moments later Zelig went down for the first of a number of sentences. The girl was never used again and soon Zelig aligned himself to the protection offered by Eastman. From there on, his career was for some years an upwardly mobile one. After the division of the spoils of the Eastman enterprise, Zelig continued his leg-breaking activities as well as his protection of lower-class brothels and saloons. There is some evidence that he also included higher-class enterprises such as that on W 44th owned by Honest John Kelly, whose fame came in 1888 when he turned down a bribe of $10,000 when umpiring a Boston v. Providence baseball game.[29]

It all started to go wrong when in 1911, finding himself temporarily short of cash, Zelig robbed an East Side brothel of a modest $80. Unusually, the madam went to the police and Zelig was arrested and charged with not only robbery but also carrying a concealed weapon. He sent word to his former friends Tricker and Sirocco for help but, possibly scenting a large share of the spoils if Zelig went to prison, they politely declined and it was left to a Jimmy Kelly – again, no immediate relation of Paul – who owned a bar in the Bowery to organise the suborning of the witness. Zelig was not pleased and threatened revenge on his former partners. In turn they recruited Julie Morrell, a known killer, to dispose of Zelig. On the night of 2 December 1911 Morrell went about his work by first getting drunk and making threatening remarks. The word was passed up the line and, by the time Morrell arrived at the Stuyvesant Casino on Second Avenue where a pre-Christmas ball was taking

---

[29] Kelly was able to trade on his integrity after his decision against giving the game to Boston and opened a series of gambling and drinking houses throughout New York. He was constantly in difficulties with the police because he refused to pay for protection by them. After a particularly unpleasant raid in 1912 he moved from 44th to W 141 St. He sold out his interests to a Republican political organisation in 1923 and retired to Florida, where he died aged 70 three years later.

place, Zelig was both forewarned and forearmed. Reports are that Morrell more or less staggered onto the dance floor calling out 'Where's that Big Yid Zelig? I gotta cook that big Yid.' As was the custom at these moments, the lights went out and, when they went on again, Morrell was dead on the floor. Zelig was arrested and released. From then on he was at war with Tricker and Sirocco. For a time there was little in the way of reprisals for attacks by his men on their saloons and brothels and gradually he became bolder, finally launching a raid on a bar owned by Jack Pioggi in Doyers Street. It was there that he met resistance from Tricker and Sirocco and was forced to retreat. Zelig was arrested and after being bailed out from the Tombs prison on Central Street in downtown Manhattan, on 5 October 1912 he was shot behind the ear.

For a time, his men took enthusiastic reprisals until the police stepped in and arrested 19 men on both sides. Tricker was himself arrested but released without charge. After that the war died down.[30]

On the labour front, soon to be controlled by both Jewish and Italian criminals, in 1911 a fire at the Triangle Shirtwaist Company in Greenwich Village killed 146 and brought 36 new labour laws within the next three years. On the top three floors of the ten-storey Asch building at the northwest corner of Washington and Green Streets, 500 mostly Jewish immigrants worked. The doors to exits were locked to keep the women at their sewing-machines. The fire began on the 8th floor at 4.30 p.m. and, fed by the fabric, spread rapidly. In the main the workers on the 8th and 10th floors escaped, but those on the 9th were unable to open the locked doors. The women died in less than 15 minutes. The fire brigade's ladders reached only to the 6th floor and the safety-nets broke as workers jumped three and four at a time. The owners were acquitted of manslaughter, but in 1912 were ordered to pay $75 to each of 23 families who had sued.

This was the beginning of the union struggles, many of which were led at the time by the Industrial Workers of the World. In

---

[30] For a fuller account of the early gangs in New York see Herbert Asbury, *Gangs of New York*; James Morton, *Gangland International*; R. A. Rockaway, *But – He Was Good To His Mother*. For a more personal account of a slightly later period see Rich Cohen, *Tough Jews*.

1912 'the Red Flame' – Elizabeth Gurley Flynn, one of the great Wobbly heroines – and Arturo Giovannitti led an unsuccessful strike against conditions in New York restaurants. This was described as 'the most tumultuous effort before World War I'.[31] Now the elements of organised crime would begin to hire themselves out on behalf of unions and owners or both.

The next decade would see the rise of both the Italian and Jewish gangsters in the golden era of organised crime. It would mark the end of the independent small but deadly operators who had run things often fairly haphazardly but usually with a great deal of panache for the previous 50 years.

---

[31] The Italian-born Giovannitti, editor of *Il Proletario*, had been acquitted of murder the same year during the textile workers' strike in Lawrence, Massachussetts, which in many ways was the peak of the IWW when it turned wage cuts into wage increases. See Patrick Renshaw, *The Wobblies*.

EPILOGUE – GRAVEYARDS

28

What Happened to Them All?

Many of them continued touring the world as they had during their careers. Some simply settled down. A very few did move into polite society with their fortunes intact, but these were very much the exceptions. The Clafin sisters were a shining example.

Victoria Woodhull was born in 1838. Her sister Tennessee Clafin, born 6 years later, was regarded as the more beautiful of the striking and difficult pair. The sisters were brought up in Homer, Ohio, until their father was obliged to leave under suspicion of arson and the townsfolk held a benefit to enable the rest of the family to leave as well. Their mother was a fanatical devotee of spiritualism and Victoria, who claimed to have had visions from the age of three, had a familiar, Demosthenes, who first appeared when she was 10 years old.

In 1853 she married Dr Canning Woodhull, by whom she had two children, and for a time the whole family travelled in a medicine show. She gave spiritualism exhibitions, and her sister's picture was on the labels of the 'Elixir of Life' bottles sold at the booth. Their brother Herbert, who posed as a cancer doctor, made up the potions. In 1864 she divorced Woodhull and married James Blood. Tennessee, who now signed herself Tennie C. Clafin, had married John Bartels who appears to have dropped quickly from the picture. There was also the small matter of a manslaughter charge following a devotee's miscarriage. From then on they cut a swathe through society.

The girls travelled to New York and met Cornelius Vanderbilt through his interest in spiritualism. Under his guidance they made a fortune on the stock market and, always keen on feminism and suffrage, became involved in the socialist movement The Pantarchy. In 1870 the sisters launched *Woodhull & Clafin's Weekly*, advocating amongst other things free love, equal rights for women and a single standard of morality. Victoria became the first woman to run for President, but before then the pair were in prison on remand for criminal libel and obscenity.

On 2 November 1872 they published details of the congregational divine Henry Ward Beecher's alleged immoral intimacy as well as an attack on Luther C. Challis, a broker, saying that at the French Ball he had seduced two maidens and boasted of it. Now Anthony Comstock struck, prosecuting them under the 8 June 1872 legislation for mailing an obscenity.

Blood was taken to Jefferson Market prison and the sisters were given bail, subject to sureties. Despite having the funds raised for them, they refused and also went to prison for a month before consenting to be released. Victoria described the Ludlow Street jail as having, 'all the appointments of a regular hotel . . . opportunities for bathing, exercise in the open air, a generous table and scrupulous cleanliness'.[1] 'Red' Leary and Harry Benson would have been amazed.

They were defended by Bill Howe, decked for the occasion in plaid pantaloons, purple vest and blue satin waistcoat, who was at his most formidable. Not one word published in *The Weekly* could be called obscene, if so:

> the transmission through the mails of the Holy Bible, the works of Lord Byron [perhaps he was on slightly shakier ground there] or any edition of the works of Shakespeare would be liable to the same penalty.

---

[1] Johanna Johnston, *Mrs Satan: The Incredible Saga of Victoria C. Woodhull*, p. 170.

Not guilty.

The Clafin sisters went from strength to strength. Blood was divorced and their friendship with Vanderbilt prospered to the extent that when he died in 1877 his children brought a suit to annul the will in their favour. The sisters sailed for Europe.

In 1883, after six years of opposition from his family, Victoria married the wealthy John Biddulph Martin, while Tennessee married Francis Cook and thus into the minor peerage. In July 1892 Victoria founded *The Humanitarian* of which her daughter was assistant editor. She had named the child Zulu Maud, thereby setting a fashion in eccentricity to be followed over the years by politicians and entertainers, of both of which she was a shining example. She died on 10 June 1927. Lady Cook had predeceased her by 4 years.[2]

Very few of the criminals of the period left anything in the way of an empire or even an estate. On the other hand the police officers did well for themselves. Indeed they always had done. Beginning at the top, the New York Police Commissioner Teddy Roosevelt went on to become President of the United States.

Much further down the hierarchy the report that one officer, James Churchill, had purchased four brownstone houses at 46th W and Broadway for a price reputed to be around $200,000, elicited the comment:

> A little more than three years ago Churchill was captain in charge of the red light district. After leaving the police force he entered mercantile life and has been unusually successful. In addition to the restaurant he conducts he has operated extensively and successfully in real property.[3]

There were many more like him, including the corrupt but highly successful Devery. He formed a partnership with the gambler Frank Farrell, and together they bought into a baseball team, the New York Highlanders, which would in due time become the New York Yankees.

---

[2] For a life of this extraordinary woman see Emanie N. Sachs, *The Terrible Siren*.
[3] 'Former Police Captain buys Big Plot in Forty-Sixth Street' in *New York Herald*, 16 May 1906.

As for the lawyer Abe Hummel, he only once returned to New York and then for a brief visit. Over the years it was reported on many occasions that he had died, but in fact his death occurred at his flat in Baker Street, London, on 21 January 1926.[4] His body was taken back to New York where his funeral was attended by a few elderly lawyers and a young man who, to the interest of the other spectators, took a rose from the coffin, kissed it and threw it on the grave. Later the boy claimed he was Henry D. Hummel, the son of Hummel's long-term liaison with the actress Leila Farrell whom his father had represented in a breach of promise suit against the vaudevillian Nat Goodwin. Henry's claim was good, but although the overall estate was sizeable the New York County part on which he had a claim amounted to only some $17,000. He soon returned to his job as a baker's delivery assistant in Portland, Maine.

What happened to members of the firm? Hummel's nephew Abraham Kaffenburgh was disbarred on 7 July 1906 for allowing the business to continue under the name of Howe and Hummel, and also for his part in attempting to smuggle Dodge out of Texas. Another lawyer Benjamin Steinhardt, indicted along with Hummel, was now suffering from *locomotor ataxia* and never stood trial. Because of his illness he survived another potential legal disaster when he was found to have represented both plaintiff and defendant in the same action.[5] An application to disbar Nathaniel Cohen failed and he joined other members of the firm, David May and Isaac Jacobson, in a practice which continued until the 1930s. As for the firm of Howe and Hummel itself, the shingle was taken down in November 1906.

The Pinkerton Agency went from strength to strength, obtaining and maintaining a worldwide reputation. Over the years the controversial industrial division which had been involved in labour spying had come under criticism, and it was closed after Congress in 1937 declared the system unfair and illegal. The Agency's great rival, William Burns, ended his career in some disgrace. He reached a pinnacle when on 22 August 1921 he became the first Director of

[4] *New York Times*, 24 January 1926.
[5] Joseph Auerbach, *The Bar of Other Days*.

the FBI. But the Bureau was not in good shape when he inherited it and he did little to improve things.

The only thing which can be said to have been to his credit during his short term in office was the 1924 prosecution of Edward Young Clarke, a leader of the Ku Klux Klan, who pleaded guilty to a violation of the Mann Act. State authorities had previously been unable to secure convictions for murders and kidnappings committed by the Klan, and the Bureau had commenced a prosecution under the Act for transporting a woman across a state line for the purposes of prostitution.

In the main, however, the agents then working for the Bureau were the tools of the politicians who made up the so-called Ohio Gang which came to power during the Harding Administration. With Burns turning a blind eye or being deceived, the gang looted the Veterans' Bureau and the Alien Property Claims Bureau. Things came to a head with the so-called Teapot Dome Scandal when Secretary of State Albert Fall sold his friends vast chunks of land on which oil had been discovered. The Attorney General, Harland Fiske Stone, demanded Burns' resignation and the mantle of Director passed to Burns' assistant J. Edgar Hoover. Another to fall in the scandal was Attorney General Harry M. Daugherty.

Burns returned to his private detective agency and fell further when, in 1927, he was indicted for jury tampering following the acquittal of the oil magnate Henry Sinclair who had been charged over allegations that he had bribed Fall. Burns had accepted an assignment to shadow jurors in the trial, something which the judge said was simply a version of jury tampering. He was convicted, but the Supreme Court set aside his term of imprisonment.

When he died on 14 April 1932 the *Washington Post* in its obituary of him wrote that he was 'probably the most famous individual in the detective business during his active years'.

Without doubt, however, he had had some extremely curious agents on his books. Perhaps the most curious of them all was Gaston Bullock Means. Burns regarded him as 'the greatest natural detective ever known', but others saw this one-time lawyer as a swindler, blackmailer and very possibly murderer. Means was born in North Carolina in 1880 and was once a towel salesman. He joined the Burns Agency in 1910 and, using a network of informers, progressed rapidly. In 1915 he left the Agency and became the personal bodyguard to the eccentric heiress Chicago Maude R. King, who in 1901 at the age of 24 had married the lumberman James C. King, some 50 years her senior. On her husband's death she embarked on a career of entertaining herself and outraging others. She threw stink bombs in the Houses of Parliament and, rather more dangerously, dropped wine bottles from the Eiffel Tower.

Means very likely came to favour with a variation of the standard 'Pigeon Drop', pretending to save her from a fake mugging. Within two years he had separated her from $15,000. That same year, despite her protests that she knew nothing of the sport, he took her on a hunting trip to North Carolina during which she was shot dead.

The story goes that the pair became separated from the other hunters and after a shot was heard Means stumbled out of the woods saying, 'Oh, poor Mrs King.' Apparently he had put his .25-calibre Colt in the crotch of a tree while he went to get a drink in a spring. Mrs King had not been thirsty and had stayed behind. At the water's edge he turned round and saw Maude twirling the gun; he shouted at her to put it down and, satisfied she had done so, he was actually cupping water to his mouth when he heard the gunshot. He ran back but, sadly, Mrs King had managed to shoot herself behind the left ear. There were strong reasons to think he had done the shooting, but the local coroner's jury made up of acquaintances of Means ruled that her death was accidental. However, he was still charged with her murder. A jury dominated by Ku Klux Klanners acquitted him, finding that Mrs King had committed suicide.

During the First World War he worked as a spy for both the German and British governments, and when America entered the War he shelved his German connections.[6] He can then be found once more in Chicago in 1920 acting for a lawyer friend, Roy D. Keehn, and separating him from $57,000. He agreed to go and collect a settlement and remit it to Chicago, but when the package

---

[6] For an account of Means' career, see Don Whitehead, *The FBI Story*.

arrived it contained a block of wood. Keehn sued Means, who in turn claimed from the Southeastern Express Company.

The case never came to court but the next year Means joined Burns in the FBI, something which displeased J. Edgar Hoover. He supplemented his salary by undertaking private work for Mrs Harding, the President's wife, investigating her husband's affairs and possible involvement in a paternity suit. Then he too was investigated and left the Bureau, being employed by Burns simply as an informant.

Means was next indicted in a bootlegging swindle pretending that he was collecting graft for the Secretary of the Treasury, Andrew Mellon, and forging his signature, selling fake protection to businessmen to whom he had sent threatening letters. By now he was also blackmailing the Hardings by threatening to reveal that the President was the father of a child by the undistinguished Ohioan poetess Nan Britton. After Harding's mysterious death in San Francisco, Means co-authored a book with Mrs Britton, *The President's Daughter*. He finally went to prison for bribery and on his release wrote *The Strange Death of President Harding* in which he implied that Mrs Harding had poisoned her husband.

He also hired himself to Mrs Finley Shepherd of Tarrytown, New York, a committed opponent of Communism. He had written her a letter promising that she and her family would be killed; it was signed 'Agents from Moscow'. Now, on her behalf, he would devote his life to tracking down the agents. He was so successful in obtaining money that he set up a nationwide service earning $1,000 a week from similar letters and offers.

His final coup came in 1932 when he removed some $104,000 from another heiress, Mrs Evalyn Walsh McLean, telling her that through his Underworld contacts he could recover the kidnapped Lindbergh baby. He maintained that he repaid the money, but the members of the firm of lawyers had not given him a receipt. Could he have one now? Instead he received 15 years.

Means died in 1938 in the prison hospital in Leavenworth after a heart attack. FBI agents were sent to his bedside to ask him to disclose the whereabouts of Mrs McLean's missing money but, at least so the story goes, he simply smiled and died.

James McParland, the Pinkerton agent who had broken the Molly Maguires, retired shortly after the Haywood fiasco and the last years of his life were not happy. He married twice and died in the Mercy Hospital, Denver, in 1918. Probably through a combination of drink and diabetes, he had lost a leg and an eye. He had had high walls built around his home, and inside the walls attack dogs were always on the loose. In addition, there were bars on all the lower windows and indoors a hand-gun on every table. He also carried a gun constantly and got up frequently during the night to patrol the house. Apparently, he was in constant fear of being assassinated by descendants of the Molly Maguires.[7]

Back in England, the receiver Cammi Grizzard found conditions in prison little to his liking and he began trying to scheme his way out. Like so many thieves, he came to a long prison sentence late in life and discovered that prison takes the stuffing out of many a man. There is a theory that those who have received regular sentences can cope better than those who have perhaps served only a few months. Jimmy Lockett knew and understood what penal servitude was all about. Grizzard did not and, while Lockett appears to have accepted his sentence and conditions stoically, Grizzard became an informer on some of his former competitors. He was now in his fifties and apparently in poor health because he spent much of his time in the prison hospital. In any event Grizzard was an old man by the standards of the day; he had a heart condition and was suffering from eczema. He wanted out and now, reneging on the principles which had kept so many men loyal to him, he wrote to the authorities naming George Hanlon as a man wanted for three robberies. Hanlon was well known, having done 3 years in Paris and 5 in England. Grizzard hoped that when his wife lodged a petition for his release it would be supported.

Grizzard may have been a master crook but spelling was certainly not his strong suit. On 11 October 1915 he wrote from Parkhurst giving information that an American whom he knew only as Yankee Johnny and a German whose name he did not know were two of the best burglars in London. The German was kept under cover by

[7] See Patrick Campbell, *A Molly Maguire Story*.

a Jim Trott in Manchester and Yankee Johnny was a great friend of Harry Snell:

> The German may have his mustarsh off -Oftern- nows A man Rogers used to live in the Westend has a money lender.

As for his health, Grizzard was suffering from 'diebertus' and 'skin diesiese'.

Certainly Grizzard was giving good information. Yankee Johnny was John Talbot, an American safe-breaker who lived in Darwin Street in the New Kent Road. The German was Max Baum. James Trott did live in Manchester and had a police record. Harry Snell lived at 83 Hungerford Road, Holloway, and was a bookmaker suspected, rather like Grizzard, of being a financier and putter-up.

Grizzard's gang had been relatively quiet since the arrest of Grizzard and Lockett, but George Hanlon was indeed wanted for stealing a mailbag from St Pancras station on 24 August 1913. He lived at 14 Wroughton Road, Wandsworth, where the bag minus the contents was found. And, for that matter, the house was also minus Hanlon who was now thought to be living in Streatham. Rogers, believed to be Swiss and certainly an associate of Hanlon, was thought to have gone back to Switzerland.

Sergeant David Goodwillie recommended that Grizzard have a reduction in his sentence. Nothing came of it, but Grizzard was not finished and in 1917 he wrote again, informing this time on a Bernard Hedgis, who was serving 3 years, alleging him to be one of the most dangerous criminals in the country. He also disclosed some of his own past. Hedgis had come from Africa at the end of the Boer War and knew a foreigner, Idleman, who lived in a boarding-house in Russell Square kept by his wife. Moreover, Hedgis was a dealer in stolen jewellery. Grizzard had been summoned there and later went over to buy jewellery in Paris for some £4,000. In fact this was a trick. Grizzard had been 'put out' and robbed. Hedgis, he claimed, also robbed the English in South Africa and then later went to South America, living off women.

Sadly, apart from naming Hedgis and another prisoner, 0394*, he peached on his old friend Silverman saying he had been working with Lockett for about 10 years. He hoped that his letter would be of assistance. The country, he thought, should be protected from the likes of Hedgis. At least he did try to row Lockett out, writing that neither he nor Lockett knew anything of the pearl necklace before it was stolen. Indeed, according to him, Lockett had apparently been recruited to save the gems after they had been taken.

Again the police made inquiries and found that Hedgis and Samuel Morris Natenson had been recommended for deportation when they were sentenced to 3 years penal servitude on 8 December 1914. They would have been entitled to 9 months' remission. Further police checks found that the men had not yet gone to Brixton to await their deportation and Natenson was not in fact due for deportation; he was to be allowed to join the British Army, and did indeed join the Royal Artillery. Hedgis was to see a recruiting officer with a view to enlistment, and on 14 April he too joined the Artillery. He denied even knowing Grizzard and Detective Inspector Wensley, now having one of his most talented opponents in custody, was implacable. Poor Cammi was to be told that in his view the information was of no value to the police. He would remain where he was for the rest of that sentence.[8]

On his release Cammi Grizzard just could not stop. In 1922 he was charged with receiving the proceeds of an ingenious fraud on a firm of London jewel dealers which netted some £10,000, and again Richard Muir prosecuted him. Grizzard had arranged for Major Harrison – actually ex-Major Harrison since he had been cashiered – to purchase jewellery on approval from Bedford & Co. in Aldersgate High Street. He advanced Harrison £3,000 to establish a line of credit and Harrison played his part well. The jewellery was to be shown to a Colonel who would shortly be returning to India. It was a simple, well-established confidence trick. The initial purchases were paid for; more jewellery was bought and paid for, and then £10,000 of jewellery was handed over for approval. The idea was for it to be smashed, or sold at a discount, on the Continent; but after a quick attempt to sell it in Hatton Garden, Grizzard and another member of the conspiracy, the American-born Michael

[8] MEPO 3 236B.

Spellman, received only £900 for it in Antwerp. Foolishly the Major returned to England where he was found to have another collection of stolen jewellery in his possession, and more gems were traced to Grizzard.

In August 1922 Grizzard was arrested and in the October received 12 months, as did Spellman. The gallant Major fled to Canada where shortly afterwards he received 2 years for a similar fraud. While awaiting trial Grizzard was found to be suffering from both tuberculosis and diabetes in an aggravated form. He was taken home where he died on 15 September 1923, aged 57.

He wrote a note for Spellman, leaving him, 'all the spoils you have done me out of and my place in the Underworld as Prince'.[9]

On his release, unfortunately Spellman did not behave as well as Grizzard had done towards those from whom he bought. Operating out of Hatton Garden and Duke Street, Houndsditch, he was known to screw burglars down for the last penny. But he had his come-uppance. It was from an anonymous tip-off that the police arrested him in the autumn of 1925, and he received a further 12 months with hard labour for receiving.

Grizzard's long-time helpmate 'Blonde' Alice Smith continued working and writing her memoirs telling how she had given up crime. She was in the dock in Durham receiving 3 years in November 1923, still working with Harry Grimshaw, and was convicted again in 1927.

Another of Grizzard's associates was George Martin, long regarded as the prince of warehouse thieves. He had been a burglar king for over 20 years and now received 3 years penal servitude. His technique was to dress well with a silk hat as a potential purchaser, and to survey the layout of premises. The stolen goods would be sold to Grizzard and other Jewish dealers. Martin was thought to have been worth in excess of £100,000 and had his children educated at good schools. He had also been involved in the theft

[9] Spellman and Grizzard had worked together over a number of years. They first met in America when Grizzard absented himself from London for a period. It was thought that Spellman had backed out of participating in the Great Pearl Robbery because his wife was ill. There are suggestions that Grizzard was born in America. His brother Abe was a noted pimp. *Empire News*, 25 October 1925.

of jewels worth £30,000 from the Princess of Thurm and Taxis. This time a replica had been made of her jewel-case, which was switched.[10]

James Lockett, released from penal servitude in 1919, married for a second time and became a bookmaker. While he was inside there had been a curious incident over his house at 7 Powis Gardens, Golders Green. It had been sold for £425 to a Mrs Saxby who wanted to use it as a bed-and-breakfast; now she reported to the police that the estate agent, an S. Bowyer from 25 The Parade, Golders Green, was pestering her to buy it from her. What was the reason for this? The police did not know, but they certainly knew that Bowyer did not have a good reputation. They had searched the place – throughout which there was a host of electric alarms – when Lockett was arrested, and they could not believe his family had left anything behind when they moved out. They advised Mrs Saxby to search the house again and report back, but there is no record that she did so. Lockett died in North London in March 1923.

Some, such as James Robert Duncan, known as Duncan the Devil, carried on working despite old age. His penal career had begun in 1903 when he received 5 years for the theft of £100 in Glasgow. After that he began forging and picked up 10 years in 1912. In September 1925 he received 3 years penal servitude following a series of thefts from London hotels; he was then 71. Some were coming to the end of their careers and found life and the prospect of more long sentences too hard. Lionel Arnold Singleton, the noted safe-breaker, killed himself in Paris on 29 August 1925.[11]

Others took up advisory positions. In 1920 Charles Ney received 3 years penal servitude after being caught in yet another burglary. As part of his early training he learned the trapeze – as indeed had the criminal-turned-detective Vidocq – and how to get up and walk away after falls. By 1897 he had served sentences of 6 and 18 months and two of 10 years. By then he was regarded as one of

[10] S.T. Felstead, 'Master Criminals of London' in *Empire News*, 19 August 1922.
[11] *Empire News*, 3 October 1925.

the top burglars and held court in a public house off Drury Lane where he provided advice for a fee.

In Ney's earlier days he was another who was regarded as being extremely attractive to women, a number of whom would attend court with him. One story of him is that his second 10-year spell came after he had gone to Brighton with a woman and the proceeds of a jewel theft, leaving behind his *inamorata* Rosa who promptly betrayed him. Perhaps fortunately for her she died from tuberculosis during his sentence.[12]

As for von Veltheim, with whom we began, he continued to try to work the Kruger millions scam and was deported from South Africa to Germany where in March 1925 he was sentenced to 3½ years in Magdeburg for false pretences. He was then aged 68.

There had long been a tradition of military gents, and on 2 May 1904 Colonel Bowden alias James Turner appeared at Brighton Police Court charged with the theft of diamonds worth some £1,500. He had followed the usual pattern of the jewel thief by visiting the shop of William Pearce in King Street and buying a trifle. Now, he asked, would the jeweller bring some samples to the Grand Hotel where he was staying? His daughter was soon to marry and he wished his wife to see some pieces. The jeweller obliged and was shown into the Colonel's suite. Apparently Bowden's wife was in the bedroom and he did his best to persuade her to come out, saying that she really must look at this or that piece. Finally, when she did not emerge he took three diamonds and went into the bedroom, followed – too slowly – by the jeweller who said he regretted he could not allow the stones out of his sight. The door had closed and by the time the man was able to open it there was no sign of the Colonel and even less of his imaginary wife. Turner was arrested a week later in Droitwich and denied having any knowledge of the affair.[13]

Fashions in crime changed. Now with the First World War came a variation in the form of a new market of injured officers. It was no longer necessary to pose as a gent. War wounds would do

[12] *Empire News*, 2 May 1920; *The Times*, 3, 24 April 1920.
[13] *Morning Leader*, 3 May 1904.

nicely.[14] On 12 September 1915 Sam Rutherford, a cheque fraudsman, received 21 months. He had enlisted on 10 March 1915 and deserted in June 1917, by which time he had been promoted to sergeant. Now he posed as a V.C. holder, rubbing metal polish on his skin and claiming it was caused by gas burning. He had, it was said, made love to several women impressed by his war record. He was only one of many.

At the other end of the scale there was a modest living to be made out of German atrocities of the bayoneting babies kind. Alice and Ellen Bowman appeared at Bow Street charged with fraud. Alice had been exhibiting her daughter at fairs with the hype:

> First German atrocities shown in England. See what a mother will suffer for her children. Only ladies allowed to touch the body.
> Because this Belgian woman would not tell where she had hidden her daughters she was 'arrested' as a spy and for the sport of two German officers a young Frenchman was forced to tattoo her from head to foot.

Apparently the girl was in a mask and the upper part of her body was swathed in a sheet. The lower part was tattooed with various designs. PC Mizen told the court, 'When I questioned her she admitted she was a London woman who had never been to Belgium.' Fined £1 and the daughter bound over.[15]

In America the prospect of Prohibition and all that would bring was looming. England was seeing the rise of the racecourse protection gangs such as the Sabinis from Clerkenwell who would, in due course, extend their interests to all forms of protection in the capital and establish a dynasty which lasts until today. Life would no longer

---

[14] Stripes indicating wounds were sewn onto the sleeves of uniforms. It was this that led to the capture and execution of George Walter Cardwell for the murder of Rhoda Walker on 16 August 1918. He and Percy George Barrett had deserted and were on the run when they decided to rob the widow who died from injuries received. They had changed into their uniforms to do the job and a witness had seen six wound stripes on Cardwell's sleeve. Wounded five times and gassed once, he had in fact had an heroic war, being recommended for both the Military Medal and the Distinguished Service Medal. He was 22.

[15] *News of the World*, 10 September 1922.

be recognisable for the nineteenth- and early twentieth-century players.

In a way many of these early career criminals, from Ned Velvet to the Bowens, were what we would consider today to be almost amateurs; some of course were better than others. These people were not organised as we have come to understand the term relating to the Mafia and Al Capone, let alone the late twentieth- and early twenty-first-century criminal empires which have almost imperceptibly, and certainly inextricably, merged with what might be called the Overworld. Perhaps that is the charm of Adam Worth, Sophie Lyons, James Lockett and the many others who did what they could to separate fools from their money.

Bibliography

Alcorn, R.H., *The Count of Gramercy Park* (1955) London, Hurst & Blackett.

Anderson, F.W., *Bill Miner: Stage Coach and Train Robber* (1982) Surrey, Heritage House Publishing.

Anderson, R., *Criminals and Crime: Some Facts and Suggestions* (1907) London, Nisbet.

——*The Lighter Side of My Official Life* (1910) London, Hodder.

Anon, *I Die a True American: The True Life of William Pool* (1855) New York, William L. Knapp.

Anon, *Life in the New York Tombs* (1878) New York, The Great Publishing House.

Asbury, H., *Gangs of New York* (1928) New York, Alfred A. Knopf.

——*All Around the Town* (1934) New York, Alfred A. Knopf.

——*The French Quarter* (1937) London, Jarrolds.

——*Gem of the Prairie* (1940) New York, Alfred Knopf. Reprinted as *The Gangs of Chicago* (2002) New York, Thunders Mouth Press.

Atholl, J., *Prison on the Moor* (1953) London, John Long.

Bean, J.P., *Crime in Sheffield* (1987) Sheffield, Sheffield City Libraries.

——*Brave as a Lion* (2002) Sheffield, D. & D.

Begg, P., *Jack the Ripper, The Uncensored Facts* (1988) London, Robson Books.

Bennett, De R. M., *Champions of the Church* (1878) New York, D.M. Bennett.

Berrett, J., *When I was at Scotland Yard* (1932) London, Sampson Low & Co.

Berry, J., *My Experiences as an Executioner* (1982) Newton Abbott, David & Charles Reprints.

Bertillon, S., *Vie d'Alphonse Bertillon* (1940) Paris, Gallimard.

Bidwell, A., *From Wall Street to Newgate* (1893) Hartford, The Bidwell Publishing Co.

Biron, C., *Without Prejudice* (1936) London, Faber & Faber.

Bland, J., *The Book of Executions* (1993) London, Warner Books.

Bleackley, H., *Hangmen of England* (1929) London, Chapman and Hall.

Booth, J.B., *Old Pink 'Un Days* (1924) London, The Richards Press.

————'Master' *and Men: Pink 'Un Yesterdays* (1927) London, T. Werner Laurie.

Borowitz, A., *Blood & Ink* (2002) Kent, Ohio, The Kent University State Press.

Bowen, C., *The Elegant Oakey* (1956) New York, Oxford University Press.

Bowen, E., *72 Years at the Bar* (1924) London, Macmillan & Co.

Brandon, C., *The Electric Chair* (1999) Jefferson, North Carolina, McFarland & Co.

Bristow, E., *Prostitution and Prejudice: The Jewish Fight Against White Slavery* (1982) Oxford, Clarendon Press.

Britton, N., *The President's Daughter* (1927) New York, Elizabeth Ann Guild.

Broun, H. and Leech, M., *Anthony Comstock: Roundsman of the Lord* (1927) New York, Boni.

Browder, C., *The Wickedest Woman in New York* (1988) Hamden, Conn., The Shoestring Press.

Brown, M. (ed.), *Australian Crime* (1993) Sydney, Lansdowne.

Burns, W.J., *The Masked War* (1913) New York, George H. Doran.

Burrows, E.G. and Wallace, M., *Gotham* (1998) New York, Oxford University Press.

Byrnes, T., *Rogues' Gallery* (also called *Criminals of America*) (1888) Secaucus, N.J., Castle.

Caesar, G., *The Incredible Detective: The Biography of William J. Burns* (1968) Englewood Cliffs, N.J., Prentice Hall.

Callow, A.B. jnr, *The Tweed Ring* (1966) New York, Oxford University Press.

Caminada, J., *Twenty-Five Years of Detective Life* (1895) Manchester, John Heywood.

Campbell, P., *A Molly Maguire Story* (1992) Jersey City, N.J., Templecrone Press.

Campbell, H., Knox, T.W. and Byrnes, T., *Darkness and Daylight* (1899) Hartford, Conn., Hartford Publishing Company.

Cancellor, H.L., *The Life of a London Beak* (1930) London, Hurst & Blackett.

Carlin, F., *Reminiscences of an Ex-Detective* (1927) London, Hutchinson & Co.

Casal, M., *The Stone Wall: An Autobiography* (1930) Chicago, Eyncourt.

Cassellari, R., *Dramas of French Crime* (1930) London, Hutchinson & Co.

Caunt, G., *Essex Blood and Thunder* (1967) Liford, George Caunt.

Chancey, G., *Gay New York* (1995) London, Flamingo.

Cherrill, F.R., *Cherrill of the Yard* (1954) London, Harrap & Co.

Chesney, K., *The Victorian Underworld* (1972) London, Penguin.

Chinn, C., *Better Betting with a Decent Feller* (1991) Hemel Hempstead, Harvester Wheatsheaf.

Claretie, G., *Drames et Comédies Judiciaires: Chroniques du Palais* (1911) Paris, Berger-Levrault.

Cobb, B., *Critical Years at the Yard: The Career of Frederick Williamson of the Detective Department and the C.I.D.* (1956) London, Faber.

——*Murdered on Duty* (1966) London, Brown Watson.

Cohen, D., *The Encyclopedia of Unsolved Crimes* (1988) New York, Dodd Mead & Co.

Cohen, R., *Tough Jews* (1999) New York, Simon & Schuster.

Collins, J.H., *The Great Taxi Cab Robbery* (1912) London, John Long.

Comstock, A., *A Defence of Detective Methods* (1892) New York, The Christian at Work.

Cook, F.F., *Bygone Days in Chicago* (1910) Chicago, A. G. McClurg.

Corbitt, R.L., *The Holmes Castle* (1895) Chicago, Corbitt & Morrison.

Cornish, G., *Cornish of the Yard* (1935) London, The Bodley Head.

Corps of Specially Appointed Commissioners, *Chicago's Dark Places* (1891) Chicago, The Craig Press.

Costello, A.E., *Our Police Protectors* (1885) New York, A.E. Costello.

Crapsey, E., *The Nether Side of New York* (1872) New York, Sheldon & Co.

Croker, R., *Some Things Richard Croker Has Said and Done* (1901) New York, City Club of New York.

Dalton, E. and Jungmeyer, J., *When The Daltons Rode* (1931) New York, Doubleday & Co.

Dilnot, G. (ed.), *The Trial of the Detectives* (1928) London, Geoffrey Bles.

————*The Bank of England Forgery* (1929) London, Geoffrey Bles.

————*The Trial of Jim the Penman* (1930) London, Geoffrey Bles.

Divall, T., *Scoundrels and Scallywags* (1929) London, Ernest Benn.

Dizikes, J., *Yankee Doodle Dandy* (2000) New Haven, Conn., Yale University Press.

Drachline, P. and Petit-Castelli, C., *Casque d'Or et les Apaches* (1990) Paris, Renaudot et Cie.

Drimmer, F., *Until You Are Dead* (1991) London, Robert Hale.

Dubofsky, M., *We Shall All Be: A History of the IWW* (1969) New York, Quadrangle.

Dubois, C., *Apaches, Voyous et Gozes Poilus* (1996) Paris, Parisgramme.

Dugan, M. and Boessenecker, J., *The Grey Fox; The True Story of Bill Miner, Last of the Old-Time Bandits* (1992) Norman, University of Oklahoma Press.

Duke, T.S., *Celebrated Criminal Cases of America* (1910) San Francisco, The James H. Barry Co.

Eldridge, B.P. and Watts, W.B., *Our Rival the Rascal* (1897) Boston, Pemberton Publishing Co.

Ellis, J., *Diary of a Hangman* (1997) London, True Crime Library.

Engel, H., *Lord High Executioner* (1996) Toronto, Key Porter Books.

Farley, Phil, *Criminals of America, Tales of the Lives of Thieves enabling everyone to be his own Detective* (1876) New York, published by author.

Felstead, S.T., *Shades of Scotland Yard* (1950) London, John Long.

Ferrier, J.K., *Crooks & Crime* (1928) London, Seeley, Service & Co.

Fiaschetti, M., *You Gotta Be Tough* (1928) Garden City, N.Y. Doubleday.

Fielding, S., *The Hangman's Record, Volume One, 1868–1899* (1994) Beckenham, Chancery House Press.

————*The Hangman's Record,* Volume Two, *1900–1929* (1995) Beckenham, Chancery House Press.

Fitch, H.T., *Traitors Within* (1933) London, Hurst & Blackett.

Fitzgerald, P., *Chronicles of Bow Street Police Office* (1888) London, Chapman and Hall.

Folsom, de F., (ed.), *Our Police* (1888) Baltimore, Maryland.

Fuller, R.A., *Recollections of a Detective* (1912) London, John Long.

Gallagher, D., *All the Right Enemies: The Life and Murder of Carlo Tresca* (1988) New Bruswick, N.J., Rutgers University Press.

Gallagher, E.J., *Robber Baron* (1967) Laconia, New Hampshire, published by author.

Galton, F., *Fingerprints* (1982) New York, published by author.

Gardner, C. G., *The Doctor and the Devils: The Midnight Adventures of Dr Parkhurst* (1931) New York, published by author.

Gee, T., *Up to Scratch* (1998) Harpenden, Queen Anne Press.

Gilbert, M., *Churchill: A Life* (1991) London, William Heinemann.

————*Fraudsters* (1986) London, Constable.

Gilfoyle, T.J., *City of Eros* (1991) New York, W.W. Norton & Co.

Gorm, E.J., *The Manly Art* (1986) Ithaca, N.Y., University of Cornell Press.

Goron, M-F., *Behind the French CID* (n.d.) London, Hutchinson & Co.

Grant, D., *The Thin Blue Line* (1973) London, John Long.

Greenham, G.H., *Scotland Yard Experiences from the Diary of G.H. Greenham* (1904) London, George Routledge.

Greenwall, H.J., *The Underworld of Paris* (1921) London, Stanley Paul & Co.

Griffiths, A.G.F., *Mysteries of Police and Crime* (1898) London, Cassell.

Guerin, E., *Crime: The Autobiography of a Crook* (1928) London, John Murray.

Harrison, H., *Hell Holes and Hangings* (1968) Clarendon, Texas, Clarendon Press.

Harrow, A., *Old Bowery Days* (1931) New York, D. Appleton.

Hastings, M., *The Other Mr Churchill* (1963) London, G. G. Harrap.

Heppenstall, R., *A Little Pattern of French Crime* (1969) London, Hamish Hamilton.

————*French Crime in the Romantic Age* (1970) London, Hamish Hamilton.

————*Bluebeard and After* (1972) London, Peter Owen.

Hibbeler, R., *Upstairs at the Everleigh Club* (n.d.) Chicago, Volitair Books.

Honeycombe, G., *The Murders of the Black Museum* (1988) London, Mysterious Press.

Horan, J.D., *The Pinkertons* (1967) New York, Crown Publishers.

Horn, T., *Life of Tom Horn: Government Scout and Interpreter, written by Himself* (1964) Norman, University of Oklahoma Press.

Howe, W.F. and Hummel, A., *In Danger* (1888) New York, J. Ogilvie.

Hummel, A., *The Trial and Conviction of Jack Reynolds for the Horrible Murder of William Townsend* (n.d.) New York, published by author.

Humphreys C., *The Great Pearl Robbery of 1913* (1929) London, William Heinemann.

Huxley, A., *Four Against the Bank of England* (1969) London, John Long.

Hynd, A., *The Pinkerton Casebook* (n.d.) New Jersey, Penguin Signet Books.

Innes, M., *Great Crimes of Scotland Yard* (1947) London, Reader's Digest Publishing.

Jackson, J., *Leavenworth Train: A Fugitive's Search for Justice in the Vanishing West* (2001) Toronto, Carrol & Graf.

Jeffers, H.P., *Commissioner Roosevelt* (1994) New York, J. Wiley & Sons.

Johnston, J., *Mrs Satan, The Incredible Saga of Victoria C. Woodhull* (1967) New York, Putnam.

Joselit, J., *Our Gang: Jewish Crime and the New York Jewish Community 1900–1940* (1983) Bloomingale, Indiana, University of Indiana Press.

Katz, J., *Gay American History* (1976) New York, Crowell.

Lambton, G., *Men and Horses I have Known* (1924) London, T. Butterworth Ltd.

Langford, R., *The Murder of Stanford White* (1963) London, Victor Gollancz.

Larner, J. and Reppetto, T., *NYPD* (2000) New York, Henry Holt.

Laurence, J., *A History of Capital Punishment* (1963) New York, The Citadel Press.

Lawes, L.E., *Life and Death in Sing Sing* (1928) New York, Garden City Publishing Company.

Leach, C.E., *On Top of the Underworld* (n.d.) London, Sampson Low.

Leach, J., *Sods I Have Cut on The Turf* (1961) London, Victor Gollancz.

Leeson, G., *Lost London* (1934) London, Stanley Paul.

Lewing, G., *The Dark Side of New York* (1873) New York, F. Gerhard.

Lewis, A.H., *Nation Famous New York Murders* (1914) New York, G.H. Dillingham.

Lewis, Arthur H., *Lament for the Mollie Maguires* (1964) New York, Harcourt, Brace and World.

Lindberg, R.C., *To Serve and Collect* (1991) New York, Praeger Publishers.

———*Chicago by Gaslight* (1996) Chicago, Chicago Academic Publishers.

Long, G.H., *The Arch Fiend* (1851) New York, A. R. Orton.

———*The Great Louisiana Murderer* (1855) Baltimore, A. R. Orton.

Lucas, N. and Graham, E., *Myselves* (1934) London, Arthur Barron.

Lyons-Burke, S., *Why Crime Does Not Pay* (1913) New York, J.S. Ogilvie Publishing Company.

Macintyre, B., *The Napoleon of Crime* (1997) London, HarperCollins.

Macnaghten, M., *Days of My Years* (1915) London, Arnold.

Marjoribanks, E., *The Life of Sir Edward Marshall Hall* (1929) London, Victor Gollancz.

Mayhew, H. with Binney, J., Hemyng, B. and Halliday, A., *London Labour and the London Poor*, Vol. IV.

McKenzie, D., *Hell's Kitchen* (1930) London, Herbert Jenkins.

McLoughlin, D., *The Encyclopedia of the Old West* (1977) London, Routledge & Kegan Paul.

Means, G. B., *The Strange Death of President Harding* (1930) New York, Gold Label Books.

Mendham, R., *Dictionary of Australian Bushrangers* (1975) Melbourne, The Hawthorn Press.

Montarron, M., *Les Grands Procès d'Assizes* (1967) Paris, Plon.

———*L'Histoire du Milieu* (1969) Paris, Plon.

Moore, L., *His Own Story* (1893) Boston, Langdon W. Moore.

Morn, F., *The Eye That Never Sleeps* (1982) Bloomington, Indiana University Press.

Morris, N. and Rothman, D.P. (eds), *The Oxford History of Prison* (1995) Oxford, Oxford University Press.

Morton, J., *Gangland International* (2000) London, Warner.

————*East End Gangland* (2001) London, Time Warner.

————*Manhunt* (2002) London, Ebury Press.

————*Gangland, The Lawyers* (2002) London, Virgin.

Moylan, J., *Scotland Yard and the Metropolitan Police* (1929) London, Putnam.

Munro, J.J., *The New York Tombs Inside and Out* (1909) Brooklyn, Munro.

Nash, J.R., *Hustlers and Conmen* (1976) New York, N. Evans & Co. Inc.

Nicholls, E., *Crime within the Square Mile* (1935) London, John Long.

Nott-Bower, W., *Fifty-Two Years a Policeman* (1926) London, Edward Arnold & Co.

O'Connor, J.J., *Broadway Racketeers* (1928) New York, Liveright.

O'Connor, R., *Hell's Kitchen* (1958) Philadelphia, J.B. Lippincott Company.

————*The Combative Career of William Travers Jerome* (1963) Boston, Little, Brown.

Osborne, T.M., *Within Prison Walls* (1914) New York, D. Appleton & Co.

Owen, D., *Hidden Evidence* (2000) Willowdale, Ont., Firefly Books.

Parmer, C.B., *For Gold and Glory: The Story of Thoroughbred Racing in America* (1939) New York, Carrick & Evans.

Pearl, C., *Wild Men of Sydney* (1958) London, W.H. Allen.

————*The Girl with the Swansdown Seat* (1980) London, Robin Clark.

Pearson, G., *Hooligan* (1983) London, Macmillan.

Phelan, J., *The Underworld* (1953) London, George G. Harrap & Co.

Pinkerton, A., *Professional Thieves and the Detectives* (1880) New York, G.W. Dillingham Co.

————*The Spy of the Rebellion* (1888) New York, G.W. Dillingham.

Potter, H., *Hanging in Judgment* (1993) London, SCM Press.

Quinn, J.P., *Fools of Fortune* (1892) Chicago, The Anti-Gambling Association.

Radford, P., *The Celebrated Captain Barclay* (2001) London, Headline.

Renshaw, P., *The Wobblies* (1967) Eyre & Spottiswood.

Rhodes, A.J., *Dartmoor Prison* (1933) London, John Lane.

Rixon, A.H., *Captain Thunderbolt* (1951) Sydney, published by author.

Robin, M., *The Bad and the Lonely* (1976) Toronto, Lorimer.

Robinson, J., *Claret and Cross-Buttock* (1976) London, George Allen & Unwin.

Rockaway, R.A., *But – He Was Good To His Mother* (1993) Jerusalem, Geffen Publishing House.

Roston, W.W., *British Economy of the Nineteenth Century* (1948) Oxford, Clarendon Press.

Rovere, R.H., *Howe and Hummel* (1986) London, Arlington Books.

Rowan, R.W., *The Pinkertons* (1931) London, Hurst & Blackett.

Rumbelow, D., *The Complete Jack the Ripper: Notable British Trials* (1987) London, W.H. Allen.

Russell, J.S.F., *My Life and Adventures* (1923) London, Cassell & Co.

Sachs, E., *The Terrible Siren* (1928) New York, Harper & Brothers.

Samuel, R., *East End Underworld* (1981) London, Routledge Keegan Paul.

Sante, L., *Low Life* (1992) New York, Vintage Books.

Sawyer, E.T., *The Life and Career of Tiburcio Vasquez* (1875) San Francisco, Bacon & Co.

Selvaggi, G., (trans. Packer, W.A.), *The Rise of the Mafia in New York* (1948) Indianapolis, Bobbs & Merrill.

Sharpe, M.C., *Chicago May – Her Glory* (1928) New York, The Macaulay Company.

Sifakis, C., *The Encyclopedia of American Crime* (1982) New York, Facts on File.

———*Hoaxes and Scams* (1994) London, Michael O'Mara Books.

Sloan, T., *Tod Sloan, by Himself* (1988) San Diego, NP.

Sloat, W., *A Battle for the Soul of New York* (2002) New York, Cooper Square Press.

Smith, H., *From Constable to Commissioner: The Story of Sixty Years, Most of Them Misspent* (1910) London, Chatto & Windus.

Smith, Horace, *Crooks of the Waldorf* (n.d.) London, John Long.

Smith, P.J., *Plutocrats of Crime* (1960) London, Frederick Muller.

Stead, W.T., *If Christ Came to Chicago* (1894) Chicago, Laird & Lee.

Steffens, J. L., *The Autobiography of Lincoln Steffens* (1938) New York, Harcourt Brace & Co.

Stein, L., *The Triangle Fire* (1962) Philadelphia, J.B. Lippincott.

Stevens, C. L. McC., *Famous Crimes and Criminals* (1924) London, Stanley Paul & Co.

Stokes, F., *London III* (1904) London, Greening & Co.

Stone, I., *Clarence Darrow for the Defense* (1941) New York, Doubleday & Co.

Styles, T.J., *Jesse James* (2002) New York, Alfred A. Knopf.

Sutherland, D., *The Mad Hatters* (1987) London, Robert Hale.

Sutton, C., *The New York Tombs* (1874) San Francisco, A. Roman & Co.

Sutton, I. *From Constable to Commissioner* (1910) London, Chatto & Windus.

Thomas, D., *The Victorian Underworld* (1998) London, John Murray.

Thomson, B. H., *The Story of Dartmoor Prison* (1907) London, William Heinemann.

Thorwald, J., *The Marks of Cain* (1965) London, Thames and Hudson.

Totterdell, G., *Country Copper* (1956) London, George. G. Harrap & Co.

Train, A., *My Day in Court* (1939) New York, Charles Scribner & Sons.

———*True Stories of Crime* (1908) New York, Charles Scribner & Sons.

Tullet, T., *Inside Dartmoor* (1966) London, Frederick Muller.

Tumblety, F., *The Kidnapping of Dr Tumblety* (1866) Cincinnati, Tumblety.

Underhill, L.B., *The Woman Who Ran for President* (1995) Bridgehampton, NY, Bridge Works Publishers.

Walling, G., *Recollections of a New York Chief of Police* (1887) New York, Caxton Book Concern.

Washburn, C., *Come Into My Parlour* (1934) New York, Knickerbocker Publishing Company.

Welcome, J., *Cheating at Cards* (1958) London, Faber & Faber.

Wensley, F., *Detective Days* (1931) London, Cassell & Co.

Werner, M. R., *It Happened in New York* (1957) New York, Coward-McCann.

White, G. M., *From Boniface to Bank Burglar* (1907) New York, The Seaboard Press.

Whitehead, D., *The FBI Story* (1956) New York, Random House.

Whittington-Egan, R., *Liverpool Shadows* (2003) Liverpool, The Bluecoat Press.

Wilkins, P.A. (ed. and trans), *Behind the French CID* (n.d) London, Hutchinson & Co.

Willemsee, C., *Behind the Green Lights* (1931) New York, Alfred A. Knopf.

Williams, D.R., *Call in Pinkerton's* (1998) Toronto, Dundurn Press.

Williams, M., *Leaves from a Life* (1892) London, Macmillan & Co.

Wilkins, P.A., *Behind the French CID* (n.d.) London, Hutchinson & Co.

Wilson, C., *Written in Blood* (1990) London, Grafton.

Wilson, C. and Pitman, P., *Encyclopaedia of Murder* (1984) London, Pan.

Wolfe, H.A., *Outlaws of Modern Days* (1927) London, Cassell.

————*The Underworld* (n.d.) London, Hurst Blackett.

Wooldridge, C.R., *Hands Up! In the World of Crime* (1986) Chicago, Stanton & Van Vliet.

Wyndham, H., *Crime on the Continent* (1928) London, Thurton Butterworth.

Zimmermann, J.T., *America's Black Traffic in White Girls* (1912) Chicago, Chicago Women's Shelter.

Articles etc:

The Report of the Special (Mazet) Committee of the Assembly appointed to investigate the Public Offices and Departments of the City of New York and of the Counties Therein Included (Albany, 1900).

'Adam Worth alias Little Adam' published by Pinkerton's National Detective Agency, New York, 1901.

Anon., 'The Epic of Incendiarism' in *Leslie Illustrated Weekly*, Vol. 82, 18 February 1897.

Anon., 'Chicago as seen by herself' in *McClure's*, May 1907.

Anon., 'In the World of Graft: Chicago – an honest city' in *McClure's*, February 1901.

Anon., 'The Truth about the Third Degree' in *Reynolds Illustrated News*, 8 April 1925.

Donald Bell, 'Jack the Ripper – The Final Solution' in *The Criminologist*, Vol. 8. No. 33, 1974.

Albert E. Brager, 'The Pinkertons and the Bank Ghosts' in *True Detective*, 13 February 1945.

W.F. Burns, 'American Dynamiters' in *The Spectator*, 6 January 1912.

———'Hotel and Bank Crooks' in *Saturday Evening Post*, 6 June 1925.

———'Trial of the Bank Swindler' in *Saturday Evening Post*, 16 June 1925.

Harry Cox, 'Some famous cases from my notebook' in *Thomson's Weekly News*, 15 September 1906 and subsequent weeks.

Daniel Czitrom, 'Underworlds and Underdogs' in *Journal of American History* 78 (1991), pp. 536–58.

George Forbes, 'The Last Highwayman' in *Scottish Memories*, February 2001.

'Forgers in Toil' in *New York Herald*, 14 May 1896.

Henri Fremont, 'Mémoires ou Histoire de Casque d'Or raconte par elle-même' in *Fin de Siècle*, 5 June 1902 et seq.

Annie Gleason, 'My Life as the Queen of Crooks' in *Empire News*, 15 August 1925 and subsequent issues.

Herbert Grimshaw, 'A Famous Jockey's Downfall' in *Thomson's Weekly News*, 12 September 1925 and subsequent issues.

Stephen Hobhouse, 'The Silence System in British Prisons', April 1918.

'Darkie Hutton's Remarkable Life Story' in *Thomson's Weekly News*, 12 March 1910 and subsequent issues.

John Landesco, 'The Criminal Underworld of Chicago in the '80s and '90s' in *The Journal of the American Institute of Criminal Law and Criminology*, May–June 1934 and March–April 1935.

Francisco Xavier de Santa Cruz y Mallen, 'Historia de familias Cubanas' in *Editorial Hercules* 1940, Vol. III.

Arthur Newton, 'Secrets of Society' in *Thomson's Weekly News*, 16 September 1922 and subsequent issues.

Richard E. Nicholls, 'Thoroughly Bad Guy' in the *New York Times Book Review*, 27 October 2002.

'The Wages of Sin, Being the Authentic and Remarkable Story of Charles Peace' in *Thomson's Weekly News*, 20 October 1906, and continued in subsequent issues of *The Red Letter*.

Robert A. Pinkerton, 'Forgery as a Profession' in *The North American Review*, April 1894.

'Blonde' Alice Smith, 'The Truth About My Double Life' in *Thomson's Weekly News*, 10, 17, 24 April, 22, 29 May 1926.

Norman Smithson, 'Those Bygone Days of Pitch and Toss' in *Yorkshire Life*, August 1975.

Dot Swarc, 'Background and conditions contributing to Jewish prostitution in the East End of London 1890–1914' (1987). Unpublished manuscript deposited in the Jewish Museum at the Sternberg Centre, Finchley, London.

'The Trial of Madame Restall, alias Ann Lohman, for abortion and causing the death of Mrs Purdy' (1841) New York, reprinted from the *National Police Gazette*.

Henry Thomas, 'Harry the Valet' in *Thomson's Weekly News*, 27 March 1926 and subsequent issues.

Basil Thomson, 'My Years as Governor of Dartmoor' in *Thomson's Weekly News*, 4 February 1922 and subsequent issues.

George Kibbe Turner, 'Tammany's Control of New York by Professional Criminals' in *McClure's*, 33.

———'The Daughters of the Poor: Jewish Prostitution in New York' in *McClure's*, 34.

———'The City of Chicago: A Study of the Great Immoralities' in *McClure's*, April 1907.

Richard Whittington-Egan, 'Jack the Ripper, I Presume' in *New Law Journal*, 29 September 2000.

———'The Netley Lucas Story' in *New Law Journal*, 30 June 2000.

Index